UPROAR
at Dancing
Rabbit Creek

Noxubee County
MISSISSIPPI

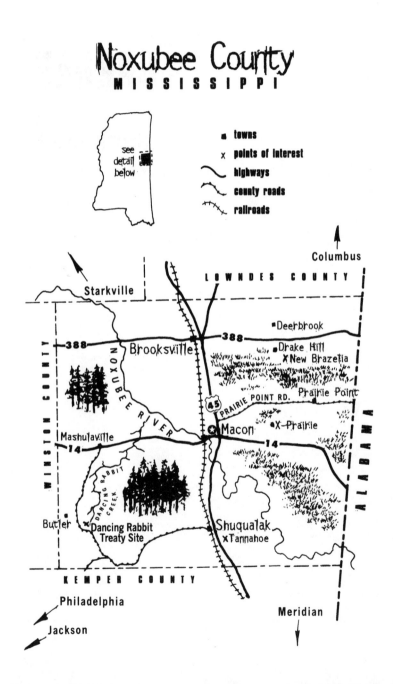

see detail below

- ■ towns
- x points of interest
- ～ highways
- ～ county roads
- ＋＋＋ railroads

Columbus

LOWNDES COUNTY

Starkville

■ Deerbrook

388   Brooksville   388

■ Drake Hill
X New Brazelia

NOXUBEE RIVER

WINSTON COUNTY

US 45   PRAIRIE POINT RD.   Prairie Point

X Prairie

Mashulaville

★ Macon

14   14

DANCING RABBIT CREEK

ALABAMA

Butler

Dancing Rabbit
Treaty Site

Shuqualak
x Tannahoe

KEMPER COUNTY

Philadelphia

Jackson

Meridian

UPROAR
at Dancing Rabbit Creek

■   ■   ■

Battling
over Race,
Class,
and the
Environment

COLIN CRAWFORD

▲▼▼ ADDISON-WESLEY PUBLISHING COMPANY, INC.

Reading, Massachusetts   Menlo Park, California   New York
Don Mills, Ontario   Harlow, England   Amsterdam   Bonn
Sydney   Singapore   Tokyo   Madrid   San Juan
Paris   Seoul   Milan   Mexico City   Taipei

Selections from Loyle Hairston's short story "The Revolt of Brud Bascomb," in Chapter 3, and selections from his essay "Growing Up in Mississippi," in Chapters 7 and 8, reprinted by permission of the author, © Loyle Hairston, 1984 and 1985, respectively. Quotations in Chapter 3 from V. O. Key, Jr. from *Southern Politics in State and Nation*, reprinted by permission of Marion T. Key, Esq., © Alfred A. Knopf, 1949 and Asalie Key Price, W. Cecil Key, Luther S. Key, and Marion T. Key, 1977. Permission to reprint selections of the untitled history of the Magnolia Mennonite Church, discussed in Chapter 3, courtesy of Edwin Knepp, Bishop, Magnolia Conservative Mennonite Church, Macon, Mississippi. Portions of John A. Tyson, *Historical Notes of Noxubee County* reprinted courtesy of Noxubee County Historical Society, Inc. The excerpt from William Ward's "Come to the South," which appears in a footnote for page 81, reprinted courtesy of the *Beacon*, copyright © Macon Beacon Press, 1933. The Eudora Welty quotation in the Acknowledgments reprinted courtesy of Random House, Inc., © Eudora Welty, 1971.

Many of the designations used by manufacturers and sellers to distinguish their products are claimed as trademarks. Where those designations appear in this book and Addison-Wesley was aware of a trademark claim, the designations have been printed in initial capital letters.

Library of Congress Cataloging-in-Publication Data

Crawford, Colin.
    Uproar at Dancing Rabbit Creek : battling over race, class, and
the environment / Colin Crawford.
        p.   cm.
    Includes index.
    ISBN 0-201-62723-X
    1. Noxubee County (Miss.)—Environmental conditions.
    2. Environmental policy—Mississippi—Noxubee County.   3. Noxubee
County (Miss.)—Politics and government.   I. Title.
GE155.M7C74   1996
363.72'87'09762955—dc20   96-6140
                                                                              CIP

Jacket design by Alexander Knowlton
Jacket photograph by Birney Imes
Text design by Karen Savary
Set in 11-point Minion by Shepard Poorman Communications Corporation, Indianapolis, IN

 2 3 4 5 6 7 8 9-DOH-0099989796
First printing, July 1996

FOR MY PARENTS

Sheila Eigeman Crawford

and

Malcolm Douglas Crawford

CONTENTS

INTRODUCTION

NOXUBEE. IT WAS THE name that caught my attention. Noxubee, Mississippi. A queer name in that most maligned and neglected of states. The name alone seemed impenetrable: how even to pronounce the odd configuration that formed the three syllables into a single word? Nox-YOU-bee? NOX-uh-bee? *Noxubee*, I would learn, was a Choctaw Indian word meaning "stinking water." A popular local legend has it that the name Noxubee derives from the massacre of several hundred Choctaw and Creek warriors after a disputed gambling match between the tribes turned violent. A local historian wrote that: "The unearthly stench of decayed human flesh hung a fetid cloud over the area for weeks," thus meriting the name. A more likely explanation stems from the fact that when the Noxubee River recedes, it leaves in its wake large pools of still water that reek in the long, hot, humid Mississippi summer. But a myth locating the area's history in a brutal massacre provides an account that is at once horrifyingly repulsive and more seductive than the likely reality. The story is typical of the dark fables that locals will tell you about Noxubee's history. As Dante wrote: "Names are the consequences of the things they name."

Noxubee County's history is steeped in a struggle for control of the land; its single most famous site is the bucolic Dancing Rabbit Creek. It was there that, in 1830, the Choctaw nation was forced to sign one of the most oppressive treaties ever foisted on a native tribe by the U.S. government. The treaty led to a forced exodus that cost the tribe many lives, as they, like the Cherokee and other tribes, followed their own Trail of Tears outside their ancestral lands. After the forcible Choctaw removal, Noxubee flourished for decades under the rule of King Cotton, a domination that meant the enslavement of thousands of blacks, many of whose descendants live there today in situations not vastly better than those of their ancestors. A white descendant of the county's landed gentry described Noxubee's uniqueness like this: "I guess for a long time this county was looked upon as goin' back toward feudal England as any county in the South was. The relationships that existed between whites and blacks were different from what I've heard in other places. I guess what would be the paternalistic-type society that's set up in most places—maybe it's a little slower to come out of it."

Noxubee is a place where people are especially eager for change but doubtful it will come. One local Baptist preacher explained: "People start to have such a low opinion of themselves that they will do anything to get some fast money. People will say things like 'no decent industry will come here because this is sort of the cesspool of the country.' "

I first read about the controversy in Noxubee County in late 1992. While researching for a consumer advocacy group, I noticed an article in a trade journal about a thinly populated, heavily African American county in east-central Mississippi. For several years, three companies had been locked in fierce competition for the right to build there one of the nation's largest complexes for hazardous waste dumping and incineration. What piqued my interest initially was not so much the corporate rivalry but the fact that one of the companies had proposed an outlandish scheme to have a parcel of Noxubee land declared part of a distant Choctaw reservation in order to evade state environmental regulation. I then made several phone calls. Issues unrelated to the Choctaw quickly proved to be even more astonishing.

On that first day of inquiry I spoke, minutes apart, with two remarkable people, both of whose perspectives could not have diverged more sharply. The first was a white woman of privileged and conservative background. She was hungry to talk; clearly she saw me as a channel of communication to the world beyond her home in Prairie Point, Mississippi. She spilled out an extraordinary tale of corporate chicanery, race-baiting politics, likely corruption and deception (including the expenditure of tens of millions of dollars in a race for *approval* to build and run a toxic dump—this in a county with an annual operating budget of little more than $1 million). We talked for over an hour. What especially intrigued me about Martha Blackwell was that she revealed herself to be in the throes of a struggle that was as much personal—spiritual almost—as it was civic minded.

Several things about Martha Blackwell struck me as unusual. She spoke with surprising frankness about what she knew of her county's troubled racial past. My father's family were southern farmers, and from visits to them I knew that white southerners remain defensive on the subject, anticipating from their northern counterparts hypocritical, holier-than-thou sermonizing; conversely, I knew that white northerners (me included) are inclined to exactly the sort of self-righteous moralizing our southern counterparts fear.

Martha's account was also slightly naive, astonished. Although then in her mid-thirties, her political education had been recent. She expressed hope that things were changing and explained how she thought reforms could be made. And her explanations did not seem especially self-serving.

Some of what she had to say did seem wildly improbable. The local chapter of the National Association for the Advancement of Colored People (NAACP) had, she told me, endorsed the attempt by a Hughes Aircraft subsidiary to place one of the nation's largest toxics disposal facilities in her overwhelmingly black county. A branch of the nation's preeminent civil rights group endorsing a hazardous waste dump? Were things so desperate that they were willing to sacrifice health and safety concerns for the few jobs a waste facility brings? Finally, I wondered why this was the only business that the people of this rich agricultural land could attract.

Martha also told me that the NAACP was opposing efforts by a Union Pacific subsidiary to site a similar facility. Her explanation again begged more questions than it answered. Why did the NAACP support one and not the other? And why was a white woman of the planter class leading the charge for environmental justice? Was she a mere political opportunist, worried that her land might be devalued if a waste dump came, or a paternalistic do-gooder, condescending to make her county's poor, unlettered black majority understand the peril they faced? Or was hers a sincere effort to try and heal the county's racial fissures?

Improbably, Martha had become not only the leader of a fight to oppose a massive hazardous waste dump and incineration site—that was not unlikely for someone of her background—but also the county's primary source of information on the subject of environmental racism. That struck me as completely out of character. I knew scattered bits and pieces of information about the cause with the cumbersome label of environmental racism. I knew, for example, that the term (less confrontationally called "environmental justice") referred to the claim that racial and ethnic minority areas— primarily African American and Latino ones—are unduly burdened with toxic industrial activities. I knew that several studies had documented the persistent tendency to put everything from waste dumps and lead smelters to other kinds of undesirable, heavy industrial activity in poor communities of color. I knew, too, that the movement had focused inordinately on toxic dumping, rather than on other activities at least equally threatening to the environment (and probably more so), such as oil refining and chemical manufacturing. But oil refineries and chemical plants offer more employment than a hazardous waste dump or incinerator; protesting becomes more complicated when large numbers of jobs are at stake. Toxic waste dumps, which manufacture nothing, are also particularly potent symbols of our society's willingness to perpetuate the racial inequality that has plagued our history.

One could scarcely find a better example of this reality than Noxubee County, Mississippi. By every measure, Noxubee County is hurting, as evident in everything from high black mortality and morbidity statistics to stratospheric rates of welfare dependence and appallingly low levels of literacy and educational achievement. As a result, Martha Blackwell's urgent message was compelling, even if she seemed to be an unusual messenger to announce it.

■ ■ ■ I SPOKE next with a black political organizer named Ike Brown, a loyal Democratic Party operative who spearheaded the local NAACP endorsement and actively campaigned for one of the waste companies in the county's poorest black areas. Martha Blackwell had told me he was paid for his support. Yet I soon realized that his financial interest explained only part of his involvement. This was a man with a political philosophy focused above all else on remedying persistent racial inequality. Supporting hazardous waste was for him a means to an end—to get political and economic power for some of the nation's most dispossessed citizens. True, he supported the Hughes affiliate in part because they paid him. But it was also the company that directly sought his and other blacks' support in a majority-black county. This was, I learned, a rare event in Noxubee, which was then still white controlled.

Where Martha Blackwell had been critical but temperate in her descriptions of him, he was vehement in his contempt for her. Martha represented to Ike a class that had kept blacks down for generations. No act of contrition would ever absolve her of the taint of past oppression.

In Martha and Ike's mutual dislike I had my first glimpse of the extent to which the controversy to site a huge hazardous waste dump and incinerator in Noxubee County was rooted in its history of domination and servitude. Environmental justice activists tend to blame industry and government for the discriminatory burden of toxic operations. But Martha's and Ike's mutual dislike—and my subsequent study of the county's history—suggested that the fault for igniting such controversies is far more complicated than people usually acknowledge. Noxubee County is its own worst enemy. For such places to fend off government and corporate predators looking for easy and cheap solutions to looming environmental (or other) crises, they will need a better-educated population and a well-trained workforce. But the cost of securing these goals is one that, deep down, neither the white elite in Noxubee County nor the nation at large may be willing to pay.

■ ■ ■ WHAT people in Noxubee County called "the" hazardous waste ignited a fierce political struggle. As a result, unbiased, reliable information about the waste proposals was hard to come by locally. I therefore set out to understand just how hazardous waste disposal works. The best explanation I found came from Peter Montague, who left a tenured post at Princeton University to work as a health and environmental crusader. In the often shrill and emotional politics of antiwaste campaigns, Montague is not some fringe Cassandra but an exceptionally dispassionate observer. He likens a landfill to a bathtub covered by an umbrella. To build the modern landfill, such as those proposed by the companies who battled it out in Noxubee County, a big hole is dug in the ground. Engineering then improves on the natural advantages of a site by putting in manmade liners. The liners are usually made of high-density polyethylene, a hard plastic widely used for packaging. The variety used in landfills is about the thickness of a quarter and the hardness of a floor tile. A "leachate collection" system is then installed to gather any fluids, such as rain and decomposed organic waste, that find their way into the bathtub. The hole is then filled with solid or liquid hazardous wastes.

Hazardous waste–generating industries include nearly every type of manufacture, from the biggest generators of toxic materials such as the chemical, oil, steel and transportation industries to home appliance, furniture, perfume, food preservative, and household disinfectant makers.

Once the hole is filled, another liner, typically of the same substance, is placed on top of the fill—Montague's umbrella. The umbrella is covered with soil and prettified with a ground cover, usually one that flowers, intimating that what lies below poses no threat to biological life.

Montague argues, however, that both the plastic cover and the liner eventually will deteriorate and hasten the leaking of the landfill. How? Both barriers will be eroded by rain and wind, the synthetic materials will gradually degrade with age and the force of regular contraction and expansion due to varying temperatures, or the barriers will be burrowed into by rodents and other soil-dwelling creatures. Meanwhile, the leachate collection system will clog with sand and silt, the growth of slimes and molds, or simple mechanical failure. Finally, he concludes, "humans, in their marvelous unpredictability, will sooner or later forget where the umbrella was located, and sometime after that they will build trailer parks, roads, homes, schools, factories or other structures on the site." Then "the bathtub will fill with rainwater, spill over its sides, and contaminate the surrounding environment." The U.S. Environmental Protection Agency (EPA) has more than once agreed in print with Montague's pessimistic assessment of landfill technology.

Landfills give further cause for concern because they mix all sorts of individually toxic materials in the same bathtub, with unknown results. True, liquid wastes no longer get poured straight into a fill, as was once the case. (Today they are usually solidified in part by adding something like sawdust.) Wastes are now placed in metal drums that at the time of disposal can be identified as to producer and contents. But drums eventually rust, corrode, and leak, potentially creating a toxic brew. Even the conservative U.S. Public Health Service has admitted that the toxicity of these combined chemicals is largely unknown and therefore cause for concern.

Moreover, landfills are built on the dubious assumption that a company will remain solvent and able to fulfill its financial and maintenance obligations for a long time. These obligations are guaranteed for about 100 years at most (and probably much less than that, closer to 50 years). Montague therefore concludes that in the long term an environmental disaster is not only possible but likely. Since "it is impossible to accurately predict future patterns of land use, water use and habitation by humans, prudent planning requires that we assume the worst: whenever we dump toxic chemicals, someone, somewhere, will be harmed."

This sort of reasoning has given rise to what proponents of stringent environmental protection call the precautionary principle, the notion that an activity should be avoided until we can be sure of its actual environmental effects. By this logic, even if, as a society, we were to conclude that landfills of some kind were necessary, it would be especially ill advised to put them near the rich soils covering much of Noxubee County—some of the nation's best farmland and a future source of our food security.

In the face of such criticism, hazardous waste generators and the people who dispose of the stuff they create typically point to an item—say, a home entertainment center—and piously intone, as one of the combatants in the Noxubee waste wars did to me, that, "unfortunately," hazardous wastes are a by-product of good living. Thus, the waste company apologist proceeds on the principle that people will be shamed into silence if they are made guilty about their reliance on the conveniences of modern life. Billy McCann, a Noxubee lumberman and prominent backer of one of the waste companies, handed me a flyer one day that read: "Due to conservation efforts in the Pacific Northwest, wood and paper products are no longer available. We suggest you try wiping your ass with a spotted owl." This is the choice that defenders of our current waste disposal practices would have us make: we can either keep enjoying our downy, bleached-white tissues and hairspray and TV dinners and individually wrapped slices of processed cheese, or we can move to a commune and start buying legumes in bulk and getting around by human-powered transport.

This is becoming something of a false choice. In the past decade, heavy industry has greatly reduced the volume of toxic material it produces, in turn creating a decreased need for landfill space and incinerators. Even once such information became available in Noxubee, however, it did not stem the uproar over hazardous waste that gripped Noxubee County for five years. Above all, this was because the hazardous waste became a way to settle old scores—between a politician derided as a poor redneck and the powerful lumbermen who had once employed him, between the local white gentry and angry, dissatisfied black politicians fresh to power, between brothers with different ambitions, and between friends and families who had grown apart as some became more successful.

■ ■ ■ IN a 1937 autobiographical essay titled "The Ethics of Living Jim Crow," Mississippi native Richard Wright inquired: "How do Negroes feel about the way they have to live? How do they discuss it when alone among themselves? I think this question can be answered in a single sentence. A friend of mine who ran an elevator once told me:

'Lawd, man! Ef it wuzn't fer them polices 'n' them ol' lynch mobs, there wouldn't be nothin' but uproar down here!' "

As I spoke with more and more people in Noxubee County, I came to see the struggle over hazardous waste as part of the uproar Wright's friend had predicted. Gradually, talk about the environmental consequences of hazardous waste was subsumed by endless recriminations and the opportunity to express deep-seated and long-standing hatreds. Thirty years after the passage of the civil rights laws, why were old animosities so resistant to healing? What of the oft-trumpeted claims about the transformation of the old Deep South into the New South—the sunny home of Atlanta's gleaming office towers, Raleigh-Durham's high-tech science parks, and the busy ports of the Mississippi Gulf Coast? Part of the answer lies in the fact that the media's New South is a sales pitch, like a glossy tourist brochure hiding a more complicated reality. Although bordered on all sides by examples of the New South ideal, Noxubee County remains mired in the manners and behavior of an earlier time.

At first, it was easy to distance myself from Noxubee's social pathologies. Mississippi is a well-worn liberal punching bag; I easily explained away the racial divisions that persist in Noxubee County as a permanent shadow cast by what the historian C. Vann Woodward famously dubbed Jim Crow's "strange career." Noxubee County's white elite is a familiar and easy target, the upholders of a tarnished code of southern gentility and racial subjugation that has devolved into a cultural caricature.

Yet the more time I spent visiting Noxubee County and

following developments in the local hazardous waste wars, the more familiar its struggles seemed. In New York City, my white friends and I seldom—if ever—venture north of Ninety-sixth Street, into Harlem. I am frequently in cars with other whites when the driver suddenly locks all doors at the sight of blacks or Latinos gathered on a street corner. Like most other whites, I tolerate jokes and disparaging comments about "welfare mothers" and "violent youth"— references that are understood to be colored black. In sum, I knew that in New York and other cities where most of the U.S. population lives, discussion about race is scarcely more candid or less prone to recrimination than in Noxubee County. People of different races in New York or Los Angeles or Chicago or Miami are as unlikely as in Mississippi to mix in any but the most superficial of contexts, a division that breeds chronic suspicion and often mutual dislike. Small wonder that among the country's white majority a mere generation of civil rights protections and affirmative action preferences is widely thought to have been sufficient recompense for generations of state-sanctioned policies of racial inferiority, or that a majority of African Americans are more suspect of police motives than of the black men arrested for criminal acts. We make few opportunities for ourselves collectively to discuss and understand the nature and causes of our differences. As I watched the standoff over hazardous waste, race, and class develop in Noxubee County, I could not help but admit that many of its least appealing aspects mirrored life in the urban America I know best.

One of the most dispiriting aspects of the Noxubee waste wars was how little will existed for people of different races and economic circumstances to work together. In Noxubee County, this was truer of those who opposed hazardous waste than of their adversaries: there were separate protest groups for blacks and whites. This is a pattern, I learned, repeated throughout the rural South. Like a good northern liberal, I shook my head in dismay at the wasted energy of divided, simultaneous efforts. Yet during the same years, in my home of New York City, the New York Environmental Justice Alliance, a prominent collection of grassroots activists united to fight for environmental justice, spent the better part of two years bickering about whether whites should be permitted among their number.

■ ■ ■ THUS, the uproar in the stinking water of Noxubee County, Mississippi, presented itself to me as an example of what happens when shortsighted federal and state environmental laws intersect with bitter state and local politics and long-running personal feuds. This confluence of factors opened the way for corporate outsiders with no apparent long-term interest in the county's future. Yet even when it would have been to their mutual advantage to work together, Martha Blackwell and Ike Brown—two people who shared an intense interest in Noxubee's future—would not talk to one another. There were moments when Noxubee residents stepped outside the confines of their prejudices of race and class, to try to understand others vastly different from themselves. But as the story unfolded in "Stinking Water" County, Mississippi, these moments—and the people who made them—were few and far between.

1
AN ARISTOCRACY
OF THE SOIL

O N A LATE WINTER DAY IN 1992, Martha Mullins Blackwell and Ike Brown arrived for the same board of supervisors' meeting at the Noxubee County courthouse in Macon, Mississippi. It is an unremarkable, red-brick, neoclassical building with a white, columned porch and a small, functionless cupola on top, indistinguishable from similar county seats across the South. The white exterior trim had been peeling badly for over a year. Inside, the ceiling paint was mottled from dampness, plaster had fallen away in big chunks, and broken light fixtures dangled in their sockets.

That morning was rushed for Martha, as mornings had been for over eighteen months. She got up early, then fed her husband, Drew, and her two young children, Drew Jr. and Mary Katherine. She saw Drew off to work at the feed mill he runs for Deerbrook Farms, drove the twelve miles from her home out on the family plantation in the county's eastern prairie to get little Drew to Central Academy, the county's all-white private school, and delivered Mary Katherine (then two and a half) to a babysitter. This left her just enough time to get to the supervisors' meeting at the courthouse.

A hearing had been called to examine proposals to address a looming local crisis, namely, what to do with Noxubee County's garbage. A multinational corporation was offering to dispose of local trash at no charge, provided the county would also agree to support its effort to site one of the nation's largest hazardous waste landfills and incinerators there—the proposed operation would accept toxics from all fifty states and abroad. Though Martha hardly realized it then, these were subjects that would eventually consume several years of her life and radically change its direction.

Martha entered the courthouse and headed straight for the courtroom upstairs, which the supervisors use for public hearings. Her path took her right by the supervisors' regular meeting room. Above the safe inside the cramped room sits a framed photograph depicting her father and the board of supervisors over which he presided. In the picture, Martha's father, William Sylvester Mullins Jr., who had served the county as a supervisor for twenty-eight years (and for eight of them, as the board's head) stands smiling stiffly, dressed in the pleated khaki trousers and khaki shirt he wore nearly every working day of his seventy-nine years. That morning, she hardly had time to glance at the photo or reflect on her father's long service. Nor, as she turned to climb the stairs, did Martha so much as glance at a plaque commemorating her ancestor Joel Barnett and the five other Revolutionary War soldiers buried in Noxubee County. Martha Blackwell's identity is deeply entwined with Noxubee County, but she is not one publicly to celebrate her family's deep roots in its history.

With her small, fast, deliberate steps, Blackwell quickly reached the dimly lit second floor and entered the courtroom on the building's south side, which is painted an improbably demure pastel green. With its carved wooden benches and soft light, the courtroom resembles a Puritan church or meeting hall as much as a place of municipal business. She slipped into a bench on the room's far side, near the tall windows overlooking the courthouse's leafy square.

Just after she sat down, Ike Brown entered the nearly empty room, crossed over to the far side where Martha sat, and slid his serpentine frame right next to her, giving her a big, open grin and nodding hello.

"Ya'll," Martha stood up and called to the supervisors as they prepared to begin, "can we open the windows or turn on the air conditioners in here? It's startin' to get hot." She sat down again. Ike looked down at her, still smiling, and said: "I ain't hot. It mus' be a cu-u-u-l-tural difference." His jibe had the desired effect. Blackwell fumed. "Mr. Brown, if I said that to you, you would call me a racist and have it all over town. What is *that* supposed to mean?"

When Martha Blackwell recounted this story to me nearly two years later, the thought still enraged her. She remembered that, even after her remark, Ike just smiled smugly and turned his head to the front, not even responding to her ire as the meeting began. I asked Ike Brown about the incident. Didn't he force such encounters precisely to devil his antagonists? "Sometimes, yeah—if they stupid enough to go for it. It really wasn't hot. What she really was mad about 'cause she was sitting next to me. She just didn't want to be next to a black, next to me. If she had asked me in a nice, right manner, I probably would have moved."

Martha Blackwell and Ike Brown are almost contemporaries, but in nearly every respect they could not be more different. Though both are prominent citizens in this forgotten pocket of the old Deep South—Noxubee County's 694 square miles are populated by just over 12,500 people—their lives and experience barely intersected until late 1990, when they first collided in a fight over the siting of a massive hazardous waste dump and incinerator. For opponents of the project, the odds were formidable: the locals were up against two multinationals, one a subsidiary of Hughes Aircraft and the other a division of the railroad giant Union Pacific—not to mention other venture capitalists lurking around waiting to cash in on a possible Mississippi toxic waste gold mine.

The fight over whether hazardous waste would come to Noxubee County arose just as the nation began a period of soul searching about the ethics of siting operations like hazardous waste facilities in poor, mostly African American and Latino communities. The foot soldiers of this grassroots movement fashioned themselves the advocates of "environmental justice." Adherents to the environmental justice cause, who have been rallying behind that banner since at least the early 1980s, claim that the nation's racial and ethnic minorities are disproportionately burdened by the presence of what are (or at least are perceived to be) America's most environmentally threatening activities, amounting, they say, to a sustained program of "environmental racism."

Because the population of Noxubee County, Mississippi, is nearly 70 percent African American and poor, it would seem to provide the ideal example of the injustices asserted by those who decry the phenomenon of environmental racism. Yet Ike Brown, the county's most influential black political organizer and the vice-president of the local NAACP chapter, was an early and vocal supporter of bringing the hazardous waste to Noxubee County. He played a key role in getting the local NAACP chapter to issue a resolution endorsing the Hughes project. Brown was also a paid "consultant" to the project he supported.

Ike. Utter that single syllable in Noxubee County and anyone, black, white, or Choctaw, will know who you mean. Ike Brown is Noxubee County's political power broker par excellence, and his activities engender no lukewarm judgments. Depending on who you talk to, Ike Brown is the county's Al Sharpton, or its Savonarola, or its Boss Tweed. He is rumored to have amassed a small private fortune, a claim he makes no attempt to dispel. Such suppositions are reinforced by the fact that he holds no steady job and is always free to throw himself into the political fray.

Ike's successful politics of racial grievance and reward is especially remarkable because he is single and not a Noxubee native, in a place where social relations are based on family connection and tie to place. Born and raised in Canton, Mississippi, southwest of Noxubee County and sixty miles north of Jackson, the state capital, Brown migrated to Noxubee County in the early 1980s.

Ike Brown invites controversy. "My Bible tells me to shun the very appearance of evil," offered a woman who attends the same church as Brown, explaining why she avoids speaking with him. An elderly white man who, uncharacteristically for someone of his race in Noxubee County, spoke enthusiastically of his affection for Brown, lowered his voice to a whisper and insisted that he not be quoted by name for this one confession only: "I just wonder how he stays alive."

Whenever he sees him, the older man added, his first question is always, "Who'd you provoke today, Ike?"

Ike is evasive about his family and upbringing and quickly changes the subject when asked about himself. I asked whether his passionate advocacy of African American interests sprang from any childhood experiences. As in a politician's campaign biography, he answered in a self-consciously homespun way, revealing little about himself:

"Oh man, I been in politics since I was born—it's just a natural-born instinct to deal with people. I mean, I was in politics when I was a little kid. The bigger kids used to have the little kids elect me like their leader to deal with the bigger kids, 'cause they would always try to beat us up and everything like that, and you know, I started off then. We gotta stick together. I said, 'If they separate us they can get us and beat us up, but if all of us hang together we can catch them.' Stuff like that. Leadership. And even in high school, same thing. . . . I find you can lead people, as long as that's where they want to go. I've always been in politics on everything."

Born the sixth of twelve children, Brown was eleven when Martin Luther King Jr. marched through his hometown of Canton; one of Brown's brothers was injured slightly in a racial melee that resulted. Canton, the heavily black seat of Madison County, was a hot spot of civil rights activity. Brown remembered: "During the civil rights movement I was real young, so I wasn't in that at first, and then I did voter registration work in '71. I was sixteen years old when Charles Evers run; we registered three thousand people in Madison County." (Charles Evers, the brother of the assassinated civil rights leader Medgar Evers and something of a gadfly in Mississippi politics, ran for governor of Mississippi in 1971, greatly threatening the powers-that-be in then-still-segregated Mississippi.) What at sixteen had drawn him into the still-risky business of registering black voters? Once again, Ike was evasive on personal details, turning the youthful memory into the most general of explanations of why he does what he does: "I wanted to, I've always been interested in people, that's automatic politics. And in order to be a successful politician, you have to be able to read people. What are they sayin'? What do they really mean? What makes this person do this? Who don't like who? All these factors go into cummin up with a candidate." With that, we were off the subject of Ike Brown and onto a discussion of tactics he had used successfully in organizing a recent political race.

Ike Brown's guardedness about his personal history is one way he strengthens the mystique of his political and social power. Because he is at the center of most public events in Noxubee County but reveals so little about himself, he is the sort of person about whom legends abound. In addition to the claims of his supposed wealth, and speculation about its sources, I heard a range of suspicions about his education. Some said he had not graduated from high school. Others said he was a lawyer, and they mumbled suspicions about why he was no longer allowed to practice. The truth turned out to be less dramatic.

Ike Brown graduated from Jackson State University, with a degree in business. The Mississippi public university system historically educated white and black students at separate universities. Whites had two main choices: the University of Mississippi ("Ole Miss") or the state agricultural school, Mississippi State University, which sits on the edge of the Mississippi–Alabama prairie, not far from Noxubee County. Blacks were left with the option of attending a number of less prestigious, underfunded schools, the best of them being Jackson State University and Alcorn State University. In theory, admissions are now race-blind, but tradition is hard to break. Even today, Jackson State's student body is 98 percent black and Ole Miss' is 81 percent white.

Brown then attended the first year of law school at the Mississippi College of Law, but never finished. Founded in 1975 and accredited only in 1980, the school is the state's second law school, trailing far behind Ole Miss in terms of career-building opportunities.

In his forty-one years, Brown has carefully cultivated a detailed knowledge of the mechanics of politics, with a focus on statistics—percentages and numbers of voters. Whether discussing national electoral trends, Mississippi contests, or local school board elections in Noxubee County, he prides himself on being able to recite the racial and ethnic breakdown of political representation down to the last percentage point.

Brown's excitement about electoral numbers, plus his ability to rattle off the who and where of each local election, has an ingenuous, irrepressibly boyish quality, as if he is trying to impress his elders with his prodigious skills. When the subject is Noxubee County elections, Brown is the undisputed master, as even his many detractors admit. District by district, polling place by polling place, he can tell you exactly how many votes are needed to win for a particular candidate and how the voting will break down by race. He knows just how many absentee ballots will be needed from the poor and mostly elderly black voters who live in dilapidated shacks and trailers far out in the country along the hundreds of miles of Noxubee County's back roads, in order for his candidates to win. Wilbur Colom, a well-known African American lawyer from adjoining Lowndes County, was arrested several times as a teenager during the civil rights years. Colom spoke admiringly of Ike Brown: "Ike is like me when I was 13, 14, 15 years old." Colom, who has both defended Brown in criminal and civil matters and sometimes been a Brown combatant, observed:

"Ike still has this youthfulness more than most of us. Ike is truly willing to die in the trenches for what he believes. I mean, he could be much more successful because he's smart. He gets things done. He's disciplined in elections. Ike loves to campaign in one of the most disciplined fashions I have ever seen. He knows down to the exact number how many absentee votes he has. He can tell you within three or four votes how close he is to winning. He knows what boxes are weak. I mean, he is precise. One of the—probably the best in the state, the country. He normally would go ahead and let greed and other things take hold and become successful, settling in and make all the necessary compromises." Despite unsupported gossip about ill-gotten gains, Ike Brown has most definitely not "settled in"; his time is devoted most visibly to political wrangling.

Ike is characteristically vague about the circumstances that led to his arrival. Noxubee County, he says, "needed leadership. It needed someone who knew, needed someone to show them how to do what they wanted to do, and I did that." What seems more likely is that Noxubee County, with its impoverished, aging, majority-black population, provided some of the most fertile ground in the state for his racially confrontational politics. Ike came to Noxubee County specifically to work on the successful 1979 campaign for superintendent of education of a woman named Reecy Dickson. Dickson, who is now one of the county's representatives in the Mississippi House of Representatives and herself no stranger to local political controversy, thus became one of the first black elected officials in the county since Reconstruction. Dickson acknowledged that Brown taught her "everything he knew about absentee voting, which turned out to be the key in winning the 1979 election." In that campaign, Ike first recognized that Noxubee County well suited his political aims: "It's where I wanted to start my machine at." Self-conceived as a latter-day ward heeler of the kind that once flourished in Boston, New York, or Chicago, Brown dreams eventually of building his machine throughout east-central Mississippi, then throughout the state, and finally the entire South.

He could not look less like a political power broker. Brown stands at almost six and a half feet tall, but his lanky frame is resolutely nonimposing; he cannot weigh over 170. His mien is friendly. His unlined face, round and open, is bisected by a wide mouth covering a tangle of stained, yellowing teeth. Brown likes to be liked and seems eager to secure one's favor, the way a politician does. To most whites in the county, however, he is hardly a benign presence and is viewed by many as a hopelessly divisive, hate-mongering figure.

Noxubee County's poor, badly educated, rural African American majority forms the bedrock of Ike Brown's political machine, a machine fueled by a mixture of small-time patronage and service, the promise of political redemption and racial resentment. "Now let me ask you somethin'—Who you can perceive as bein' in your best interest?" Ike said, beginning an explanation of his approach to political organizing with one of his typical rhetorical questions. Taking the example of a schoolteacher (a traditional path for black economic advancement in the rural South), he offered: "When he gets off work, he goes home to his house and reads a nice book, sits curled up in a nice chair, he's so smart. Now you got Ike Brown. I make more money than all of 'em do. I don' need nobody's money. I got my own tax business, I got businesses everywhere, I got real estate. Got Ike Brown, who gets up in the mornin' time, goes to the post office, stops on the street and talks to everybody who gotta problem, and don' get to bed till late at night, because people always callin' me about some kinda problem they got with a government agency or private individual, whatever." With a characteristic flourish, he observed with satisfaction: "Now who do you think they—the people—gonna follow?"

People ask: How is he always free to attend official meetings to defend what he sees as the rights of his constituency? Why does he not have a regular job, yet maintains a home and a car? He has been known to do everything from running a little grocery truck on the county's back roads (an indispensable means to cultivate the support of the county's disenfranchised, elderly majority, many of whom lack regular transportation) to selling insurance, doing accounting, and preparing taxes. He variously described himself to me as a professional "income tax preparer" and "political consultant." He has a business selling heavy fuel oil to the county government. People regularly identify him as "the convicted felon, Ike Brown," referring to his 1980 loan-fraud conviction, for which he received a suspended sentence and probation. His probation expired in 1989, and the following year his civil rights were restored by order of Governor Ray Mabus. Restoration of his rights meant that he could vote, but not hold public office—making a necessity out of his aptitude for being the power behind the throne.

Ike refuses to dignify questions about his crime or his pardon: "If a man's done a crime, repaid everything he owed, made an example outta his life, why shouldn't you pardon him?" His enemies' frequent allegations of his manipulation of absentee ballots to commit voter fraud only prove their hypocrisy: "We got some votes for the black candidate. But *we* fraud now—*we* gonna steal votes. But they fine. Now why is you so much better than me? They don't say nothin' about that." Ike thus refines the myth of his own martyrdom.

Ike Brown's detractors also decry his central role in bringing the evil of liquor to this corner of the Bible Belt, in the early 1980s. Others similarly worry about his threats to solicit proposals for casino gambling. One woman solemnly noted that this sort of thing had been prophesied in Revelation: "As it was in the days of Noah so shall it be in the last days before His coming."

Despite his presumed wealth, Ike Brown does not look rich. His dress is unremarkable. On two of my visits with him—separated by eight months—he wore the same olive green sweater whose polyester fibers had pilled all over the garment. If he is vain about any aspect of his grooming, it is his hair, the style of which he changes frequently. When we first met, he had a "Marcel," with elaborate curls plastered to his scalp in wavelike patterns, preserved in the glistening hold of a firm hair gel. More recently, he has been keeping his hair in a natural style, meticulously cropped close to his scalp.

Like any other savvy political operator, Brown lives among his constituents. Giving directions to his home, he will tell the visitor not to worry if he gets lost on the way. "Everybody knows me." And they do. Ask most any African American man, woman, or child from one edge of the county seat to another, and they can direct you to Ike Brown. His dull brown double-wide trailer is perched on a small hill in Macon at the end of one of the gutted, curbless roads in the ramshackle black section of town north of Baptist Hill (the epicenter of the county's black population). It sits across from fading, two-room clapboard shacks enlivened outside only by trailing rosebushes or, in the early spring, the violent pinks and reds of blooming azaleas.

Like his little Honda car and his clothes, Brown's home is unpretentious. Inside his trailer, clad throughout in a cheap wood veneer and dominated by a mammoth television screen, nothing betrays position or wealth—certainly not the mud-colored shag carpet or the living-room set, upholstered in an olive and gold acrylic plaid. The only sign of his political connections is an autographed photograph on top of the television—his most impressive piece of furniture—of him and Ray Mabus, Mississippi's one-term, Harvard Law School–educated governor, a New Democrat in the Clinton mold. It reads simply: "With Best Wishes, Ray Mabus." Mabus, appointed by President Clinton as Ambassador to Saudi Arabia in early 1994, acknowledged to me that Brown did yeoman's service for him in Noxubee County and east-central Mississippi, but declined to speak about him for the record. Brown is uncontrollable and controversial enough that no ambitious politician is likely to nurture the perception that they are close. On his part, Brown stresses his good service to Mabus and other political notables in the state. He told me, for example, that he and a white woman staffer who used to work for Mabus's office remain "like sisters" they are so close.

Brown's critics have a ready response to the suggestion that his activities are conducted as much for a selfless desire for political change as for material gain. "He jus' wants you to think he doesn't have anything," said one. "Thas how he does," said another. "He can't live better and get support from the kinda folk who support him." Yet they cannot provide ammunition in support of these charges. A shrewd political operator willing to line his own pocket in the service of his realpolitik, yes. But it is difficult to countenance the

frequent suggestion of his critics that Brown serves his own
bank balance above all else.

■ ■ ■ MARTHA BLACKWELL subscribed to the latter
view as she battled Ike and what he came to stand for. Blackwell is a small, trim, solidly built woman with aquamarine
eyes and a prominent nose slightly rounded at its tip. Her
affable, alert face is framed by a magnificent corona of prematurely gray-white hair. And although Martha Blackwell
may have moved home to rural Mississippi, she still takes
care with little touches—a bit of makeup, earrings that work
with her outfit. She has not entirely left behind the woman
who dreamed in college of becoming a big-time interior designer in Houston or New York.

Scion of one of the county's oldest and most respected
white families, Blackwell became the waste projects' most
vocal opponent. Improbably enough, Noxubee County's Junior Miss for 1974; a lifelong but not especially political Republican; a daughter of the Old South who majored in
interior design at Mississippi State, where she worked as the
house manager for her Delta Gamma chapter; and a born-
again Christian active in her all-white Presbyterian church
has done more to publicize the environmental racism cause
than anyone else in Noxubee County. Nothing in her background or upbringing fits the stereotype of a politically correct, wooly-haired, tofu-munching environmental activist,
much less a campaigner for civil rights. When I asked a former sorority sister if Martha had been political in college,
she responded: "Yes, in a way. When she got into something,
she would do all the work." For example? "She would walk
the halls asking people to vote for someone for homecoming
queen." As another sorority sister explained: "At Mississippi

State University in the late seventies, we didn't talk about social issues at all. Current events were just not widely discussed. Current events meant 'weather.' "

However, there is in Martha Blackwell's background a commitment to the land and future of Noxubee County and the state of Mississippi. George Poindexter, a paternal ancestor, served as the state's second governor, from 1820 to 1822. More important still, her family has deep and illustrious roots in county history. Her paternal ancestor, Joel Barnett, was a decorated Revolutionary War captain who had participated in the siege of Yorktown. A local history reports that in 1797, Barnett trekked from Georgia to what would become Noxubee County, with a small fortune to invest "in the rich prairie land in the eastern part of the county."

Another paternal ancestor played a central role in the early history of Noxubee County. In the early 1850s, William R. Poindexter founded the "Calhoun Institute for young ladies" with "its site in Macon, Noxubee County, Mississippi." He noted, "Macon is a healthy, flourishing village, promising to be the most important town between the termini of the Mobile and Ohio Railway." The Mobile and Ohio ran through Macon up from the Alabama coast, moving straight through eastern Mississippi and turning west just south of Tennessee, and continued from there over to Memphis and on up to Ohio. The line was completed in 1856. Had the Civil War not rudely interrupted his dream, Poindexter's gamble that Macon would become a prosperous regional center would have been an intelligent one. The years before the Civil War, when Noxubee County was served by both rail and steamship travel, were especially vibrant, prosperous ones in the inland county, a natural stopping point between Mobile and points north.

By 1858, Poindexter and his wife, Martha (there has

been a Martha in the family for as long as anyone can remember), had built the most beautiful structure the county would see to this day. The Calhoun Institute was "to Macon what the Parthenon was to Athens," in the words of one of the building's early enthusiasts. A contemporary advertisement described it as "truly an elegant edifice." And it was. An illustration of the Calhoun Institute depicts the graceful, three-story Greek Revival building. Pairs of young ladies sporting elaborate millinery confections promenade down a wide semicircular drive. Swathed in layers of petticoats, the ladies shelter themselves from the unforgiving Mississippi sun with frilly parasols. The Calhoun Institute was determinedly for the Finer Sort: girls were taught French, German, Latin, mathematics, and rhetoric. "People were too aristocratic to permit any industrials; in fact, they were never thought of." Music was required, but only harp, guitar, or piano. "Violin was tabooed for a lady, postures and movements being regarded as undignified."

During the Civil War, the Calhoun Institute became first a hospital and, from July 1863 to May 1865, after the fall of Vicksburg, the Mississippi statehouse. The house of representatives met in the girls' main salon; the senate, in an adjoining red-brick building on the institute's grounds. Poindexter acted as the personal secretary to Mississippi's governor, Charles Clark, who may have been arrested by federal troops on the grounds of the institute upon the Union victory. Poindexter's blind son, John Quarles, was elected a Mississippi state senator, and he advanced the cause of building a state tuberculosis sanitarium. "The Blind Senator" thus continued the family tradition of public service.

But it was not only male ancestors who figured large in forming Martha Blackwell's sense of who she is and what her responsibilities are. Older white people say that she takes after her mother, Maureen, who, while not in the least political, was "very social-minded"—that is to say, a great hostess. Maureen Mullins was raised in the plantation culture of the Mississippi Delta, in one of the farming counties on the opposite side of the state, on its western border. Martha Blackwell's octogenarian aunt, Elaine Mullins, explained to me that Miss Maureen's sociability came from her Delta roots and was therefore well adapted to the plantation culture of eastern Noxubee County. "Delta people are real social-minded, so that part comes natural to Martha." Elaine Mullins said that Martha's mother's people were always going off to the Peabody (referring to Memphis's famous hotel), "the way Delta people do." This characterization of the ways of Delta whites has a venerable heritage. William Faulkner once wrote that "Mississippi begins in the lobby of a Memphis, Tennessee hotel and extends south to the Gulf of Mexico."

But when asked where Martha got the wherewithal to throw herself into the hazardous waste fight—sacrificing friendships and threatening the stability of her family and marriage in the process—her aunt articulated a view echoed by other family and friends. She insisted that Martha's single-mindedness derived neither from her father, who, despite his service on the board of supervisors, was by all accounts a shy man, nor from her mother, who took no active interest in social and political disputes. Martha's doggedness came, she said, from the strong women on her father's side, from her great-aunt, Weenonah Poindexter and from her grandmother, Ethel Poindexter Mullins.

Weenonah Poindexter aimed in the late 1800s and early 1900s to put Mississippi on the musical map. In 1894, she became the first head of the music department at the Mississippi Industrial Institute and College, the nation's first state-supported college solely for women. (In 1920 the name was changed to Mississippi State College for Women, renamed Mississippi University for Women in 1974. Throughout the state, the name has long been shortened to "the W" (pronounced "the DUB-ya").) When Ignace Paderewski, the famed Polish-born pianist, toured the United States during World War I to raise funds for war relief, "Miss Weenonah," as family members still speak of her, was determined to have the most famous musician of the age visit east-central Mississippi. The closest to Mississippi he was scheduled to come was Birmingham, Alabama. Miss Weenonah petitioned both the W's administration and the state legislature to fund his Mississippi tour, and she was twice refused. She then risked her personal savings to pay for his visit. Her gamble paid off: she netted a thousand dollars from ticket sales and used the total to establish a regular fund that brought internationally recognized musicians to the W for the rest of her 50-year tenure; the music building there bears her name today.

Martha Blackwell's paternal grandmother, Ethel Mullins, was equally steel willed, if less flamboyant. Widowed in her mid-twenties with three sons to raise, she took over the newly purchased, eponymous family hardware business, in the middle of Macon's main street, and built it into a local institution, in addition to managing the family plantation and serving as a trustee for the Macon city schools. As Martha's cousin Andy, now a professor of education at Ole Miss, recalled: "My grandmother was a firm believer in women gettin' college degrees and standin' toe to toe to fight it out with the men of the day. So in her way she was a feminist before her time. For Noxubee County she was unusual." Although conventional in many respects, Mullins and Poindexter women always determined to be heard.

■ ■ ■ MARTHA BLACKWELL's family history does not solely explain the absorption with which she threw herself into the county's fight against hazardous waste. Martha's efforts also owe much to the prairie culture in which she was raised.

Between 1936 and 1938, a history of Noxubee County was compiled under the auspices of the Works Progress Administration. In it a local writer described the county as "rich in the traditions established by an intellectual and cultured citizenship of the Old South." Noxubee County, she explained, "is a land of ideals, tenaciously adhered to down through the years since the early days of the nineteenth century. Noxubee is a story of an aristocracy of the soil." Few Noxubeeans, black or white, would disagree that the ideals of its planter class have been tenaciously adhered to since the county was first settled. Practically, this has meant that, until the last decade, all political and related decisions about county life were controlled by a small circle of white families. For over 150 years—until the local hazardous waste wars—Noxubee County has been a place controlled not by poor, rednecked white scratch farmers from the western hills, and certainly not by blacks, but by a tiny white elite, most of whom are cotton planters, concentrated in the county's eastern prairie.

Like most other natives, Martha pronounces the name of her county "KNOCK-shu-bee." This in itself is a sign of the county's insularity: as close as thirty miles away, people pronounce the name as "KNOX-uh-bee." But KNOCK-shubeeans cling as tenaciously to their pronunciation as to their historical patterns of behavior.

Martha Blackwell was born to the upper tier of the county's aristocracy of the soil. Despite her previous lack of interest in things political, the sense of entitlement that accompanies her station emboldened her to lead the waste dump opposition. In the traditional way of things in Noxubee County, if it was anyone's birthright to speak for future uses of the land, it was hers. Yet this legacy would also burden her as she strove to gain black supporters for her fight.

While the values of this aristocracy of the soil persist in Noxubee County, the realities of late-twentieth-century life mean that its black majority is increasingly impatient with them. To put it simply, the old aristocratic order rendered their voices mostly silent. As a result, for most people in Noxubee County today, nearly every political choice continues to turn on questions of racial control. This is not to say that every issue involves racial conflict. On the contrary, superficially, racial relations are, if not harmonious, at least generally cooperative. But just beneath the surface, questions of power—of racial power—are omnipresent in Noxubee County. This is largely because a small segment of the white minority continues to own most of the land inhabited and the businesses patronized by a black majority. But the roots of Noxubee County's political and social discord involve more than a simple case of the mostly white haves versus the mostly black have-nots. To understand Noxubee County, an observer must understand how the land has shaped the area's people and their history.

■ ■ ■ AN abundance of Choctaw place names in Noxubee County reflects the fact that it was once the center of Choctaw culture. It was in present-day Noxubee County that the tribe was finally pressured into surrendering any claim to its traditional lands. The Treaty of Dancing Rabbit Creek, negotiated from September 27 through 29, 1830, was the last of four treaties in which the Choctaw ceded their lands to the U.S. government. Dancing Rabbit Creek, the site of the actual treaty signing, forms a natural amphitheater for a large meeting. Beside the creek, in the hilly pineywoods of the county's extreme southeastern corner, United States Army commissioners met Choctaw leaders, surrounded by thousands of the land's indigenous people. The U.S. representatives, instructed by President Andrew Jackson only to "fail not to make a treaty," secured most of the vast swatch of central Mississippi—fully twenty-five of the state's modern eighty-two counties. In fact, an early chronicler of the event concluded, "Fear, intimidation and coercion, all more or less combined, were the causes that prompted the Choctaw councilmen to sign the treaty." Historians of the event agree that the principal incentive for the Choctaw to sign was the treaty's infamous Article 14, which allowed those who desired to remain within traditional lands to do so.

Article 14 derived its notoriety from the fact that it proved to be a false promise: subsequently, most of the Choctaw were forced to move from their ancestral lands to a radically different, semi-arid terrain in present-day Oklahoma. Those who remained in what is now Mississippi were relegated to several small settlements about forty miles southwest of Dancing Rabbit Creek, near what became Philadelphia, Mississippi. So began the cycle of land transfer about which Faulkner wrote in his short novel "The Bear." The land he said, was "bought with white man's money from the wild men whose grandfathers without guns hunted it. . . . " Whites in turn tried to tame and cultivate the land with the labor of black slaves over whom they held complete power, trying to grow something new on the land—first to recoup their investment, and then to make a profit. This was so, Faulkner recognized, even though the Indian chief who sold white men the land "knew . . . that not even a fragment of it had been his to relinquish or sell."

This is part of what Faulkner called the "curse" of "this whole land, this whole South." Faulkner's bear-hunting protagonist, a white man named McCaslin, disagrees with a black stranger (more prosperous, better dressed and spoken than he), about this curse, conceding that whites had brought the curse: such that whites could at best expect to "endure and outlast it until the curse is lifted. Then your people's turn will come because we have forfeited ours."

Although the black stranger demurs, insisting that a new era insuring freedom, liberty, and equality for all is beginning in this "new Canaan," McCaslin's lament more aptly describes the history of Dancing Rabbit Creek since 1869. As the fight over hazardous waste would demonstrate time and again in Noxubee County, McCaslin's real world descendants found themselves embroiled once more in a fierce battle over who should profit from the lands once freely hunted by the native Mississippi tribes, and how. Arrayed against them were the real world descendants of the black stranger with whom McCaslin spoke, allied with previously powerless whites, seeking their "turn" with the land.

■ ■ ■ BUT for its eastern border, which juts out to the northeast, Noxubee County forms an almost perfect square. The county sits along the Alabama–Mississippi line in east-central Mississippi, along one edge of the Alabama–Mississippi black prairie belt, a huge tract of rich alluvial soil that arcs toward the northwest from just above Montgomery, Alabama, to Tupelo, Mississippi, forming a thick crescent. The phrase *black prairie belt* refers to the thick black soil that distinguishes the area. The county farm agent boasted in the

1920s that "Noxubee County contains the largest acreage of any county in the belt." This natural feature of Noxubee County's landscape has done much to shape the direction of its troubled social history.

U.S. Route 45, which runs up and down about two-thirds of eastern Mississippi, from south of Meridian north to just below Tupelo (Elvis's birthplace), today separates Noxubee's eastern prairies from its western hills. The road runs more or less straight through Noxubee County, gently curving up and down like a piece of ribbon candy for much of the county's thirty-or-so-mile length. For years now, signs have promised that the road will go from two lanes to four, as part of a statewide highway improvement program (anyone who has driven Mississippi roads knows how desperately this is needed). However, although there has been work to the south and north, completion of the four-lane stretch through Noxubee County has proceeded at a snail's pace. This is not especially surprising, because there is not much reason to go there. It has been easy for Noxubee County to hide itself from the outside world's gaze.

In 1977, construction of a bypass was completed that diverted U.S. 45 from around Macon, the county seat. As a result, the casual visitor can easily pass through Noxubee County without realizing it, and certainly without knowing that it contains much of a town at all. Though once dotted with dozens of settlements large enough to have a post office and a cluster of shops, the county today has but three settlements that can be called towns. Macon, the largest of the three, with a population of twenty-five hundred, is now hidden from view of the highway. Shuqualak (pronounced "SHOOG-a-lock," which means "hog wallow" in Choctaw), the major town in the county's southern section, looks more like a ghost town than a place that a thousand people call home. From a speeding car, an outsider would be struck only by several lines of rail siding and perhaps some truckloads of freshly hewn pine waiting for processing at the milling and planing operations run by the Thomas brothers at Shuqualak Lumber, or the sight of hardwoods en route to Billy McCann's Prince Lumber Company. In the northern portion of the county, the town of Brooksville, with a population of fifteen hundred, is only a bit more lively, but it is largely invisible from U.S. 45. An outsider might easily suppose that it consists mostly of large farms spread out over the endless acres of Kansas-like prairie north and east of Macon, and dense pineywoods and grazing land south of its biggest town.

But reminders of a rich and conflict-ridden history lie hidden behind stands of pine, leafy oak, and hackberry, or rows of low-lying, gnarled bois d'arc (pronounced "BO-dock" by locals) along its unpaved back roads, or concealed by tall stands of grass and cane. One such reminder is New Brazelia. In its heyday, the main plantation house, now partially shielded by overgrown brush, could be seen for miles around. It stands out in the middle of the prairie, near the ghost hamlet of Prairie Point, with few other buildings for miles around, just off the Buggs Ferry Road.

Finding the Buggs Ferry Road is no easy task. Road signs are not a local government priority in Mississippi, and Mississippians are used to giving detailed directions that require the recipient to appreciate minor changes in the landscape. A typical set of directions might go like this: Turn left at the first graveled (but not the dirt) road, and look out for the cluster of hackberry trees with the biggest one closest to the road. Turn left again. When you see the rusted combine about two miles on, next to the unused silo, then you'll know you've gone the right way.

Getting to the Buggs Ferry Road is something like that. If you turn right off U.S. 45 just north of Macon, head east toward Alabama, go over a small bridge after about three miles, and then make a few more turns to the northeast on rutted, unpaved roads, you'll eventually end up along the Buggs Ferry Road, which once led to a trading post on the Tombigbee River.

The Tombigbee River, once a major trading artery for this part of Mississippi, was cannibalized in a 1979 U.S. Army Corps of Engineers project first recommended to Congress in 1938. The Tenn-Tom Waterway (pronounced "TEEN-Tom" locally), the nation's largest inland water link, joined the Tennessee and Ohio Rivers and the upper Mississippi River valley with the Tombigbee River, which runs from north of Noxubee down to the Gulf of Mexico, emptying out at Mobile. The idea was that the Tenn-Tom would thus reduce transportation costs from the gulf ports to mid-America. Its series of locks and dams—bridging the thirty-nine-mile gap between the headwaters of the Tombigbee and the nearest portion of the Tennessee—never resulted in the hoped-for increase in commerce in northeastern Mississippi and northwestern Alabama.

In Noxubee County, the effects of the Tenn-Tom make it hard to imagine that there was once a thriving ferry culture in this inland portion of Mississippi, far from the state's eponymous river. But an active river trade did once flourish in eastern Mississippi and Alabama counties like Noxubee. Cotton and other crops were shipped to ports along the Tombigbee, including Mobile, and other merchandise was shipped back up river. The main Noxubee port was not far from the end of the Buggs Ferry Road, at Memphis, Alabama.

New Brazelia stands just off the Buggs Ferry Road, a few miles from the site of an old ferry stop that served plantations in the area. The centerpiece of a plantation said locally to have been one of the largest in this part of the state, New Brazelia is a rambling, two-story house with a high gabled roof. The land around it is today somewhat overgrown and unkempt. The last resident, a woman now in retirement, moved into Macon a few years ago, although she still goes out to the prairie to spend several days each week in her family house.

In 1882, New Brazelia's long-leaf pine timbers were sawed and framed in Mobile, and then shipped up river from the port. The architect and twelve assistants moved to Noxubee to erect the grand house over the course of the next eighteen months. Ironically, few states other than Mississippi have greater timber resources with which to build wood housing. But the state was growing so fast—especially in the mid-1800s, before the Civil War—that there simply wasn't the industry to process wood for building timber.

New Brazelia's most distinctive feature is the four-sided cupola that sits atop the house, with wide-paned windows looking out in every direction across the flat prairie land. Descendants of John Cockrell, the man who first built up the plantation and erected the house, learned as children that the cupola was a design element copied from the grand houses nestled around Mobile Bay, with views across the bay and to the Gulf of Mexico beyond. But the myth I heard time and time again in Noxubee County was that the cupola was designed to allow the plantation overseer to keep watch over every slave hand laboring on the plantation's thousands of acres. Which story represents the truth about New Brazelia's cupola is not likely ever to be known. Yet the persistence of the local explanation for the cupola's existence, with its suggestion of a watchful, demanding white overlord, speaks volumes about local perceptions of the power of the plantation culture that flourished in Noxubee County's eastern prairie into the 1960s.

Whites in Noxubee County's black prairie belt still say that its people are more like those in the Delta than in any other part of the state, echoing the comments of Martha Blackwell's aunt about the similarity of the two cotton-based plantation cultures. Even today, with so many of the county's grand properties in disrepair, it is easy to imagine lavish entertainments at New Brazelia and similar houses that still dot the prairie, or in one of the handful of sumptuous antebellum homes that line Jefferson Street, Macon's principal thoroughfare. As in the Delta, the descendants of Scottish, Irish, and German immigrants streamed into the area in the late 1830s and 1840s. The savvier ones began acquiring large tracts of land, sometimes eventually amassing thousands of acres in the black belt. Their descendants—Evanses, Fieldses, Cunninghams, Missos, Tubbses and Ferrises—can still be found living in Noxubee County. Martha Blackwell's parents, too, would eventually settle out in the dark-earthed eastern flatlands, near the Prairie Point community, as had her eighteenth-century forebearer, Joel Barnett.

Also like the Delta, the rich soil proved ideal for cotton production. In a premechanized agricultural age cotton was a labor-intensive crop, and this fact led to the acquisition of large numbers of slaves. In 1860, on the eve of the Civil War, Noxubee County was inhabited by 15,496 slaves and but 5,171 whites—roughly the same proportion of blacks to whites as today.

By contrast, in surrounding Mississippi counties, the reported census figures showed a significantly lower proportion of blacks to whites in three of the four Mississippi counties adjoining Noxubee, reflecting the special characteristics of the prairie land in Noxubee County and the determination of its new white settlers to maximize their financial gain there. Noxubee County was also the only one of these five counties that recorded no "free colored"—the census designation for freed slaves—in its 1860 population. Each of the others, like most Mississippi counties outside the Delta, registered a handful of freemen.

I spent an afternoon with Robert Hunter, a ruddy-faced lumberman in his mid-forties. Hunter is a descendant of John Cockrell, the man who built New Brazelia, and when he speaks about landholding patterns in eastern Mississippi, Hunter's enthusiasm turns him into something of an over-grown puppy. He carefully laid out the land maps of Noxubee and surrounding counties for me. The differences in land-holding patterns between adjoining counties were astonish-ing. Noxubee County—similar to western Sumter County, Alabama, which adjoins it to the east—has large tracts of flat prairie land, ideal for big plantations. In the pineywoods to the west, the tracts that have not been consolidated by big lumber companies remain broken up into small farms of a few dozen acres each. Looking at the land maps with Hunter, I could see quite clearly how none of the Mississippi counties near Noxubee—Lowndes and Oktibbeha to the north, Winston to the west, Kemper and Neshoba to the south and southeast—contained a similar concentration of large planta-tions. It was the black prairie land, which required large num-bers of hands to work it profitably, that made this section of the Mississippi–Alabama border a demographic black belt as well as one so named for the color of its soil.

One of the things that makes Noxubee County unique, and quite unlike the Delta, however, is that the prairie oc-cupies only slightly over half of the county's area. Drive through the Delta and the horizon is endless, unarticulated by any rise or bulge in the terrain. But most of the western half of Noxubee County is thick with towering loblolly and other southern yellow pines, a portal to the vast forests of central Mississippi. The county's pine forests stretch back to Mashulaville, the settlement—today little more than a handful of houses—that takes its name from the Choctaw chief Mashulatebbe, who negotiated and signed the Treaty of Dancing Rabbit Creek.

Writing in the 1920s, John Tyson, the Noxubee County clerk and a local historian then in his seventy-first year, explained that the natural division of the county's prairies dated back to the use of the land by its indigenous occupants, the Choctaw. Tyson reported that the Noxubee River, which bisects the county in a diagonal running from its northwestern tip down to its southeastern corner,

> was wholly within ancient Choctaw territory and was, generally speaking, the dividing line between their permanent homes in the pine lands to the south and their summer hunting grounds to the north and east of the river, embracing the prairies of Oktibbeha, Lowndes and Noxubee counties, in which fish and game abounded.

It was in this part of the county that white men first settled as well. Tyson continued:

> It is a well known fact, that the early settlers of Noxubee County did not locate in the prairie section of the county by reason of the scarcity of water, but passed them by and settled in the western part of the county, notable [*sic*] in the neighborhood of Mashulaville, where wood and water were abundant.

The county's western landscape is marked by clusters of small, steep hills that give way to narrow fields, on which some people eke out a hardscrabble existence. Human habitation on this side of the county is a far cry from the antebellum homes that line Macon's main street and distinguish the prairie's terrain. Interspersed between steep logging roads traversed by gargantuan trucks owned by paper giants like Weyerhaueser and Georgia-Pacific sit small, weathered houses that have gone too many years without a fresh coat of paint or needed repairs to sagging roofs and windows. Many people live in trailers and some in the tar-paper shacks that are indelibly imprinted in the national memory as a symbol of the Deep South's poverty. A general feeling of meanness, of struggle, emanates from these dwellings. Listless children dawdle at the door, endless rows of laundry are strung out to dry, and trash burns perpetually in oil drums—as if serving as each clan's own eternal flame. Inevitably, a host of small animals—mangy dogs, chickens—roams about. This is Faulkner's Mississippi, the land of Snopeses. Here begin the vermillion-colored clay hills that run through neighboring Winston County and then down to Neshoba County, which produced the men who, in 1964, killed three civil rights workers—James Chaney, Andrew Goodman, and Michael Schwerner—near Philadelphia, Neshoba County's seat. One white Macon businessman confided to a group at a dinner I attended that this is one part of Noxubee County where he was afraid to drive at night. Sometimes the boys "back there" drank too much, he said, and he wouldn't trust them not to get uncontrollable.

Most of the faces one sees in this part of Noxubee County are white. Some blacks live in western Noxubee County, to be sure, but that area is largely white or, to invoke the terms used interchangeably by Noxubeeans when describing the people of this part of the county: redneck, hillbilly, trash. I knew them instantly. Theirs are the faces of my

Kentucky relatives: prematurely aged, badly nourished, and drawn from years of too much sun; they wear pinched expressions masking resentments deeply felt but usually unexpressed. They are reserved, their eyes watchful and guarded. And they have reason to be suspicious, for the prairie's bounty has not been shared with them.

■ ■ ■ RALPH HIGGINBOTHAM, who became the head of the county's five-member board of supervisors, was born and raised in the hilly southwestern section of Noxubee County. It is hard to imagine a man who seems more ill suited for public service in a democracy; for Higginbotham, stubbornness is a virtue. At a board of supervisors meeting I once attended, Higginbotham was being challenged by an angry group of citizens about his decision not to appoint a man's wife to fill the term of her recently dead husband, a supervisor, in keeping with Mississippi custom. Rather than explain himself, he simply walked out of the room. Supporters and enemies alike assured me that this was standard behavior.

Higginbotham represented District Four, Noxubee County's largest and least densely populated. The geographic size of a district matters a great deal to a supervisor, one of whose primary functions is regularly to drag and gravel roads. Elected supervisor in 1987, Higginbotham became the board's head in 1991. Both developments were surprising to the people whose families had traditionally been the dominant forces in Noxubee County politics. Here was a man from the hills, with a ruddy face and tightly drawn lips, a man of little education and no means, a man from out in the Butler community, a place Martha Blackwell described as "real backwoodsy"; to her ilk, Butler is "a different world."

Higginbotham and his wife, Sue, attend a Pentecostal church in Butler, near where he was raised as one of over ten children, most of whom have left the county. A young lawyer in Macon reported Higginbotham relating to him with some bitterness stories about the poverty in which he grew up. Higginbotham recalled that he and his family had been without refrigeration into his young adulthood (he is in his mid-fifties) and so had been forced to buy large blocks of ice, which they then wrapped in blankets to keep cool in the summer. Others told me that he will not drive in Jackson because of the traffic. The state capital is a city of but two hundred thousand, and the metropolitan area twice that big; Jackson is not one of the nation's major urban traffic headaches.

Higginbotham's rise to power signaled the near-end of a major tectonic shift in county politics, one begun nearly two decades earlier. Joseph Wayne, the county's first black supervisor in this century, was elected in 1971. Martha Blackwell was sixteen that year. She remembers hearing in those years that her father had to help lead and guide Wayne, because he did not know the first thing about being a supervisor. "It was just real awkward. Mr. Wayne expected Daddy to help him, and Daddy helped him." As a novice, Wayne would naturally have looked to more experienced people for guidance. And the relation must have been uncomfortable in a place where the social hierarchy had for so long been clearly delineated. But the paternalism of Blackwell's characterization—one I heard frequently repeated about different black officials today—makes it suspect. Still today, a supervisor's job is often a half-time one for a farmer, and supervisors mainly see to it that roads are cleared and that the county's budget is balanced. High-level managerial skills are not required.

Blacks were similarly thought to be ill prepared for the responsibilities of freedom after the Civil War. But with emancipation, the historian Eric Foner has noted, "specific aspirations" were underpinned by "a broader theme: a desire for independence from white control, for autonomy both as individuals and as members of a community itself being transformed as a result of emancipation." Similarly, for Wayne and the black officials who were to follow him in twentieth-century Noxubee County, office holding intertwined not only personal ambition but also the aspirations of a majority community ill understood or held in contempt by the minority white population.

It was in the 1971 local election that Martha Blackwell and her older siblings began to urge their father not to keep running. But they said he insisted; there was no one else. Another candidate, a white man, was widely viewed by stalwarts of the community, by people like William Mullins, as an unacceptable choice. In fact, a black man—and not the other white candidate—ran second to her father in 1971 and again for Mullins's last campaign, in 1975. Notably, Martha Blackwell's recollection, one informed by the dinner-table conversation of her parents and their friends before she could vote, lacked this important detail.

Wayne was succeeded in 1979 by another black man, Joseph Stevenson, who for the next generation served District One, which covers the county's northeastern prairie and has the largest black population. In the next decade, another black man, George Robinson, was elected supervisor to represent District Three, which includes the heavily black town of Macon. By the late 1980s, this left Higginbotham and two other white supervisors, ones with long and celebrated roots in the county: Johnny Heard, a farmer of modest means whose family was nonetheless an established presence in

District Five, comprising Brooksville and the surrounding area in the northwest, and Kenny Misso, a farmer descended from some of the family's earliest settlers. Misso represented District Two, covering much of the county's black prairie land. He farmed out in Prairie Point, near New Brazelia and Martha Blackwell's place.

What was novel about this quintet is that Higginbotham became a wild card. He could not be counted on to support the views of the white-minority segment—the aristocracy of the soil—that had traditionally directed the county's political affairs. This was a fact that Ike Brown, with his detailed electoral calculations and racially inflammatory political style, would ruthlessly exploit for almost five years. Ike Brown was in luck. As it turned out, Higginbotham was more than ready to align himself with newly empowered black politicians and turn against the powerful, prosperous whites in the county. For nearly a generation he had nursed a grievance against what came to be identified as "the white power structure." His vendetta found a perfect opportunity for expression when, in the summer of 1990, Ed Netherland came to town and proposed building one of the country's biggest hazardous waste dumps and incinerators. Like a latter-day snake-oil salesman, Netherland was offering the promise of a new life for Noxubee County.

2
THE LAND OF MILK AND HONEY

E DWARD H. NETHERLAND
could model for the figure of
the groom on the top of a
fancy, picture-perfect wedding cake. Standing at well over six
feet, he exudes that combination of confidence and friendliness, calculation and enthusiasm that the world associates
with Anglo-Saxon men from the United States. A group of
women I knew in law school had a name for men like this:
"Leaguers," shorthand for members of the "League of Identical Men." The moniker carried with it the derogatory impli-
cation that Leaguers were also the types who accepted
uncritically the assumptions and ground rules of American
business. Leaguers were those who were interested in their
own short-term financial gain ahead of any other concerns.

■ ■ ■   ED NETHERLAND hails from Murfreesboro, Tennessee, about a half hour south of Nashville, just north of Tennessee walking horse country. Five minutes with him and it's clear that good living is his vocation, with no small desire to impress. Netherland is the quintessential check grabber, the kind who picks up the tab with a flourish: Stick with me, kid, and you'll be in the money, too. Ed often brags that in his early thirties he became a top insurance salesman for one of the nation's biggest insurers, working out of a family agency started in 1934. In this business, Netherland had cultivated a lot of rich, powerful clients. His run as a hazardous waste baron began when some of those clients agreed to support his decision to try and make a mint promoting hazardous waste disposal.

In 1988, Netherland remembered, he was contacted by an insurance client who was himself a friend of Tennessee's former commissioner for health and the environment, Jim Word. Netherland was told that Word believed the southeastern United States needed more disposal capacity for its hazardous waste. The men knew some venture capitalists who had raised money for this sort of thing. As the head of a new hazardous waste disposal company, Word—the chief environmental regulator for two governors—would give respectability to the project.

At the time, such a business proposition looked promising. Nationally, fears of a national waste crisis—of mountains of toxic garbage with nowhere to go—were mounting. In 1987, the Mobro garbage barge, carrying Long Island, New York, trash, was turned away by six states and three nations. Similarly, the "poo-poo choo-choo," a sixty-three-car train of human waste, traveled between Baltimore and the Gulf Coast for several weeks in late 1989.

In the Southeast, these worries were particularly intense. The growing sense of crisis developed out of Alabama's desire no longer to serve, in the pungent phrase of one state politician, as "America's biggest industrial pay toilet." The pay toilet in question was the nation's largest hazardous waste landfill, in Emelle, Alabama, run by the nation's biggest toxic waste disposal concern, Chemical Waste Management, often called Chem Waste. The Emelle landfill, in Sumter County, sits near Alabama's west-central border, not thirty miles from Noxubee County. Like its Mississippi neighbor, Sumter County is in the black prairie belt, and shares a nearly identical demographic profile. In 1988, the Emelle dump was accepting hazardous residue from all forty-eight continental states; in some years more than 90 percent of the waste dumped at Emelle was produced out of state. Emelle's waste volume grew exponentially from the mid-1980s, fueling Alabamians' fears. From 1985 to 1989, the tonnage of hazardous waste landfilled there more than doubled, from 341,000 tons in 1985 to 788,000 tons in 1989.

What would happen if a state like Alabama limited access to the huge disposal facility within its borders? In 1989, Alabama tried to do just that, when Alabama state representative Jimmy Holley introduced a bill that aimed to alleviate Alabama's increasing anxiety that it was becoming the nation's hazardous waste litter box. The Holley bill strictly limited the waste that could be dumped at Alabama's only commercial hazardous waste facility, in Emelle. Under it, Emelle could accept only wastes generated in states that had their own hazardous waste disposal facilities. Because Emelle is one of only fifteen U.S. commercial hazardous waste disposal facilities, the bill's success was nervously monitored by industries across the nation.

The Holley bill challenged a central tenet of federal hazardous waste law, a concept known as capacity assurance planning, by which each state is required to show that it has sufficient capacity to dispose of waste produced within its borders. Since it is not cost effective for each state to install the often-expensive technology needed to dispose of different kinds of toxic trash, federal law allows states to enter into regional agreements, by which they agree to accept others' disposal responsibilities. Many Alabamians had come to realize that regional agreements allowed other states to produce capacity assurance plans, or CAPs, that complied with the law—and still left Alabama holding the short end of the stick. Despite—and maybe because of—the way the CAP process had worked out, a disproportionate amount of the nation's toxic garbage continued to be dumped in one of the poorest and blackest areas of Alabama.

The Holley bill's message to the rest of the country was clear: Take care of your own damn mess. Soon after enactment, the bill was challenged in federal court by Chem Waste and its trade association. The waste industry challenged the Holley bill as an unconstitutional interference with commerce across state lines. In an August 1990 opinion, a federal circuit court reluctantly agreed with Chem Waste and declared the Holley bill unconstitutional. But by then, Chem Waste's victory meant little: in April 1990, the Alabama legislature had passed a law imposing high taxes on out-of-state wastes headed for Emelle. It was not until June 1992 that the out-of-state tax law was in its turn declared unconstitutional by a sharply divided U.S. Supreme Court. In the meantime, energetic entrepreneurs like Ed Netherland had reason to think that they might make a killing in hazardous waste speculation.

■ ■ ■ ONE of the people Netherland approached for possible financing was another client, Gary Neal, the chief operating officer of the Danner Company, one of the Southeast's most legendary business empires. The company's founder, Ray Danner, is famed in the Southeast for his Shoney's chain restaurant success. Danner, the quintessential self-made American man, is also a figure followed by innuendo and controversy. In 1993, Danner and his company were sued for widespread racial discrimination at his Shoney's and Captain D restaurants. Top-placed Danner associates testified that Danner's own racial views were widely known: Danner believed blacks were not qualified to run restaurants and should not have jobs where customers could see them. A former chief executive officer recalled that Danner spoke of contributing to the Ku Klux Klan and implementing a corporate "matching gift" program for Klan donations. The denouement of the class action lawsuit was that Danner agreed to pay a $132.5 million judgment, without admitting guilt. Most of the money came from his own pocket. He refuses to comment on the case; under oath, he said he "couldn't recall" when confronted with specific employee accusations about his racism.

Neal went off and considered Netherland's offer. "He came back to me," Netherland recalled. "And for them it looked like a good proposition. The Danner Company is very well capitalized. With only about eight companies in the [hazardous waste] business, they could afford to try and compete. Mr. Danner said that 'it's a difficult entry business, but it's legitimate, something America will need, and a growing field.' " The Danner Company committed itself to give Netherland $1 million.

Netherland was off and hustling. Federated Technologies, Incorporated, or FTI, was born in the summer of 1989. Jim Word was its president and Ed Netherland its chief promoter. No one could have predicted then that this $1 million would turn out to be but seed money. There was a condition on the investment, too: Netherland was not to reveal its source.

Netherland then had a couple of false starts. One of his tries was to site a facility in Marion County, Tennessee, in the south-central portion of the state, next to an industrial site with river access. But news of his plans was leaked before he had a chance to build support with local business and political leaders. Public opposition was swift and heated, forcing the local authorities to come out against the project. This doomed it. Almost one year later, with nothing to show for his efforts, Netherland began looking for alternative sites for his venture.

Then, on March 20, 1990, every plan in Netherland's life took on a new urgency. Netherland was out clearing trees on a farm he had bought outside of Murfreesboro when he noticed a big lump under his arm. He went to his doctor, who aspirated it and took cell samples. Worried, the doctor sent the samples away for further tests. Netherland was diagnosed with a malignant melanoma. He was told that someone of his age with a diagnosis of malignant skin cancer had but a 3 percent chance of living over two years. Ten days later, on March 30, he entered St. Thomas Hospital in Nashville, where doctors cut out twenty-eight lymph nodes, two of which were deep enough to confirm that he had little hope of recovery.

No proven treatment for melanoma exists. Netherland was 35 years old, married, and had two infants and a new farm. His doctors advised him not to have any more children and to sell the farm. The week after surgery, Netherland was back at work on the FTI project. "Otherwise," he mused, "I'd just a-been sitting back waiting to die."

■ ■ ■ NETHERLAND recalls that people began calling him from all over Tennessee, asking him to consider bringing his untested hazardous waste business to their county. One of those Netherland remembered contacting him was Tillman Knox, a sixty-five-year-old mining contractor with land to sell in south-central Tennessee.

Knox remembered his introduction to Netherland and FTI differently. "The first thing that happened was that I was approached by FTI, and they were interested in some land that I had." That was in March 1990.

Knox, whose office walls are covered with hunting trophies and pictures of his days as an infantry mess sergeant during the Korean War, is a genial, unassuming man who built up a comfortable mining business in Mount Pleasant, Tennessee. Nestled among beautiful rolling hills, Mount Pleasant was once the home of a thriving phosphate-mining industry. The back roads near Mount Pleasant are dotted with visual reminders of the now-dormant strip-mining operations, with descending coils of gray-green rock exposed, looking like some kind of B-movie set for a moonscape. The Mount Pleasant/Maury Phosphate Museum, complete with cheap manikins dressed as miners, their wigs askew, remains the town's principal tourist attraction, although phosphate mining no longer contributes much to the local economy. The environmental push to remove phosphates from laundry detergents signaled a decline in demand for phosphorus, and the last company still mining in Mount Pleasant closed in February 1991.

Knox talked to FTI because he knew James Word,

having dealt with him as a regulator overseeing the conduct of Knox's phosphate business. FTI proposed to build a $40 million hazardous waste incinerator on Knox's land, which was no longer good for much else. The site was also less than an hour from Nashville, not far from General Motors' new Saturn plant at Columbia, and near a rail line. In other words, it appeared to have a ready market. The wastes, which could have included oils and solvents, paint residues, leftover plastics, infectious medical waste, and municipal garbage, were not to be disposed there. After incineration, blocks of toxic ash would be shipped off-site for disposal.

Tillman Knox subscribes to what might be called the states' rights view of hazardous waste disposal. "I do personally think that each state should take care of their own. Some day, some of the states that are allowing stuff to come across the state lines, I think that's gonna be stopped before it's over with." What Knox did not realize is that Alabama's endorsement of this approach to hazardous waste disposal encouraged people like Ed Netherland to seek him out. As a result, Knox was drawn into the biggest nightmare of his business life.

In May 1990, Word came to look at a possible site near Mount Pleasant, in Maury County. Knox insisted in advance that if they bought the land, they would have to obtain permission from the town of Mount Pleasant. He lived there, after all, and wanted to preserve his good name. "Mr. Word walked over that down there, and there was some question in his mind about, uh, wetlands, which of course you know you cannot disturb wetlands. And so they did not like the site. And they asked me if I had anything south of, or anywhere around." In fact, he did. Several years earlier, Knox and a partner had bought scattered parcels of unreclaimed mining land in the region, including sixty-four and a half acres of unreclaimed mining land in neighboring Giles County. Phosphate strip mining of the Giles County tract, known locally simply as "the Mines," began in 1914, and the rail transportation access was good. For years, a phosphate-based animal feed supplement was produced at the Mines. But in the 1940s, efforts began to extract fluorine, causing local complaints about fluorine gas emissions. Strip-mining operations at the Mines ceased in 1965; Knox and a partner bought the land in the late 1980s for the grand sum of $36,000, or about $550 an acre, a bargain price for land in that part of Tennessee.

"[FTI] had told me, and I believed them, that they were going to be extremely modern in everything they did, that there would not be any fumes or contamination or anything that would affect the community. So I told them about this land in Giles County. So, they went and looked at it, and we priced the land to them." Knox's scruples about having town permission for a sale if it was to proceed in his home county suddenly evaporated when the possible sale concerned land in an adjoining county.

"So anyway, one day I was playing golf, and they came out to the club that afternoon . . . and they wanted an option on it. And I told them, I said, 'I'm playin' golf and I'll be through in an hour or so, and if some talkin' needs to be done, I'll talk to 'em at that time.' "

The day was June 13, 1990. That morning, Netherland had pressed Knox's partner, a lawyer, to draft an option agreement on the spot and had rushed it out to the golf course for Knox's signature.

"See," Knox continued, "we had told 'em what we'd take for it. I think we told 'em we'd take $150,000." This would mean a potential profit to Knox and his partner of over 400 percent on their investment.

"They wanted an option on it for $1,000. And they called on me after I got through, and they, uh, sort of high-pressured me . . . "

He paused to correct himself. "I won't say high-pressured me. And I said, 'Well, I wouldn't give anybody an option for a thousand dollars.' "

But Netherland, typically persistent and pressed for time, insisted, waited for Knox to say when he would sign the option agreement. "And I ended up givin' 'em one for three thousand dollars. Don't misunderstand me, now. I'm not downgradin' any of these people. So I went ahead hurriedly and we"—Knox and his partner—"gave him a sixty-day option."

Knox quickly came to worry about what he had done. How quickly? "Well, immediately. I was mining on Rusty Horne's place at that time." Horne is the president of First National Bank, Giles County's largest, and a local power broker. "So the next day my son and I made an appointment with Rusty and went down there and told him what we had done. It sort of shocked him, but he said to me, 'Well, I know, Tillman, that this is just a business deal with you, and I can understand your situation of doin' this.'

"We were mining on his property, and I felt like—and still do—that Rusty Horne is a friend of mine, and . . . I didn't want this thing to come out all—a sudden. And he says, 'I don't know how involved I'll get into it,' but of course we don't, we don't want an incinerator in Giles County.' "

Horne is not a man given to understatement. He is assured enough of his power and position in his community that he speaks his mind, he expects to see his views implemented. But when he told Knox, "We do not want an incinerator in Giles County," Horne wildly underestimated the forces of protest that were about to be unleashed in this scenic part of south-central Tennessee.

■ ■ ■ IN the early 1960s, when Carol Puckett was a little girl growing up in Decatur, Alabama, a port city along the Tennessee River in northern Alabama, her family would drive north on the weekends into southern Tennessee. At Elkton, Tennessee, the first town across the state line, where the expanse of flat Alabama–Mississippi farmland uplifts into the gentle, rolling hills of walking horse country, there used to be a sign that read: WELCOME TO GILES COUNTY, THE LAND OF MILK AND HONEY. The sign is gone now, but still today, the slogan is one locals freely appeal to when trying to drum up neighborly support for a worthy cause in Giles County. The memory of those signs, and the place they celebrated, stuck with Carol Puckett into adulthood, making her determined that she would someday make her home there.

Giles Countians are intensely proud of the natural beauty of their place, with its well-tended white fencerows, abundance of stately antebellum brick homes with manicured yards, and a vigorous commercial center in the county seat, Pulaski. Pulaski (pronounced "PEW-las-ki") is dominated by a gracious three-story neoclassical courthouse that adorns one of Pulaski's many hills. It is made of blond brick articulated with granite Corinthian columns to the east and west, and corresponding granite pilasters to the north and south; each side of the building is surmounted by a pediment containing an elaborate frieze. Atop everything rests a working bell encased in a freshly painted, copper-clad bell tower. Taller than it is wide, the courthouse towers over the surrounding buildings, only one of which is three stories high. The spacious central square where the courthouse sits is planted with an abundance of elms, oaks, and flowering crabapples, and evokes feelings of quiet confidence, of comfortable prosperity. Radiating out from the central square is an active business district. There is a McDonald's in a commercial strip down in a valley on the northwestern side of town, but otherwise there are few reminders of the predictable commercialism that dominates most American cities and towns. A Wal-Mart came and succeeded, but unlike the sorry story in so many small towns, where the merchandising behemoth drove out local hardware stores, Wal-Mart's local competitors continue to thrive. Pulaski's success in holding onto some of the best of its past, sustaining itself as an active small town into the late twentieth century, is symbolized by the fact that Reeves Drugstore, which has been operating continuously on the northeastern corner of the square since 1893, still sells Cokes for a nickel, amidst its thriving pharmacy and gift business.

Pulaski's visual tidiness is echoed throughout the county. Dozens of small, well-kept farms visible in all directions from the hills of Pulaski would warm the heart of any movie scout seeking locations for a Typical Southern Scene. The closeness of the verdant hills, row upon row receding toward the horizon and lushly decorated with leafy deciduous trees, recalls southern England or Normandy.

Locals work hard to polish the image of both town and county. They delight in the fact that it is not merely rural, but offers some culture as well. A small Methodist college is still going strong after 100 years, even attracting foreign exchange students from Japan and Europe. Uncharacteristically for a town of nearly eight thousand (about a third of the county's population), Pulaski boasts an accomplished dinner theater, rather oddly housed in the back of Rusty

Horne's bank, through a door just behind a row of loan offi-cers. The theater has had a professional, full-time staff and puts on as many as five productions a year, drawing tens of thousands of theatergoers.

It is not only the theater-hungry who flock to the county, however. Giles County shelters as diverse a mix of groups as one is likely to find in rural America. The outlying areas of Giles County are populated not only by a concentra-tion of poor white farmers but also by an eclectic collection of folks seeking different things. They include wealthy retirees drawn by the natural beauty, mild climate, comparatively low taxes, and proximity to a major cultural center and transpor-tation hub like Nashville. One tenured professor of hydrology and fluvial geomorphology at the University of California at Los Angeles prefers to spend the bulk of his time in the pas-toral idyll that is Pulaski and commutes regularly to work. Greg McDonald, a transplanted New Englander and the au-thor of the "Fletch" mysteries, lives and works there full-time (having been sold on the place during a chance meeting with the brother of a Pulaski banker in the bar of the Beverly Wil-shire Hotel, no less). Stephen Gaskin, a onetime San Fran-cisco State University instructor who, in the psychedelic spirit of the times, ventured southeast in 1970, complete with a converted school bus and hippie band, lives in a neighboring county. He and his followers started the Farm—once de-scribed as "the archetypal hippie commune"—nearby. The acolytes and sympathizers of Saint Stephen, as he is caustically known in the area, have settled throughout Giles County. The area is also attractive because it is near two major artistic and intellectual centers. Many people commute an hour or more to Nashville or Huntsville, the latter having boomed as a high-tech center through the 1980s because of the NASA rocket-manufacturing facility there.

Pulaski itself has developed a thriving base of mostly light manufacturing, in addition to its agriculture. Unlike Noxubee County, Mississippi, whose industrial park sits empty and overgrown with weeds and field grass, Giles County has a full, and expanding one. In campaign stops and advertisements Giles County politicians wear ties and suits, a personal presentation almost unimaginable in Noxubee County. While the Noxubee County Chamber of Commerce has tried rather feebly to market itself as the "best of both worlds," meaning a rural area hospitable to industrial development, Pulaski and Giles County legitimately can make such a boast.

Giles County also has—again, rather atypically for a town this size in the South—a significant Jewish population. Fading advertisements for Cohen's groceries can be seen on turn-of-the-century brick warehouses near downtown Pulaski. Cohens and Cohns and other Jewish mercantile families were active in the county's business and civic life from before the Civil War, and they continue to be active today.

In short, Giles County combines a higher percentage of highly educated, business-savvy professionals who have lived elsewhere and seen the world outside than is true in most comparable rural areas. At its core, however, Giles is typical of a rural southern county with an indigenous population of large, extended families that stretch back generations, families that hold fiercely to libertarian notions of their rights to protect themselves and their land. Giles County's eclectic mix was one that confounded Netherland's plans to do business there. He appeared not to have taken demographics into account when he had rushed to buy Knox's Giles County land. If there was any place where citizen opposition was sure to be loud and fierce, it was Giles County. And the people of Giles County had worked together to oppose far more powerful, unwanted guests.

■ ■ ■ GILES COUNTY is a magnet for the Ku Klux Klan. On Christmas Eve, 1865, the Klan was born in Pulaski, in a law office just off the courthouse square. The six young men who dreamed up what became the nation's most infamous secret society had, in the words of one not entirely unsympathetic local historian, "all served in the Confederate army, and after they got back home, and while they were adjusting themselves to the new conditions of life, time hung heavy on their hands." The group came from the county's most respected white families. From their yuletide meeting grew the risible and eventually terror-inspiring costume, the earliest surviving version of which can be found in the Pulaski museum. Within five years, the Klan's intimidating, violent tactics led to widespread anxiety about its activities. In 1869, retired Confederate General Nathan Bedford Forrest, then the Grand Wizard, issued an order that the Klan disband.

Some Giles Countians even today endorse the judgment of the local writer who, in 1951, wrote that the Klan "served a definite purpose, the protection of Southern white people during the years when they had no other protection." Officially, however, the county labors to overcome its identification with the Klan. Some white Giles Countians insist that the original Klan was different from its more recent incarnation, less interested in racial intimidation than in protecting whites from the panic caused by newly freed blacks. The "real" Klan, they say, was organized in Stone Mountain, Georgia, in 1917, adding nativist hatred of Jews and Catholics to its racist foundations. This sort of self-serving account of the ugliest chapter in local history aside, it is true that, for much of this century, race relations in Giles County have been remarkably smooth. A black physician, for instance, headed the local medical association as early as 1956. Giles Countians boast that they have "the first public school system in the South to be fully integrated" without a court order. (In May 1965, the local school board unanimously voted to integrate.) The county is not without its racial brushfires, but they do not burn with the intensity seen elsewhere. This is explainable in part by the fact that only about 15 percent of its population is black.

Nonetheless, like the chiggers that reappear in the South every summer to burrow into people's skin, the Klan has selected Giles County as its symbolic home. Since 1986, Klan members have returned to the county every January—when the rest of the country is preparing to celebrate Martin Luther King Jr.'s birthday—and march through town, garnering more media attention than anything else in the town's year. This profoundly irritates locals, although the Klan's parades were for the first years tolerated with a resigned shrug, an acceptance that the Klan legacy was Giles County's unavoidable historical baggage.

Matters came to a head when Aryan Nations, the Idaho-based white supremacist group, announced in mid-1989 that it intended to march through the Klan's birthplace. The date they chose for their march was October 7, to commemorate the birthday of Sam Davis, a young Confederate courier who was caught and hanged in Pulaski on November 27, 1863, by occupying Union troops. On the south side of Pulaski's courthouse square stands a granite monument to Davis, a dreamy-eyed statue of the youth that commemorates the county's Confederate dead. Erected by the United

Daughters of the Confederacy in October 1906, the base of the monument bears an inscription reading: "Though a Confederate soldier in the line of duty he was executed as a spy by the Federals at Pulaski." Davis is something of a local hero, but the paramilitary character and violent rhetoric of Aryan Nations (committed to the overthrow of the United States' ZOG, for "Zionist Occupied Government"), who extended a welcome for skinheads, the Klan, and all other white supremacists to join them, terrified many in Giles County.

In response, a group including "Fletch" creator McDonald formed Giles County United, an activist group, and spent the summer and fall before the march planning an organized response. They coordinated a citywide business shutdown on the Saturday for which the march was scheduled—no small achievement in a county seat that, like any rural center, depends on Saturday traffic from people in outlying areas. They also draped storefronts in orange banners protesting the march, and strung orange bows and wreaths from street signs and car antennas. Even the hand of Davis's statue held one of the orange wreaths. Orange was chosen as a symbol of unity and brotherhood, borrowed from Dutch peace organizers (who must never have traveled to Northern Ireland). For their efforts, Giles County United received extensive national publicity, including being named ABC News's "Person of the Week."

■ ■ ■ FOR all Giles County's strengths as a community, however, one thing it did have in 1989, months before Netherland arrived, was unemployment in the double digits. From 1975 through 1989, twelve hundred manufacturing jobs had been lost in the county, including the recent departures of both a shoe and a shirt factory. Giles County—not forty minutes from Netherland's Murfreesboro base—had acquired a reputation for aggressively recruiting and keeping industry, its recent unemployment problems notwithstanding. As a result, in the late spring of 1990, when Netherland finally set his sights on Giles, at least superficially it looked as if the county might be receptive.

In the meantime, Netherland was working just as hard to fight his cancer. He visited four of the best oncology treatment centers in the country—the University of Texas in Houston, Sloan-Kettering in New York, Duke University in Durham, North Carolina, and the University of California at Los Angeles—exploring radical melanoma treatments. He figured that he was young and otherwise healthy, and stood as good a chance as anyone of beating it. He ended up opting for a radical form of immuno-therapy at Duke. Once a month for the next eight months, he would visit Durham religiously for treatment.

Netherland also determined not to repeat the mistakes of his experiences elsewhere in Tennessee. He resolved to keep his Giles County plans secret until he had secured an option on some land. On June 20, exactly one week *after* he had secured Tillman Knox's agreement to option his land, Netherland approached Pulaski's mayor, Dan Speer, as well as the Giles County executive, members of the Economic Development Commission, and a few others, including Joe Henry, a powerful local attorney whose family had been influential in Giles County for generations. Netherland recalled that the group was "relieved" to know he intended to build an incinerator, and not a landfill. They told him that they wanted to investigate the project further before going ahead, and that they intended to contact other communities with such facilities. Netherland's Nashville public relations consultant, himself a Giles County native recommended to Netherland by Speer, would later report that "the result of those contacts was a feeling that initially such a facility is very controversial, but over the long run, the plants become good corporate citizens" and that "they were in no position to support the project publicly but did not see how they could stop it." The group also said that they would wait to take any public action until after the upcoming August primary election—nearly six weeks away.

Just four days later, on June 25, Netherland received a call at home from Speer. Speer, who looks like a youngish, bespectacled Mr. Magoo, was calling to say that the deal was off, and that the county and city would publicly come out against him and his project the next morning. For Netherland, "It was clear that we had been double-crossed, big time."

On June 26, Mike Curry, the cochair of the Economic Development Commission and Rusty Horne's deputy at First National, read a prepared statement saying that local officials did not support FTI and had never requested a meeting with them. Speer called a public meeting for June 29, a Friday, to discuss people's concerns about FTI.

■ ■ ■ ENTER Carol Puckett. At five feet four inches tall, Puckett exudes boundless energy. Puckett's demeanor is friendly and open, her round features circled by a tousled mess of auburn hair. If Martha Blackwell retains traces of the more gracious, hierarchical pre–Civil War South, Puckett is more determinedly a product of the 1960s. But for her accent, you would never guess that she was nurtured in the same soil that gave birth to that once vehement segregationist, former Alabama Governor George C. Wallace.

In describing her to me, people routinely described Puckett as something of a zealot. Speer called her "overdramatic and a little paranoid." But her critics always take care to qualify that judgment with the recognition that without her drive and effort, FTI might today be operating an incinerator in Giles County.

Puckett grew up in Decatur, Alabama, in a well-to-do family—the kind that counted among its friends all of the local power brokers. For a privileged white woman from the Deep South she is something of a political anomaly because, when she was nine years old, her family's Methodist church got a new pastor, John Rutland. Rutland had been Birmingham police commissioner Eugene "Bull" Connor's pastor. As a girl, Carol learned that Rutland "drove Bull crazy" with his liberal ideas and that the segregationist had the minister exiled to Decatur. The Rutlands moved a few houses away from Carol's family, into another of the stately brick homes on their wonderfully shady, oak-lined block. The Rutland's only daughter was exactly Carol's age, and they became close friends. Hours spent in the progressive pastor's household became the beginning of her education in social justice.

As a student at the University of Alabama in the early 1970s, Carol designed her own major, concentrating in journalism with a minor in a new subject, environmental studies. She married a computer software designer, a man even more voluble and gregarious than she—no small achievement. When they talk together, Carol and Chuck Puckett create enough energy to propel a city bus.

For the first years of their marriage, Chuck's career as a software designer kept them in Huntsville, Alabama. In April 1989, the Pucketts moved as a family back to Giles County, with their two girls, Rosemary and Ruth, then five and two, respectively. They settled into a stately Victorian house behind the Methodist college, on the outskirts of Pulaski. The price of the move was that Chuck would have to spend nearly two hours a day commuting, or, to be more exact, "fifty-four minutes and thirty-three seconds" each way. "But, you know, I never noticed it really. 'Morning Sedition' on the way in, and 'Some Things Considered' on the way back," he explained, playing on the names of the popular National Public Radio news programs, Morning Edition and All Things Considered. The natural beauty of their new home justified the inconvenience.

The Pucketts returned to Giles County just as plans were under way to oppose the Aryan Nations, and they joined the opposition effort. Throughout the following winter, they continued to work in community affairs. Carol became vice-president of the Giles County Historical Society and helped organize an arts council. She became pregnant again. Then, in the last week of June 1990, she read about the proposed FTI incinerator in the Nashville paper. Puckett is not one to wait for anything. Her reporter's training and her environmental knowledge were instantly put to use. That very day she called her mentor at Alabama, an environmental studies professor, who put her in touch with national groups that help communities oppose proposed hazardous waste facility sitings. She called friends all over Pulaski to alert them to what she saw as an unacceptable threat to their home.

Like Carol Puckett, Pat Miles had recently moved to Giles County with her husband, Jerry, a retired AT&T vice-president who had worked for that company for thirty years. She remembers being cornered by Carol in the produce section of the supermarket. It took Pat Miles a few minutes to grasp the problem. She and her husband had lived in posh suburbs of major cities—Dallas, Chicago, New York—cities with zoning. The threat of an incinerator was not one the communities she had lived in had ever faced.

Miles remembered that Puckett just followed her around, up and down each aisle, from produce through to frozen foods, until she agreed to do what she could to help. By the eve of the June 29 public meeting, Puckett—who used military metaphors throughout the coming months as a way to marshall support—was armed and ready with information for her troops, most of whom she had recruited just the way she cornered Pat Miles.

"On Tuesday night before the meeting, I had spent all day doing a lot of research, getting a lot of information, and I was ready," explained Puckett. She documented Netherland's foray into two other Tennessee counties and contacted his opponents there. She knew Mayor Speer from her peripheral involvement in the opposition to the Aryan Nations. "He knew that we were activist sorts of people. And outsiders. Very key. Very key. Don't know anything about us, and probably don't need to. So I called the mayor at home on the Tuesday night before the meeting.

"And I said 'Mayor Speer, this is Carol Puckett,' . . . and he said, 'Yes?' And I said, 'I would like to share some information with you that I have gathered about FTI, and I've put together quite a bit in the last twenty-four hours. And I'd like to talk to you, and maybe . . . I could address the group that shows up tomorrow? I think I've got a lot of information that people could use.'

"He said, 'Uh, well, thank you, but we don't need any help.' Because Carol Puckett grew up in Decatur "the same way Dan Speer grew up here," she was used to people accepting her help and respecting her abilities.

"And I said, uh, 'Wha-a-a-t?' I just—" Carol's eyes

bugged out as she recalled her astonishment. "And he said, in his slightly nervous, hurried way, 'I don't think we're gonna need any help on this. Thank you a lot. I appreciate it. I think we've got it under control. Thank you very much.' And he hung up the phone. I turned around to my husband, and I was stunned. Maybe I stun easily, but I was ST-U-U-U-N-NED. I-could-not-be-lieve-it!"

The public meeting was scheduled for the next afternoon at the city hall, a squat, functional, modern red-brick building catercorner from Mayor Speer's insurance agency, a five-minute walk from the courthouse square. "So," Puckett continued in her efficient, staccato delivery, "went over to the meeting. I would say there were about sixty people there. And so, I went up, and I was *very* pregnant. I went up and I sat down on the front row.

"It was real interesting. By that time the little group had it—they had appointed who was going to be the cochairs of the group that's gonna fight this." The cochairs of the group that became Citizens against Toxic Incineration, or CATI, were the bank president Rusty Horne, the lawyer Joe Henry, and Merry Merle Sigmon, in Carol Puckett's eyes the "token woman," a court reporter who depended on Henry for much of her business. All three were white, and all were born, bred, and well established in Giles County.

Puckett, whom a friend described as a "kick-butt take-names" person, would have none of it. Her family's income came from Chuck's work as a software designer in Huntsville. Not only did she not depend on the county for her economic well-being but, as an outsider, she also had no allegiance to the ruling powers in Giles County and their trickle-down approach to combating this threat. She also had enough anarchic 1960s idealism in her veins not to respect authority for its own sake.

Puckett knew only that Horne was the president of the bank. Before that day, she would not have known him, had they passed on the street. "Well, these three were introduced to the people as the people who were gonna fight this. There were lots of questions from the audience. The mayor was very obviously trying to overlook this pregnant woman on the first row who kept raising her hand. And he would not ever let me say anything.

"And finally, this man in the back—"Carol lowered her voice and imitated a man's shout: " 'LET THAT WOMAN SPEAK!'

"And, you know, Dan said, 'Oh! Did you want to say somethin'?'

"I said, 'Mr. Mayor, would that be okay with you?' " Carol pursed her lips together as she repeated the question, her voice heavy with a false, saccharine tone. "This was the beginning of our relationship." She then laughed her big, throaty laugh, triumphant in the recollection of how she put the mayor in his place. "I just stood up and turned around with my back to him and answered all the questions, and I told everybody everything that I knew, that I could help them with. And that's the way it went from there. It was great.

"Well, what happened from that meeting, it was just wide open at that point." CATI's cochairs recognized Puckett's talents. At church the next Sunday, Joe Henry asked Chuck Puckett if his wife "would give them some direction." She sent back word that she would. The Pucketts observed that this was in keeping with the traditional social politesse of Giles County: a man-to-man inquiry about the little lady's availability.

"I made a list, and it was a wonderful list." Carol Puckett shared it the next day. The list contained thirteen items—

"points, suggestions." She explained: "One of them, the top one was, Never turn down anyone's help. That was the number-one thing. You *must* include everyone that wants to be included, because that's the clue to the whole thing." Puckett was aware that the anti–white supremacist efforts of Giles County United, the previous year, had raised the hackles of many who saw it as an effort organized by a powerful elite dictating the terms and manner of participation. "The people that were kind of in charge had not included everybody and had excluded people, and there were kind of bitter feelings." In her view, born of nearly two decades in progressive politics, the self-appointment of the CATI troika was the first step in a wrong direction, and she was not prepared to let that uninclusive management style go any farther.

One unwritten item on Carol's list was that she did not need to talk to her enemy to know she was right. To this day, Carol Puckett has never seen Ed Netherland, never sat down at a table with him, never taken the measure of his abilities and weaknesses in the flesh. For Netherland's part, she is an equally unknown quantity. When asked about her, he did not recognize her name.

Puckett threw herself into action. Within three days, the first of a series of public meetings was held. About a hundred people showed up. Puckett provided information and research but stayed in the background, always the éminence grise. After their recent encounter, the mayor, she recalled, "stayed out of my way, always," and overnight became a vocal opponent of FTI's proposal.

Puckett continued to mobilize her "troops" for "battle" in the "war" against FTI. Within days, a local businessman with the Dickensian name of Fagan Sneed donated use of the old opera house for CATI's headquarters. The opera house faces the courthouse on the east side of the square; its dome is a local landmark. Headquarters became an operational command center under the direction of Jerry Miles. As a retired corporate manager, Miles had no problem directing people about when and where to act. The center was staffed from early morning until evening and was open on weekends. Carol and Chuck Puckett prepared a series of inflammatory, information-packed fact sheets and press releases.

Carol Puckett's style was direct, head-on, confrontational. One handout listed the names, addresses, and phone numbers of all the players, from Knox and FTI's board of directors to every Tennessee politician with a possible interest at stake. She recognized immediately that the fight was to be won at a personal, emotional level, and she directed that various actors be attacked differently: "Women, write their wives appealing to them as wives and mothers." Fifty copies were made of a Greenpeace anti-incineration videotape (which, the Pucketts said, combines just the right mix of fact and outrage) for people to check out and watch at home. People responded to this inclusive, participatory style. "You'd go down to headquarters one morning, and laying out in front would be forty bundles of sticks for signs— somebody had made tomato sticks for signs and bundled 'em up and dropped 'em off. Then you'd have somebody come down and bring a staple gun. It was a true grassroots movement." Because it was summer, timing was also on CATI's side: school teachers provided an essential core of support in manning headquarters and doing what work was necessary.

Other sources of help for CATI were the former phosphate workers and the farmers who had lived near the Mines. They came with stories of cattle raised near the Mines with "phosphate mouth," so parched they could never get enough water, so weak they could not graze except when kneeling. These stories helped draw support for the feeling that a past harm should not be repeated in a modern disguise. Carol Puckett said she would never forget the image of Mahlon Peden, then in his eighties, who had farmed near the Mines for years, showing up religiously throughout the FTI fight, staple gun in hand, to do his bit attaching anti-FTI protest signs to tomato sticks—all because he did not want to see another environmental disaster visited upon Giles County.

These stories also underlined another respect in which Netherland had not taken stock of Giles County. Out in the country of Giles County, where for years the state's Department of Health and Environment had been viewed as falling short in fulfilling its duties to regulate phosphate mining, Jim Word's credentials as the head of that department did little to build people's trust in the start-up operation.

No tactic was unacceptable in what Puckett, Horne, and Henry insisted was a high-stakes, life-or-death battle for the soul of the county. They assaulted the character of FTI's directors by playing with their names: Ed Nether-land wants to turn your county into a Never-land; Jim Word does not keep his. Doesn't Robert Culbreath's name sound like "kill breath?" That's what his incinerator will do to the life of our county if FTI comes.

Meanwhile, Horne and Henry took Puckett's facts, and her emotional tactics, to the county's business leaders. On July 5, FTI planned a luncheon meeting at city hall for local industrial leaders. After a brief presentation, all but one of the fifteen businessmen who came to hear what Ed Nether-land had to say walked out, leaving their free lunches untouched. Netherland was quoted in the local newspaper as saying that the meeting had been "very positive."

The bank president and the lawyer were also instrumental in securing resolutions—as Carol Puckett had urged—from every conceivable business. Opposition to FTI began pouring in. The city of Pulaski, the Giles County Chamber of Commerce, and the Giles County Livestock Association were among the first publicly to denounce FTI's plans. Each day would bring a new resolution decrying FTI's invasion: first the Deerhunters, then the Rotary Club, the Arts Council, the Giles County Medical Association, the Retail Merchants' Association, Hillcrest Country Club, the Frito-Lay plant, and the Historical Society (which was worried that "within a radius of a few miles of the proposed incinerator is situated one of the South's largest concentrations of antebellum homes, other historic structures and properties listed on the National Register of Historic Places, as well as beautiful rural scenery as is now seldom seen in America").

The crisis spirit that Puckett and CATI had created was everywhere. The heads of the county's Democratic and Republican Committees issued a joint "proclamation" gravely intoning: "The FTI incinerator must never be located in Giles County, and . . . what amounts to a state of war exists between the people of Giles County and FTI. . . . We do further jointly proclaim that the threat of said incinerator creates a crisis unparalleled in Giles County since the Civil War, and we urge all Republicans and Democrats in this county to band together against this common foe."

Wearied by these attacks, Netherland observed the same day, on Tuesday, July 17, that CATI consists of "a small and very vocal group that is doing everything it can to oppose us. . . . It smacks of Greenpeace and some other very radical groups. We actually feel there has been an improvement in the public perception of our plans."

The locals knew better. The *Pulaski Citizen* ran a "late-breaking bulletin" announcing that Governor Ned Ray McWherter had publicly come out against the project and had met with two board members, including his former appointee, Jim Word, to make clear his displeasure with the brouhaha. FTI's plans had not even been public for a month and it was clear: Ed Netherland was losing the war.

But Carol Puckett knew not to claim an early victory. Her calculated public relations battle continued unabated. One week an advertisement would appear in the local papers warning that "life as we know it" was "threatened" in Giles County, complete with a photo of a bucolic mist rising from the Elk River, below which appeared the following warning: "IF YOU ASSUME THAT SOMEONE ELSE IS FIGHTING THIS BATTLE FOR YOU, FTI WILL COME." The following week, as if to show fulfillment of the prophecy, CATI would run ads depicting a wasted landscape dominated by a billowing incinerator-scape.

Later ads would skillfully market children's fears in support of CATI's war. "HEAR OUR CHILDREN'S CRIES," one proclaimed, showing a child's drawing of a dark-suited, mustachioed figure with horns, who had coins dripping from one hand and a wad of cash clutched in the other. "Greedy Men Trade Our Lives for Money," wrote one elementary school artist, below whose drawing appeared plaintive letters to Netherland, like one from 10-year-old Elizabeth Cesarini, reprinted in her labored child's cursive: "Mr. Ed Netherland Sir, About the Toxic Waste Incinerator . . . your precious time plotting to kill whole towns at a time, whole counties even. We flat out DO NOT WANT THE INCINERATOR! . . . Please I'm on my knees begging of you not to build it in our senic [sic] town. . . . You don't know that we might have a child here that will be renowned all over the world. But if FTI comes here she or he might get cancer and die, never to be known."

If, under the guidance of some skillful public relations operative, Netherland had published similar drawings celebrating his project, cries of protest about children being ruthlessly manipulated and terrorized in support of a cause would have resounded. But CATI was on a roll.

If CATI's efforts were sometimes pitched just short of hysteria, they always zeroed back in on two key concerns: FTI's lack of experience and its mysterious financing. With a flourish that would do a Madison Avenue account executive proud, CATI convinced the public that Netherland had sneaked into the county, as if in the dead of night, and continually questioned why the sources of FTI's finances had to be kept secret ("FTI's financing is a stone wall," Chuck Puckett was fond of saying), hinting at alleged connections between the Mafia and the hazardous waste industry. When they got wind that Ray Danner was behind the project, Rusty Horne announced without any hesitation at one of CATI's big public meetings: "Well, don't eat at Shoney's!"

Carol Puckett's exhortations for people to harass those involved in the possible arrival of an incinerator in Giles County were paying off but teetered on the brink of becoming violent. The outside of Tillman Knox's office in Mount Pleasant began to be papered with signs protesting his efforts. He began to receive threats, anonymous phone calls and letters, from people who warned him that he and his children or property could be hurt if he did not rescind the sale.

Puckett recalled one of her "favorite stories." "I get a telephone call at home. I was getting a lot of telephone calls. Every night someone would call with somethin'. And it was a man, he wouldn't tell me who he was. And he said—they would always say—'Are you that incinerator woman?' "

She chuckled at the recollection. "Yessir."

And he said: "Miz Puckett, I was jus' thinkin'. You know, there's . . . a hundred-year-old train trestle, a wooden train trestle that goes over" to the Mines. "You know, that train would have to go over there. What if we jus' went out there and blew that thing up?"

"And I say, 'Well, now, let's think about that for a second.' And I said, 'You know, if we did that, if someone did that, the government would just pay for it to get built back a whole lot sturdier than it is now.'"

"Ya know, I hadn't thought about that—yer right. Thank ya."

"And he hung up."

For Knox, these threats brought sleepless nights. He investigated possible ways to transfer his option to CATI, but lawyers said this was impossible; Knox and his partner had a contractual obligation. Knox explained that after FTI paid them: "Then the pressures really started. I mean, it got right rough. And I was mining in Giles County and had probably a million dollars' worth of equipment down there, and trucks running and everything. I even had threats of dynamiting my equipment. They'd call my children and say that we were allowing something to be that would kill their children and grandchildren, and this that and the other. And I've always been an even-tempered sort of a person, and I don't like problems and troubles at all."

In the second week of July, Knox gave CATI a check for $94,000—his share of the sale proceeds. Knox thus became CATI's largest single contributor.

"And really, the reason I did all this is that I just couldn't stand the pressure that was being put on me." Yet if Knox's conscience was cleared, his feelings were still equivocal:

"But I still say, and I said when I made the decision to do that, there's gonna have to be some places, somewhere, to take care of waste. It's gonna have to be somewhere, and it's gonna have to inconvenience somebody. So I do say that even though I've gone through all of this, I still think that they're gonna have to be places for it. Now, I don't want it in my backyard either, and nobody else does, but I was just caught in the middle of that thing and probably didn't give it the thought, because of the way I was approached that day, and what had happened to me that day.

"If I had it all to go over, I would talk to some people in Giles County prior to doing it. But still—and I've thought about it a lot of times, whether I did the right thing or not—I have peace of mind, and that's worth more than money, ya know. I done lived all my life to have a good reputation, and I don't want to do anything any differently."

Knox's costly, nontax–deductible gift was seized upon by Puckett and CATI. They ran full-page ads reprinting his letter of apology and companion ads denouncing his partner for failing to do the same. Here was tangible proof that their tactics would prevail. But Puckett and CATI were also walking a fine line. The inclusionary strategy, which united Giles County's eclectic population around a single goal, was constantly threatening to erupt, moving from indignant, educated protest to unrestrained, possibly violent expressions of anger.

Momentum in the fight against FTI continued to build, and for all intents and purposes, in the third week of July the fight was won, just over a month from when it had begun. On July 21, 1990, several thousand people—the largest crowd ever assembled for a single event in the county's 181-year history—gathered on a light, warm Saturday night beneath the flowering crabapples and elms of Pulaski's courthouse square to rally against FTI. The speakers included the county's representative in Congress, Jim Cooper, the man who for a time in early 1994 would become President Bill Clinton's most outspoken Democratic opponent in the health-care debate (and a casualty of the November 1994 Democratic slaughter at the polls). A CATI member provided a twin-engine plane to bring down Corinne Whitehead, a grandmotherly environmental activist from Calvert County, Kentucky, the site of a hazardous waste incinerator allegedly linked to widespread local health problems.

The crowds filled Pulaski's spacious square: retirees in folding chairs, the disabled in wheelchairs, young couples toting babies and dragging stray children—most wearing one form of anti-incineration T-shirt or another.

Joe Henry, the lawyer, who had a week earlier been quoted as calling Netherland "one of the biggest liars" he had "ever met," opened the program. In the style of Carol Puckett, he tore into Ed Netherland, demonizing the man to cast doubt on the integrity of his project. Calling him "Honest Ed," Henry threw out a series of rhetorical questions about Netherland's motives to the assembled crowd, each dripping with sarcasm and louder than the one before.

The rally's success stemmed not only from the solidarity of gathering together with at least a tenth of the entire county's population, but also from its simple, educated message. Speaker after speaker emphasized that no need for another incinerator existed, that the nation had sufficient incineration capacity, and that the best solution was to reduce the volume of industrial pollution at its source.

It was the beginning of the end for "Honest Ed's" plans in Giles County. And just three days later, his cause was further undermined when McWherter made clear that the state of Tennessee would never sanction his plans.

McWherter went to Giles County to pay a political debt. He was to be the featured speaker at a rally for an old crony, state representative C. E. DePriest, who was facing a tough reelection battle. The governor arrived in the early evening at the new National Guard Armory, near the Industrial Park. As soon as he got out of his car, he knew that the subject was going to be hazardous waste, and not DePriest's campaign. The instant he set his foot on the parking lot, still steamy after the blistering July day, the governor was beset by Giles Countians who opposed hazardous waste. Their welcome was cordial but their message unmistakable: most were toting homemade anti-incineration placards. Girl Scout troops in their uniforms assembled to greet him and politely stated their fears of a waste-filled future. Television and print journalists from Alabama and Tennessee milled about. Inside, the armory was packed, everyone waiting expectantly for the governor's word on waste.

"You've got one thing on your minds—I can see that by your signs," the governor said once at the podium inside. The crowd roared its approval. Questions began popping out at him from the audience. And the questions were informed, about complicated issues of state and federal toxic waste and environmental planning.

The governor played to the crowd: "There is no need for a hazardous waste incinerator to be constructed here or anywhere else in the state. We do not want Tennessee to become a dumping ground for anyone—for hazardous waste or household garbage. We're not going to be dumped on in Tennessee. We'll join the fight in any other county they go to. I'm sure they'll try us, but we're gonna stop them."

All the cameras were trained on big, blustery, baldheaded, rotund McWherter. Reporters scribbled furiously on their steno pads. Rusty Horne knew Carol Puckett well enough by then to worry that she might introduce a confrontational note: "I had been warned to keep my tongue," she recalled.

The governor then made a statement that gave Puckett the entry she was looking for. Someone asked, "Governor, will a toxic waste incinerator be built during your term of office?"

"Whatever rumors are spread, I came here to tell you that as governor, I will use every resource available to support you in your fight to not have an incinerator brought here by FTI or any other company. In simple language, I came to tell you we will join in the fight—go all the way to the U.S. Supreme Court—whatever it takes. The state has resources, and we will use all that are available to keep the incinerator out of Giles County."

Carol Puckett, five feet four inches tall and eight and a half months pregnant and sweating heavily under the summer heat and the television lights, stepped forward. "And I raised my hand up, and I said, 'Governor.'" A collective gasp, nervous and excited, issued from portions of the crowd. "Governor, thank—you—so—much," she said, stretching out her words for emphasis. "We really appreciate your word on this. So now could you please tell me, should we just all stop and go home now? And he said, 'Oh, no ma'am. You keep up the fight, just like you're fighting now, keep it up, keep it up—and SIGN ME UP!'

"And at that point, the chairman of the Republican Party walked up with the petition that we had been circulating," a petition addressed to McWherter himself, "and said, 'Sign right here.' And so, instantly, right in front of all those people, he signed the petition."

The movie director Frank Capra could not have scripted better. It was a lead story on Tennessee and northern Alabama television stations that night and in the papers the next day. Two of FTI's board members—including Word, the board chair and former state health and environment commissioner—immediately announced that they were "reassessing" their FTI affiliations. The *Nashville Banner* quoted Word as saying: "For my part, I'm probably as disturbed as anybody about what's going on. It's beyond out of control. It has caused us to sit down and sort of be reflective about who is involved and what their involvement is."

■ ■ ■ NETHERLAND's plan to establish a small waste empire in Giles County was crumbling. The high-profile members of his board of directors resigned. And just as the fact that some of his funds came from Ray Danner was revealed—courtesy of a high-placed CATI source in the governor's office—the Danner Company announced the withdrawal of its support.

Unbeknownst to the people of Giles County, however, Netherland was testing other waters. In the months that "Honest Ed" was being attacked by the people of Giles County, he was busy learning from his mistakes, plying his charms upon and becoming a hero to some, down farther south, in Noxubee County, Mississippi.

3
WHITES, BLACKS, AND MENNONITES

WHEN ED NETHERLAND started scouting around for a place to do business in Mississippi, he could not remember having visited the state. Several months before, a chance encounter with a Democratic fund-raiser from Mississippi—whom he met in the kitchen of Senator John Glenn, of Ohio—had disposed him, Netherland recalled, to give Mississippi a serious look. Worries about where to send Mississippi's toxic trash, comparatively little though it was, were heightened after the Alabama scare. Mississippi was the only southern state, and one of only eleven states nationally, without a hazardous waste facility. *Facility* is an ambiguous word in this context, since it can refer to everything from a massive landfill (as at Emelle) to a modest transfer station or storage depot. The fact—often obscured in the Noxubee debates—is that, nationwide, only sixteen states had (or have) commercial hazardous waste *landfills.*

In Mississippi, Netherland determined not to repeat his Tennessee mistakes. This time *he* would be the one to line up local civic and grassroots support. He could not have anticipated the extent to which his appearance and activities in Noxubee County would give expression to a simmering struggle for its future, releasing generations-old hatreds and resentments in the process.

■ ■ ■ MISSISSIPPI's history of racial violence, from the lynching of Emmitt Till for allegedly whistling at a white woman, to the slaying of Medgar Evers and, later, the murders of James Chaney, Andrew Goodman, and Michael Schwerner, the three civil rights workers murdered during Freedom Summer 1964—to cite only the most infamous examples—continues to color national perceptions of the state, despite its best efforts to shake public memories of those times. Even in neighboring Alabama and the rest of the South, Mississippi is still widely viewed as backward and dangerous. Every time I left for a Mississippi trip, friends would pull me aside and, in conspiratorial tones, urge me to exercise caution. It was as if they worried that latter-day incarnations of sheriff Lawrence Rainey and deputy sheriff Cecil Price, the Ku Klux Klan members charged with the brutal murders of the civil rights workers in Neshoba County (not forty-five miles from the Noxubee County line) would ride me off the road because I wore glasses and did not speak with a drawl.

In fact, Mississippi, like the South in general, is in important respects now much better integrated than the rest of the country. The typical white student in Mississippi, for example, now attends a school where over 30 percent of the students are black. In Illinois and New York, by comparison, the typical white student goes to a school where just under 7 percent of the students are black.

Mississippi has a black population of nearly 36 percent, far and away the highest percentage for any state, and it has nearly a comparable percentage of black legislators. Walk down a street in Jackson—where you are much more likely to see blacks and whites eating together than in New York or Los Angeles—and every single person, black or white, is likely to greet you with a warm "hi" or "how ya' doin'?" To be sure, this surface cordiality can mask deeper disaffection (this is the state, after all, where the third Monday in January is a legal holiday celebrating the birthdays of *both* Martin Luther King Jr. and Robert E. Lee). However, just as children who attend integrated schools are less likely to stereotype others because of their race, this geniality shatters the usual racial distance.

By contrast, Noxubee County remains solidly segregated. A stranger of any race is unlikely to be greeted by passers-by on the street and will not receive the hospitality Mississippi boosters insist is the state's forte. In part, this is because the county protects its own above all else, as illustrated to me most vividly at Martha Blackwell's house one evening. A group of her high school classmates and their spouses gathered for dinner shortly after New Year's Day. The conversation turned to planning their upcoming twentieth high school reunion and the question of whether they would invite a particular woman. Opinion was divided. The men tended to think not: "She" had not been in their class. The women disagreed: she was, they insisted, the same person inside.

The woman in question, who had recently moved back to Noxubee County, had left soon after high school graduation a score years earlier—as a man. Even those who felt she should be invited were overwhelmed at the thought. As one woman cried with exasperation: "What are we gonna do about prizes? We can't hardly give [a formerly obese classmate] the Most Changed Award because he lost fifty pounds when Arthur became Nancy!" "Perhaps," someone else intoned, "we could change the name of the award to 'Most Changed by Natural Means.'" The room erupted into laughter.

In the end, the prodigal son/daughter was invited to the reunion but could not attend: her new business making elaborate cloth toys had its official opening the same day as the reunion. By the end of the year, she was again fully integrated into county life, receiving extensive local newspaper coverage for her craft and an award as the chamber of commerce's businessperson of the year. That in the heart of the Bible Belt a home-grown transsexual could be embraced with such welcoming arms spoke volumes to me about the nature of tolerance in Noxubee County.

This quality was illustrated in countless other ways. Among whites in particular, people who had moved to Noxubee from outside the county as long as thirty or forty years earlier, individuals who had ended up making major contributions to county life, were routinely identified as "not from here." This suspicion of outsiders is the typical parochialism of all isolated subcultures. But in the particular case of Noxubee County, I came to see it as emanating from the white elite's desire to hide its secrets from the outside world. The desire to uncover those secrets, to speak frankly about past and present realities, is one of the things whites hate most about Ike Brown and his supporters (feelings admittedly fueled by his especially accusatory, in-your-face style). What Ike Brown's presence made constantly, uncomfortably clear in Noxubee County was that, despite exterior genialities, suspicion and division characterize local relations. This results largely from the willingness of many to keep the place just as it has been for generations, a square of the pre–civil rights Deep South preserved in intellectual and emotional amber.

Noxubee County has two Boy Scout troops, two Girl Scout troops, and two Little Leagues: one of each all black, one of each all white. In the summer, the public swimming pool is patronized by blacks, who are unwelcome at the American Legion pool. "Hell," the mayor of one of the three towns said to me, lamenting the state of the county's race relations, "it wasn't but four or five years ago that they took the wall out of the doctor's office in Brooksville that divided between where blacks and whites sat."

Cockrell's, the county's principal funeral home, continues to bury blacks and whites at separate and unequal locations less than a mile apart. This racial divider is invisible but understood: blacks go to the cramped location behind the courthouse, where the bereaved sit on metal folding chairs. Whites visit the elegantly appointed old home on Jefferson Street, one in a row of stately antebellum houses. W. E. B. DuBois's color line, what he famously called "the problem of the twentieth century," has for most intents and purposes not been crossed in Noxubee County, Mississippi. Blacks grumble about the unequal quality of such services. But resentments run so deep that the county's black citizens voice no greater desire than do whites to combine resources and share facilities and activities.

On Jefferson Street sit a couple of black-owned businesses, including T & J Johnson Beauty Supply and Glass

House Fashions, owned by state representative Reecy Dickson. But Dickson's business is closed more often than not, while she is down in Jackson for the legislative session. Wilbur Colom, the black lawyer from nearby Columbus, has a storefront satellite office across from the courthouse, but it is mostly there for show and is seldom open. Some blacks work at the white-owned grocery store on the street's north end, where old black men in overalls and black women in faded sundresses or nylon exercise suits gather under the awning to visit late into the afternoon. One waste company executive is reputed to have said that he did not realize Noxubee was a majority-black county when he first came through. His statement was widely derided as poppycock, yet I came to realize that such a misperception was quite possible. Blacks' economic invisibility helps make their numerical dominance yet another of the county's secrets kept well hidden from the outside world.

Walk down Jefferson Street in Macon and you will hardly see a black face at work, not in the law offices or the drug stores or the bookstore. Of the two banks, one has a black teller, but no black officers. This is not because blacks are out in the fields, either. Farming is now so highly mechanized that the 1990 census recorded but 322 agricultural workers in the county, and most farmers are white. In general, blacks with jobs in Noxubee County work in a lumber mill or in a factory, at Shuqualak or Prince Lumber, for Weyerhaeuser or Georgia Pacific, or at Delta Brick, GSI Plastics, or the Cal-Jack plant, making cheap jackets for men and boys. Many others, jobless and untrained, stay at home and collect from the county's largest single income source: public assistance.

Noxubee County is the poorest county in one of the poorest regions in the country. Most years, over 35 percent of the county's population receive food stamps—a percentage between one-third and two-thirds greater than that in any of the six surrounding Mississippi counties. Throughout the 1980s, Mississippi registered the highest percentage nationally of need for food stamps and emergency assistance. Noxubee County's percentages were always significantly higher than the state averages, sometimes by as much as 100 percent. For nearly two decades, Noxubee's level of assistance to poor single mothers through the federally funded Aid to Families with Dependent Children program, or AFDC, has usually reached 15 percent—and has never gone below 10 percent. Looked at another way, since 1983 no other surrounding county ever distributed monies to 10 percent of its population, as was always the case in Noxubee County. This condition is a source of despair for the county's small black middle class. One older black man articulated a view common among more prosperous blacks when he observed: "People used to come up the hard way. The government and the way things is made people lazy. It used to be you would have to kill a hog, kill a kid [to eat]. You can control folks when you keep them on welfare." Yet despite the gospel of self-reliance that undergirds these sentiments, the county's small black middle class doubts that the situation will change.

For his part, Ike Brown sees the situation as part of a system of social entitlements that needs to be rethought at every level. Noting that whites in the county regularly deride black welfare dependency in Noxubee, he sneered: "You talkin' about welfare programs—these folks put their land on what they call crop rotation and collect a big check for it. That's welfare! And you talk about cuttin' that out and see what happens. These folks hypocrites."

■ ■ ■ FOR a city dweller, the unnerving thing about the rural poverty of a place like Noxubee County is its evidence: disintegrating pine shacks and collapsing trailers abut stately homes, which in turn can face an industrial plant. Poverty is an unavoidable condition of life, something never tucked away in a distant neighborhood or across a county line. The visitor consequently can't help but wonder, How can people tolerate this inequality when it is so inescapably present? So too, in Noxubee County racial divisions startle and unsettle the visitor mostly because of the intimate scale of the county's commercial and social life.

On reflection, its racial divisions should not surprise an observer, because they mirror America's national experience. The American workplace may now be integrated, but for most of us, living in large, racially and ethnically heterogeneous cities and towns, the intimate parts of our lives, the moments that fill photo albums and shared recollections, are lived largely among people of our own color. It is another of our collective dirty secrets: we are willing to tolerate the divisiveness and mistrust bred by racial separation in exchange for the comfort and peace of mind that comes with living among those we understand best, namely, the mirror images of ourselves. As Wilbur Colom said to me: "It's natural for me just to surround myself with black people, those are the people I go to church with, those are the people I socialize with. I mean, the easiest thing in the world would be all black, and it's a struggle not to. It takes that extra effort."

Paradoxically, the generation in Noxubee County that lived with Jim Crow experienced more intimate and routine interaction between the races than is true today. When Martha Blackwell was a small child "coming up" out in Prairie Point, her regular playmates were all black, the children of the dozen or so families living on her family's place. Nashville relatives were horrified when little Martha, upon seeing a cat chasing a squirrel, exclaimed in a dialect that sounded to them distinctly Negro, "He gwin ketch dat 'kwirl."

Like many other white rural southerners, Blackwell's early life was populated more by blacks than whites—those who labored in kitchens, cleaned around the house, and worked the land. Her parents employed an older woman, Anna, whose sole task in her dotage was to churn buttermilk on the porch. Blackwell remembers being wakened every day by her softly singing "come butter, come butter" to the steady beat of the churn. Blackwell's affection for the woman, despite the oppressive hierarchy on which the relationship was based, is a warm one, solidly fixed in the firmament of her recollections of a secure and happy childhood.

Her children will not have similar memories because they have virtually no regular contact with Noxubee County's African American majority. In this, the experience of children in Noxubee County has since the mid-1960s been like that of children in the nation's large northern and coastal cities.

A number of factors, including regular increases in the minimum wage laws, made it prohibitive for many whites to keep black workers. As a result, blacks who had lived in a state of peonage moved not only to large northern metropolitan centers but also to nearby towns, where ghettoes sprouted beside the central business areas. Despite their proximity, they became no less separate from their former overlords and ladies than their relatives who had migrated north. Whites can get quite sentimental about this change. A descendant of the county's aristocracy of the soil tenderly remembered a black woman that worked for his family and helped raise him: "I mean, I loved her as much as you'd love your mother. Probably didn't even pay her minimum wage.

But she ate breakfast, she ate lunch, she ate supper. She was clothed in nice clothes every day. She was taken care of when she was sick. She can't have that today because nobody can afford it, so she's on the welfare rolls. So what's a better way of life?" In part, the man clearly longed for the return of a paternalistic idyll, for severely compromised and unequal plantation relations, and his comment underscores the extent to which a resistance to sharing power perpetuates suspicious race relations. But I did not doubt his regret at the passing of a human connection between blacks and whites that is now as little possible in the rural South as in big cities.

This is not to say that the divide between the races makes for openly hostile relations. On the contrary, with a low crime rate, a slower pace, and instant access to outdoor recreation, including exceptional deer and wild turkey hunting, many residents sing the Noxubee praises. In November 1958, Medgar Evers, the state NAACP head who would be slain in the driveway of his Jackson home in 1963, wrote an essay titled "Why I Live in Mississippi." Although Evers made civil rights his life's work, correcting racial injustice was not the reason he gave for his continued residence in his native state. Instead, he observed, in lines rendered tragic for dreams denied him:

> It may sound funny, but I love the South. I don't
> choose to live anywhere else. There's land here, and a
> man can raise cattle, and I'm going to do that some
> day. There are lakes where a man can sink a hook
> and fight the bass. There is room for my children to
> play and grow, and become good citizens—if the
> white man will let them.

Except for the suggestion that whites hold blacks back, these are sentiments most Noxubeeans of any race would still endorse today, over a quarter century since they were written. Just as Manhattanites bewail New York City's crowds, conflict, dirt, and noise but love its excitement and energy, so too Noxubeeans treasure the land's variety and tranquility, even while decrying the way use of that land has poisoned human interactions.

Yet the tension of racial separation is never far from the surface. Reflecting on the virtues of its small-town life, a white secretary for a waste company told me that it was so nice and neighborly, that people were just so friendly and helpful to one another. Although she mourned the absence of employment opportunities, which had affected her directly (she was trained as a schoolteacher, and there were no jobs), and would lose her job again within the year when the company closed its Macon office, she nonetheless told me she hopes the county stays that way, "just like Andy of Mayberry." After she'd left for lunch, her black contemporary (unlike the local norm, the waste companies hired one black and one white secretary) told a different story. The black woman mordantly observed, "I don't remember any black folk on *Mayberry, R.F.D.*"

This exchange underlines a basic point about Noxubee County: its aristocracy of the soil did not—and still does not—nurture black talent. For most whites, blacks continue to be largely faceless and nameless, despite their numbers. If, for example, you stopped in at the Noxubee County Historical Society, you could buy a booklet published in the Confederate Centennial Series on the horrors of Negro rule in the black belt during Reconstruction, but not one about local civil rights struggles. At the museum, you could visit a room devoted to Noxubee-born James C. Windham, once the president and CEO of Pabst Brewing. If you visited the library and inquired about famous Noxubeeans, you might learn that the Civil War historian Shelby Foote had family roots in Noxubee County (although their history is mostly tied to the Delta) or hear of Ben Ames Williams, a white historical novelist popular from the 1920s through the 1940s, or of the minor and long forgotten late-nineteenth-century poet William Ward—all of whom were white. The librarians also might tell you about the recital career of the white pianist Creighton Allen, born in Macon in 1900, who made his New York debut at age twenty-two.

However, a visit with the library's all-white staff would not inform you that Margaret Murray Washington—the third and last wife of Booker T. Washington, who distinguished herself as the head of the Women's Division of Industrial Work at the Tuskegee Institute—was born in Macon. You would not learn that Frederick O'Neal, of Brooksville, helped establish the American Negro Theater in New York before World War II. You will certainly not hear about Noxubee's own Alexander K. Davis, Mississippi's lieutenant governor during Reconstruction. And you would not be told about Loyle Hairston.

Hairston, a writer and journalist who now lives in New York City, was born in Macon in 1926. He lived there with his mother and brother until he was fourteen, when, like thousands of others, they moved north to St. Louis. By the time he reached New York, he joined a writer's workshop and eventually became a founding member of the Harlem Writers' Guild. Hairston's memories of Noxubee County are crowded by the dualisms that characterize so much African American thinking about the pre–civil rights Deep South. He recalled the Macon of his childhood as a "lovely town," and he praised the South and southerners for the "surface thing," the "hospitable, folksy flavor." At the same time, however, he said, "Even as a kid, Macon had a reputation as one of the most notorious places to live because of the extreme hostility whites had towards what they called 'nigger impudence:' meaning blacks wanting to be treated with dignity and respect." Cousins in Lowndes County, adjoining Noxubee to the north, used to tease him and his brother mercilessly "that it was just a terrible place for black people to live." He recalled:

> One day when I was about ten years old, I saw this white man on his lawn. The way he was dressed, his pleasant, friendly demeanor told me he was a preacher. For some inexplicable reason I suddenly had the urge to ask him how come whites were so mean to colored folk, or something to that effect. But when I approached him I lost my nerve because to a black boy of any age he was still a white man, who in Macon was someone to be feared.

As a young man, Hairston attempted: "to erase all traces of my deep South origins. I hated Mississippi. I had no desire ever to return there, even to visit relatives or childhood friends in my old hometown, Macon, a particularly dreadful place for blacks to live." Yet he has returned over the years to visit the place that continues to fire his literary imagination.

When he was sixteen years old, Hairston visited Macon, and stood in front of the offices of the newspaper, the *Macon Beacon*. He was wearing a suit: "I was literally kicked off Jefferson Street in the presence of two women friends and a mixed crowd of people. Having passed two white soldiers earlier and heard one say, 'there go a goddam nigger with a zoot suit on,' we crossed the street to avoid them on our return home." Later, "I encountered these two white soldiers again. One of them said: 'Why don't you niggers git outta the middle of the street and let white folks pass?' I stood to the side but the worthy young Aryan wasn't satisfied. . . . He kicked me as I turned to leave. Now to have turned and challenged him on Jefferson Street in Macon, Noxubee County, Mississippi on a busy Saturday evening would have been flirting with a lynching. Any black person from Mississippi would know this." In Macon, he added, "ordinary whites behaved pretty much as members of the Klan."

Variants of this story were frequently shared in Noxubee County: black men recalled times in the fifties and sixties when they were repeatedly challenged because they were wearing a white shirt and tie, or a dress hat. Painful memories of those experiences remain acute. Even after passage of the civil rights laws, one black man remembered returning home in the early seventies, after a tour of duty in Vietnam. He was not allowed to enter a restaurant from the front door—even though he was wearing his freshly pressed army uniform.

Hairston's most recent trip back was in 1992, in the midst of the hazardous waste wars. Physically, Hairston noted: "it's a completely different place now. I didn't even recognize it." He was delighted to find that some blacks had nice homes and jobs other than as boot blacks and porters.

Hairston also stopped in at the library, an imposing, neo-Romanesque heap of red sandstone that was formerly a jail. The building, which faces the courthouse and is now listed as a national historic landmark, was the county jail in his childhood (today the holding pens and hangman's chamber, complete with trapdoor, must be passed to get to the collection's stacks). "As a kid, you could stand on the corner and hear black people being beaten" there. Hairston met the head librarian "She was perfectly civil to me. But during the course of our conversation I got the impression that she was an unreconstructed Rebel."

■ ■ ■ ONE of the means by which Noxubee County remained a white Potemkin Village for most of its history was through its local press. The *Macon Beacon*, which has published continuously since its inception in 1849, even throughout the Civil War, scarcely mentioned the majority of the county's population until well into 1993, when it was sold to Scott Boyd, a young journalist from Jackson. Other than a few announcements of goings-on in the public schools, or notice of the occasional award or other distinction, news about its black citizens simply did not appear in the paper's pages. Their marriages, births, deaths, and other social activities were censored.

But one aspect of Noxubee County's de facto racial apartheid has wrought the most devastating, long-term consequences on the county's social and economic well-being and continues to poison its roots: the complete segregation of Noxubee's schools. Despite the Supreme Court's 1955 order in *Brown v. Board of Education of Topeka* to desegregate public schools with "all deliberate speed," it was not until the late 1960s that federal court rulings finally mounted a direct assault to separate schools, in Mississippi and throughout the nation. In August 1968, on the eve of a new school year, in the case of *Adams v. Mathews*, Noxubee County and several dozen other school districts in Mississippi and Louisiana were ordered to begin taking steps to desegregate their schools in compliance with the spirit, and not just the letter, of *Brown*. In that case, Judge John Minor Wisdom—famously one of the southern federal judges most committed to dismantling institutional racism—reaffirmed the view that "freedom of choice" plans, by which students were given the option to integrate, had largely failed "to bring about an integrated, unitary school system in which there are no Negro schools and no white schools—just schools." His opinion reiterated the imperative that each school board's desegregation plan eliminate racial discrimination " 'root and branch' " and had to be one that " 'promises realistically to work now.' "

As in many other communities nationwide that faced such orders, Noxubee County's white minority reacted by forming a private school. The southern rural variant of northern urban white flight to suburban school districts was the creation of the private academy—often deceptively identified by that oxymoron: private *Christian* academy. Allegedly built to enshrine the principle of free choice, the private academy was really a sanctum of retreat: nearly everyone with the economic wherewithal to make a choice was white; no nonwhites would have been welcome in any event.

Still today, a central justification of the academies has to do with educational quality. The explanation is one familiar to parents in northern cities. When the academies began, black students were less well educated. How—the logic goes—could children's precious years be compromised by mixing them with those who, at best, were less academically advanced? Thus was spawned a cycle of inequity out of which few are willing to break. There are other, less prettified justifications as well. One man observed to me: "All of us draw the lines somewhere on the race issue. Are you gonna date 'em? Are you gonna . . . " My subject's voice trailed off and then, after a reflective pause, he continued: "And I don't think just black, but Chinese—whatever. And some of us draw those lines earlier than others. I may say,

'I'm not gonna let it happen.' Big deal." The man, a white opponent of the waste companies, might as well have been speaking in 1964 as in 1994.

In the summer of 1968, leading whites in Noxubee County formed an entity called the Noxubee Educational Foundation, which would establish a new school. The *Beacon* cryptically reported on August 8 only that the as yet unnamed school had found a head: "Polk Farrar, head of the Noxubee Educational Foundation, stated today that John L. Barrett has accepted the position as headmaster of the private school which will open in September." The first head of the school had for a decade been the superintendent of the public schools, and earlier the sometime football coach, English and driver's ed teacher, and a Cub Scout master. (The grandfatherly Barrett, now a deacon at Martha Blackwell's church, was the school's headmaster for twenty-one years. Today he does several odd jobs, including running the local golf course, because his pension is insufficient to support him. In this he is something of a casualty of integration: he left the public schools to head the private academy, where he received no retirement benefits. Later, when he wanted to return to work in the public schools, he could not get hired because resentment against him was so strong. As a result, he could not work in the public schools for the number of years necessary to merit an adequate pension to support himself in retirement.)

The new school was assembled so hastily that it remained unnamed at its opening. Housekeeping details like the school colors (blue and gold) and the team name (the Vikings, in this land that seldom sees snow) would not be settled for still another month. Despite this monumental change in the social landscape, the school discontents were not discussed by the *Beacon,* even though the paper was written almost exclusively for the white minority; to do so would have been an indecorous recognition of the trouble, it would have aired shared understandings for wider inspection.

Instead, the paper was full of the usual miscellany of small-town life: a white elephant sale on Saturday, August 24; news of the—still all-white—fall 1968 football squad, featuring its "fine" tight end, "Little Tiny" Heard; the Pilot Pancake Party to be held on Saturday, October 24; a twenty-point buck killed near Artesia in early December.

Meanwhile, like many other school boards, the Noxubee County Board of Education did not comply with the federal order. The school system earned yet another year's delay for its white students through litigation. In the summer of 1969, the U.S. Court of Appeals for the Fifth Circuit concluded in yet another case: "The Noxubee County School District, along with two dozen others, continues to operate and maintain its all-Negro schools. The record compels the conclusion that to eliminate the dual character of these schools alternative methods of desegregation must be employed." At the time this decision came down, the black enrollment in Noxubee County's traditionally white schools achieved through freedom of choice was still only 3.2 percent—only 95 of 3,002 black students—a number kept low through intimidation and harassment. Noxubee's 829 white students continued to attend the three "predominantly white" schools, while the vast majority of black students went to the three "all Negro" schools. White students had not flocked to the new private academy (it had started with 228 students), because there had not yet been a need for them to do so.

The court ordered that freedom of choice would no longer be an acceptable method for "disestablishing their dual school systems." It ordered that each school board defendant develop an "acceptable" plan of desegregation before August 11, 1969, to be implemented for the district court's approval no later than August 27, 1969.

In Noxubee County, the school board dragged its feet; interim desegregation plans for the 1969–70 school year were proposed by the Office of Education of the U.S. Department of Health, Education and Welfare, and were rejected by the school board. "The board maintains that these plans are unworkable and would not be to the best interest of Noxubee County and would seriously injure the academic standing of the Noxubee County schools," reported the *Beacon.* The subtext understood by the *Beacon's* white readership was that the plans would force their better-educated children to be thrown into classrooms with ill-educated black students.

As if to reinforce the impression of the rabble with which white students would suddenly be associated, the *Beacon* ran two stories about local African Americans on its front page. At a time when blacks rarely received attention in the local press, this coverage was exceptional. The first story, on October 9, reported that a forty-three-year-old Negro sheriff's deputy, "known around the courthouse as 'Peanuts,'" had died the previous Saturday after having been shot in a disturbance on Baptist Hill—Macon's largest black section—the previous August. The other story, on the bottom of the same page, was uncharacteristically lurid for the usually staid local paper. "Berserk Negro Kills Wife, Mother-in-Law" read the headline for a story about a bricklayer named Richard Hopkins who had been placed in jail after stabbing his wife and mother-in-law to death.

By early November 1969, in the face of the board's intransigence, the Fifth Circuit Court of Appeals again intervened, ordering the complete integration of the county's schools. It directed that HEW's interim plans become permanent, effective the spring semester: "This activity shall commence immediately. The Office of Education's plans will result in the transfer of thousands of school children and hundreds of faculty members to new schools. Many children will have new teachers after December 31, 1969." The desegregation plan ordered the closing of black schools and the consolidation of facilities. This was easier said than done: the HEW plan ordered that Noxubee High take all 1,171 students in grades nine through twelve; the school had facilities for only 280.

The *Beacon* gave this order more extensive coverage than any previous event in the conflict. Its account of this latest development, opening wounds that still fester in Noxubee County, was remarkably restrained and passionless: "Involved in the huge transition are 4,800 student [*sic*], approximately 4,000 of whom are Negroes, as well as 225 teachers and 82 bus drivers. With a deadline of December 31, 1969 to make changes, there is lots of work to be done in a very short time." More emotionally, the paper waxed enthusiastic over the naming of Jay Chancellor—who would, over two decades later, become a prominent backer of the hazardous waste opposition—as the best-dressed man on the still overwhelmingly white Noxubee County High School campus. But the public schools would never be the province of whites again. When the new term began, Central Academy's enrollment skyrocketed. John Barrett remembered: "Friday evening we had 279 students, and Monday morning we had 650. And I had to make room for all of 'em."

When the newly reorganized Noxubee County schools opened in January 1970, most black students did not attend. Accounts as to why this boycott happened are contradictory, and it is difficult to get people in Noxubee County, black or white, to summon up memories of that time, a time of great drama and heightened social tension. Or at least, it is difficult to get them to share memories with an outsider.

The reason for this conspiracy of silence probably resides in a reality that no one in Noxubee, white or black, is proud of today. Whites disclaim any knowledge and explain that they were not the ones doing the boycotting. The man Ike Brown calls his "mentor" told me that blacks kept out of school because they thought it was the "right thing," with "so much controversy in the schools." Two powerful black ministers, he reflected, may have sold out by accepting bribes from whites to help keep blacks out until the start of a new school year and completion of the new academy. Essie Spencer, an older black woman and a retired teacher with whom Ike Brown regularly fights, repeated this view. Her daughter, Darlene Cole, now an official in the public schools' administrative offices, could remember only that she had had to make up classtime the following summer. State Representative Reecy Dickson, herself a product of the Noxubee schools and a former teacher educated in Noxubee, had but the vaguest recollection of children not attending schools that year. Memories of the boycott, I concluded, were but another of the secrets that the people of Noxubee— white and black—so scrupulously hide from the outside world.

Characteristically, the *Beacon* did not live up to its name, and once again participated in this deliberate, collective amnesia. Future historians could return to Noxubee County and, on the basis of contemporary news sources, have not the slightest inkling of the turmoil its schools underwent in those years. The paper remained virtually silent on the subject of the school boycott, which kept as many as

3,500 of its school-age children—out of a total of almost 5,000—out of the classroom for an entire term. In the January 21, 1970, issue the paper reported that the white superintendent had resigned, adding simply: "Meanwhile, attendance figures continued on a low level. There were 705 white students enrolled in the Noxubee County Public School system and only 509 were in attendance on Tuesday of this week. Of the 4000 odd Negroes enrolled, only 25 attended classes on Tuesday." This was the only mention ever made in the local press about a boycott that kept the "odd" majority of its schoolchildren out of the classroom for an entire term, allowing white students who remained to finish out their school year much as they had started it.

Twenty years ago, the constitutional law scholar Derrick Bell remarked that "irrationally, an 'integrated' school, work force or neighborhood is one with no more than a 25 percent black population." In general, his observation may hold true. But in predominantly African American pockets of the South like Noxubee County, whites would consider a 25 percent black population so small as to be palatable. At the end of the 1969–70 school year, the ideological tug of war continued, with the school board this time proposing that a sixty-to-forty white-to-black ratio for the schools be implemented. With a black population of over 70 percent, some all-black schools would have had to remain if this plan had been put into effect.

"The colored citizens of Noxubee County presented a plan" calling for the pairing of white and black schools, and the consolidation of all high school students in a single location. A plan very much like the one presented by the county's "colored citizens" was ultimately enacted, with federal court approval. By September 3, 1970, 3,268 students were enrolled in the schools, only 102 of whom were white.

In its by now familiarly cryptic manner of addressing the issue, the *Beacon* observed that in September 1969, "by way of comparison," enrollment had been 4,216. One week later, white attendance declined to 71 students. In grades nine through twelve, there were but 23 white students—only two in the senior year.

For that school year, enrollment at the newly-named Central Academy quadrupled, to nearly eight hundred—almost all of the white student population. Analyzing these figures, the *Beacon* articulated a view that still holds weight with some whites in Noxubee County: "From the above figures, it would appear that the order of the Fifth Circuit Court of Appeals has created an almost totally segregated system in Noxubee County." This was the last the newspaper would utter about the school crisis. It would not be the last time, however, that the county's residents would blame the federal government and disclaim any responsibility for their own troubles.

Within a couple of years, Noxubee County's public schools would become almost totally African American, and they have remained that way ever since. In the 1992–93 school year, for example, there was one white student at the public high school. As Brooksville's mayor, Brad Moore, put it to me: "In '68, if the schools had integrated, if we'd thought it out, we could have more industries now. We have rail, productive land, a good workforce." But, he added, now it's "too late. We have a whole generation raised on hating each other."

■ ■ ■ SOME of the last white students to leave the public schools were Mennonites. They justified the construction of separate schools for their children on religious grounds. "By

1969 conviction arose within the hearts of our brethren," explains a history of one of the conservative Mennonite congregations in Noxubee County, "for the need of our own school, where Bible doctrine and principles could be included in their educational curriculum." Why the Lord waited to make this conviction arise in the hearts of Noxubee County's Mennonite brethren until the schools were integrated remained unsaid. By the summer of 1970, the Magnolia Mennonite School had been built, yet another structure firmly in place to guarantee the long-term segregation of the Noxubee County schools.

Mennonites first began moving into Noxubee County and nearby parts of the black prairie belt in the early 1960s. They discovered Noxubee County through the ads of H.E. "Hap" Bollar, a thin, rosy-cheeked, jocular man now in his late eighties, who stands over six feet two inches tall. He is the sort celebrated in the early years of the Reagan administration for making the country what it is: a wildly patriotic veteran, who had been successful in business, involved in his community, married to the same woman for sixty-four years, and the sire of three children, twelve grandchildren, and twenty-three great-grandchildren. Alert and energetic in conversation, when he speaks he seems a much younger man than he is. Raised in Illinois and Ontario, Canada, Bollar always wanted to farm. His father lost their family corn farm in the Great Depression, and for years Hap could not afford to get started himself. He flew for the air force in the Pacific theater during World War II and then became the personal pilot to J. Walter Duncan, a multimillionaire Oklahoma oilman and aviation pioneer. Duncan made it possible for him to save a comfortable sum, and at age fifty he kept a promise to himself by finally becoming a farmer and moving to the black prairie belt. In the late 1950s, Bollar began putting ads in *Prairie Farmer* magazine promoting his services as a purveyor of black prairie land.

The Mennonites came as pioneers, as if on a religious mission, to "colonize" parts of the South; they also came in search of cheaper land. At least two midwestern Mennonite congregations had begun to explore the possibility of moving south in 1959 and after some research had concluded that Noxubee County offered the best bargain. At between $85 and $105 an acre, Noxubee land was cheap, even by comparison to nearby areas in Mississippi and Alabama, and it was about a quarter of the price of the rich corn-producing land from which they had come, mostly in Illinois and Indiana.

Mennonite is the generic name for several Christian denominations tracing their origin to Simon Menno, a seventeenth-century Dutch priest; Noxubee County is home to four of them. Mennonite denominations share the same basic beliefs, notably, their renunciation of most political activity and military service, because of their belief that the kingdom of God—and not worldly governments—merits their full allegiance. There now exists a wide spectrum of Mennonite belief, ranging from extremely conservative denominations like the Amish (none of whom trekked south to the black prairie belt), many of whom abjure all trappings of modern, mechanized life, to a variety of congregations that permit their members to participate in civic activities, vote, and even earn higher degrees—instead of the usual practice of educating children only until about age sixteen.

Most Mennonite men are identifiable by their beards, which are trimmed to frame their jaws and chins, and their lack of mustaches; the women wear thin, loose-fitting cotton dresses year-round and sensible, orthopedic-looking shoes. The women also sport small woven caps ("head coverings" to Mennonites), the color of which identifies their sect: black for the more conservative Holderman Mennonites, white for a more moderate denomination. Even those who were born and raised in Mississippi tend to speak in the flat, uninflected tones of the midwestern prairie. A chorus of their spoken voices would sound like an opera by Philip Glass.

Had it been strange to move to Noxubee from Indiana in the early sixties? Harvey Miller, a seed dealer and catfish farmer, answered: "Yes, it were. You wouldn't see blacks eating in a restaurant where the whites would be." Today, he continued: "You go to . . . McDonald's and all the eatin' houses in Columbus and black couples, black families . . . have their relatives in there . . . and I like to see that. God made it all, like we say, human beins, and they're just as pretty as we are. We ain't got no right to discriminate against 'em." Despite their comparative tolerance, Mennonites often hold racial attitudes that seem anchored in an earlier time. Many of them refer freely to "colored people" without the slightest inkling of political incorrectitude.

Since the Mennonites moved south, some have broken off and established more liberal denominations, and others have moved to nearby counties, making difficult an exact count of Noxubee County's Mennonite population. But the number is at least a thousand—about a quarter of the local white population.

There is a curious schizophrenia in the way others in Noxubee County think and speak about this 10 percent to 20 percent of the county's total population. On the one hand, they are prized as neighbors by blacks and other whites alike. The county had many absentee landlords when they arrived in the early 1960s, people who had grown too old to farm and had moved away. For others, the land's traditional cotton crop was no longer lucrative because of federally mandated increases in the minimum wage, and some land had fallen into desuetude. Mennonites came in and began working derelict farms, reviving the county's agricultural life, bringing with them different values and practices. They were surprised at how undeveloped the county was. Many of their farms did not receive rural mail delivery when they arrived; garbage was collected by an old mule-drawn wagon. When Harvey Miller arrived in the early sixties, he was startled to see lines of as many as twenty black people, moving in sync as they chopped cotton and moved across the horizon like a giant scythe.

It became a game for me to try and identify the Mennonite farms. Theirs were on average more carefully tended than those of native farmers. They worked the land to the edge of the property and cut away weeds and shrubbery that had grown up between fields or next to roadsides and outbuildings. Mennonites introduced new crops and products to Noxubee County—notably, soybeans and catfish—as well as modern farm management practices, and they emphasized the values of crop rotation and diversification. This also meant more intensive use of agricultural chemicals. I. D. Conner, a retired black man who has lived all of his life in Noxubee, was not alone in tracing a change in the landscape to the Mennonites' land use. Before their arrival, "peach and plum trees used to be all over the land in Noxubee County," as well as more "creeks and streams."

On the other hand, many native whites despise the Mennonites because the vast majority of them do not vote, to honor their rejection of what they see as worldly values. J. P. Hoover, a husky dairyman in his late 30s with the chubby, cheery features of the Pillsbury Dough Boy, flushed slightly when he rather sheepishly admitted that his white neighbors had cursed at him: "If you," he whispered the next word, "*damn* Mennonites don't vote, why don't you just get out of the county?" This view contributes further to the county's social and political polarization. One family told me that they changed their congregation's name to Cornerstone Community Church largely to avoid the locally negative "Mennonite" connotation.

Because they do not vote and so have absented themselves from local power struggles, Mennonites are treated as a different race entirely, as if they are not white. When native Noxubeeans of any race limn the social contours of their county, they explain unblinkingly that it is populated by "whites, blacks, and Mennonites."

Mennonites are determinedly uncritical and generally affect a pleasant, if bland and rather reserved, demeanor. Nevertheless, it does not take long to discover an undercurrent of dissatisfaction with Noxubee County. The majority of Mennonites I spoke to testified to their longing to leave the county, if they could. Soybeans, a crop they introduced, boomed in the 1970s, but prices collapsed in February 1981, when President Jimmy Carter threatened a Soviet grain embargo. Farmers in Noxubee and across the nation were suddenly getting less than half the price for a bushel of soybeans than they would have earned the previous month, leading to widespread bankruptcies. The fall in soybean prices especially hurt Noxubee's Mennonites. Although some Mennonites are among the county's most prosperous farmers, many of them were left so heavily mortgaged and now run such small operations that the possibility of moving back north has been rendered impossible.

A sentiment echoed time and again in my conversations with Mennonites was that many of them do not agree with the values of the dominant white community. They came to Noxubee County with fresh sets of eyes, eyes accustomed to a different, more homogeneous culture, to be sure, but nonetheless eyes unaccustomed to the inequities and imbalances of power they discovered in Noxubee County.

One Mennonite farmer, a lanky, long-faced man now in his mid-fifties, recalled how, as an adolescent fresh to Mississippi in the summer of 1964, National Guard patrols, equipped with klieg lights, combed the fields near his family's home at night, searching for the bodies of the three civil rights workers who had in fact been murdered and buried in an earthen dam near Philadelphia, Mississippi. The man was fifteen years old when, the next year, he saw a neighbor's hired hand being beaten: "The Civil War had been fought 100 years before, but I was reminded that it was not too far removed when I saw a man with a board paddle his thirty-year-old married hired man. He ended up running away sometime later." Other Mennonites told me similar stories, of seeing grown black workers being bullwhipped by their employers in the 1960s.

In the Midwest, it was Mennonite custom for everyone working on a farm to take their meals together. In Noxubee County they likewise would have their help, black and white, in the kitchen to eat dinner at noon and supper at day's end. This created discomfort, too; local custom was for black laborers to eat outside the door. Some Mennonites were threatened for their breach of local behavior.

In a thirty-year retrospective of their congregation's fortunes in Noxubee County, an unnamed author shared a recollection entitled "Times Have Changed":

> The labor force has also changed. There was an abundance of colored labor that were working for $2.00 to $2.50 per day in the cotton fields. Regular farm help was paid $20.00 to $25.00 per week plus

a house or shack to live in, also milk and meat. But when the minimum wage went into effect, a farmer could not pay that price for labor in the cotton field, as it would cost more than he would receive for his crop. The farmer went to machinery and let the colored help go, they went on welfare and food stamps, etc. Only the most dependable ones are still working on farms.

Most of the Mennonite people could not understand using the colored people that way, not paying more, but most of them have learned the reason for some of the unexplained things that did not look right to them at first and still may not be right, but we know the reason for some of the ways that things were done.

The passage intrigued me for its confusion of sentiments. Simultaneously, it seemed accepting of the local status quo ("unexplained things that did not look right to them at first"), but also critical of it ("still may not be right"). Asking around, I learned that Mennonite frustration with the lack of skilled workers was widespread. Many felt that black farm laborers were badly paid and were taken advantage of by white farmers, and many said the white farmers still do not pay minimum wage by giving workers salaries of $150 to $200 a week and then requiring seventy-hour weeks. Yet Mennonites also shared the concern that those same workers were ill equipped to do much beyond the most menial tasks; and so, as employers, Mennonites could not justify paying a living wage either.

One obvious way to begin correcting this state of affairs would be through improved education and vocational training for Noxubee's black residents. Yet, like the county's white minority, Mennonites elected to withdraw from the county's overwhelmingly black public schools. And if their example in other facets of county life is a reliable guide, they were the segment of its population best equipped to help improve the schools' quality. But in the face of an enormous problem, they elected not to bother.

■ ■ ■ THE deliberate neglect of the public schools is directly reflected in Noxubee County's appallingly high rate of functional illiteracy. The April 1991 Mississippi Literacy Assessment, completed during Ray Mabus's term as governor, measured adult literacy in several categories. For the three basic measures of literacy—the ability to read and understand basic prose, the ability to work with simple documents, and basic quantitative ability—Noxubee County ranked lower than any other Mississippi county in its region. A statistical map of the figures would tell the story: Noxubee County resembles no other part of the state so much as the Delta. This is the unwanted residue of the sparkling, "social-minded" plantation culture that links Noxubee County's eastern prairies to the Delta. Large numbers of black slaves, and later tenant farmers and sharecroppers, worked the land to support whites' extravagant social habits; many of their descendants, poor and badly educated, live on in situations not dramatically improved from those of their forebearers.

The problem is everywhere, and easy to see. A librarian told me that in a federally funded literacy program she had grown men who operated heavy road equipment for a living and could not read basic road signs. My interviews with Ike Brown and other educated blacks were often interrupted by someone needing interpretation of an official notice, court document, or some other written message meaningless to its holder.

Whites and blacks alike would lower their voices when explaining to me—as if admitting a dirty secret—that industries like furniture manufacturing, which flourishes north of Noxubee, had come into the county to evaluate the possibility of locating there, only to conclude that they could not do so because the quality of the public schools was so dismal, making the county unattractive both as a potential labor pool and as a place for outsiders to move to.

Whites increasingly now complain as well about Central Academy. Distressed by the quality of education at Central, the more prosperous among them today send their children thirty or forty miles away to other private academies. Yet the notion that Central Academy should close, in order to pool dwindling local resources, is routinely rejected. What of the claim, I wondered, that the poor schools helped make Noxubee County attractive to businesses like waste companies? A white woman who has been exceptionally active in opposing the waste companies absolutely rejected the thrust of my question: "I don't think that the academy is drawing away from the public schools. The people who are going to the academy are paying academy tuition, but they're also paying taxes supporting the public schools." A relative, who had been equally vocal in opposing hazardous waste, similarly refused to take responsibility for the state of the public schools. Why wouldn't better industries locate in Noxubee? "Well, it's just not an educational system that anyone from any other area would want to come in here to—when you don't have computers in your classrooms, and you don't have a number of classes and courses that the other kids have the privilege of taking advantage of if they live someplace else." In fact, when she spoke those words, Central Academy had just been given a small computer system by a white family. The thought of those resources being shared in a public school system that serves all of the county's children is not a possibility she or others of her class are willing to entertain.

■ ■ ■ AT bottom, the refusal to end this and other divisions in the county's life is attributable to that most human of tendencies: a desire to maintain control. In the introduction to *Southern Politics in State and Nation*, first published in 1949, the Alabama political scientist V. O. Key concluded that the oddities of Southern politics can be traced back to the region's black population. In words that, almost a half century later, still resonate when discussing the politics of the black prairie belt, Key explained that Southern politics were not "chiefly concerned with the maintenance of the supremacy of white over black." Instead, he offered: "the observer must look more closely to determine which whites and which blacks give southern politics its individuality." In majority black areas like Noxubee County, Key observed, "a real problem of politics, broadly considered, is the maintenance of control by a white minority." Key went on to compare this control to that of a colonial power, like the Dutch in the East Indies, or the British in India, trenchantly adding that the white minority remains in control with the tolerance and support of the "home country."

This thesis, Key further explained,

> runs counter to the idea that many top-drawer
> southerners firmly believe, viz., that the poor white is
> at tue bottom of all the trouble about the Negro. The
> planter may often be kind, even benevolent, towards

his Negroes, and the upcountrymen may be, as the Negroes say, "mean": yet when the political chips are down, the whites of the black belts . . . are the most ardent in the faith of white supremacy as, indeed, would naturally be expected.

The South has, of course, changed irrevocably since Key advanced these views. Yet elements of his schema struck me as still extraordinarily relevant to understanding Noxubee County, which remains a time capsule of the sort of place he described, with its black majority, white planters in the eastern prairie, and white "upcountrymen" in the western hills.

Two of Key's thoughts explain the particular tumult caused by Ed Netherland. First, by approaching black and upcountry politicians for support, Netherland showed that those outside the "home country" no longer supported or tolerated—or merely disregarded—the historical dominance of the white planter class, at least so long as it stood in the way of other commercial concerns. Second, the white man who, in the 1990s, would become most closely identified with the interests of the county's blacks—contrary to local expectations—was Ralph Higginbotham, a man not from the sometimes-benevolent planter culture of the eastern prairies, but from the hills, home of "mean" whites. Key's analysis thus provides a framework for understanding how the Noxubee waste wars were but the latest chapter in a struggle for control in poor and divided Noxubee County.

It was a struggle that began, tentatively, several years after the passage of the Voting Rights Act of 1965. For years the Voting Rights Act of 1965 meant little in predominantly black Noxubee County, where the memory of voter intimidation still hangs heavy. The Voting Rights Act hardly mattered in 1968, for instance, when George Wallace carried the county in his third-party Presidential bid, receiving 1,868 votes to Hubert Humphrey's 1,429 and Richard Nixon's 225. Richard Brooks, the retired schoolteacher and NAACP chapter president who compiled the chapter's history of local black achievement, wrote of that time: "Many blacks expressed their views that they could not get a black elected even if they all voted. Many felt that a black candidate would not win even if he or she received the majority votes casted."

The August 19, 1971, edition of the *Beacon* carried an extraordinary half-page political notice trumpeting "The Black Community's Endorsed Candidate Slate for Noxubee County Election." The county had not seen anything like it for nearly a century. For the first time since Reconstruction, there were blacks in a Democratic primary runoff for some of the most important county offices—for sheriff and three of the five supervisors' posts. The ad touting a full black slate came in the wake of the overwhelming Democratic primary victory of Joseph Wayne, a black candidate for supervisor of District One, covering the northern part of the prairie, with the most concentrated African American population.

Wayne was the only African American to win in that year's election. In reporting the final results, the *Beacon* printed "August 26, *1871*" on its masthead, as if expressing an unconscious fear that the county was turning back the clock to Reconstruction, an era described by one contemporary chronicler, echoing sentiments still heard today throughout the South, as a time when "white people were desperate," having "been mistreated, insulted, degraded, and humiliated" from 1867 to 1875. The misprint also emphasized the deep-seated fear that whites were losing control: exactly a century from the zenith of carpetbagger and scalawag rule in Noxubee County, a black man would again serve in one of the county's five most visible political offices.

William Mullins, Martha Blackwell's father, was also re-elected to the board that year, and at its first meeting in January 1972, unanimously chosen as its president, a post he would occupy almost until his death in 1980. Mullins won comfortably, although his closest challenger was also a black man, Mastraw Oliver. Oliver was perhaps the county's most successful black farmer and had taken the courageous step of sending his children to the still white public schools when the feeble free choice plan was in effect. Twenty years later, his nephew, William "Boo" Oliver, would become supervisor for District Two, Mullins's old district, in the middle of the hazardous waste controversy.

For the remainder of the decade, no other blacks were elected to public office in Noxubee County. In 1975, Joseph Wayne was reelected to his supervisor's post, in which "he serviced until his death in 1978," according to an NAACP account. By time-honored Mississippi custom, a family member—in Wayne's case, his brother—was selected to serve out the remaining year of his term.

In 1979, Noxubee County politics took a dramatic turn. For over five years black registered voters had outnumbered whites, but blacks were not correspondingly represented in political office—not even close. That year—the year Ike Brown first worked in the county elections—there were African American candidates for most major offices. In the final election, Joseph Stevenson was elected to fill Joseph Wayne's spot on the board of supervisors. Another black man, George Robinson, lost to a longtime white supervisor whose district covered most of the city of Macon. Both Stevenson and Robinson would later support Ed Netherland's forays into Noxubee. Symbolically, however, the most important victory signaling the desire of the county's majority to control their own fortunes occurred when the white stranglehold on the office of superintendent of education was broken.

A tall, thin woman, Reecy Dickson has a pretty, small, round face, with regular features and bright eyes. In one statement she distributed in her successful campaign for superintendent, accompanied by a photo of herself with a radiant smile, her hair cut in a then-fashionable short Afro, Dickson began by describing her activities to help build a health clinic ("This work has encountered twelve trips in various states") and a dozen years' service as a public schoolteacher. She then outlined her concerns:

> We are unable to produce enough educated citizens.
> I feel that a school system should be based or set up
> on theories to benefit the students to the higher
> degree, and not be centered around personal benefits.
> . . . In doing this, we should consider that education
> springs from the future. There, we should have
> enough teachers, proper teaching facilities, a wide
> range of subjects, and cooperation between students,
> parents, teachers and administrators to produce an
> atmosphere conducive to learning.

Hers was a fascinating tangle of thought. Mixed in with the educatorspeak, mangled syntax, and contorted imagery, under the thicket of the paragraph's confusing logic, was an apparently heartfelt finger-pointing at the current system's inadequacies, in addition to a suggestion of corruption and favoritism.

The intimation that students' interests had been usurped by school authorities was especially provocative. One of the things whites and a few blacks in Noxubee County repeatedly claimed was that Dickson had been an exceedingly corrupt superintendent. (Charges of corruption swirled about her throughout her tenure, although audits of the schools by then state auditor and later governor Ray Mabus failed to prove any wrongdoing.) Yet as a candidate and teacher, in the forum of a mostly white-read newspaper in a majority-black county, she promised to end corruption in the schools.

Reecy Dickson went from being superintendent to serving as state representative for a district that includes most of Noxubee County. A soft-spoken woman, she radiates a slightly dreamy, far-away quality. I first met her during a recess of the Mississippi House of Representatives, in the state's magnificent house chamber; the room was flooded with multicolored light from its elaborate stained-glass windows. The house chamber, outfitted in oak wainscoting and capacious leather seats, is at once clubby and grandiose, the very image of a legislature one expects to see in a junior high school civics textbook. Because of her anti-corruption promises as a first-time political candidate in 1979, I asked Dickson about the charges of political payoffs and dirty dealing then being hurled about in the Noxubee waste wars. The political tables had turned since 1979: the anti-waste forces now accused mostly black and dispossessed poorer white politicians of corruption. She slumped her listless frame back into her roomy leather chair, sighed heavily, and looked away. There was silence for what seemed an hour; it was probably only a minute. Dickson's gaze drifted up to the ceiling, as if looking to summon a spirit, an angel to help her explain the obvious to this inquisitive, if uncomprehending, Little White Boy from the North. Eventually, she breathed heavily again and pulled her right hand from her lap, her eyes following its path as she drew it up and around her in a wide arc, as if it were the arm of a compass that would direct her to face me.

Dickson's languid composure suddenly broke. Her elegant face tightened as she spat out her response: "An excuse. Noxubee County has always looked for an excuse to justify their attitudes, their expectations. Small-town garbage. An excuse to remain in the past." As if an afterthought, again distracted, and no longer even distantly responding to my question, she sighed and added: "Not one day was Noxubee County integrated. Not for 30 years."

■ ■ ■ IN short, when Netherland arrived in the summer of 1990, Noxubee County was like a constellation inhabited by three stars—black, white, and Mennonite—all of them sharing the same space, endlessly circling one another, their paths intersecting in their daily rotations, but never colliding.

"I will go to my grave swearing this," Netherland insisted. "Had no clue about the demographics of this. On my mother's grave, I swear that. Okay?" To this day, he denies that his company picked Noxubee County because it is a poor, majority-black area. How then did he end up in east-central Mississippi, a forgotten part of a neglected state?

his associates, putting down roots in the black prairie belt of Mississippi.

In the late spring of 1990, Mike Goff, the garrulous aide who was at that time Governor Ray Mabus's special assistant for natural resources, met with Netherland and a couple of his associates; top environmental regulators; and the heads of the senate and house conservation and water resources committees, the state assembly's key environmental legislative oversight committees. It was Mabus's policy that his administration meet at least once with every representative of a waste company until some decision had been reached. Goff remembered the meeting as a courtesy call. He said it lacked any detailed discussion of specific proposals. Goff also said he never trusted Netherland, and recalled that "Ed was bragging that he'd just sited in the home of the KKK and if you can do it there, you can do it anywhere."

Of course, Netherland actually had no guarantee that he could build his incinerator in Giles County in the spring or summer of 1990. Netherland's braggadocio with Goff and other Mississippi officials was a vintage example of his well-honed sales technique: Overinflate the nature of your accomplishment with prospect A to woo prospect B. Turn around and use the slightest hint of prospect B's support as leverage to build more support with prospect C. The suggestion that he had overcome the Sisyphean task of siting in the home of the KKK is of special interest, however, for another reason. Specifically, it contains the germ of a self-image Netherland would cultivate in Mississippi, namely, of himself as a kind of business evangelist, answering a call in the face of almost insurmountable odds. In Mississippi, the self-image he would thus cultivate was of one determined to improve the lot of the Defenseless Negro against his White Oppressor, and so to help guide a pocket of the poor, afflicted, struggling Deep South into the late twentieth century.

Having already spent $900,000 with little to show for it, after meeting with Goff and others Netherland used his time in Mississippi to, in his words, "sniff around for a day or two." He observed that Mississippi was in the throes of a hazardous waste crisis. Despite the fact that Mississippi was generating a mere 2.6 percent of the national hazardous waste total, the state was suddenly worried that it might be left holding the short end of the political stick. Mississippi had no treatment facility for any kind of hazardous waste and, thus, no leverage to bargain with other states. Just two years earlier, when Mabus had been elected governor, this had not been a concern. Goff recalled that the nation's largest hazardous waste dump, at Emelle, Alabama, was "rollin' and blowin' at the time." The Mabus administration reasonably assumed that Mississippi's comparatively small amount of hazardous waste could be sent right across the Alabama line, where there was ample capacity to dispose of it.

But that had all changed with Alabama's 1989 decision to play political hardball and attempt to restrict the flow of hazardous wastes to Emelle. Suddenly, the Mabus administration was looking for options to a possible impending waste management crisis, brought on by Alabama's national brinkmanship. Mabus and his staff set out to consider possible options. Goff and others on the governor's staff concluded that since Mississippi was a comparatively small waste producer, the strongest and most politically palatable card they could play was to offer the other southeastern states a specialty service. In the world of waste "management" (the industry's euphemism for hazardous waste treatment, storage, and disposal), that meant something like a metals recovery facility, which the industry giant Chemical

Waste Management offered to build in Flowood, Mississippi, where Mississippi Steel was located. Another alternative was an aqueous treatment facility for nonsolid hazardous wastes. Mississippi could then say to other states in the Southeast that it offered a waste treatment service they did not, thereby earning an invitation to enter a regional waste management pact and so satisfy its federal capacity assurance planning obligations. Tennessee had done this by offering aqueous treatment capability in exchange for the provision of other disposal services in sister states. But the Mabus people had a hard time convincing Mississippi industry to support either one of these options. With Alabama's door still open, there did not seem to be much reason to worry—yet.

Serving a waste niche market was *not* what Netherland understood Mississippi to want. At his meeting with Goff and the other Mississippi officials, Netherland remembered: "I asked them for a wish list. I said, 'What d'you want?' The discussion was all off the cuff, all couched in 'ifs.' They were very specific about wanting incineration and landfill." Netherland's exploration of possible landfill construction seems odd, since he had weeks before told the *Pulaski Citizen*: "We don't want to be in that business. Everything we handle will eventually go to Emelle or Barnwell, S.C." (Barnwell is one of the country's two licensed low-level radioactive dumps.)

Thus, if Netherland's recollection is accurate, the Mabus administration must share some of the blame for encouraging him to think as big as he did for Mississippi. Alan Huffman, a former journalist who succeeded Goff as Mabus's environmental adviser, admitted that the administration's "position was a kind of Pontius Pilate exercise," meaning that they did not want the state of Mississippi to be in a position either of "promoting hazardous waste" or, conversely, favoring a particular company or particular disposal option. With the state's leadership hedging its bets, an eager entrepreneur had wide latitude to see how far he could push.

■ ■ ■ WHOEVER'S recollection is accurate as to what Mississippi wanted or needed—Goff's niche market or Netherland's Mother of All Waste Facilities—Netherland prepared for a Mississippi assault.

He returned to Tennessee. "I reported to my board that we had fertile soil. I also outlined what I had learned from the Mabus people about the possible sites in chalk and clay formations." The traditional wisdom in the waste disposal business is that building a dump on a mass of chalk or clay serves as a guarantee against contamination of water supplies. Netherland continued: "With our engineers, we then proceeded to set up maps over where we could find rail access, chalk, and a significant land mass." Just chalk? What happened to clay? In his recollection, the possibility of siting in clay formations—most of which are in central Mississippi, near the state capital and Mississippi's most heavily populated areas—had disappeared.

Between the states, things were getting tense. Goff traveled to Alabama with other Mabus staffers. They met in Montgomery with the head of Alabama's Department of Environmental Management, who Goff says simply did not warm to the idea of a niche market. Goff remembers him saying that "Alabama wanted to quote 'share the pain,' unquote."

This made it look ever more likely that Mississippi would be forced to come up with its own facility. Ray Mabus recalled later the concerns that this raised. A small man, Mabus has an alert, somewhat tense manner; when we met at his office in downtown Jackson, he was dressed like an aging preppie, in topsiders and a blue blazer; none of his salt-and-pepper hairs (he is forty-six) is ever astray. He would not be out of place in George Bush's family photo. Mabus ran in Mississippi as a New Democrat reformer; in a February 1988 cover story, the *New York Times Magazine* glowingly described him and his youthful administration as Mississippi's answer to the Kennedy White House. Though appointed by President Clinton to be the U.S. ambassador to Saudi Arabia in 1994, he continues to nurse the pain of his political defeat to a boorish political neophyte, Kirk Fordice, in 1991. An inexperienced candidate, Fordice nonetheless had some able handlers who relished slinging the mud. In the last weeks of the campaign, for example, they ran a television ad saying that while Mabus had studied at an eastern university patronized by Kennedys, Fordice had attended a state engineering school. What the ad did not say is that Mabus, who had attended public schools in Mississippi through college, had gone to Harvard for law school only and that the state school Fordice had attended was outside of Mississippi. Quentin Compson, the doomed young man in Faulkner's *Sound and the Fury*, was not the last Mississippian to suffer from a Harvard connection.

Throughout Mississippi, Mabus is now widely reviled for his "arrogance," studied self-promotion, and insistence on pushing his vision instead of listening to the concerns of his constituents. Even his admirers and former associates criticize him for these, his tragic political flaws, and identify arrogance as the fuel for his particular hubris. Despite this reputation and the fact that I had been warned that Mabus was always watching his words, looking over his shoulder for political opportunity, his reflections on Mississippi's 1990 waste situation made eminent sense.

Mabus remembered: "The focus at the state level was on three things: first, whether we needed a hazardous waste facility and, second, if so, what kind of facility. Third, we were concerned to protect the process to keep shenanigans from happening." In the end, these concerns were the ones that were not addressed.

Mabus recalled further: "We didn't want Mississippi to become the repository of hazardous waste simply because it was Mississippi. . . . Economic development does not mean taking anything that comes down the road." Resisting any business proposal can be a formidable task in Mississippi, especially if the prospect is a business—like a hazardous waste facility—that this state, unlike many others, lacks. Mississippians are acutely conscious of ranking "last" by all sorts of measures. They can recite chapter and verse of the different areas in which they fare poorly by comparison with the rest of the nation. What was for Democrat Mabus a concern that the state not become a hazardous waste repository "simply because it was Mississippi" became a virtue to the probusiness Republican Fordice.

After Ed Netherland landed in Noxubee County, with his grandiose visions and a big stack of cash, the Mabus administration's openness to different options gradually eroded, overwhelmed by the momentum of a titanic competition for a waste disposal permit, a competition made more intense by the apparent loss of Alabama as a cheap market for hazardous waste disposal.

However, Netherland did not arrive in Noxubee County with a splash. In fact, to hear him tell it, he almost happened upon the place by accident. Netherland made a couple of false starts when looking for a Mississippi site, including one a couple of counties south of Noxubee. It was judged unacceptable because the water table was too low. Yet Netherland recalls having felt confident. He was receiving a "great reception" from public officials in Mississippi, welcome relief after the aggressive rejections he had suffered in Tennessee.

His scout continued the search for locations. Driving down U.S. 45 in eastern Mississippi one day that summer, his emissary stopped when he saw the first of a series of roadside billboards in Noxubee County that advertised in three- and five-feet high letters: "BLACK PRAIRIE LAND. H. E. Bollar Realty."

■ ■ ■ HAP BOLLAR is the sort of well-rehearsed raconteur who speaks without pause in a loud stage whisper, as if sharing a stream of titillating secrets—a conversational style betraying his Irish-Catholic roots. A pendulous dewlap sways from side to side as he speaks. He professes great love for Noxubee County, which he calls "the last stand of the Old South," but his religion and northern roots make him eternally the outsider, despite his thirty-five years' residence. When he first moved to Noxubee County, he recalled, blacks still did all of the farm work, and would nearly stop dead in their tracks to watch a white man pass by on a tractor.

In Bollar's third and fifth years farming in Noxubee County, he produced the county's highest cotton yield, an impressive feat for one without a long farming history. He credited this not to his own skill but to other whites' lack of ability. The old cropping system, he told me, produced little love for the land either among whites, who took it for granted, or among blacks, who resented their servitude. In one of those early years, his father, who had moved down with him, came out to him one day as he worked the fields. As they spoke, Hap absent-mindedly reached down and picked up a clump of soil, which he began breaking up through his fingers. His father stopped in midsentence to declare: "I haven't seen a white man do that in years."

In addition to farming, Bollar sells real estate. In August 1989, then entering his ninth decade, Bollar contracted to sell his business to Brad Moore, a twenty-six-year-old native of Brooksville. Personable and energetic, Moore grew up on a soybean and cattle farm in northern Noxubee County. At five feet six inches, Moore looks rather like a shrunken version of the Leaguer Ed Netherland—handsome in a forgettable way. His looks are almost pretty, with his long, full eyelashes, which may account in part for the different roles he seems to play: alternately tough guy and good ole boy. When Netherland came to town, Moore had had his real estate license for only a year; he was still finishing up a degree part-time at a nearby junior college. He had three young tow-headed boys to support, and his priority was making a life for them and his wife, his high school sweetheart.

Netherland's scout visited Bollar Realty, spoke with Moore, and reported back to Netherland, who was not pleased and later recalled: "I was kind of pissed off. I had this image of a brand new realtor who didn't know his butt from first base." But when Netherland and Moore met, they instantly hit it off. To Moore, Netherland was a "jam-up guy . . . never met a nicer person in the world." He was also the image of a type in short supply in Noxubee County: young, entrepreneurial, and rich. It is not hard to imagine Moore warming to Netherland. Noxubee County has a dearth of young white people. And because whites and blacks do not socialize in Noxubee, as in most of the rest of the country,

Moore's social circle was severely limited. Netherland has the salesman's ability to be all things to all people. He can play country boy one minute, transform instantly into a hard-nosed business negotiator, and then affect the mien of the most courteous of country club hosts. Tim Gowan, a lawyer who wrangled with him repeatedly in the waste controversies, later said of him with grudging admiration: "Ed will say anything to anybody. And deny it. I've seen him. He's good. He'll deny it the next week and have you doubting your own memory. He will promise you, he will offer you, he will threaten you, and then he will beg."

For the unsophisticated, ambitious Moore, here was someone who could put him at ease with country charm and yet seemed deeply fixed in the firmament of American Business and Finance, flying in on corporate jets and rushing out to meetings in Nashville or Washington, D.C. Netherland was extravagant in his entertainments too, at least for Noxubee County, and could be counted on for a good meal at the Oak Tree Inn, one of two restaurants in the county at which both blacks and whites can have supper and a drink. Into the world of Brad Moore, Ed Netherland introduced a whiff of the 1980s, a sense of boundless economic possibility.

For Netherland, Moore provided a vital link to the life of Noxubee County; his family had deep roots there. The Giles County experience had showed him that he badly needed a solid local friend from the start.

Netherland was looking for about five hundred acres. He says that he told Brad that he could neither reveal the purpose for which he wanted the land nor the source of his funding and that the realtor never pressed him on the subject. Over the course of about a week, they looked at several locations together, but none of them were ideal, either because they lacked sufficient rail or highway access or because he would have had to assemble one parcel with purchases from several different landowners.

One day, the pair set out from Brooksville for lunch in Macon at the Oak Tree. They took the back way, along old U.S. 45. Netherland noticed big signs advertising the Martin Conrad ranch.

"What's that?" Netherland asked.

"Oh, you wouldn't be interested in that, Ed. It's too big. It's almost six thousand acres, and they won't let it be split up. Besides, it's too expensive. They're asking five to six hundred an acre." Comparable farmland in Noxubee County was going for half that at the time.

It turned out that the Martin Conrad ranch belonged to the Indiana University Foundation. Martin Conrad, an Indianapolis lawyer, first started buying land in Noxubee County in the 1960s through Bollar, whom he knew through friends in the Midwest. In 1975, Conrad and his wife, Opal, gave their Noxubee County ranch to Indiana University with the understanding that the land eventually would be sold, but only as a single parcel. The sprawling ranch begins in the flat, west-central part of the county and reaches north and west into the hills. Some of it is suitable for row cropping, but extensive limestone deposits on the property make it better suited for pasture, the use to which it had been put for nearly fifteen years.

For Ed Netherland, the proposition of paying $3.5 million for the six thousand acres appealed to the visionary in him. In Giles County, he was only proposing an incinerator. In Mississippi, he could become the King Of Hazardous Waste. His memory of the meeting with Mike Goff, Governor Mabus's advisor, is that they wanted everything: landfill, incinerator, who knew what else? Here he could do everything.

Surrounding acreage could continue to be used for pasture-land; some could be used as a public hunting preserve. And the price seemed low, at less than a fifth of what he would have been paying per acre in Tennessee. He obtained approval from his backers to buy an option to purchase the Conrad ranch.

In late September 1990, just before Netherland signed the option agreement, he maintains that he first told Moore about the reason he wanted to buy:

"Why else would you be down here?" Moore responded.

"And I will never forget this speech," Netherland recollected. "Brad said, 'Ed, I know it's controversial. But the majority of the people supported the other one and will support this one. This county is dyin'. My friends have moved to Atlanta or Houston or Washington. And I'm convinced that properly done, this is a good business.' "

The other one? Netherland claims that this was the first he knew—despite having been in the business for over a year—that seven years before, Chem Waste, the nation's largest handler of hazardous wastes, had tried to site a Noxubee facility similar to the one he was proposing. And there hangs a whole other tale.

■ ■ ■ CHEM WASTE is a subsidiary of the nation's largest waste hauling and disposal concern, WMX. (The WMX label cleverly blurs image and activity, avoiding mention of the company's central purpose. The company's original name, Waste Management, was more straightforward in stating its corporate mission.) WMX's story is one of being in the right place at the right time. Formed in 1968 out of an amalgam of three small haulers, two in Chicago and one in

Florida, the company grew with the need to handle the detritus of America's burgeoning consumer culture. The fact that one of the companies from which WMX was formed was called Ace Scavenger Service—suggestive of a more frugal time, when waste had to be sought for recycling instead of "managed" because it had become a daily result of good living and a lucrative commodity in its own right—speaks volumes about the changing patterns of consumption to which the new entity responded. In 1971, WMX went public and since then has constantly been expanding its network of services.

In 1977, Alabama Governor George C. Wallace's son-in-law, James Parsons, and a couple of other investors formed Resource Industries of Alabama. The year is significant. In 1976, Congress passed the Resource Conservation and Recovery Act, commonly referred to by its initials, RCRA, and pronounced "RICK-ra." RCRA provides for "cradle-to-grave" management of hazardous waste, meaning that it requires every producer of hazardous waste to insure that hazardous waste created as manufacturing by-products is accounted for from creation until disposal. Most of this gets treated or disposed of on-site. But to accommodate companies without the capacity or technology to handle their wastes on-site, a commercial hazardous waste treatment and disposal industry was born. Only about 4 percent of the nation's waste stream actually goes to commercial off-site facilities, generating controversy out of all proportion to its volume.

Resource Industries seems to have been a calculated business venture to capitalize on RCRA's new waste-handling requirements. Although never confirmed, widespread speculation is that the investors formed it with an intention to sell once they had a permit to operate a facility in Alabama.

Within a year of opening, Resource Industries, permitted to operate and then headed by Parsons, sold its operation to Chem Waste. Of the 2,400-acre tract in Emelle, Alabama, about 350 acres are used for the waste disposal operation.

The history of Emelle's siting could not be repeated today. Local residents would later recall that they had no idea the site would be used for a hazardous waste dump. Wendell Paris, who for much of his life has been a labor and civil rights activist in Sumter County, remembered that locals began hearing rumors about a "new use" for the area's Selma chalk deposits, layers of calcified rock that occur in this and surrounding black belt counties. Selma chalk, they were told, could be used as insulating material, and as a liming agent to reduce the soil's acidity for agricultural use. The words *hazardous waste*, he remembered, were never uttered, although the waste companies had identified Selma chalk deposits as ideal sites on which to site their facilities because of the deposits' supposed impermeability.

By the early 1980s, pressure was building in Alabama to restrict the flow of toxins on state highways for dumping at Emelle. To the public, Emelle became a subject of ridicule and suspicion because of perceived political preferences and sweetheart deals agreed on with the tacit endorsement of Governor Wallace.

There were other concerns as well. A 1980 study by the Conservation Foundation revealed that Alabama spent only thirty-nine dollars per person for pollution control; the national average was seventy-one dollars. Given what that figure said about the comparative limitations of Alabama's Department of Environmental Management, people began to ask whether the state really wanted to be accepting almost a quarter of the nation's hazardous wastes to be disposed of off-site.

Chem Waste started to get a lot of pressure from the Alabama legislature, and its operations were scrutinized in the state press. In 1981 and 1982, reports also emerged of trouble at other facilities and, eventually, of company cover-ups in Vickery, Ohio; Denver, Colorado; and elsewhere.

It came as no surprise to many, then, that the company began to scout around for alternatives to Emelle—or at least spoke of doing so—as a way of forcing Alabama authorities to appreciate what Chem Waste was bringing to an impoverished part of the state.

Brad Moore had good reason to be intimately familiar with Chem Waste's earlier efforts to site in Noxubee County. From 1983 to early 1985, the man who would become his father-in-law, Sam "Tiny" Heard, had played a role similar to the one he himself was to play in the later fight over FTI. Tiny Heard (or "Big Tiny" as he is known to his intimates, to distinguish him from his son, "Little Tiny") is a man of average height and weight so as hardly to live up to his nickname, but for his impishness. Although over sixty and bald, Heard is an elfish presence, at once mischievous and playful, impetuous and feisty. One almost expects him to appear in a puff of smoke, spin a tall tale, cast a spell or two, and disappear.

Heard's reputation in Noxubee County is complex. Something of a dreamer, Heard as a twenty-five-year-old conceived and executed the idea of building Land-o-Lakes, a 160-acre lake in northern Noxubee County, near his Brooksville home. But he is also a bit of a schemer, and by his own admission, his standing was damaged by unproven claims that he took out fraudulent crop insurance—buying big policies, planting the crop, purposely letting it go unattended, and then collecting when it failed.

In 1981 or 1982, Heard says, he received a call from

a man responsible for management of the Tennessee-Tombigbee Waterway, which manages barge transportation through east-central Mississippi. Chem Waste needed someone to do a report for them on the ideal site for the location of a hazardous waste facility in one of four eastern Mississippi counties, the idea being that the waste would be moved by barge instead of the politically less popular alternative of highways. In Heard's account, he was hired for the job and slanted the report to favor Noxubee County, hoping eventually to land a permanent position.

As it turned out, several waste companies were scouting the area for possible sites, presumably encouraged by the success of Chem Waste's cash cow across the Alabama border. By the end of June 1982, Gus Evans, a prominent local landowner, confirmed publicly that an entity called Noxubee Management Corporation had an option to purchase around 540 acres of his land for possible use as a hazardous waste treatment and disposal facility. Evans's announcement generated little notice.

■ ■ ■ AUGUSTUS T. EVANS is the last remaining descendant in Noxubee County of what was once the county's most distinguished, and probably its richest, family. He is a big, white-haired man who speaks softly and deliberately, in the gentle tones associated with the Virginia Tidewater rather than the plangent drawl of east-central Mississippi. Though he does not seem nervous, his hands shake a little as he talks.

The name of Evans's maternal ancestor, E. F. Nunn, is fading now, but it still dominates the brick warehouses and storefronts facing the railroad tracks in Shuqualak, where the family's wealth was concentrated. I met Evans in one of those buildings, a closed-up supply shop. Behind a half-empty storeroom filled with dusty bits and pieces of agricultural machinery, Evans's office is a surprise: majestic and serene, paneled in dark hardwoods, and elegantly furnished. He sat behind an expansive hardwood desk, beneath the portrait of his most famous ancestor.

Legend has it that E. F. Nunn built his fortune on a canny business judgment made during the Civil War. Gus Evans knew the story well: "It was during the early part of the war when the South looked like they were winning. And he saw that the South did not have the industrial capacity to keep going. And his wife was here, and he wrote her and told her to sell all the slaves except two and put [the money] in either cotton or gold. And there's some woods right back here called the Pitwoods, and they put runners down there and put the cotton down there. And then the Yankees came through ten miles west of here on Pontotoc Ridge and didn't find [anything]. So after the war he had the cotton and the gold." This story even made its way north. Several years ago Evans was contacted by a Chicago genealogist, who had been hired by a black professional to research his roots. "And he had descended from a Nunn. And that was the only story that he knew, was about that gold and cotton."

After the Civil War, Nunn prospered and the family built a plantation of nearly twenty thousand acres. By the middle of this century, when Gus Evans himself was growing up, there were still over 450 families living on the Nunn place—close to four thousand people by Evans's estimate. "People" on a "place" of course means black sharecroppers and tenant farmers.

Gus Evans's mother, Gladys Evans Powe, was an extravagant and famed figure in Noxubee County for much of this century, and she built a home atop a small rise in her property, in the county's southeastern section. She called the house Tannahoe—(Choctaw for "green acres")—and it could serve as a double for the Tara that David O. Selznick built. (The family dropped the name Tannahoe with the advent of the goofy 1970s TV sitcom *Green Acres.*) Like his own children after him, Evans was sent north for "finishing." He completed college at Cornell University—a fact that sets a person apart in this most regionally conscious part of the nation. After getting a graduate business degree at Ole Miss, Evans returned to the county and, in the 1950s and 1960s, became one of its most successful farmers. In 1968, he was named Mid-South Cotton Farmer of the Year for growing "1,477 acres of the fluffy white stuff," and in the same year, *Cotton Farming* magazine named him its man of the year. Twelve years later, in 1980, Evans received the Mississippi Man of the Year in Agriculture Award.

Evans distinguished himself in other ways. The most privileged son of this undeveloped backwater, he was among the first in east-central Mississippi to join that now nationally common species, the farmer as big businessman. In the mid-1960s he was among the first in Noxubee County to apply chemicals to all of his cotton crop on the by-then twelve-hundred-acre family plantation. His practices were unusual enough to make him a local celebrity. In November 1966, the *Beacon* ran a front-page story about him, which began:

> Gus Evans wears an old and very comfortable-looking pair of shoes, but he's not afraid to try new things in the field.
>
> For example, he used chemical weed control in every one of his 1,200 acres of cotton this year. . . . "It's the only way we could make a crop," says Gus

when speaking of using chemicals to control the money robbing weeds and grass in cotton.

"Chemicals control the grass and weeds much better, and it's cheaper than labor," says Gus. "You can't afford labor when you can find it."

Twenty-five years later the practices he employed are unremarkable. A Mennonite farmer kept repeating to me the observation that "cotton farming is chemical farming—that's what a lot of folks say."

As an early advocate of chemical-intensive farming Evans was inclined to be receptive to the possibility of a hazardous waste operation in Noxubee County, having extensively used substances that produce waste needing to be landfilled. In 1981, he joined the board of the Mississippi Chemical Corporation, a farmer-owned cooperative that produces nitrogen fertilizer. As a result, he had a more sophisticated understanding of the risks and advantages of such materials than many of his neighbors, and he had faith in America's ability to handle them.

Evans had some difficult times, and by the early 1980s he needed an influx of cash. His Shuqualak property lies but twenty miles from Chem Waste's Emelle facility and straddles the same Selma chalk formation celebrated by the waste industry as an ideal base on which to build a toxic dump.

A June 22, 1982, public meeting was held to discuss the proposals concerning possible construction of a hazardous waste landfill in Noxubee County. About 225 people showed up. A Meridian paper quoted one local man as saying: "We're backwards down here and we prefer to stay that way—that seems to be the consensus here." In a portent of things to come, Ike Brown spoke. Characteristically, he made a splash.

Brown had been living in Noxubee County only since 1980, so he was not yet a well-known figure, especially among whites. Identifying himself only as "an NAACP member," at the June meeting, Brown made his inaugural public defense of a waste facility, giving basic shape to an argument that he would refine over the next decade. Hazardous waste may not be the best industry to bring into the county, he said, but people face a greater hazard in being poor. Here was a chance for some of the county's black majority to get some jobs. For too long, moreover, whites in the county were opposing "industrial development" as a way of keeping blacks down.

Tiny Heard recalled that someone stood up in back and said, "Don't listen to him. He ain't nothin' but a nigger." A ruckus ensued. Tiny chuckled when he thought back to that night. Once the recriminations ended and apologies were offered, Heard said: "We had a real quiet meetin' after that." When, at the evening's end, a vote was taken to get a show of support for the project, Ike Brown's was one of the only hands to be raised.

By August, the board of aldermen of the town of Shuqualak, which then counted Gus Evans as a member, issued a resolution endorsing the project. By December, Chem Waste formalized its plans by filing an application with state regulators to build the Noxubee Treatment Center in Noxubee County. On December 15, the state Department of Environmental Quality scheduled a public meeting to allow for public discussion of the project. Linda Thomas, who would shortly become one of the project's most visible opponents, reflected that "they thought they were going to come to a quiet little country town and have a quiet peaceful hearing, and it got rather heated."

■ ■ ■ BY the end of December, a group was formally chartered to oppose the possible siting: Protect the Environment of Noxubee, or PEON. Linda Thomas, the wife of Charlie Thomas, a wealthy lumberman, explained the name's genesis: "We were hashing over names. We realized we needed a catchy name. Gus Evans has always been a wealthy landowner, and we said, 'We're just peons in comparison to Gus Evans,' and it stuck. The mansion on the hill, and here we are down in the valley."

As white Republicans in a majority-black Democratic district, the early members of PEON were not political power brokers of consequence. But they were among the best-heeled residents of Noxubee County, including a good sampling of people whose family names had dominated county life since it was first settled in the 1830s. Charlie and Bill Thomas descend from Captain C. M. Thomas, one of the county's most celebrated Civil War heroes and its first postwar sheriff; Robert Field is the seventh generation of his family to work a large farm next to Nunns and Evanses. From the start, PEON was backed with local economic, if not political, muscle, a reality that would always compromise its effectiveness with the county's majority-black population.

In fact, Gus Evans also lives "down in the valley" today, in one of the sprawling ranch-style houses favored by people in the southern section of the county. It is Tannahoe, his mother's house, that stands atop the hill. But every self-proclaimed David needs a Goliath, and PEON it was.

Grassroots success in these community environmental struggles usually results from the efforts of women, as was the case with PEON. Although the men were initially named officers of the new group, the driving forces behind PEON in the early 1980s were Linda and her sister-in-law, Peggy Thomas, the wife of Charlie's younger brother, Bill.

The Thomas brothers run and partially own Shuqualak Lumber, one of the county's few large, locally owned businesses. Like Martha Blackwell after them, Linda and Peggy Thomas could not have been more reluctant or less skilled activists when PEON was formed in late 1983. Their involvement began with a summons from Charlie, in January 1984. Linda thought back to that day: "The men were at the office on a Sunday afternoon, and Charlie called and said, 'Come down here—we need to have a little meeting.' " The women learned that they were to go to Jackson that week, to carry out instructions from their lawyer. They thought they would be acting as gophers. Linda had never even stepped foot inside the state capitol. The attorney's list directed them to have a series of personal meetings. "It was rather overwhelming. It was the lieutenant governor, the speaker of the house, and committee chairmen of both houses. Charles Ray Nix, then the head of the Mississippi Senate's Environmental Protection, Conservation and Water Resources Committee, came out and said he had never seen a more forlorn-looking group of people in his entire life. There were four of us, I believe. I guess we looked so pitiful that he decided he would take us under his wing."

■ ■ ■ LINDA THOMAS went to visit Gus Evans early in 1984; she was then in her mid-forties. Thomas is thin and blond, with sharp, angular features; her voice has a slightly nervous, brittle edge. "Gus, I can't believe your ancestors would want you to do this," she screeched. Given the traditional respect accorded the county's Old Families, the appeal to the wishes of his ancestors was smart, diminished in its effectiveness only by the fact that Linda Thomas is not "from here," not a Noxubee native. "And I just told him it was a sin and a disgrace to do this to the land his family had obviously loved over the years. I cried and he laughed." There was more: "I had told him I felt like that if one person died as a result of this hazardous waste coming into this county that the blood would be dripping from his fingers."

She reflected on the outburst. "He thought I was a hysterical housewife. I heard later that he went to a cocktail party in Alabama and mocked me as just that—a hysterical housewife." Gus Evans demurred, remembering the encounter in less emotional terms and insisting that he would never repeat it mockingly at a social event. "I told her I thought she was way overestimating the damage, and she was the one that was going around laughing about it."

Unlike Carol Puckett in Tennessee, who had finely honed skills as an organizer and political activist when FTI entered Giles County, at first Linda and Peggy Thomas's only weapon was raw emotion. A whole education lay ahead of them, as it would for Martha Blackwell at the beginning of the next decade. By the time they were through, they would be known throughout Mississippi, and particularly in the state capitol, as "the Toxic Twins" for their single-minded advocacy. But before they had earned that nickname, used with teasing affection by allies and with patronizing disdain by foes, Linda and Peggy Thomas had much to learn. The pair had led conventional lives of prosperous upper-middle-class American women of their generation, lives focused around church, school, children, and their husbands' work. It was not a world marked by open animosity or confrontation. In their world, the highest compliment one can pay a man is that he is a "fine Christian" and "good businessman"; women are admired if they keep a "nice" home or have "good taste." Those found disagreeable or odd are described merely as "different."

The Toxic Twins call themselves grandmothers and country housewives, conjuring up an image of kindly sorts with bluish hair, and attired in calico frocks and orthopedic shoes. The reality is different. Though in their mid-fifties, they can both exude a winsome, coquettish charm. Tall, angular, and fair, Linda can seem more determined and unforgiving. A brunette with high cheekbones and a Pepsodent smile, Peggy is petite and more self-effacing than Linda.

Speaking out did not come easily, as Linda was the first to recognize: "At the time of women's lib, everyone was burning their bras and demonstrating and all the Vietnam demonstrations and all, I was home baking cookies and havin' Cub Scout meetings or doin' whatever I was doin'. Now here I am in my fifties. And I've marched from the courthouse to the city hall, and I've marched from the capitol to the governor's mansion, and this is . . . just such a far-out thought for me. I've always been so conservative. But, you do what you have to do."

In retrospect, the battle against Chem Waste, which was until then the most all-consuming activity they had engaged in as a family, looked like a warm-up for the next decade's struggle against Ed Netherland and FTI. They did not know it when they began in late 1983, but the entire showdown would be done within eighteen months. Over a decade later, with the Chem Waste fight long since behind them, the struggle against hazardous waste in Noxubee County had simply, in Peggy's words, "become a way of life." Her sister-in-law echoed that view: "It's become a *way* of life."

■ ■ ■ THE Toxic Twins became PEON's designated lobbyists. Their early efforts at the state legislature were laughably amateurish and sometimes comical. They spent their days roaming the halls of Mississippi's state capitol, grabbing lunches—a pimento cheese sandwich and a pint of milk—from the little food counter beneath the capitol steps, and making supper of warmed-over steam-table offerings at the endless political receptions to which, helped by their girlish, flirtatious good manners, they received regular invitations.

Ever sensitive to the criticism that they were well-heeled housewives on a sort of extended holiday with a political twist, the Toxic Twins insisted that they were always minimizing expenses. PEON's charter did not allow the organization to lobby, so they went on their own tab. "We go on the poverty program," explained Linda. *Economy program* would have been a more accurate term; these are not women who live life on a shoestring. Peggy interrupted to describe the motel they stay at in Jackson as "kind of a dump. And we do get a kind of a discount there," she giggled, "because we begged for it."

Linda and Peggy Thomas and the other "PEONs," as people began to call them, scrambled to acquire as much information as they could. What they learned left them scared. Chem Waste's literature assured them that its technology was state of the art. But the more research they did, the more their doubts about the long-term safety of dumping in the Selma chalk grew.

They unearthed a February 1979 letter from a Tuscaloosa, Alabama, resident. Tuscaloosa is about forty miles from Emelle and is served by the same aquifer. The man wrote to Alabama environmental regulators: "The soil in that area is of such a nature that the 'stored' waste could easily percolate throughout the whole region." Locals knew that no matter how deeply anyone dug into the Selma chalk, a hole could fill with water, like an artesian well. Wendell Paris had been working to provide plumbing to Sumter's poor in the late seventies, about the time the pits at Emelle started to be dug: "About a third of the septic tanks in northern Sumter County are situated in the Selma chalk. And so here they were sayin' that it's totally impermeable. And I said, 'Well, hey, it gotta be a little off base here, because clearly the septic tank systems are percolatin.' Here were these folks sayin' it's a totally compacted soil—six hundred feet of pure limerock without any cracks, crevices, or anything in it." But Paris and others who had been closely following the development of the Tenn-Tom Waterway understood that the Corps of Engineers was "behind in schedule because they had run into cracks and crevices in the Selma chalk, sometimes large enough to drop a bulldozer off in."

Charlie Thomas organized an outing for Mississippi environmental regulators. A handful of them dutifully trekked up from Jackson and set out in little skiffs for a ride along the Noxubee River. Thomas is a large, gruff, chain-smoking, sometimes short-tempered man. His aim was to convince the regulators that scientific claims about the supposed impermeability of the hundreds of feet of Selma chalk in the black prairie belt contradicted what generations had known about the area's geology. "We'd be goin' down the river, and here would be a 150-foot bluff of exposed Selma chalk, and 125 feet below the surface would be water just gushing out. And they all agreed with us. . . . I guess the point we were trying to find out is: Is it impermeable or not? 'Cause we didn't really know. I don't really know what their official conclusion was, but I know they took pictures of it— they saw the water coming out, 125 feet deep."

What they saw on the Noxubee River was supported by some of their digging into official documents. An EPA hydrologist who studied the Emelle site concluded that there was inadequate knowledge about the environmental impact of the Emelle operation and acknowledged the severe limitations of scientific knowledge about such activities. But as Charlie Thomas commented later, "The fact that we unfortunately have Selma chalk was really not material."

PEON and the Thomases were astonished at their own ignorance. They learned that major expansions of the Emelle facility had received no public comments. In early February 1984, Bill Thomas wrote a letter to the editor that summarized their collective amazement. Even-tempered and courtly, Bill is a striking contrast to his larger, louder, more brusque older brother.

"We respectfully request," the letter decorously began, "that you publish this letter and ask that all who read it join with us to fight location of a hazardous waste dump in Mississippi soil." Thomas went on to relate the results of their research, specifically, that "man does not know how to make a container that will not leak." If the absence of leaks was the measure of success, he said, no successful dump had ever been built. The answer was not dumping but spending more to reduce the volume of waste created. The letter concluded as modestly as it had begun, with the following, rather ingenuous appeal: "Many states now have organized groups organized to fight hazardous waste dumps. We need such an organization in Mississippi. If you are interested— and we feel you MUST be—please contact me at my address above."

The gracious tone of Bill's letter typified PEON's genteel tactics throughout 1983 and 1984. In Giles County, Tennessee, Carol Puckett had said that her success—along with her take-no-prisoners style—had come from being an outsider. Bill and Charlie Thomas had deep roots in Noxubee County, where a cardinal rule of social interaction is not to be contrary. It was inconceivable for them to demand that people support them.

■ ■ ■ THE skirmish of 1983 and 1984 was mostly limited to the southern part of the county, around Shuqualak. Peggy Thomas observed of those years: "A lot of people in the north end of the county felt that this was *our* fight. They would help us fund a little bit perhaps, but actively you probably could name the families that really worked with us. Because so many people in the county would ask you, 'What in the world is going on?' without understanding the fight, really."

Politically, the struggle was a rude shock for the Thomases and other PEONs. They had all supported Ronald Reagan in 1980 and 1984; in theory, they favor less government. Yet they also had tended to believe uncritically that government had the best interests of its citizens at heart. If asked, they would have said that government would not take risks with incalculable effects on the population. They simply were not people given, like Carol Puckett, to suspicion about corporate or governmental action. But the more they read and learned, the more they were forced to reexamine this trust. They found a 1979 letter, for instance, in which their regional EPA administrator admitted: "The state-of-the-art for predicting discharges or releases from landfills is poor and, thus, [EPA] believes that the only option available to ensure protection of human health and the environment is to prescribe design and operating standards which will provide maximum containment in landfills."

Robert Field, one of PEON's first officers and the descendant of 170 years of Fields in Noxubee County, gave firsthand testimony to the limitations of science. He trained as a chemical engineer in the late 1960s and worked in the

plastics industry in Texas for three years following his graduation from Mississippi State University in 1970, before the
land pulled him back to Mississippi.

"I have no memory of ever hearin' the term *hazardous
waste* when I was a chemical engineerin' student b'tween
1966 and 1970." Although Field is in his mid-forties, his
boyish good looks, tousled brown hair, and lean, wiry frame
give the impression of someone much younger. As a chemical engineer, he worked in low-density polyethylene, the
manufacture of which created hazardous waste oil.

"We would collect the oil, and we were disposin' of it
by Bill's Waste Oil Company of Lake Charles, Louisiana. The
first year, there was an old truck, painted green, and it
looked like someone, a nonprofessional, had lettered on the
side of it BILL'S WASTE OIL SERVICE. The driver of the
truck was Bill's father-in-law. A year later the green truck
was gone. The father-in-law was gone. And there was a
young driver, in some coveralls with a company logo on,
drivin' the truck. That was in the early seventies, that was.
And my point? *This is a new field.*"

Field's three years of professional experience made him
PEON's science guru. At public meetings he would stand up
and display sheets of low-density polyethylene he had used
ten years earlier to cover a building foundation on his property. Chem Waste was trying to assure the people of Noxubee that there would be no contamination because the
landfill cells would be "enclosed in a synthetic membrane"
out of the same stuff. Field brought pieces of the liner for his
building and held them up for the crowd; they would crum-
ble in his hands. He aimed merely to show, he said, that this
was "not a forever material."

The PEONs' alarm increased as they began collecting a
litany of infractions at Emelle, all the result of human error:

leaks, overturned equipment, fires from inadvertent mixing of incompatible substances. The Toxic Twins took these details to Jackson. But by the late spring of 1984 and the end of the legislative session, no bill had been passed to stop Chem Waste from coming. Linda and Peggy Thomas and the other newly minted PEON activists spent the remainder of 1984 gathering more information, traveling over the state, and speaking to anyone who would listen: women's groups, agricultural cooperatives, and Rotarians.

Charlie Thomas and a friend drove to Emelle and took some test samples of their own. In its public pronouncements proclaiming the safety of its operations, Chem Waste stressed that materials disposed at Emelle did not escape its carefully monitored precincts, and especially could not harm water supplies. Early on a May evening, the men scrambled down into a ditch adjoining the Emelle site. They took some Mason jars and collected water samples from sediment in the ditch, and sent the samples out of state for testing. The results revealed concentrations of potentially deadly polychlorinated biphenyls, PCBs, in negligible amounts—only two parts per million. The amounts were not sufficient to cause worry about human health, but nonetheless contradicted the company's assurances.

PEON produced its first newsletter that summer, which resembled nothing so much as a Sunday church bulletin. "TAKE HEED TO THIS AND REMEMBER!!" it warned. "With CONFIRMED groundwater contamination there are NO REQUIREMENTS that a facility be closed until the leak is found and collected, nor to even find or stop the leak." Biblical syntax then gave way to a progress report: "[PEON members] have been traveling around the state to inform our fellow Mississippians of the dangers facing our county. They have many engagements in the next few months. Thus far they have been warmly received and everyone has offered to join in the fight to keep Ms. from becoming the dump of the nation!"

The decisive achievement of those months was a tangible victory. In the late spring of 1985, their second year of lobbying, the Toxic Twins helped push through a bill that put a five-and-a-half-year moratorium on the siting of commercial hazardous waste facilities in Mississippi. The bill was introduced by Senator Eddie Briggs, a smooth political operator who would maneuver himself through the thickets of Mississippi's back-slapping—and back-biting—politics into the lieutenant governor's office within a few years. Briggs was also an extremely well known quantity to the Thomas family, as a friend and neighbor from eastern Mississippi, with farm and timber interests in Kemper County, adjoining Noxubee to the south. He is also a director of Macon's Merchants & Farmers Bank, along with Bill Thomas.

Publicly, the bill was credited with postponing the battle over whether Mississippi wanted or needed a commercial hazardous waste facility. In fact, there may have been other reasons. "After it was all over," Evans told me, "I found out Chem Waste never had any intentions of coming over here anyway. That was just a power struggle with the government of Alabama." Evans said he had learned this from high-placed Chem Waste officials. A Chem Waste official demurred: "I would disagree with Gus on that. It was not a ruse to scare the state of Alabama."

When the moratorium bill passed into law, the PEONs assumed they were done fighting waste in Noxubee County. In five and a half years, they supposed, the political landscape could change considerably, to say nothing of new technologies. As Linda Thomas put it, they could again look forward to worrying not about hazardous waste but instead about whether she could babysit for her children.

In contrast to the struggle that would be repeated, longer and louder, in the early 1990s, PEON's 1980s fight did not tear the county's population apart, since it was confined mostly to the county's southern portion. Notably, it was also not a divisive struggle along race or class lines. PEON had several vocal black members—notably, Essie Spencer, a woman who would endure her share of derision from other blacks for affiliating herself with the mostly white organization—but its identity was not routinely linked to the race of its members. Some people whistled Ike Brown's tune, suggesting that whites did not support Chem Waste because they wanted to keep blacks economically disadvantaged. At yet another public meeting, he once rose to say that white opposition was evidence that whites wanted to keep blacks poor. People in the largely white audience objected; Brown's racially divisive comments distracted attention from the Chem Waste threat. Bill Thomas, who was chairing the meeting, immediately shied away from any conflict. "That's good advice. Injecting race into this is just stirring up a mess."

In a speech she gave after the moratorium was well in place, Linda Thomas originally included the following words: "Let me tell you a little about the typical H.W. treating facility. High minority population, low educational level, high unemployment in the area. How many poor uneducated people have been exploited!" But she crossed the comments out of her final draft. Better to leave well enough alone.

5
ED NETHERLAND'S DOG AND PONY SHOW

BY EARLY 1990, WITH THE Mississippi hazardous waste moratorium set to expire, it was impossible to disregard the racial implications of locating toxic businesses. The issue had achieved national prominence from groups like the United Church of Christ's Commission on Racial Justice, which issued an influential 1987 report documenting the link between toxic waste sites and racial and ethnic minority populations. In Noxubee County, blacks and a white man from the hills were poised to dominate county politics. Their views on whether a toxic dump should come to the poor, largely black, segregated county would now be sought—and would matter. Moreover, with the moratorium about to expire, Mississippi became vulnerable to inspection by every waste business in the nation. In 1985, Linda and Peggy Thomas and other PEON members, exhausted from fighting, had hoped that the issue would just disappear for good. But as the Mississippi county the industry giant Chem Waste had tried to conquer, Noxubee was something of a known quantity. Furthermore, from 1985 to 1990, the county's employment situation had improved only marginally; unemployment remained at a disturbingly high 13 percent. Any job-producing prospect would have been taken seriously.

With the moratorium period about to end, some of the county's leading white citizens—notably, Gus Evans, still the owner of thousands of acres of pastureland atop a big hunk of Selma chalk—had been quietly recruiting waste companies. Evans explained why he sought out waste firms: "That's about the only thing. You know we don't have a blue-chip situation here where you're gonna get a whole lot of different things in. This seemed to be what would do the most for the county and for me individually." And into this potentially incendiary situation entered Ed Netherland, with a personality simultaneously magnetic and unctuous, determined to win over the good people of the black prairie belt.

■ ■ ■ GLASS. Slick as glass. That's the way people in Mississippi remember Ed Netherland. A person need spend but two minutes with him to understand that he is a spectacularly gifted salesman. Geraldine Harris, a pixieish older white woman and a resident of Noxubee County for forty-eight years who thoroughly disapproved of his activities, once said to Netherland: "You've missed your calling. You should have been selling sand to Saudi Arabia." At that, she remembered, he turned red. "In case you're wondering, Mr. Netherland, that's a compliment."

Netherland's seemingly boundless confidence and prosperity are hard to resist. Tim Gowan, a Macon lawyer, mused in late 1993, nearly a year since he had last seen him, that despite everything he knew about Netherland and his way of doing business, he still would not trust himself tomorrow not to buy an "EEN-shu-rance" policy if Netherland walked through the door hawking one. Allen Hunter, Macon's longtime mayor, once a supporter of Netherland's who later came to feel that the county had been had, echoed Gowan: "Ed was his own biggest enemy. He would do almost anything to get a permit for his facility. But he was a great salesman. I hate to admit it, but I fell for it."

Lawyer Tim Gowan moved to Macon just before Ed Netherland's show rolled into town. "This [law] firm had for many years represented the board of supervisors. I kinda became the attorney for the board of supervisors by virtue of cummin into this firm and taking the place of the person who was leavin'."

The firm is the fiefdom of Charlie George Perkins. Housed in a little red-brick building oddly adorned with periwinkle-colored shutters, the Perkins firm sits right beside the courthouse, protected by a row of giant oaks. It thus occupies a spot in Noxubee County's life assuring both physically and figuratively that its members have a finger on the local political pulse. Its lineage stretches back almost a century, its power rooted in the possession of title abstracts for most of the county's land. As the county's only title company, Charlie George's firm stands to close most of the county's land sales, giving it a steady stream of both business and influence. In an oligarchic society based on control of the land, Charlie George plays the role of its financial and political Cerberus, jealously guarding the interests of its top strata. This role has done little to endear him to the county's black majority: his former partner defended the county's resistance to federal integration orders, and he himself represented Noxubee's white elite in subsequent efforts perceived by some as an effort to dilute black electoral strength.

The offices of Perkins and Gowan are cramped and cluttered with paper. A Bible concordance is the only reading matter on a little side table crammed between the two chairs reserved for visitors in a crowded front office shared by the lawyers' wives, who do its paralegal and secretarial work. When we spoke in his windowless office—brightly lit by overhead fluorescent lamps and clad in a blond, faux-ash veneer—Gowan was nearly obscured by stacks of paper. Slightly rumpled at the end of a day, his tie askew, Gowan stretched back. A smile drew across his chubby cheeks as he began to recount his involvement in the waste wars. He could talk about it all night if you let him.

"Um, I came in on Joo-lie the first of 1990. I'd been practicing law in Jackson for ten years, the fast lane. Mr. Netherland showed up about a month and a half, two months later. This is one of the first stops that I'm aware he made, in Macon. He came in here and tried to hire us to represent him. Charlie and I talked about it, but, you know, we represent some of the largest people who oppose it, we represent some people who favor one company, so we basically took the position that we were not goin' to take a position, you know, any more than was necessary."

Any more than was necessary. Sentiments like this were routinely confided to me by businesspeople in Noxubee County. No one wanted to run the risk of offending Gus Evans and Billy McCann, who favored it, or Charlie and Bill

Thomas, who opposed it, and possibly lose business. Besides, in the rural South, it is thought indecorous to "call out the name" of others in your milieu. It is just plain bad manners.

Tim Gowan's initial impression of Netherland and his grandiose vision had been positive. "I kinda regretted, in the back of my mind, sayin', 'I know we're conflicted out, but I really wish we could represent that guy.' "

On August 1, just a month after Gowan began his new job in Macon, the U.S. Court of Appeals for the Eleventh Circuit issued its decision holding that an Alabama law taxing out-of-state hazardous wastes at higher rates than toxic material produced in-state amounted to an unconstitutional attempt to control commerce across state lines, in violation of the U.S. Constitution. This meant that Mississippi's toxic trash could again be assured a resting place across the border from Noxubee County, in Emelle, Alabama.

A federal court decision was not about to change the course of a salesman like Ed Netherland. With investors who believed there was still money to be made in hazardous waste disposal, there was little incentive for him to pull back, even though the Alabama case had substantially reduced the need for his project. Building a hazardous waste facility was turning into his holy quest; he later acknowledged, "It became, for me, almost a type of crusade." In Mississippi, ignoring the Alabama case also was easier because, by September 1990, Ray Mabus and his staff were gearing up for what looked sure to be a difficult reelection campaign. Mississippi's hazardous waste planning was not the administration's top priority.

Netherland's zeal to build a hazardous waste empire resulted in ever-grander plans. Not only did he propose to build an incinerator that would burn annually up to 50,000 tons of toxic materials, but he also promised to build a hazardous waste dump that could accept up to 350,000 tons per year—nearly matching Emelle's capacity at the time and promising to make it one of the nation's five largest hazardous waste dumps. He imagined a research-and-development center that would experiment with new ways to dispose of hazardous waste.

From late September until November, Netherland began holding meetings all over the county to explain his vision. Brad Moore recruited his old friend Ben Tubb, who had coached him in Little League, to help organize the meetings. Tubb is a short, eager, nervous man who smokes constantly; a PEON leader described him to me as "tookie lookin'." If he were an animal, he would be a woodchuck, with his small head, diminutive features, prominent front teeth, stout build, and generally bushy appearance. Although Tubb is not native to Noxubee County, his grandparents were from Shuqualak. He spent summers there as a child and is nearly treated as a homeboy.

Tubb was selling insurance and training dogs when Netherland arrived in 1990. He had long been active in civic affairs and had served without pay for the county's Economic Development Authority and as commissioner to the regional solid waste management authority. He takes pride in having been named the chamber of commerce's 1990 Man of the Year. Like many who have not been raised in Noxubee County, Tubb's interest in community service was born of his ability to imagine a different place. He recognized the county's advantages—the slower pace, the appeal of hunting and outdoor sports at your doorstep—but he also knew that people could live together more happily. His parents' working lives had been spent in more prosperous, more densely populated parts of southern Mississippi. His wife had been a military brat who moved frequently as a child. She later became a journalist for the Meridian newspaper. In the scheme of things in Noxubee County, the Tubbs belonged to its informed, progressive bourgeoisie.

Netherland hired Tubb to handle FTI's local public relations: $2,000 per month, a tiny voting share in the company, and the promise of long-term employment. It was Tubb's idea to arrange a series of public meetings all over the county. In Giles County, Tennessee, Netherland had been hounded by the claim that he and FTI were secretive, deliberately circumventing the public by dealing with elected officials and business leaders in closed-door meetings. To avoid being burned again, Netherland wanted to be publicly visible in Noxubee from the start.

Netherland told Tubb to organize an open public meeting at the courthouse and to advertise it in the *Beacon*.

"And I said, 'You're crazy if you do.' "

"Why?"

"First of all, you've already got an organization that's put together to fight a hazardous waste facility." PEON had been dormant since 1985, but, Tubb knew, a public meeting would only galvanize its members into action.

"As soon as you put that ad in the paper, you'll never get a chance to tell your story. You'll never get a chance."

"Well, what would you suggest?"

"And I said, 'I would suggest meetin' with groups of twenty-five or thirty people, and let's start with those that are reasonable and willin' to listen to your side before they make up their minds.' And we went ahead and had probably sixty of those meetings all over the county, and we done it in churches, at the restaurant, beer joints, wherever an audience would listen. And when you do it like that . . . the people that really want to know aren't intimidated to stand up to ask a question."

Tubb's recollection masked his knowledge of the county's polarized racial relations. Small meetings would allow FTI to build unity out of social division. The beer joint, the juke joint, is an African American venue. Those meetings were for blacks—often poorer, unemployed men. Church meetings were also organized to convince blacks, especially middle-class and older working people. Meetings at "the restaurant" meant gatherings at the Oak Tree Inn—outside of the all-white country club, the county's fanciest locale—and those were primarily for whites.

Going out and speaking to the county's African American majority, on its own turf, was a revolutionary act in Noxubee County. As Tubb explained, "Quite frankly, in this county, a lot of people don' like you includin' the blacks in decisions that are made. I hate to say that because I'm from here, but that's the truth. And um, I happen not to be one of those that believes that way, so we set up meetins for the blacks just like we did for the whites.

"We've got support in this county that's never been heard from because they've been intimidated into stayin' out of it—for fear of their businesses bein' boycotted by PEON members, for fear of losin' their jobs because they work for PEON members. But they'll call me at ten o'clock at night and say, 'I'm with ya, but please don't mention my name.'" This was an extraordinary confession from a white person in Noxubee County, although one I heard frequently repeated by blacks. And it was not idle rhetoric. The Mennonite owners of a ready-mix concrete operation confided to me that certain PEON leaders had threatened to give them no more business if they supplied products to a waste company.

To help galvanize black support for the project, Tubb and Brad Moore led Netherland to Ike Brown, whom they hired as a consultant to woo the support of the county's black population. Brown's mission was to treat FTI like a political candidate. As Tubb observed: "Ike can reach a segment of the population of Noxubee County that nobody else can reach, 'cause they don' trust anybody. You or I could go out there and you could ask for somebody that was livin' in their house, and they won't tell you because they don' trust you. And probably rightfully so. Ike helped us set up some of those meetins out in the country, and let us give presentations that we would have never known who to contact or how to contact, and even if we had, they wouldn't have bothered to come."

In a small county, news of efforts to stage-manage support quickly got out. Linda Thomas learned of a "ladies' luncheon" to promote FTI. It was to be held at the Oak Tree Inn and was to be cosponsored by the chamber of commerce. She called Dorothy Baker, the chamber president: "Dorothy, I understand you're having a luncheon on Friday, on hazardous waste."

"O, Linda, Linda, we've got your name down, we plan to have you later," she remembered Baker telling her.

"Well, I want to come Friday."

"Well, Linda, I promise you we're going to have you and Charlie to a meeting, we're going to have you for coffee and tell you about this company that wants to come in here."

"Dorothy, I doubt seriously that there is one woman coming to that luncheon Friday that knows one thing about hazardous waste, and I want to come."

That afternoon, Dorothy Baker called Linda Thomas back. Linda Thomas could come to the lunch. Such encounters fostered the very impression of FTI that Netherland had wanted to avoid, of being less than open with the public.

At the meetings, Netherland, Moore, or Tubb would describe the project, give a slide show, serve up some refreshments, and, depending on the crowd, pass out employment applications. In the hardscrabble context of Noxubee County, the meetings had an air of sophistication. Here was Netherland, tall and handsome, friendly as could be, outfitted in a smart, pressed blue blazer and flannels or one of his spanking-clean work shirts, the kind you get at Abercrombie and Fitch. He was always prepped for the meetings. Knew peoples' names before they introduced themselves.

Tim Gowan was one of many who attended the meetings. "You know, he had these nice meetings out at the Oak Tree 'n all that, and I was well impressed. And I'm not young enough or naive enough to fall off in it, you know. I view everything with skepticism, having been through the years of litigation experience I've been through. . . . But my impression was positive." Gowan stretched out the syllables in his high squeal: "PAH-suh-teev." "And I was wonderin' what the big deal was. You know, I was sayin' that if it's a positive economic tool and then the trade-off might well be worth it, let's study it."

Most Noxubeeans, less skeptical than Gowan, swallowed whole the razzmatazz Netherland served up. FTI's propaganda promised that "about 80%" of its workers would "be hired from the local labor pool." Within several months, FTI's "Job Opportunities" office had collected over seven hundred job applications. The applications were simple, many of them cut out from a half-page advertisement in the weekly *Shoppers' Guide* mailed to every family in the county. County unemployment was then at its highest in four years—13 percent; seven hundred applicants amounted to about 15 percent of the employable workforce.

Ben Tubb saw nothing unethical in this practice. "Why does anybody consider that unethical?" Passing out the job applications, he insisted, was justified for two reasons. "First of all, we have every confidence that we're gonna get a permit." Second, the applications were, he said, an information-gathering device: he had spent "months" analyzing them to understand the local labor force. "It's also helped us identify people who are interested in the project. We couldn't make the statements that we make about usin' local labor if we didn't know they're out there."

Yet the applications would hardly matter several years down the road. A toxic dump takes many years to get permitted and built. Opposition inevitably occurs, and the permit review drags on at length. The last new commercial hazardous waste landfill to open did so in 1979, in a place named—unbelievably enough—Last Chance, Colorado. More recently, an Ohio hazardous waste incinerator took over thirteen years to begin burning, due in no small measure to community resistance.

By the end of October, the carefully scripted meetings came to be characterized by Netherland's opposition as secretive, underhanded attempts to build support for FTI by sneaking around those who could ask the hardest questions. In response, on November 6, the open letter that Netherland had wanted to run in the first place finally appeared, not in the mostly white-read *Beacon* but in the weekly *Shoppers' Guide.* Addressed to "our neighbors in Noxubee County" by Netherland and Fred Wynn, FTI's president, an engineer who seemed bland next to the brashly confident Netherland, the letter touted the "news that FTI has taken a strong position in the economic development of Noxubee County." Netherland and Wynn wrote: "The purpose of this letter is . . . to say 'thank you' to all of you who call this area 'home' for the hospitality you have extended to us as we consider locating here." To readers who had not attended one of over thirty public meetings that FTI had held, they said, "You should know that progress is afoot." Progress meant "more than 180 jobs when fully operating." (The top figure promised in Giles County had been 100.) "This translates into an annual payroll of more than $4,500,000. And, we will be spending an estimated $10,000,000 each year just on local purchases once the plant is operational."

For everyone from Ralph Higginbotham, the white supervisor from the county's impoverished hills, to Ike Brown, these figures formed their principal public justifications for supporting FTI: numbers that promised jobs, services, and economic development. In response to the criticism that a hazardous waste dump provides relatively few jobs (the one at Emelle employs only about three hundred), Brown and his disciples maintained that, unlike local enterprises, outside businesses could be used to foster black business development. Said Brown: "It's not so much they were gonna bring jobs, but we talkin' about bringing independent black businesses into the flow. That equalizes the structure." Yet in a place with high adult illiteracy and a woefully undertrained workforce, most of the better-paying jobs could not be filled locally, even if FTI sincerely meant to do so. The top twenty-five or so best-paying jobs required people with advanced degrees in chemistry, chemical engineering, or administration, none of which could be filled locally. The second tier, managers and supervisors, required people with industrial waste management experience, which the county lacks.

In Noxubee County, finding people who could even satisfy FTI's most rudimentary job requirement—"interpersonal communication skills along with fundamental reading and writing skills"—presents a challenge. Farmers routinely complain that they cannot find local laborers sufficiently skilled to perform the most basic operation of increasingly sophisticated, computerized farm machinery. (An error can be expensive: a four-row cotton picker costs upward of $180,000.) Lawyers and doctors in Noxubee regularly give directions to their offices using visual markers because the caller cannot read the most basic street signs. Essie Spencer, the retired black schoolteacher and staunch hazardous waste opponent, summed up the reality: "They gonna have cooks to prepare meals, they gonna have laundry where they wash the clothes, and they gonna have main-te-nance—you know, landscaping to keep up the yard, clean up the yards and trim the hedges. Now those will be the majority of the jobs that Noxubee County will be able to do. We have no engineers. We have no people for what they are callin' for."

FTI's open letter further assured that its facility would be "state-of-the-art," meaning an operation "that is safe, secure and 100 times more effective than the most stringent EPA standards." FTI further guaranteed that its toxic disposal methods had "been accepted and endorsed by offices, agencies and entities ranging from local mayors and civic groups to the hallowed halls of higher learning and government." Martha Blackwell and other PEONs would eventually ridicule this rhetoric, arguing, for instance, that FTI's guarantees—like the promise that the facility would be "100 times more effective" than EPA standards—were chimerical, unverifiable. But their objections were largely ignored; many in Noxubee had little choice but to hope that FTI might help turn around their county's sorry prospects.

One of the open letter's details was entirely correct, namely, the representation that "virtually every elected official" had "been in attendance at one meeting or another." Brad Moore had made good on his promise to provide political access, and Netherland was well on his way to enlisting the support of most local politicians.

■ ■ ■ IN retrospect, Netherland's self-description of his activities in Noxubee County made him sound like part misunderstood business visionary and part champion of civil rights, come to redeem a static pocket of the old Deep South. It is therefore striking that the closest contacts Netherland would make in Noxubee were with whites. His most stalwart supporters were Moore and Higginbotham. For Higginbotham, Netherland may have provided an opportunity to settle some old scores.

The pairing was an unlikely one: Netherland was suave, poised, and confident; Higginbotham, unworldly and suspicious of outsiders. Yet they proved to serve one another's interests in unusual, unexpected ways, creating a loyal bond that would only grow stronger in the next four years.

In the story "Barn Burning," William Faulkner told the tale of Abner Snopes, a man from the Mississippi hills. Snopes is a man of few words and stubborn resentments. The story chronicles his family's moves from place to place after Snopes, in silent rage, burns the barns of the landlords on whose property he works as a poor tenant. For Snopes, "fire spoke to some deep mainspring" of his being, "as the one weapon for the preservation of integrity." With fire Snopes exacts his own justice, defies the social hierarchy that keeps him poor and powerless, and rages at a lowly rank in a system he cannot change.

Faulkner's characterization of Abner Snopes could describe the impact Ralph Higginbotham makes on outsiders:

> There was something about his wolflike independence and even courage . . . which impressed strangers, . . . a feeling that his ferocious conviction in the rightness of his own actions would be of advantage to all those whose interest lay with his.

A word that recurs in Higginbotham's self-description is *stubborn*. It is a characterization others endorsed without reservation; once his mind is made up, he is closed to further consideration of an issue. Wilbur Colom, the black lawyer who would later defend Higginbotham's reputation in court, related that: "He is one of the most stubborn people I've ever met. Inflexible." For Higginbotham, Colom suggested, rigid thinking was a matter of principled action.

Ralph Higginbotham's loathing for the Thomas family was notorious and enduring. Twenty years before Ed Netherland showed up in Noxubee County, Higginbotham had worked for Bill Thomas at Shuqualak Lumber. But the ornery, quarrelsome Higginbotham had stirred disagreements among his fellow workers and had not respected the workplace hierarchy. He had been fired. For two decades he had the opportunity to nurture his resentment of the Thomases.

When Netherland sought Higginbotham's support for an operation that the Thomases were sure to oppose—having been the county's most prominent opponents of Chem Waste just five years earlier—he provided Higginbotham with the opportunity, figuratively speaking, to burn the barn in which the Thomases stored their hopes and plans for their future in Noxubee County. Netherland would later exult, recalling Higginbotham's unwavering support: "I got a freebie there."

Higginbotham was not Netherland's only freebie. Netherland also found support from George Robinson, the board's junior African American supervisor. Years before, Robinson's brother died while in the custody of Cecil Russell, a white sheriff the mention of whose name still brings angry glares from the county's black residents. The story endlessly repeated in the black community is that Bascom

Robinson was murdered by his jailers; the official story was that, suffering a case of the d.t.'s, he killed himself by banging his head against a wall. In discussions with black FTI supporters, Bascom's death became an explanatory shorthand: the implicit suggestion was always that the people fighting FTI were the people who had killed him. Why listen to them? As with Ralph Higginbotham, the wound of this memory—combined with hundreds of other indignities real and perceived—predisposed George Robinson to show an interest in any project opposed by the county's well-to-do whites.

Robinson and Higginbotham remained Netherland's staunchest supporters on the board of supervisors. By early November, after but two active months, Netherland was well on his way to having sewed up the support of most of the county's elected officials. Ben Tubb's idea of a series of low-key meetings was paying off. PEON had not geared into action. In fact, many people—including Martha Blackwell—knew nothing of the renewed interest in Noxubee County as a toxic waste dump site.

■ ■ ■ FRIDAY is Martha Blackwell's regular day to spend in town, when she connects with her professional dreams of life as a fancy interior designer, working at Miss Anise Chancellor Howard's shop, Antiques and Collectibles, the only one of its kind in the county. "Social-minded" like her mother, she also uses Fridays to catch up with high school friends like Bill "Taco" Bell, who now runs City Drugs, and Philip "Buzzy" McGuire, who inherited his father's jewelry business. For a conservative, religious southern white woman, Martha is somewhat unusual in that most of her soulmates are men. She admits: "Sometimes I wish I were a man. I've never been a tomboy, but I think have some real male characteristics." In her world, that means being willing to agitate, to make some noise.

On Friday, November 10, 1990, running some errands on her lunch break, her two children in tow, Martha ran into her best woman friend, Laurie Flora, whose flawless, cream-colored complexion, abundant chestnut locks, and comely manner provide a picture-book image of the southern belle. Laurie began talking about the waste dump news. Martha had only vaguely heard of the "waste dump thing coming in" and hadn't been to any of the meetings; she was not sufficiently involved in county affairs to merit an invitation.

Martha recalled Laurie saying that she was worried because such businesses can "really split communities, and we can't afford to be divided."

"Laurie, you're overreacting. Surely no one is going to lose a friendship over a *waste dump!*" Martha replied.

The friends finished their speculations, caught up on other local gossip, and Martha went into Senter's Hardware to pay her bill. Senter's replaced Mullins' Hardware as the county's preeminent emporium after Martha's uncle Ike closed up the shop that he and his mother, Miss Ethel, had built up over decades. Senter's is a mixture of old-fashioned hardware store—with bins of nails, light fixtures, nuts, bolts, and washers—and fancy housewares shop, with lines of china, crockery, glassware, and cutlery. Like all of the shops along Macon's main street, Senter's is nothing much to look at. Its windows just open the store to light; there is nothing so elaborate as a display in them. The Jefferson Street store stands right across from McGuire's Jewelry, the name spelled out in black letters on its faded orange awning. As children, Martha and her friends spent endless hours there confiding their hopes and worries to Buzzy's dad, old Mr. Phil. It is next to Chancellor's Wholesale Groceries, still run by Anise Chancellor Howard's family, and catercorner from Perkins & Gowan's law offices.

Martha stopped in the back of Senter's, as she often did, to chat with Bill in accounts receivable. Bill was always good for a bit of local gossip, but that day he told her a story that left her stunned. He said that her family's longtime neighbor, Earl Skinner, was fixing to sell Chem Waste a chunk of land abutting her catfish ponds, for use as a hazardous waste dump.

Martha and Drew Blackwell had moved back to Noxubee County in 1983; Chem Waste's effort to gain a foothold happened just after they returned. Martha had been so busy having and raising children and getting reestablished that she had not been involved. The news worried her. If a waste company were to come to Noxubee County and locate its operation next to her land, it would threaten all of her most important life choices.

■ ■ ■ IN 1978, when Martha Metcalf Mullins from Macon, Mississippi, graduated from college, she had big ambitions. Personable, gregarious, and energetic, she was pegged by her friends and family as someone headed for important things. Frances Lucas-Taucher, a close college friend and now vice-president of student affairs at Emory University, in Atlanta, reported: "Nobody thought she'd be in a farmhouse. I thought she'd be president of the United States. I say that glibly, but the point is that she's very talented—a designer, a very productive person. So her life has surprised me." Martha imagined that her career as an interior designer was going to take her to Atlanta, Houston, and New York. She began with a job at a fancy Nashville home-furnishings and antiques store, in the city's tony Green Hills neighborhood. The promise of a sophisticated future looked clearly within her reach. For a girl from Prairie Point, Mississippi, these were three and a half wild years. This might have meant, Lucas-Taucher said, staying out past midnight or dating more than one man at a time.

They were difficult years for her family. Maureen Mullins, Martha's mother, had been diagnosed with Parkinson's disease at age forty-eight, when Martha was just five. (Martha was an unplanned child. Her father was fifty-three at her birth; her oldest sibling, Bill, was 19 when she was born.) The degenerative nervous system disorder became acute when Martha was in college, and was one reason she decided to attend nearby Mississippi State, with its roots as a conservative agricultural college, only thirty miles away in Starkville. She had been expected to attend Millsaps College, a small, respected, progressive liberal arts college in Jackson, as had all of her siblings and cousins.

The day she graduated from Mississippi State and moved her things back home, her mother crawled into bed and never alighted from it again. From Nashville, Martha would commute back every third weekend—a six-hour drive each way—to see her. It was during that time that she met Drew Blackwell. She had been casually dating his brother, who was in a near-fatal car crash. Drew, born and raised in southern Mississippi, was in Nashville to keep watch at his brother's hospital bedside. Martha met Drew as he came off the hospital elevator; he would say, "When I first met Martha, I heard bells—elevator bells." It was love at first sight. Martha was drawn to Drew's stolidity, and they were both intensely committed to Christianity. Family and friends noted that, like Martha's father, Drew is a man completely without artifice: what you see is what you get.

Martha's family balked at their plans to marry. Drew had not yet finished college; Mullinses valued higher education, and many of them had completed graduate degrees. A cousin had taught at Mississippi State College for Women— "the DUB-ya"—in Columbus; the music building was named for their talented, eccentric ancestor Weenonah Poindexter.

But Martha and Drew were determined, and in April 1981, they were married in her Uncle Ike and Aunt Elaine's stately, turn-of-the-century brick house on the fanciest stretch of Macon's Jefferson Street. With its delicate leaded glass and capacious sleeping porches, the Mullinses' home presents the very image of southern gentility.

Six months later, in October 1981, Martha was still in Nashville when her mother died, leaving William Mullins alone, but not isolated, on Rock Hill Plantation. There were still people living on the place, but his three other children had moved away. Bill was a lawyer in Laurel, Mississippi; Tom was an engineer with IBM in Birmingham, Alabama; and Mabel was a teacher in Virginia. They were all in their late thirties or early forties, with families of their own. Her father's own health quickly deteriorated, and he was unable to perform most of his duties without help, including his work as president of the board of supervisors.

In the meantime, Martha and Drew Blackwell had moved to Lafayette, Louisiana, deep in the heart of Cajun country, where Drew got a job. He was still taking some classes at a community college, in computer science, but school "wasn't Drew's thing." When her siblings began to talk about selling Rock Hill, Martha and Drew decided to move back. They could live rent-free. With Martha's standing in the community, it would be easy for Drew to find a job, and as she later mused, a blue-collar worker has a higher social status in the country than in the city. Martha would be freed from the responsibility of being the family's primary breadwinner, and she could concentrate on raising a family.

In deciding to move back, Martha demonstrated her fundamental conservatism, deferring her ego and desires to the needs of her mate and to their partnership. Her college friends, most of whom had gone on to professional careers, were dumbstruck by her move. As one mordantly noted: "Some of us didn't buy into the southern religious ritual that the man be the head of the household."

But with her mother dead and her father in Jackson at a nursing home, Martha felt rootless. There was no longer any Mullins family tie to Noxubee County except for Aunt Elaine, who was then in her early seventies and could not remain living alone indefinitely. Martha felt heartbroken at the thought of losing that connection to the land and the role her family had played in shaping it. Her sister Mabel, thirteen years her senior, remembers Martha saying at the time that they decided to move back, "I moved back as much for the grandchildren"—meaning her siblings' children—"as for myself." In our highly mobile, transient society, this kind of identity with place is rare. But for the rural southerner, connection to family and place still exerts a powerful pull. Even Dr. Lucas-Taucher, who confessed her surprise at the direction of Martha Blackwell's life, acknowledged that "the typical southerner is very interested in lineage," adding that, for Martha, "the very fabric of her being revolves around her roots."

So Martha and Drew moved back, with little money, to the two-story farmhouse, with its gabled windows and wide front porch. Drew got a job at a feed mill, and Martha set about reintegrating them into the community.

The transition was not easy. The main house needed

repairs, and the outbuildings were in worse shape. Many of them needed to be torn down, but that cost money the Blackwells did not have. Gradually, they razed most of the decaying structures. But Martha left standing the old Negro commissary just behind the main house, where black tenants had come to settle up with her father at the end of every week and get their store of provisions. In a distant corner of the property, she also kept one of the "colored shacks" that used to cover the area—two small rooms for twice as many families who shared a common fireplace and insulated the dwelling with old newspapers and magazine pages plastered on the walls.

There was the problem of the one black family still living on the place. The parents and their son had helped her parents around the house. "It was a real issue for us what to do," she recalled. The parents were getting older. "We simply didn't have the means to support them."

Keeping a colored shack on the property for old times' sake was one thing, but for Martha, dealing with the world that her parents' tenants represented was quite another: "I don't know if you know about it or not, but I mean the whole generation of black people that came up expectin' whites to take care of 'em, and the whites expected to take care of 'em," Martha reflected. "I think they call it a 'plantation mentality' or somethin' now. And it's real—it has been very bad. . . . And I suppose it is bad in that . . . you spawn people that aren't able to take care of themselves. But what do you do when they're grown and they can't do for themselves? It's sort of Catch-22."

Martha soon gave birth to a son and threw herself into child rearing with the same gusto she gives any project. She was asked to join Junior Auxiliary, where southern white girls from "nice" families gather to plan parties and perform

Good Works. The Blackwells became deeply involved in the life of their Presbyterian church.

Thus, the news that a waste dump might be at her own doorstep produced the most extreme of NIMBY—not-in-my-backyard—reactions from Martha Blackwell. Her identity, her family's livelihood, and the choices she had made individually and as Drew's wife were intimately tied to the Rock Hill Plantation. From the second she heard the rumor of Earl Skinner's plans, she was determined that this must never be.

The story told by Bill at Senter's proved incorrect: a start-up venture called National Disposal Systems, out of Florence, Mississippi, just south of Jackson, was looking for land to be used for a hazardous waste dump, and they had approached Skinner. An agent of a Jackson entrepreneur named Richard Partridge had been scouting out farms in the prairie. The man was rumored to have said that he was relocating from Jackson and wanted five hundred acres. His wife had just died, and he wanted to be closer to his daughter, who was attending Mississippi State. Some heard he wanted to plant corn. Everyone remembers that he said he was looking for wide open space.

Richard Partridge, National Disposal Systems' president, is a jowly, blustery entrepreneur. He runs a business called Environmental Waste Management, which digs pits to specification to bury waste—mostly paper-mill and oil refinery refuse. Following oil spill disasters as with the *Exxon Valdez*, Partridge also developed an oil skimmer to speed cleanup from spills. Partridge's work in the waste business meant that he knew of the potential for developing a lucrative hazardous waste dump in Mississippi in the late 1980s.

Through a friend, Partridge met Philip Martin, the elected chief of the Mississippi Band of the Choctaw for two decades and celebrated in the national press for becoming the "czar of economic development in Indian country." Under Martin's leadership on the Mississippi Choctaw reservation outside Philadelphia, Mississippi, fifty miles from Macon, the tribe has become host to plants that assemble circuit-board parts for General Motors, Ford, Xerox, AT&T and Navistar; entered a joint venture to produce automobile speakers for Ford and Chrysler; and opened a factory that churns out prepackaged sentiment for American Greeting Cards. In mid-1994, the Choctaw broke ground on Mississippi's first inland casino. Their pregaming annual sales reached at least $60 million—no small achievement for the five thousand Mississippi Choctaw, who as recently as 1983 had an unemployment rate as high as 70 percent.

But many of Martin's own people view him as hopelessly self-serving. His Choctaw critics in the Mississippi Band point to the fact that the tribal administration is largely Anglo, as is a substantial portion of the ownership and staff of the businesses on the reservation. They complain that Martin personally appoints the eleven paid members of the sixteen-member tribal council, which includes his brother-in-law and cousin. Also, they grouse that he is among the highest paid Indian chiefs in the United States: in addition to an expense account, he earned over $97,000 in 1992, the highest for any Indian leader in the United States that year, despite budget deficits and a tribal debt of over $30 million. The pregaming per capita income of the Mississippi Choctaw sat at $3,048; many of the band's members were poorly educated and lived in substandard housing.

Partridge remembered that he first began speaking to the Choctaw in 1988. His idea was simple: His new business entity, National Disposal Systems, would buy land and give it to Chief Martin and the Choctaw in exchange for a lease from the Choctaw to operate a hazardous waste dump on the property. In exchange, the Choctaw would also get a half million dollars for the right to operate the facility plus 10 percent of gross receipts collected in the facility's operation and a five-year rental fee totaling $125,000. Partridge predicted that the Choctaw could earn as much as $1 million a month in the bargain, and he thought that the deal would be attractive to them. Jabbing his finger into the air for emphasis, Partridge explained its principal advantage to the Choctaw: "number one, it would never be on Indian land."

That is, not on land traditionally classified as Indian land. The appeal for Partridge and his investors was the possibility that the land would be declared Indian trust land. As the property of a semiautonomous nation, it theoretically would be exempt from state regulation. National Disposal Systems thus hoped to "avoid the bullshit of Mississippi politics"—and the demands of state environmental regulators and tax authorities.

Partridge had sent his scout up to Noxubee County in 1989. Because Partridge was in the waste business himself, he knew that the black prairie belt had been favored by the state Department of Environmental Quality because of the presence of Selma chalk. He also knew that Chem Waste had tried to site there earlier in the decade. Partridge's man went first for the two best sites, those atop large formations of Selma chalk with ready access to railroad spurs. They included the Martin Conrad ranch, on which Netherland would shortly take an option. The ranch was owned by the Indiana University Foundation, and Partridge recalled that the asking price was too high.

The other prime tract he looked at was the land owned by Gus Evans, near Shuqualak. Partridge approached Evans about his property. "Evans is smart," Partridge observed. "He's just sitting there waiting for something to happen." But Evans was "real vague" about Partridge's possible purchase, so he kept on looking. That's when Partridge began scouting property along Mississippi 14, the state highway that runs to the Alabama line across Noxubee County's eastern prairie.

This led the scout to Skinner, the Mullinses' longtime neighbor. National Disposal Systems bought 483 acres from Skinner and, by the summer of 1990, put together a deal with the Choctaw.

In retrospect, the Choctaw episode of the Noxubee hazardous waste wars is noteworthy mostly because it played out in miniature many of the themes, tensions, and events that would in the next couple of years surface in the county. First, the Choctaw plans came to be widely viewed as a closed-door deal, made and approved in secret by Choctaw leaders, outside the purview of the tribe's members. On June 21, 1990, the tribal council issued "A Resolution to Enter into a Contract for a Business Venture." The 135-word resolution nowhere hinted at the nature of the "major industrial venture" that "the tribal government [had] for some months . . . been pursuing" and proceeded to turn over the power "to negotiate, sign, and deliver a contract with National Disposal Systems, Inc." to Martin and his close associate, the Mississippi Choctaw's secretary-treasurer, Frank Steve. The tribal council thus relinquished its power under the tribal constitution to approve contracts negotiated by the chief. On July 5, 1990, Martin and Partridge signed a contract committing both parties to keep its terms secret.

The Choctaw episode also prefigured later experience in the Noxubee hazardous waste wars in that, superficially, the National Disposal Systems agreement looked like a bonanza for the Mississippi Choctaw. The tribe was to receive a nonrefundable sum of $300,000 just for signing, and the agreement exempted them from responsibility for defending any lawsuit or other claim arising from the operation of National Disposal System's facilities. The company promised to hire Choctaw workers whenever possible. The contract even created a fund consisting of 2 percent of gross revenues to curry favor with the "host county/community," an undefined term clearly understood by the parties to refer to Noxubee County.

Third, its financial benefits were uncertain on close inspection. National Disposal Systems' promise to indemnify the tribe, protecting it against any lawsuit or other legal claim, was only as good as its backer. The company was merely a shell corporation, without substantial assets. The indemnity contained no promise that Partridge, the other directors, or other corporations would be responsible in the event the new venture could not cover any liability. Thus, if National Disposal Systems faltered, the tribe would likely have become responsible for any legal claims. The contract did not require National Disposal Systems to disclose its assets and long-term financial plan to the Mississippi Choctaw until ten days *after* the contract was signed. In other words, nothing in the contract assured that the indemnity was backed by any financial muscle. The contract further allowed National Disposal Systems to assign its rights after only seven years of operation, meaning that the Mississippi Choctaw had no guarantee that the people with whom they negotiated would be the ones eventually operating a controversial facility on "their" land (as happened in Emelle, Alabama, when George Wallace's son-in-law bought the land and sold the permit to Chem Waste for a small fortune several months after he obtained it).

The contract's most troubling feature, however, was perhaps the fact that the term of the surface lease, by which the band was to lease the property back to Partridge's start-up company, was only for twenty-five years. Thus, even if National Disposal Systems remained solvent, the tribe could easily have been left responsible for the upkeep of a hazardous waste dump if the company had not renewed the lease. In short, the deal that superficially looked beneficial to the Mississippi Choctaw, was one that depended largely on the confidence of the parties in one another's reliability and integrity.

In November and December of 1990, details of the secret agreement were leaked to some of Martin's opponents. On December 21, the superintendent of the Choctaw Agency (the tribal representative of the Bureau of Indian Affairs) recommended that National Disposal Systems' Noxubee County land not be classified as Indian trust land. Although couched in a bureaucrat's bland diction, the memorandum took full note of the deal's outrageous aspects. To begin, the superintendent observed, the nearest reservation land was fifteen to twenty miles away, with no significant Choctaw settlements in Noxubee County. "The residents of that site have not been apprised of the proposed use of the land," he wrote, and "may object to its proposed use, which in turn would put the tribe in a very bad light." The superintendent expressed a further concern: "The membership of the Mississippi Band of Choctaw Indians has not been apprised of the proposed site either. It would have been an ideal situation if there were to be a referendum vote by the membership of the Band." The superintendent also doubted "very seriously that the proposed site will attract very many Choctaw laborers." As in Noxubee County, members of the poorly educated tribe lacked the qualifications needed for such an operation's best-paying jobs.

It was the superintendent's final comment, however, that contained the baldest recognition of the contract's dangers:

> The liability of the proposed site and the proposed use is too high. The Choctaw Tribe depends upon its labor resources in the operation of its facilities and they don't own very much money. What they own is about 22,000 acres of land. If something should go wrong with the facilities, the Choctaw Tribe can not [*sic*] handle the liability.

Choctaw opponents of the deal later reflected that their ancestors had ceded millions of acres to whites and that, consequently, most of them had been forced to relocate to Oklahoma. Their chief's secret machinations had opened the way for the possibility that they could lose the remaining land they held, further perpetuating the cycle of abusing the land for selfish ends.

■ ■ ■ BY the end of December, Martha Blackwell was beginning to gather the rudiments of this story. What disturbed her most was her sense that the project's potential dangers had been hidden from the public for the financial benefit of a few: Martha can be secretive and cagey when she wants, but she does not dissimulate. What she viewed as National Disposal Systems' deception—sending out a scout who misrepresented himself to effect a crazy, clandestine land swap designed to avoid state environmental regulation—planted the seed for her distrust of all hazardous waste ventures.

■ ■ ■ ON November 7, 1990, the Tuesday before Martha Blackwell was first wakened to what she would come to perceive as the hazardous waste threat that could destroy her county, Ralph Higginbotham won a whopping victory in his bid for reelection to the Noxubee County Board of Supervisors, beating his nearest rival by almost three votes to one. Blackwell had no prior experience with Higginbotham. He came from the hills, a "different world" to her. Like other members of Noxubee's aristocracy of the soil, she had "only known a handful of people out there and never knew anyone real well." One of the first things she began hearing after the election was the widespread rumor that a waste company had financed Higginbotham's reelection. Martha then learned that National Disposal Systems was not the only company trying to site a waste dump in Noxubee County, and that a man named Ed Netherland had been smiling, smooth-talking and glad-handing his way up and down the county for several months.

The first major skirmish in the Noxubee hazardous waste wars occurred on Monday, November 20, 1990—ten days after Blackwell's involvement began. On that day, Netherland nearly got the county's board of supervisors to give him its exclusive endorsement. The endorsement was essential for Netherland not only because he was determined not to repeat his Giles County fiasco but also because he wanted to elbow out the other companies he knew were vying to operate a Mississippi hazardous waste dump. And his most serious competition came not from National Disposal Systems, an untested start-up venture. Netherland's biggest business threat came from one of the nation's major hazardous waste disposal firms, namely, the Union Pacific subsidiary United States Pollution Control Incorporated (USPCI). Like Chem Waste, USPCI expanded to provide commercial waste services in the 1970s and became one of the nation's few major waste "management" firms. In early 1988, it was acquired in full by railroad giant Union Pacific (chemicals transport is big business in railroading today, making the pairing a logical one). USPCI's hazardous waste disposal operations have experienced the troubles typical of toxic materials management—leaks, spills, and mishandling of dangerous substances. Between 1987 and 1992, the company paid over $3.5 million for environmental fines; one $0.5 million fine was assessed in connection with a 1988 groundwater leak from a landfill disposal cell.

Gus Evans and a group of business associates operating under the benign corporate identifier of Mississippi Farms had been looking for a suitable waste company that would again take out an option on some of Evans's family's land. They had been making inquiries at least as far back as Partridge's visit with Evans in 1989, knowing that the moratorium expired in 1990. Mississippi Farms actively solicited a number of firms. They convinced Houston-based USPCI that Noxubee County deserved a look.

The endorsement Netherland tried to get the supervisors to sign that day reflected FTI's desire to fend off this competition. The tone was defensive; the "Resolution of the Board of Supervisors of Noxubee County, Mississippi Declaring its Opposition to the Siting of More Than One Hazardous Waste Management Facility within Noxubee County" began with what his opponents came to recognize as the familiar litany of justifications for locating a hazardous waste operation in Noxubee County, namely, Mississippi's desire to have such a facility and the fact that "Noxubee County is located in a geological formation which is favorable for the development of an environmentally sound hazardous waste treatment facility." But for Netherland, the endorsement's most important words were these: the board "desired" that Mississippi regulators "consider the application from no other . . . facility until it has finally determined to issue a permit to [FTI] or finally to deny its application."

The extraordinary thing about this endorsement is that it promised nothing concrete to Noxubee County. That Monday morning, Tim Gowan remembered: "There was a meeting called, and they had the meeting. And somebody, one of the supervisors, called and asked Charlie to come over. They knew I was gone. They asked my partner to go over and cover for 'em. Ed Netherland was over there with a document and wanted them to enter this agreement. And they were ready to enter it." Charlie George Perkins scarcely had a chance to review the document, which the two black supervisors and Ralph Higginbotham, a bare majority of the board, were prepared to sign. Perkins is a slim, slightly fussy man, with not a strand of his straight brown hair ever out of place. Even when casually dressed in khakis and a white oxford-cloth shirt, he has that freshly pressed, brushed, and shampooed look of the professional, as if ever ready to counsel a client. Perkins also bears a rather weary, irritated air.

Ralph Higginbotham's dislike for Charlie George Perkins was widely known. Higginbotham often spoke openly of his loathing for the man many view as the gatekeeper to the county's landed elite. It was no small feat then, in the face of Higginbotham's enmity and the suspicions of two black supervisors about this particular educated white man warning them not to jump into a job-producing venture, that he persuaded them to postpone further discussion of the endorsement. Perkins wrested from them but a two-day postponement on their vote. By Wednesday, at least, Tim Gowan would be back.

Gowan instantly recognized that the endorsement

aimed to head off the competition. And as the board's law-yer, he was to ensure that the county would get the best pos-sible deal. He made it his task, therefore, to try and get representatives of the other waste companies to come to the Wednesday, November 21 meeting. He knew to contact the Choctaw because Perkins & Gowan had represented Earl Skinner in the sale of the land sought by Richard Partridge. Gowan also knew that his firm's client, Gus Evans, was con-templating a sale of property to USPCI. He asked them to send a representative to the meeting, and they did.

Gowan's other aim was to impose some order on the process, to prevent what looked like FTI's attempt to fast-talk its way past local politicians with little business experi-ence and not much education (neither Higginbotham nor Robinson graduated from high school). The Wednesday meeting was a good deal noisier than the sparsely attended affair on Monday when FTI had tried to steamroll through its initial endorsement. In addition to company representa-tives, some PEONs were there, objecting to the supervisors' haste. The board acquiesced to the request that they more thoroughly study the economic advantages of a waste com-pany coming to Noxubee. Concerned that the board was act-ing outside its authority, Gowan insisted that they document their deliberations. For the first time in its history, the board began taking detailed minutes. "This Board, when I came here, had no established procedures to amount to anything. They had always jus' done business on a handshake—all been friends, no real controversy. Decisions were made in a very informal way. There'd not been any major controversy, you know, and so they had never really set up strong proce-dural rules, or that," Gowan explained. The minutes of that Wednesday's meeting recorded the fact that they would not endorse any company before getting more information. Also

dorsement document, and within a matter of three or four minutes they had it out on the floor and had voted on it." Joseph Stevenson, the senior black supervisor, moved to adopt the document, and the motion was seconded by Ralph Higginbotham. George Robinson voted with them.

"And that was it. It was just about that simple—no discussion. I was completely taken off guard, and I jus' told 'em look, I wadn't prepared to offer a legal opinion of *any* kind at that point. And I certainly hadn't been allowed to participate in any nego——, there had been no negotiations." That they would so recklessly ignore their attorney's advice left people stunned. Wilbur Colom, the lawyer who would succeed Gowan as the board's attorney, observed that the board attorney in a community like this usually "is in a very powerful position because they depend upon you for a lot of technical expertise that goes beyond law. Generally you the best-educated guy in the room. You know, they ask your judgment, your opinion." But spectators recalled that the trio who subsequently became known as "the FTI supervisors"—the two African Americans and the white man from the hills—seemed determined to act against their lawyer's advice. And with that, Netherland got his endorsement, by the first of the three-to-two votes that would characterize every FTI encounter with elected officials in Noxubee County.

Gowan remembered telling the board: "Let's go slow. Let's cut a deal. You know, if we're gonna make a deal, let's make a helluva deal. These people are talkin' about gettin' well. Let's get this little town well. Let's build schools like you hadn't imagined in Mississippi." His other worry was that the board was ready to endorse even though—just as in Tennessee—FTI would not reveal its financial structure and the sources of its funding. And as with the Choctaw's

National Disposal Systems contract, there was no evidence that FTI could back up its promises. The resolution and agreement was signed with FTI's Mississippi corporation, a paper entity. FTI's Tennessee parent company also had virtually no assets; there was no guarantee that they could pay a million dollars or provide services like local solid waste disposal, as promised. As with the Choctaw leadership, the board thus obtained no assurance that the entity it endorsed would end up operating an environmentally sensitive operation in Noxubee County.

Some people in Noxubee County saw the board's haste in acting as the predictable naïveté of country cousins, unlettered farmers and lumber workers taken in by a quick talker. For others, the board endorsement fueled unproven suspicions that FTI had paid off local officials. Ike Brown's presence at every stage of the debate helped fuel those rumors among most whites and some blacks.

The supervisors' haste did suggest an absence of business acumen. But what few whites in Noxubee County wished to admit is that Ed Netherland and his start-up venture held out the possibility of creating a different political and economic order in Noxubee County. As Tim Gowan, the son of a central Mississippi schoolteacher and so hardly to the manor born, later reflected: "[Ralph Higginbotham] comes from a background where he perceives himself as being pushed away. He perceives those of us who have been to school and those of us who have done these things as— His perception of it is that he's been on the outside." For a time, Netherland and FTI showed how Higginbotham, Robinson, and people like them might be on the inside.

Moreover, FTI's tantalizing promises buoyed the sagging hopes of its majority. An especially celebrated commitment was FTI's pledge to "match dollar for dollar, and up to the sum of $125,000, funding to be provided" for "the construction of a civic center building and facilities to be located in the central portion of Noxubee County." Ed Netherland explained the purpose of this promise with his Leaguer's sanctimonious gravity: "There's no place in this county where a black man can go to have a public meeting. They meet in churches without air-conditioning, a lot of times without heat. That should be remedied." Netherland's explanation perfectly captured his Noxubee style—superficially generous, ever so slightly condescending, presumptuous. Not only did he arrogate to himself the role of commercial savior of Noxubee's black majority, but he also broke a local taboo: as a white man, he publicly acknowledged the county's social inequalities.

Yet there was always a delusional air about Ed Netherland. Whether encouraged by his fight with cancer and so in a hurry to see his wildest dreams realized, or merely because of the need to clinch a deal, Netherland's promises became ever more fantastical. One day that fall, for example, he entered the library, next to the courthouse. Wearing a trench-coat over a suit in a town where a jacket and tie are unusual, and trailed by an entourage of lawyers and publicists, he introduced himself to the librarian, Beth Koostre. He explained that he was coming to do business in the county. She had never seen him before.

"What do you need, Ma'am?"

"Oh, a lot of things," she replied, eyeing him suspiciously.

"Name it, it's yours."

Miz Beth recalled that he then went over and examined a rendering of the Calhoun Institute, the ladies' music and finishing school erected by William Poindexter, Martha Blackwell's ancestor. He then called over one of his attorneys, meekly trailing in his wake, and directed the man to "get the plans for this, I want the community center to look just like this." The idea that a fanciful, three-story antebellum showplace could be reproduced in the late twentieth century for a quarter of a million dollars (FTI's promised $125,000 and a matching amount from the county) would send even the most ambitious contractor into fits. Even his detractors later conceded, however, that he actually seemed to believe—if only fleetingly—that such imaginings could come true.

Undeterred by the December 3 vote endorsing FTI, Gowan continued to press the board to reconsider its hasty action. In a detailed memo he delivered that Friday, December 7, Gowan memorialized his sense that deals were being struck outside of board meetings and that recklessness, coupled with potentially self-serving decisions, could have dangerous consequences. The memo had a hurried, slightly frantic quality—far from the measured, jovial demeanor Gowan usually presents. It included signature lines for each of the supervisors to acknowledge receipt, requesting formal acknowledgment that his clients had not heeded his warnings.

The memo recorded that "Attorney Gowan" (a professional formalism still common in the South) was "taken completely by surprise at the December 3 meeting and had no idea" that the board "was anywhere near endorsement of FTI and/or any other hazardous waste facility" that day. Gowan took an especially grave tone when he addressed the board's inexplicable haste. He warned: "It is clearly premature for the board to pass a resolution stating that it wishes for Noxubee County to be designated as a volunteer host community. . . . In all due respect, no member of this honorable body has reviewed and/or obtained such facts and information as would allow them to make such a statement.

The technical part of FTI's application has not even been filed."

The board met that day and, at Gowan's suggestion, went into executive session and closed its deliberations to the public. Inside, he orally reiterated his concerns and insisted that they were exposing the county and themselves to potential liability if the endorsement's terms were not fulfilled. The board then voted to rescind the original endorsement. But a mere seventy-two hours later, on Tuesday, December 11, again by a three-to-two vote, the board reaffirmed its exclusive endorsement of FTI. This time, their endorsement set the clock ticking for the county's three towns, giving them sixty days to follow suit.

The December 11 endorsement also obtained an indemnification from FTI. Despite Gowan's loud demands, the guarantee was virtually worthless. As with the Choctaw's deal, the board was shielded by a company with virtually no assets. At the end of 1989, FTI reported a value of but $10,105—its only asset was the Nashville office it rented. When questioned about this, Netherland cheerily replied: "I'm surprised we have that much. What we have accumulated so far is several million dollars in debt. We have private capital that stockholders are putting in—we're doing some of that by loan and some of it by equity."

Netherland also declined to accept personal liability. Gowan's round frame started popping up and down, rocking back and forth in his recliner as he summoned up the memory: "There were no assets behind the indemnity. . . . It's like a teenager givin' you an indemnity—there're no assets. . . .

"I mean, it's just a nutshell corporation. It's nothin' in it. There's still nothin' in it. They've got a hope and a prayer but that's just from one check to the next. I mean, their obligation was from one check to the next."

That day, Gowan also tried to have Netherland personally indemnify the board against any claim or liability. Gowan chuckled, savoring the recollection. "He declined. Said he was on a bank board—couldn't. He didn't think that they would let him sign a personal indemnity. I put one in front of him. Ye-ah, he wadn't real comfortable with that!

"He said he did'n know what that meant. I said, 'What part of it don't you know? Don't you know *personal?* That means you personally—you believe in this project so much that you're willin' to commit your house and your car.'" Gowan's squeaky voice rose excitedly. "I mean, we got people here committin' their lives to this project, an' yer not willin' to commit one dollar of your personal assets?"

The indemnity issue would not die for several months. Gowan continued to hound Netherland and his lawyers. "We went through this indemnity business, and they ran me round and round and round and we never got an indemnity agreement from anybody who had any assets. "But they would promise. You know, I would draft 'em and send 'em to their lawyer, and then, 'Sure, we'll get back to you.' You know—'Looks good to me. Let me run it by my board.' . . . The county still dudn't have anybody with any assets, on anything. They don't have it. The agreement from the county's standpoint is not worth fifty-nine cents. They jus' were hell-bent on doin' it. I don' have an explanation for you, but I know there's no reason for it, no logical reason."

Looking back, Gowan still marveled at the board's stunning lack of business sense: "You could write a first-year law school book on all the legal issues presented. I mean, it's a first-year contracts case in and of itself. Whether there's a legal commitment, whether there's personal liability for what they've done, whether . . . they should have been indemnified by the company, whether you're even *dealing* with an entity that . . . has assets, whether you're representing the county . . ." Simultaneously amused and horrified, he shook his head in amazement at the recollection. "It's a horrible document, I mean, from a legal drafting standpoint. They're not obligated to do *anything.*"

The endorsement would become Ed Netherland's standard, waved in the faces of legislators in Jackson, unfurled before corporate executives from coast to coast, and used to guard him and his untested enterprise from attacks that he was taking advantage of a poor, largely African American area. Local elected officials had resoundingly welcomed him, he would say, and critics therefore had no leg to stand on when they questioned the business he was bringing to "Stinking Water" County.

■ ■ ■ THE remainder of 1990 and the first months of 1991 were a time of consolidation for Netherland. He sent out a torrent of thank-you letters, always with a tone at once down-home and slightly defensive ("We continue to be impressed by the fairness and friendliness of the folks we meet."). In the county's badly hurting black sections, he became something more than a polite suitor, turning himself into a shamelessly generous romancer: baskets of fruit for the holidays, a little money here and there for a club social. One widely circulated story had it that poor white hill people and elderly blacks living in trailers way out in the country got terrible diarrhea that Thanksgiving after greedily consuming FTI's fruit cornucopias. As he would put it: "Don't know how many hundreds of dollars we gave to people who were in a jam. I treated them right, and they trusted me." This palm-greasing—proof of unethical pandering to some, evidence of good business sense to others—became the mainstay of FTI's approach. All of this Noxubee activity was extraordinary, however, if for no other reason than it was a sideshow: in the end, the decisions about siting a waste dump would be made by regulators and their political bosses in Jackson.

Yet in Noxubee County, support for or against hazardous waste came to depend, to a large extent, upon lineage, upon who your people were, what opportunities they'd had—and what opportunities they had made possible for others. Ike Brown, for instance, railed: "That lady, Miz Blackwell. Mullins. Let 'em tell you about that. Old Supervisor Mullins. Yep. Her family, old family here. Uh-huh. Had black folks on they place. And they killed the ammunition plant. They gonna have five hundred people paying good jobs. They killed it." The link between Martha's daddy and the "they" who "rejected" a Remington ammunition plant is typical Brown rhetoric, conjuring up the specter of conspiratorial oppressors. It is also inaccurate. The proposed ammunition plant was rejected in the early 1980s, after William Mullins Sr.'s death, under the watch of his successor on the prairie beat, K. T. Misso Sr.

But for Brown and his supporters, ancestry was proof of moral bankruptcy. FTI provided them with the opportunity Isaac McCaslin (the white protagonist of Faulkner's "Bear") had predicted: it was time to take their turn on the land, Noxubee's aristocracy of the soil having forfeited theirs.

landmines of Noxubee County's political terrain. In time, Martha's opposition to hazardous waste would require that she educate herself not only about the biological environment but also about her own political environment.

And she had been the least political of people. For a woman of her class and background in east-central Mississippi, this was completely ordinary. Until late 1990, the only "politics" in Martha Blackwell's life had been school and college activities, small-town good works, and contests for social standing: to determine who was prettier, more popular, or most likely to succeed. In her milieu, even the example of her father's service as a supervisor was not viewed as political. As her sister emphasized: "We knew how much the community meant to him," but we "never thought of Dad being in politics so much as being very involved." And that was exactly how Martha approached her early months in the local hazardous waste controversy: not as taking a political, ideological stand, but as doing a civic duty, of being very involved.

As likely as Carol Puckett was to raise a skeptical eyebrow when faced with someone in authority, Martha Blackwell was inclined to trust Nice Men Wearing Suits. "My whole background brought me up to trust professionals, government, the establishment. I can't tell you how I was geared that way, specifically, but I was." As a result, her initial opposition left her confused and discouraged. Martha's older brother Bill Mullins, almost twenty years her senior, had always been a quasi father figure. She greatly relied on his judgment and opinions. In November 1990, she called him to talk about the waste companies and their plans for Noxubee. A corporate lawyer in southern Mississippi, Bill had industrial clients; he did not share what he came to view as her almost fanatical suspicions. She disagreed violently and found herself in tears. Business was his bailiwick, and it was unusual for her to differ with him on such an issue; she as yet had no reasoned justification for her views. Martha's initial feelings about a hazardous waste dump and incinerator in Noxubee County were visceral. Arguments, logic, facts—they would all come later.

Martha started talking to the Thomases. Charlie and Linda Thomas had a daughter her age, and so she had known them through school, but not well. Others active in the mid-1980s Chem Waste fight—Robert and Margie Field, nearly a decade older than she, and Gerry Harris, the retired bank officer who had been friendly with her mother— quickly became closer friends. Among whites her age, however, she was very much alone. Blackwell mused: "My close friends and I don't talk about waste. I just harped on it too much early on. I don't expect them to alter their schedules. Once I was with a group of probably nine or ten of my closest friends. I said, 'Ya'll *have* to come to a meetin' or somethin'.' Silence. I was fighting back the tears. 'Okay, if ya'll don't support me, maybe your grandchildren will.' " Sometimes after such encounters she would just sit at home and cry for hours.

Out there on the prairie at Rock Hill Plantation, surrounded by her parents' scuffed, heavy furniture, a battered cordless phone became Martha's information lifeline. Simultaneously, she tended to her homemaking, spent hours calling all over the country, obtained piles of information— newspaper clippings from throughout the Southeast, polemical writings by activists, scientific studies—made contacts with other people fighting toxic industries at the grassroots, and cultivated relationships with environmental regulators in Jackson. In the first months of 1991, the Blackwells' phone bill increased by 2,000 percent. They couldn't afford that kind of expense, and PEON agreed to cover her $200 to $300 in monthly calls.

■ ■ ■ FTI's momentum in Noxubee seemed to spread as fast as the kudzu in late summer, and her education had to be quick. Several big events in the opening months of 1991 challenged her abilities and newfound commitment to resist the encroachments of hazardous waste companies in the black prairie belt.

The first was the fact that Ed Netherland and FTI were determined to get endorsements from each of the county's major towns, flush with the victory of the supervisors' exclusive support. Tim Gowan continued to try and convince the board to rescind their exclusive endorsement. This pressure persisted until the first week of February. FTI had given the towns' boards of aldermen until early February to adopt their own endorsements—or forfeit the possibility of sharing in state tax revenues on hazardous wastes the county would receive. However, events confirmed that FTI's real motive was not merely the opportunity to divide the tax spoils. As the next days proved, Ed Netherland had convinced a majority of the county's politicians that, in Mayor Brad Moore's words, "this was the last train cummin through Noxubee County."

The boards were scheduled to meet the first Tuesday evening of February. Knowing this, on Monday, February 4, Gowan hand delivered a memo to the supervisors in which he made a final plea, begging them to reverse. If they did so, he knew, the town boards might not act. Gowan's memo reiterated his belief that the supervisors were risking action that could subject the county—and the individual supervisors—to civil and criminal liability. Gowan warned: "The purported indemnity agreement from FTI affords you no protection whatsoever. It is my legal duty to inform you that if you act, you act without the benefit of these protections and at your peril." The board did not change its view. The next night, February 5, each of the three town boards endorsed FTI, all of them by three-to-two margins. Only in Shuqualak—Gus Evans's home—did an entirely white town board with a concentration of the county's commercial might not vote for an exclusive endorsement, instead endorsing the applications of both FTI and its rival, USPCI. Every single black official voted to welcome FTI, as had less-prosperous whites.

What magic spell did Netherland cast over a majority of Noxubee County's politicians? A hint of his wizardry was glimpsed at Brooksville City Hall. In Brooksville that evening, Ken Jackson, a USPCI vice-president from Houston, made a last-ditch effort to slow FTI's momentum. The hostile response he received indicated just how much of a done deal the FTI endorsement was.

An unprecedented number showed up, spilling out onto Main Street in front of city hall, a rundown storefront office abutting the railroad tracks and next to a family grocery on the town's only shopping strip. Jackson urged them to enact a resolution supporting the choice of Noxubee as a site for a hazardous waste dump but not naming a particular company.

Questions from the aldermen quickly made clear that Jackson did not have a chance. The first salvo came from Alderman Tom Mowry, a big, shaggy, white telephone-line repairman. Even the clunky, ungrammatical prose of the board minutes reveals the futility of Jackson's appearance. "Alderman Mowry ask how many people would be hired full time by 1995? How many local people? Why were you so long getting to the cities?' Mr. Jackson stated that there would be about 125 full time people and only about 25% would not be local. The reason he gave for not getting to the cities was that he had ask the county to get in contact with them and they had not been heard from." By contrast, Netherland had gone to the "cities" themselves—making them feel that they had a voice.

Alderman Eva Sherrod, a retired black teacher, was in the chair and quickly redirected attention from USPCI to FTI. Given to wearing loud plastic baubles and making equally noisy pronouncements, Sherrod is strong-willed and unyielding (she is famous for repeating the phrase "my daddy's dead and he's the last one who made me do anything"). Sherrod then turned the meeting over to FTI's lawyer, Sam Begley, who "stated that FTI and Noxubee had formed a partnership and that they were asking the town of Brooksville to endorse them." Without further discussion, the aldermen promptly did just that. A PEON supporter angrily asked Sherrod "why they voted to endorse FTI without considering USPCI?" Sherrod said that they "were acting in the best interest of the people." And that was that.

In 1984, the Brooksville board had unanimously voted to oppose Chem Waste's proposal. Tom Mowry had moved to adopt the resolution opposing Chem Waste; Eva Sherrod had seconded. By early 1991, the two of them were among FTI's most ardent supporters. In part, this surely resulted from the fact that Ed Netherland has the salesman's knack for sweetening the pot. In November 1991, for instance, his new friend Brad Moore reported to the Brooksville Board of Alderman "that the Ray Danner Foundation will donate a police car to the Town of Brooksville. Alderman Gray ask if there were any strings attached. Mayor Moore stated that there were none. Motion was made by Alderman Mowry duly seconded by Alderman Sherrod all members voting aye to accept the car."

The board members' change of heart was taken by many PEONs as proof positive of payoffs and dirty dealing; the succession of three-to-two votes was identified as clear evidence that the endorsements had been stage-managed. But their new positions might just as easily be viewed as evidence of the unraveling of Noxubee's traditional social order. Arguably, the local aristocracy had failed to provide sufficient opportunity to all of the county's residents. And even if they had done so, the pent-up resentment against them was so intense that any steps to correct the county's sorry state of affairs might not have mattered.

■ ■ ■ THE second pivotal event facing Martha Blackwell and the other PEONs in the first months of 1991 was the arrival of serious competition for FTI. In March 1991, USPCI made the smartest hire in the Noxubee waste wars: as the head of its Mississippi operation, Prentiss Wayne "Printz" Bolin Jr.

Printz is a homeboy; he grew up in Noxubee County. Just thirty-one when USPCI hired him, Bolin is a local star. Like most every other white boy in the county, he graduated from Central Academy (formed when he was in fourth grade). In 1981, after attending college at Ole Miss, he faced the dilemma shared by every young adult in Noxubee County: without substantial family land, there were no good jobs. He worked for a real estate developer in Texas for a couple of years and then went to work in Washington, D.C., as the chief of staff for Trent Lott, Mississippi's junior, and arch-conservative, Republican U.S. senator.

Mississippi has the distinction, a journalist in Jackson

said to me with no small dose of sarcasm, of being the only state with two former college cheerleaders representing it in the U.S. Senate. Lott, named the majority whip after the November 1994 Republican ascendancy, was, like his protégé Bolin, a Sigma Nu fraternity brother at Ole Miss. He still radiates the male cheerleader's non-sexual enthusiasm and can smooth over any hint of disagreement behind a big, frozen smile. He is not only a member of the League of Identical Men; he could be its President.

Printz shares some of his former boss's Leaguer qualities. He is always freshly laundered and starched (people said that he single-handedly kept the county's only dry cleaner in business when he moved back to Macon). His hair appears to be as carefully ironed as his shirts, and he flashes a wide, toothy smile every few seconds. Every time we met, I had the impression that his big, warm face had just been vigorously scrubbed, glistening as if it had been polished. But there is a vulnerability to Printz Bolin that his politician mentor, the seasoned politician, does not show.

It is easy to imagine Printz as a chief of staff, as both gatekeeper and dispenser of favors. He took to the role naturally: invariably agreeable and pleasant, never anxious or hurried, Printz is the proverbial Nice Guy. His return home to promote the arrival of a hazardous waste dump thus was puzzling, perhaps evidence of naïveté or avarice, or both. Ed Netherland transparently enjoyed the challenge of convincing people to want the unwantable and of making a bundle in the process. But Printz is a softer figure, less able to duck questions and readjust his story depending upon the audience.

In early 1991, Johnny Heard, president of the board of supervisors and one of the two supervisors who consistently opposed FTI, called Printz in Washington. Johnny and his wife, Peggy, are close friends of Printz's parents. At Johnny's request, Printz made some inquiries about FTI with state environmental regulators. Soon thereafter, USPCI's Ken Jackson called Printz "and said, 'I understand the senator's interested in what we're proposing for Noxubee County, and we'd like to talk to him about it.'" Printz continued: "And I just told him, 'He's not really interested. It was a state issue, and the only reason I was calling around, checkin' on it is 'cause I'm from there.' And he said, 'Oh, you're from there? Oh, we'd like to talk to you.'"

Printz later told people that he was earning over $100,000 a year from USPCI and had a generous expense account—more than a comfortable sum anywhere in the country, and a fortune in a poor part of a poor state. USPCI gave him the chance to return home and live there as well as if he were a young executive in Atlanta or Houston or Washington, in a position that nonetheless kept him highly visible in political and business circles. Printz is enough of a Leaguer to have jumped at the chance.

Senator Lott urged him not to take the job and warned that he would become a pariah in his own community because of the inevitable NIMBY opposition. It was advice that Printz would later wish he had heeded: "I was lookin' to come home, so that all kinda worked out. At the time I thought so. If I could go back three years, there's *no way* I'd come get in this. No way. It's just too, too controversial. It was not the paradise I thought I was cummin home to."

What Printz failed to appreciate (or allowed the golden handcuffs of a big salary to distract him from) was the fact that he would not be standing as King of the Hill. He was returning to a society where, since his childhood, the holders of economic and political power had become antagonists, and no one visibly stood on top anymore. He left Noxubee

County in 1977, two years before the epochal local elections of 1979 that put so many black candidates into office. When he returned almost fifteen years later, with a college education and cosmopolitan experience that would be envied by his contemporaries across the nation, both he and the county had vastly changed in ways he did not appreciate.

His behavior very much reflected the fact that he did not understand the new Noxubee. Before news of his job change was made public, Printz made at least one call to try and prevent the string of February endorsements for FTI. Still on the senator's payroll, Printz called his old friend Tommy Campbell, a white man without substantial land who reads electric meters for a living. He was then a Macon alderman and was quite taken with Ed Netherland's charms. He was just about to cast his vote on behalf of the city of Macon in support of FTI.

"Tommy, don't do any exclusive endorsement. Don't lock yourself into something. I think there are some other options for you to look at." Printz later defended himself against the charge that he had used the prestige of the senator's office to try and stop FTI. In his mind, calling Tommy Campbell was simply a matter of doing what came naturally, of appealing to shared values and history. When asked about this perceived conflict of interest, Printz seemed slightly hurt. "Who in the *world* could have told you that?! Like I say, we've grown up together," he explained, uncharacteristically provoked. He started running over the list of people who might have shared this story and thus violated the etiquette of his youth by calling another's name.

For much of the next four years, Printz had the mien of a wounded puppy as he wondered how so many people he liked could get so vicious toward him. We first met in April 1993, for breakfast at the Edison Walthall Hotel, in Jackson.

The hotel is one of the places political people meet in Jackson, and Printz was in his element, patting backs, sharing a few words, and grinning in so many directions that it took us a good five minutes to make our way to the table. The waste wars had just finished a particularly ugly phase, full of recriminations and counter charges from both companies. Once seated, Printz was visibly weary. I asked him about an article that had appeared the previous September in the *Mississippi Business Journal*, intimating that he was exploiting his good-ole-boy connections. Although it had been printed over six months earlier, he sourly recited its description of him verbatim: "Gliding up the sidewalk like new oil in an old engine, Bolin's starched white shirt is the brightest thing on Macon's dusty, paint-chipped Main Street. It flashes as the local boy and former chief of staff for U.S. Sen. Trent Lott shakes hands with a local lawyer, calling him by his first and middle names the way he did when they were in grammar school. Pulling a merchant close, he whispers a brief joke and moves on, smiling."

Martha Blackwell, a few years his senior, met with Printz when he first moved back. She tried to dissuade him from continuing in his new job. When he refused, she stopped speaking to him. She nonetheless acknowledged: "I grew up with Printz. That's what makes fighting him so difficult. He's a hometown boy." But Martha had no time for his pouty "why me?" act. Dismissing his puzzlement as a pose meant to deflect justified criticism, she would repeatedly emphasize that Bolin had a choice about what job to take. She once speculated: "Don't you just think Printz was the kind in college who would pretend to cry if a girl refused to sleep with him? Goll-ee. Don't you just?"

In crossing the line he did, in making a self-interested call from a senator's Washington office, Printz had ineluctably compromised himself in Noxubee County. By the time the story of his call to Tommy Campbell began circulating, before he had even moved back, his local reputation had begun to tarnish, just as Senator Lott had promised.

Printz came back to represent a company that was for the next two years successfully characterized by Ed Netherland's forces as the defender of the old guard. Whereas FTI had come in and gone straight to African American neighborhoods, USPCI was said to ignore black interests, to be appeasing the county's aristocracy of the soil. Ike Brown summarized the view this way: "See, all it was, USPCI came in and figured they could take the white power structure—that's all they signed up on they board—and run the thing through. Uh-uh. Dud'n work like that." He vigorously shook his head from side to side. "The black got the power. They found out too late in the game that the blacks had the power."

■ ■ ■ THE third event that would strain the personal and emotional resources of Martha Blackwell and company to fight the threat of a megadump in Noxubee County was Ed Netherland's uncanny ability constantly to up the ante.

In late February 1991, the Pulaski, Tennessee, papers quoted Netherland as saying that he still intended to file the technical part of FTI's application in Tennessee, "although busy with the permitting for a similar plant proposed for Noxubee County, Miss." Netherland is not given to nuanced expression or small strokes of the brush, but to say that he was "busy" with the permitting in Mississippi was a wholly uncharacteristic understatement. He was consumed by it.

Following the endorsements from Noxubee's three municipalities, he waged a ceaseless campaign to secure his fledgling company's future in Mississippi, a future that, in his Napoleonic moments, he saw tied to the creation of a worldwide waste treatment empire. It was as if he had read, entranced, the speculation advanced in one of the gloom-and-doom scenarios sketched that year by Faith Popcorn, the woman invariably described as a New Age "guru." In a best-selling book she speculated: "The newly rich of 2010 will have made their money not by creating new products, but by making the garbage go away—these are the garbage barons. And the owners of any remaining landfills will have a stranglehold on the community." By the spring of 1991, would-be waste baron Ed Netherland was speculating that "an estimate of FTI building a dozen hazardous waste facilities worldwide in the next decade is 'conservative.' "

Undeniably, his greatest coup came when, on March 22, FTI announced that a Hughes Aircraft subsidiary would join FTI as its partner. The announcement came in a ceremony at the Oak Tree Inn, where James Abrahamson, a retired air force general and then a Hughes executive, was given the key to the city of Macon. Abrahamson proclaimed grandly: "Providing environmental solutions is a significant responsibility of our industry. I see this endeavor as an opportunity to benefit all mankind."

Friendly, handsome, and imposing, Abrahamson is a man given to such bombast. (Colorado's Representative Patricia Schroeder, a senior member of the House Armed Services Committee, once described him as "Cary Grant in a uniform.") At the end of his air force career, he not only ran the space shuttle program but also, after that, was the first head of the Strategic Defense Initiative, or "Star Wars" program, that monument to the inanity of the Reagan cold war. In that capacity, Britain's *Economist* magazine once dryly noted, he "proved himself good at selling ideas."

Hughes Aircraft, a leader in the defense, electronics, aerospace, and communications fields, formed a wholly owned subsidiary, Hughes Environmental Systems (HESI), in 1989. As it became clear in the late 1980s that the Reagan-era defense-industry boom was going to come to an inglorious, whimpering end, companies like Hughes began to look for places to "convert" their know-how and technology. HESI was one such endeavor.

As the subsidiary of the nation's largest corporation and Mississippi's fourth-largest employer, Hughes provided instant credibility and the impression that FTI had suddenly acquired a guaranteed financial base. Yet the extent of Hughes's support for FTI was unclear. Characteristically skilled at finessing the details, Netherland would say that it was a "50-50 partnership," implying, but never saying, that Hughes had committed itself to 50 percent of the benefits and liabilities of the project. Netherland's lawyer in Jackson, John Maxey, using a favorite legal fudge word, would say only that Hughes was committed to investing a "substantial" portion of the $70 million the plant was then estimated to cost. Both entities steadfastly avoided revealing the exact amount of Hughes's actual investment.

Although in Tennessee Netherland's secretiveness about the sources and extent of his funding had proved disastrous, this problem did not hinder his progress in Mississippi. After all, the supervisors had deliberately disregarded their attorney's urging that they learn more about the company's finances before giving an exclusive endorsement. One need not have read between the lines to realize that Hughes's role was speculative. The entity variously described itself as a "joint venture" and a "teaming agreement." Least instructively of all, the companies said they "had developed a business relationship." The filings FTI was required to make with the state Department of Environmental Quality told a more straightforward story about the new affiliation, which gave Hughes the option to acquire up to a 50 percent equity ownership in FTI's capital stock *if and when* FTI obtained a permit. In the meantime, FTI had the benefit of Hughes's name and stature. Hughes's primary commitment at the time of the March announcement was to "share technology" and "work cooperatively" to try and help FTI get a permit. Once that was obtained, their forces would combine under the banner of a jointly owned and capitalized environmental technology firm to be known officially by the clumsy acronym "HESI-FTI." But to most people, Netherland's speculative scheme became known as "Hughes-FTI," or even better yet for him, just "Hughes."

Tim Gowan expressed what became a common sentiment, with the benefit of hindsight: "An EEN-shu-rance man from Tennessee, with some money from a guy in the hamburger business, could come down here and . . . go to Hughes Aircraft and wave and say, 'Look! I've got this sewed up. I've got all the endorsements from all the government entities in this whole county.' And they throw in, with an EEN-shu-rance salesman from Nashville, Tennessee, without even checkin' him out. Hughes Aircraft did not even check him out."

Netherland's opponents in Noxubee County would berate him for having taking advantage of poor, illiterate folk. Yet as Gowan said, Netherland seemingly managed to fast-talk a division of one of the world's largest corporations into giving him its support as easily as he convinced a group of unlettered country politicians to throw in their lot with him. Bill Yates, then the Hughes official who negotiated the "teaming agreement" with FTI, expressed surprise when he heard that FTI had encountered trouble in Tennessee. "What problems in Tennessee?" he responded when asked about the Giles County episode. Yates went on to explain: "We do a very careful examination of people we do business with— their character, the warmness of the relationship. I don't know the details of Tennessee."

Yates indicated that this major defense contractor essentially does business on a smile and a handshake: "We checked things out through a process of relationships and discussions. I did not investigate Tennessee. We checked out [FTI's engineering firm] technically and found them highly capable. We assessed them as a very capable team of individuals. We did most of our checking through dialogue and cordial relationships."

It began to look as if Netherland might actually realize some of his more megalomaniacal visions. Once the permit was obtained, Hughes-FTI would establish the Center for Environmental Optimization, or CEO. Few asked what it meant to "optimize" the environment, although the CEO's principal business would be operation of the incinerator and landfill. But its selling point would be a research-and-development unit: Noxubee County would become a world-class center for toxic disposal studies.

The CEO was quickly characterized as a sort of starship *Enterprise* permanently berthed in the limestone soils of east-central Mississippi: beacon of good science and a bustling new future. Everything would be "high-tech" at the gleaming new industrial park to be built up around the incinerator and dump. Glossy brochures promised that the facility would not only be "pleasant-looking," with "attractive buildings to house the scientists," but also, gratifyingly, "clean."

The grandiloquence of the CEO's corporate promotional copy, along with Netherland's inimitable smooth talk, worked like a charm. Again and again in Noxubee County, supporters of Hughes-FTI would mumble the three syllables, "are and dee, are and dee," expressing their conviction, even long after Hughes-FTI's promises had been eclipsed and discarded, that the research-and-development facility would have remade Noxubee County, would have put the county on the nation's industrial-corporate map.

To fulfill the promise of an R-and-D component of his operation, Netherland began soliciting support for his vision from local universities. Noxubee County's isolation from the surrounding world is more intellectual, social, and emotional than geographic: in all three Mississippi directions, a college or university is located within an hour's drive. To the east, the University of Alabama's Tuscaloosa campus is not ninety minutes by car.

Hughes Environmental Systems—FTI's partner—signed a $75,000 contract with Mississippi State University described as funding research on "the most effective methods for handling and treating hazardous waste." The university president, Donald Zacharias, was adamant that the contract was signed with Hughes only and was not to be interpreted as an endorsement of a hazardous waste facility. However, Hughes-FTI's publicity machine used the Mississippi State contract as evidence of the advantages of locating a dump and incineration complex in Noxubee: "Working with the university system, they'll bring in some scientists, . . . researchers from around the world, and from, particularly, the Mississippi university sytem" a publicist insistently told me. The Mississippi State research, the man continued, "is one of the things that we believe sets this project apart in that we know this facility will stay state-of-the-art because as new technologies are developed, they will be put into place."

■ ■ ■ USPCI watched Netherland's antics with interest. Once Printz Bolin returned to Macon, he set about improving its local image. As a result, for the first months of 1991 the companies engaged in a sustained bidding war and tried to outdo one another with promises of what they would do for Noxubee County. This duel was the fourth major trial facing Martha Blackwell and the other PEONs that spring, making it hard for them to be heard above the roar of two multinationals that were swearing they would help make the hurting county well.

Initially, the companies' offerings differed little. In late 1990, FTI had said that its capital investment would be $60 million; by early 1991, with USPCI on the scene, that estimate inexplicably rose to $80 million, the exact amount put forward by its Houston-based rival. This was a pattern that would be repeated frequently over the next thirty months. Two years later, in the spring of 1993, Netherland promised that his venture would represent a capital investment in the county of $150 million. Just as he had chosen to fight the medical odds for beating melanoma with unusual treatment, so too the insatiable gambler in Ed Netherland repeatedly raised the stakes. By the end of May, USPCI promised to help build a community center to match Hughes-FTI's, to construct a municipal landfill to counter Hughes-FTI's promised garbage service, to create a trust fund to finance local community development projects to equal Hughes-FTI's "Good Neighbor" fund, and to sponsor Noxubee's championship all-state girls' basketball team—trumping Hughes-FTI's purchase of new uniforms. For Martha Blackwell and other PEONs, this battle of promises obscured entirely the issue of whether a toxic dump and incinerator were needed at all. Netherland's high-pressure hucksterism had

Martha Blackwell was mostly apolitical until Noxubee's hazardous waste wars. Here, in 1993, she warned the Board of Supervisors that, come election time, "Seventy-five witnesses won't forget" their disregard for local political traditions. The witnesses did not.

Ike Brown is particularly skilled at raising the hackles of Noxubee's white plantocracy. He fashions himself Noxubee's political savior, but he is more prophet than redeemer.
Credit: Scott Boyd/The Beacon

Ed Netherland was a superb, tireless salesman. As one man observed: "He will promise you, he will offer you, he will threaten you, and then he will beg."
Photograph courtesy of Edward H. Netherland

The Noxubee County courthouse. *Credit: Scott Boyd/The Beacon*

Through their joint waste opposition, retirees Essie Spencer (left) and Gerry Harris (right) defy local custom and see each other socially. Says Gerry, laughing: "Essie comes to my house and we drink coffee and have co-colas and she thinks I'm trash." *Credit: Scott Boyd/The Beacon*

Legend has it that the four-way cupola on New Brazelia, a prairie plantation house, was designed to allow white overseers watch black hands at work in the cotton fields. The tale is probably false, but speaks volumes about Noxubee's culture. *Credit: Scott Boyd/ The Beacon*

Ike Brown's double-wide trailer. His home shows little evidence of the riches he has supposedly amassed. *Credit: Scott Boyd/The Beacon*

Ed Netherland remembers that this billboard led his agent to the ranch he optioned for his proposed toxic disposal complex. Brooksville mayor and realtor Brad Moore worked in the office at the time. *Credit: Scott Boyd/The Beacon*

Brad Moore (left) and Prentiss "Printz" Bolin (right) were both hometown boys, but they supported different waste companies. Moore said Netherland's dump was "the last train cummin through." Bolin, a former Chief of Staff to U.S. Senator Trent Lott, had been lured back to work for the competition. They would both flee Noxubee County before the waste fight was over. *Right photo credit: Scott Boyd/The Beacon*

Hard economic times make Noxubee's towns look virtually deserted, especially downtown Shuqualak. The name of E.F. Nunn—on the building back center—was once mighty, a major post-Civil War cotton and trading fortune. Nunn's descendent Gus Evans invited waste companies to buy his property.

The Chamber of Commerce celebrates Noxubee as "the best of both worlds"—as in this downtown Macon mural—meaning an unhurried, rural life and an ideal spot for industrial development. Despite great natural beauty, the county's social divisions make it an unappealing place to most people.

Richard Brooks, President of the local NAACP, worked with Ike Brown to craft an official NAACP endorsement of Ed Netherland's hazardous waste plans. Three years later, the state NAACP removed him from office. *Credit: Scott Boyd/The Beacon*

Ralph Higginbotham—derided as a "hillbilly"—came from Noxubee's less prosperous western hills. While President of the Board of Supervisors, he threw his support behind Ed Netherland and became Ike Brown's unlikely ally. *Credit: Scott Boyd/The Beacon*

John Gibson warily allied himself with the white-led waste opposition, always keeping his distance. *Credit: Scott Boyd/The Beacon*

Martha Blackwell did most of the legwork for a series of rallies and marches in each of Noxubee's three main towns, including hand-lettering and nailing placards, shown here resting at the base of the Confederate monument (top). The march was led by Choctaw drummers (bottom) who came to show solidarity with the people who helped them fight a proposal to build a dump on Choctaw trust land.

Ralph Higginbotham (left) had little to say after a hearing determined that there was evidence of improper conduct in the exercise of his Supervisor's office. *Credit: Scott Boyd/The Beacon*

Ike Brown's send-off to federal prison was a gala political event in black Noxubee, bringing out many of his fans, including State Senator Sampson Jackson (left) and State Representative Reecy Dickson (not pictured). *Credit: Scott Boyd/The Beacon*

changed the rules according to which businesses entered Noxubee County. The question had become not if, but which one.

The Tennessean would say that Hughes-FTI's strategy was, in order of importance, to focus on solid engineering, to build local relationships, and to piggyback on those relationships to build statewide relationships (by which he meant cultivating support in Jackson). To some, focusing on local relationships before building support at the state capitol seemed to get things backwards. Authorizing a hazardous waste treatment operation for Mississippi was the job of regulators in Jackson, whose chief was appointed by the governor and whose actions were governed by state law. The shrewd corporate operator would, they observed, focus on the hallways and backrooms of the legislature and try to curry favor with regulators by assuring them that the company was meeting the legal criteria for siting such an operation. Although USPCI met Netherland's promises in Noxubee, it concentrated its efforts in Jackson.

Netherland focused on Noxubee County for at least two reasons. First, he was still playing a Tennessee game. Giles County is within commuting distance of Nashville. When he first arrived there, its representative, the soon-to-be "incinerated" C. E. DePriest, was a good friend of the governor's. Giles County also boasted a dedicated army of Democratic voters (nearly 75 percent of those registered). It made sense there to try and curry local favor at the outset in order to build support in Nashville. To a lesser extent, when the Democrat Ray Mabus was still governor, Netherland's strategy might have worked in Mississippi. Noxubee County's majority African American population had voted solidly Democratic and, with Ike Brown's help ("I done what

I'm suppos' to do"), had overwhelmingly supported Mabus in the 1988 election. Mabus's loss to a Republican radically changed that scenario.

Second, by redoubling his efforts to win the hearts and minds of Noxubee County in the first six months of 1991, Netherland strove to inflate his company's image by comparison with its national rival, USPCI. Even with Hughes's backing, the competition from an established, national firm in the "pollution control" business (as the "industry" reassuringly calls itself) presented his untested start-up with a serious challenge. Netherland knew that the local endorsements had no binding effect on anything or anyone—they were certainly not matters regulators were required to consider when examining the voluminous scientific and technical applications required before granting a permit to operate a hazardous waste disposal operation.

Nonetheless, Netherland recognized the psychological advantage to be gained with local backing. He understood that even the most bloodless bureaucrat commanded to conduct an "objective" evaluation of scientific evidence may be swayed if the public record is crammed with enthusiastic expressions of support from the people who will live near a facility.

■ ■ ■ MARTHA BLACKWELL's initial opposition to hazardous waste came from a threat to her land by the Choctaw leadership and Richard Partridge. But the success of a mountebank salesman from Tennessee—from obtaining political endorsements and making exaggerated promises to securing the cooperation of her alma mater, Mississippi State—clearly made Ed Netherland the man to beat in early 1991. Because the Martin Conrad ranch Netherland optioned was owned by the Indiana University Foundation, Martha called the Bloom-ington campus and asked for the student environmental group. She thus was connected to a small band of mostly white students who eagerly set about helping her and PEON. The call proved to be one of the most important she would make. The issue of environmental racism was percolating into university curricula in the early 1990s, and the small, tightly knit group saw that, symbolically and substantively, they could contribute to matters of national significance. They knew that poor and largely black Noxubee County fit the de-mographic profiles of typical hazardous waste dump sites, and they looked at a map to discover that the proposal would duplicate the nation's largest and (for environmental activists) most infamous such dump, at Emelle. Before the fight was over, the Indiana students would both help and complicate the debate in Noxubee County.

■ ■ ■ THESE early days were full of personal conflict for Martha. She had returned to Noxubee so that she could ful-fill her obligations as a wife and mother. Tied to these duties were the demands of her Christianity. Her husband quickly came to worry that she was not "working on her relationship with the Lord" as she became ever more deeply involved in this fight. Martha herself fretted because housework went undone, clothes piled up in baskets outside their bedroom, and dinners were hastily assembled at the last minute. More unsettling was the emotional drain: How could she be there for her young children when she was putting all of her per-sonal energy into defeating Netherland? Was she neglecting the demands of her faith, slighting her spiritual life and the central role it played in her family relations? The answers would not work themselves out for months.

In those first weeks, Martha thoroughly exhausted herself by working at home on her new cause until past midnight and rising at dawn to attend to her husband and children, week after week. From the start, her involvement required that she associate with new sorts of people and step outside the carefully circumscribed world of family, church, and school that had drawn her back to Noxubee. This meant that she had to open herself to subcultures that had long formed a part of her world, but had remained always in the background. Thus, she was introduced to a group of Choctaw who bitterly opposed Chief Martin and his designs for the band's management of a hazardous waste management facility near her home. She also was dealing with successful blacks in Noxubee County, people who had crafted moderately prosperous lives for themselves as teachers and managers.

Associating with blacks was not hard or uncomfortable—they were part of her very earliest and most secure memories of home and family. As her cousin Andy pointed out, mixing was easy because she had grown up with blacks. But, as she would acknowledge, no matter how much they seemed like family, "there was always that boundary." Educated African Americans—people who shared her middle-class values and could afford to see that a few jobs now might not be worth sacrificing the fertile black prairie forever—are few in Noxubee. She had encountered "that" kind of black person in Nashville, but never at home. These alterations in her usual social patterns would gradually redefine Blackwell's character. Still, she longed to find someone like herself, someone who shared not only her conservative values and experience but also the conviction that what was happening in Noxubee County was absolutely wrong.

By early spring, Martha began to refine her arguments against a hazardous waste operation in her county. She came to believe that the nation did not need the new landfill and incineration capacity in the first place. She understood that new, more efficient methods of disposal would have to be developed in the long run; industry and consumers would have to demand processes that produced a smaller volume of toxics. But she continued to leave one question unaddressed, and it was the most difficult of all: If not a hazardous waste operation, then what? The county's majority needed jobs. Ike Brown was clear that a hazardous waste operation was not a panacea. For him, it was one step in breaking the local white oligopoly's stranglehold on employment and opportunity. Diagnosing the county's ills, Brown excitedly declared that the problem boiled down to this: "Lacka money! So you tryin' to tell me 'bout what somethin' might happen to me like, 'You bring an incinerator in, it might kill all o' you.' Well, I'm dyin' anyway! I'm dyin' the worst kind of death—I'm dyin' of starvation! In terms not of food but of a lack of opportunity. So I'd rather take my chances, 'cause we all gonna die. So I can choose how I want to live. Now I have challenged the PEON and anybody else to the same thing." And the challenge did not disappear.

■ ■ ■ OUTSIDE Noxubee County that spring, two crucial events only intensified the fight for the right of companies to dump toxic trash in Noxubee County. The first was the unraveling of Richard Partridge's scheme with the Choctaw leadership. The second was the final push to get Ed Netherland out of Giles County, Tennessee.

■ ■ ■ ON Valentine's Day 1991, a group of Chief Martin's regular Choctaw antagonists signed a petition to rescind the band's contract with National Disposal Systems. The Choctaw constitution allows for referenda "to approve or reject at the polls any act of the tribal council" upon submission of a petition signed by 30 percent of the tribe's eligible voters. The February 14 petition was signed by only eleven Choctaw—about eight hundred signatures were needed—and so did not have the force of tribal law. Nonetheless, it did notify the Bureau of Indian Affairs of discord over the issue, and of the petitioners' "fear of future liability of tribal trust land," and especially "insurmountable" financial liability if National Disposal Systems became "insolvent and filed bankruptcy or otherwise refused to accept responsibility for its actions."

The core group behind the petition traveled to Washington on April 2, to meet with the Bureau of Indian Affairs, from which they extracted a commitment to have the bureau's inspector general conduct an investigation. This led South Dakota's Senator Tom Daschle to call for hearings by the Senate Environmental Committee on the practice of siting waste facilities on Indian lands. The group also began a door-to-door campaign among the Choctaw, eventually collecting about eleven hundred signatures for their petition, well over the 30 percent they needed to go ahead.

While organizing the opposition to Partridge's scheme, some Choctaw contacted people in Noxubee. The trail inevitably led to Martha Blackwell, who in early March went with Linda and Peggy Thomas and a smattering of other white PEONs down to the red-clay hills of the Mississippi band's reservation, just outside Philadelphia. There, they joined a group of about two hundred Choctaw and their supporters, and walked up and down the narrow, unpaved roads turned a bright salmon color by the spring sunshine, and framed on either side by woods thick with towering, spindly rows of knobbly barked pine. The event was yet another that the women from Noxubee County never, in their wildest dreams, would have imagined themselves attending. But they did march, behind taciturn Choctaw men and boys dressed in polyester imitations of traditional dress—broad-brimmed felt hats and brightly colored tunics with fringe—beating their drums.

At the end of the march, in a forest clearing much like the one where, beside Dancing Rabbit Creek, their ancestors had in 1830 reluctantly ceded their lands, the Choctaw held a brief rally. Speakers rose to warn the little crowd of the dangers of a hazardous waste dump that could become their trust. The rally was an unprecedented act for the Choctaw, unaccustomed to this sort of public political protest against their chief, an outcry complicated by the fact that he receives so much positive attention from the national press for his enterprising ways. As the rally drew to a close, the Choctaw leaders promised their new allies from Noxubee County, the current owners of land that once belonged to their ancestors, that if they succeeded in their battle against Martin, Choctaws would come and support PEONs and their sympathizers in return.

On April 19, two days after Chief Martin met President Bush at the White House with two other tribal leaders to represent the concerns of the country's Native Americans on a wide range of issues, the Choctaw rejected his deal with National Disposal Systems by a vote of 786 votes to 525. The vote relieved the secretary of the interior from having to consider the merits of the questionable land transfer from Partridge to the Choctaw and back again. Tribes all over the country had closely watched the vote. Many were similarly in the throes of deciding whether to accept hazardous or nuclear waste facilities in the early 1990s, before the replacement savior—gaming operations—began to mushroom in 1993. At the time of the Choctaw vote there were five similar proposals before the nation's three hundred tribal councils. In the two years before the Choctaw vote, it was variously estimated that between twenty and thirty-six proposals to develop incinerators or hazardous waste dumps on Indian lands had been floated among various tribes.

For the hard-headed, resilient Richard Partridge, it was just business. Partridge sought to recover the $300,000 he had given the Choctaw for signing the contract. Martin, who said before the referendum that the band might be in breach of contract if it passed, resisted. Partridge's position was that the deal turned out not to have been likely ever to happen, through no fault of his own. Between the land purchase, the $300,000, and other promotional expenses, he had lost nearly a million dollars, "real money." In the end, Partridge recovered all but about $60,000 of it.

■ ■ ■ ON March 5, 1991, exactly a month since the aldermen of Noxubee's three main towns had voted to support FTI, Joe Fowlkes, the newly elected Tennessee state representative for Giles County who had been elected to replace DePreist, met with company representatives. Fowlkes later explained that negotiations to buy out FTI's Tennessee interests began almost immediately when they learned of the success the company was enjoying in Mississippi.

By May 5, CATI, the Giles County opposition group, had formed CATI Acquisition Company. At three o'clock in the afternoon on May 7, an exultant Dan Speer, Pulaski's mayor, opened a press conference. Speer, the man who had almost exactly a year before allegedly led Ed Netherland to believe that FTI would be welcome in Pulaski, announced triumphantly that all of FTI's land had been purchased back by CATI Acquisition for $310,000. This amount represented $62,000—the unused portion of the profits Tillman Knox had given the group as penance for selling his Giles County land to Netherland in the first place; $100,000 in municipal capital improvement funds; and a $148,000 mortgage on the property, guaranteed by Joe Henry, the attorney who had been instrumental in the local fight against FTI, together with the leader of the county Republican Committee and two other prosperous local businessmen. The purchase once again demonstrated the close unity between political and economic interests in Giles County.

In exchange for the sale, CATI's cochairs—Joe Henry, Rusty Horne, and Merry Merle Sigmon—agreed in writing to Netherland's demand that they not speak about him or his business, thus limiting the benefits that others, like the PEON supporters in Noxubee County, might have gained from their experiences with FTI. When I asked one of the them whether this did not assure that FTI could continue elsewhere what people in Giles County had widely viewed as its unscrupulous tactics, I was told that they would have done "anything just to get rid of him. It was kind of like selling your soul to be rid of somebody."

■ ■ ■ THE collapse of the Choctaw deal provided Martha Blackwell a chance to retreat: her land was no longer directly threatened. But by then she was deeply, zealously involved in what she had come to see as a struggle for the soul of Noxubee. Too much was by then tied up in this fight—a fight for her land, her family, their history, and the values they were trying to preserve. These were not solely the values of the county's aristocracy of the soil, but also those of an agrarian economy not as heavily dependent as the rest of the nation on consumer products. True, people in Noxubee drive cars, wear tanned leather products, and use microwave ovens and VCRs—and the manufacture of all of these products creates hazardous waste. But, she and others reasoned, Noxubeeans consumed less of these products per capita than others. For some of them, living a life less focused on material abundance was a choice. Why then should they be saddled with a wildly disproportionate share of everyone else's detritus?

By late spring, Martha was working with all sorts of people, from the Indiana students to Greenpeace organizers from Atlanta and New Orleans to civil rights activists—mostly black—from the Southern Organizing Committee, an umbrella organization that serves a wide variety of causes and constituencies. All of them were proving invaluable to her environmental and social justice education. With characteristic enthusiasm, Martha was turning right around and feeding back suggestions for organizing in what she—even she, the apolitical former Junior Miss—was starting to call "the movement."

On many days she felt that her efforts were hopeless. Hughes-FTI's successes in the county seemed so carefully orchestrated that she often sensed she was up against something so much larger than herself that there was little point in resisting. Why had three companies focused on her county and not any other? Why had the boards all endorsed this company by three-to-two votes? "Why *have* the endorsement?" she would later puzzle. "It's completely unenforceable. Why is this so important? Why go to such lengths to get an endorsement?"

In the moments when these questions pressed forward, Martha's new found sources of support from outside the state were not merely welcome but essential. Still, these contacts were sometimes uneasy for her. The reasons for her discomfort had much to do, symbolically, with meat—big, juicy slabs of it, hot and pink, being served up at the dinner table. Deerbrook Farms, which includes the feed mill Drew Blackwell runs, includes a large livestock operation. One of the fringe benefits of Drew's job is that the Blackwells get an endless supply of meat—sides of beef, cured hams, every imaginable cut of pork. Meat forms a central role in every meal. The Greenpeacers who started coming from Atlanta and New Orleans, occupying the dormered rooms on the top floor of their farmhouse were "vegetarians, prochoicers, very different from us," Martha remembered. Their whole package of beliefs was unfamiliar and unsettling. A big roast at the table elicited grimaces instead of the expected smiles; black-eyed peas had to be cooked up in two batches, one without any ham hocks. No ham hocks? It was gastronomic heresy—like eating turnip greens without corn bread.

Arguments about sustainable agriculture sometimes ensued. The Blackwells were made to feel slightly guilty, and they did not like it. Gail Martin, a wooly haired Greenpeace campaigner in her twenties who would surely be chosen in a police lineup if the charge was to "pick the environmental activist" (she carries her own mug fashioned from lumpy bits of clay when she travels, to avoid using disposable cups), became a friend whose counsel Blackwell trusted and relied on in teaching her how to counter the suasions of the waste companies. But when Gail began to challenge the Blackwells on things like the calves they wanted to start milk feeding for a little extra cash—"You mean, like, it's going to be a vee-e—e-a-l operation?" she cried in mixed horror and disgust to Martha one day—it was just too much.

Because Martha's instincts were (and remain) basically conservative, and because she had learned not to attack people in authority, she felt uncomfortable with the denunciatory style of some of these activists. "In Mississippi," she would say, taking a leaf from a Junior Auxiliary training manual, "you're just trained to be polite and cordial to everybody." And she simply did not endorse the larger, progressive social agenda that motivated most of the activists with whom she now mixed. She was primarily fighting a hazardous waste dump in her county, not a transformative program for radical social change. On many subjects, such as abortion, to which she was and is vehemently opposed, she learned simply to steer clear of discussion, for fear of inflaming the foxhole friendships that were still such welcome expedients.

■ ■ ■ BLACKWELL therefore felt greatly relieved when, at the Choctaw rally on the reservation that day in early March 1991, she heard George Baggett speak. Baggett has become a sort of Saint Augustine of hazardous waste. "My history was that I was gonna build a hazardous waste incinerator," he explained. Baggett fought in Vietnam and returned to attend college, training as a mathematician and engineer. After graduating in 1973, he worked for three years in the fledgling hazardous waste industry for Conservation Chemical Company, a now-defunct Missouri company and notorious polluter: one of its sites remains on the EPA's National Priorities List, an annually revised list of the nation's worst hazardous waste disasters, requiring federal cleanup money. In the wake of the EPA's 1974 report urging the expansion nationwide of hazardous waste disposal capacity, Conservation Chemical sought to site a hazardous waste disposal operation in Kansas City, and the prospects for success looked good. "Because I knew the industry, they decided that I was going to be the front man," said Baggett. He was sent out to solicit community support for a hazardous waste treatment facility and sludge landfill. "I was going door to door in a real Appalachian community, right in the middle of downtown Kansas City." One day he knocked on the door of an old black lady, a Mrs. Jamie Harris.

"She has since died. It was an amazing place. It was like the country in the middle of the city. She had cows right there on the place, next to downtown. I had never known it was there before. She invited me in and sat me down, gave me some strawberry pie.

"Now I knew that one of the hazardous waste treatment facilities I had worked on, a chemical detoxification operation, had leaked, even back then. But I went ahead, telling Miz Harris that this would be a better facility than those built in the past.

"And she looked straight at me and said, 'Young man, you really don't believe a word you're telling me!' I thought a moment and responded: 'No ma'am, I don't.' And I walked out of there and went back to work and said, 'You need someone else for this.' I returned to the office and told the owner that I could not support what they were attempting to do. I requested another project, and I was fired within a few days."

In 1977, Baggett and two friends decided they would start their own incineration business in his hometown of Kansas City. But he quickly became disillusioned with the promise of incineration as a panacea for pollution reduction, and he "backed out of the project." He recalled: "At the time, my associates suggested that I was not a team player. Since then, some have thanked me for keeping them out of a dangerous venture." Subsequently, Baggett has systematically worked to articulate his own environmental theology, one that concentrates on debunking the scientific assumptions of the waste companies and their defenders. His gospel stood in stark contrast to what Martha Blackwell was hearing from activists like Greenpeace's Gail Martin, who would say things to her like, "All we've got is the high moral ground."

At the Choctaw rally that day, Baggett was scared. "Chief Martin had made it known that I would be arrested if I came onto the reservation and into his jurisdiction. There were very few white people there. Kaye Kiker and I were the only Anglos on the podium." (Kiker, a white woman from Sumter County, Alabama, plays Martha Blackwell's role there, as the self-appointed watchdog over Chem Waste's Emelle operation.) "I was thoroughly intimidated. Three or four of the tribal policemen were present, and all wore reflective sunglasses, just like in the movies."

By the time he spoke, most of the PEON members who had come down, older white women mostly, had left. Martha Blackwell was one of the few whites still in the audience. Although Baggett toned down his speech, tiptoeing around the chief's role, what he had to say was a revelation for Blackwell. "I said to myself, 'Man, this guy is speaking my language.' George was just so *normal* to me. Everybody else was so radical."

She invited Baggett back to Macon that Saturday night. He ended up staying over "in a fine old antebellum home" until Monday. Blackwell helped arrange a couple of meetings, calling "forty or fifty businessmen all around the county, not only white. Just real white-collar types."

"He's just like me," Blackwell reflected. "Raised very conservative. And he can really talk to industry. He feels that once your eyes have been opened, you can't ever turn back. It's kinda like virginity."

In a two-hour lecture in Macon that Monday at the public library, Baggett "put on a suit and tie and presented technical info. I tried to give them a thorough examination of the physics and chemistry." He tried to give straightforward explanations in an effort to cut through the public relations hype. "It's redundant," he told them, "to talk about technologies being 'state of the art,'" since the use of new technology implies as much and says nothing about reliability. He urged them not to be swayed by assurances that the material was "four-nines" or even "six-nines" clean. (Hazardous waste companies routinely insist that their operations are 99.99 percent, or even 99.9999 percent nontoxic.) Said Baggett: "These are mathematical gimmicks. There are toxics stored or burned in these things that remain toxic in a few parts per million, doing damage to hormones, the endocrine system. Hughes-FTI's engineers have a magnitude of error based on the level of a million. But you need billions, or trillions." Baggett urged them to reject company claims of minimal risk. The companies, he said, "*never* explain the difference between imposed risk and *voluntary risk*." That is, he explained, "you may be more likely to get hit by a car than hurt by waste leaching out of a landfill, but why accept the risk of leaching wastes if you don't have to?"

He also attacked the engineering. "Even when Hughes entered, they claimed they were highly technical. The PR people were excellent, but there was no evidence that Hughes was making any changes to the previous proposed incinerator. I would have liked to see them address some of the technical subjects in the literature, but they just came forth with a burner."

Baggett urged his audience to recognize that there was also a social aspect to what he was saying. When he arrived at the library for his talk, an older white woman pointed at

Richard Brooks, a retired schoolteacher, Macon alderman, and the president of the Noxubee County chapter of the NAACP. "What's that boy doing here?" she asked. The gathering turned silent; blacks in the room looked especially uncomfortable. Some of them appeared poised to leave.

"I took her to the side," said Baggett. "She was unaware of her actions. She was oblivious as to what her inflammatory remarks would mean to a black man or others not raised in the South." He suggested that the woman be more accepting of their shared interest in learning about a hazardous waste dump. Like Martha Blackwell, the Virginia-bred Baggett is well trained in the arts of cordiality and is hardly the kind of activist to make a scene. But unlike Blackwell, who was uncomfortable with such ugliness and ill equipped openly to confront it on her home turf, Baggett—the outsider—did not want the comment to destroy the fragile alliance assembled to hear him speak. "A whole dimension of this is divide and conquer. I suggested that this was a great opportunity for racial healing."

Baggett went up to Brooks and offered to share his expertise with the NAACP. As an outsider, Baggett could not have understood the intense partisanship on the issue, in large part fed by memories of past slights, abuses, and hatreds. For someone in Noxubee County, the possibility of a waste opponent making such a gesture to Brooks—who had voted to endorse Hughes-FTI—would have seemed laughable.

■ ■ ■ ONE thing Martha Blackwell came clearly to understand from George Baggett is that in Mississippi, as in most other states, companies almost entirely neglect demographic factors when locating a toxic industrial operation.

The approval process itself largely ignores frank and open discussion of racial and economic concerns and realities. As a result, community divisions along race and class lines are more easily exploited by businessmen out to make a buck with little thought for long-term community effects.

The extent to which the state site-selection process contributed to the uproar in Noxubee County in turn derived from the state's desperate attempt to address the federal mandate that each state demonstrate sufficient disposal capacity. In 1990, still uncertain as to whether Alabama would be able to exclude out-of-state wastes, the Mississippi legislature passed the Hazardous Waste Facility Siting Act. The panic felt in Mississippi and throughout the rest of the Southeast at the time is revealed by the fact that the siting act assumed there would be an in-state hazardous waste facility and mandated no inquiry into whether one was necessary. In the late summer of 1990, Governor Ray Mabus anxiously wrote to the regional EPA administrator and assured him that this "landmark legislation sets in motion a process that will ultimately lead to the siting of a hazardous waste management facility" in Mississippi, a reaffirmation of the state's "willingness to participate in interstate agreements with other states in this region." The act's purpose was to be fleshed out by a twelve-member Technical Siting Committee. The committee's carefully circumscribed duties included the obligation to solicit interested communities and identify three "candidate sites" that might agree to "host" a hazardous waste operation. The list of factors the committee was obliged to consider focused on geology and environmental impact. But, as with most such laws, it required no detailed study of the human environment—despite the prominence that the environmental racism issue had by then attained in civil rights and environmental circles, and despite the fact that Mississippi had (and still has) more African American elected officials than any other state.

Moreover, the committee was badly underfunded as it sought to identify candidate sites. Duane Gill, a social scientist at Mississippi State University who served on it, explained: "I think most people had no idea what the committee was doing. People didn't come to the public meetings. We rarely had more than a half dozen there, including reporters." The result was that all three candidate sites recommended by the Technical Siting Committee were within seventy miles of Macon, because of their proximity to Selma chalk.

Along with George Baggett, Duane Gill proved to be a crucial figure in Martha Blackwell's environmental education. Gill, a lithe, athletic Iowan in his early forties, has a casual, youthful manner belied by his prematurely gray hair. He concluded that the committee did a good job with its limited resources. For instance, its choices could not be confirmed with test drills to make sure that the geology would work, because there simply was not enough money. As for the committee's selection of sites in or very near Noxubee County, Gill remains philosophical: "I sincerely and fully believe that we arrived at Noxubee County because of strict, objective standards. Maybe those standards need to be widened to include social, economic and demographic factors."

In fact, Duane Gill had tried to include some consideration of those factors, even though the law did not require it. He had chaired a subcommittee looking at other factors, which concluded: "Ideally, all segments of the community should have input, particularly with regard to compensation for perceived inequalities and community stigma." The subcommittee stressed that "community" meant more than elected officials, concluding that "you must look at leaders as well." Gill advised that by involving as many voices as possible, people would not be suspicious about ulterior motives and would understand how they might benefit. To a great extent, Ed Netherland and Hughes-FTI were doing exactly that: looking not only to Noxubee County's elected leaders but also to the self-appointed truth tellers like Ike Brown, people whose power went beyond electoral support. However, because Netherland was not disinterested, he excluded those voices that disagreed. Thus, the absence of a regularized process skewed the result. Underfunded and pressed for time, the ideas advanced by Gill's subcommittee just "didn't catch on very well."

No PEON members attended the committee's hearings, but Baggett submitted comments on PEON's behalf. In a seven-page, single-spaced letter, Baggett attacked the officially sanctioned scientific evidence and also urged authorities to consider concerns outside of their mandate. Baggett's style is prolix and rambling; he does not use headings or subheadings to break up ideas and points. But in his analysis he hammered away at the contradictions and unexplained assumptions of the siting process, of which Mississippi's is a typical example.

Baggett began by attacking the conviction that geology should be the controlling factor. Although the committee's criteria were not due until April 1, Baggett noted that two weeks before the criteria were released, Sam Mabry, the state Department of Environmental Quality official then responsible for overseeing the hazardous waste facility permitting process, had been quoted as saying that Noxubee County had the best geology in the state for a facility.

Did Mabry's comment suggest that the committee's results were a foregone conclusion? Baggett intimated as much: after evaluating the circumstantial evidence, he concluded, "It could also be said that there was some certainty that Noxubee County would be determined the host community."

Some of his arguments were sophisticated and technical ("polycyclic chlorinated organic and heavy metal contaminated soils can be detoxified without volatilization of heavy metals"). But much of Baggett's discussion was common sense stuff, such as his attack on the chalk's claimed impermeability. Baggett explained that the impact of toxic chemicals on the limerock is not known: "The rate at which water percolates through clay or chalk formations has no relationship to the percolation rate of inorganic and organic chemicals." He added that EPA studies on solvents and pesticides (the residues from which typically go into hazardous waste landfills) concluded that such substances "percolate through soils like 'WD-40' after many state-of-the-art landfills were found leaking into groundwater."

Finally, Baggett stepped beyond scientific disputes and urged the committee to examine the sort of social and economic concerns looked at by Gill's subcommittee. He asked the committee to consider the conclusions reached by a California environmental consulting firm, Cerrell Associates, in a 1984 report it prepared for the California Waste Management Board. The Cerrell report is routinely cited by environmental and civil rights activists as proof of the calculated decision of U.S. industry to burden racial and ethnic minorities and the poor with America's most environmentally threatening activities. The report examined "certain criteria for site selection that will result in the least amount of political resistance for a waste management project." The criteria included communities of under twenty-five thousand people, rural communities, low-income and poorly-educated areas, places populated mostly by long-time residents, places with few migrants (who, like Carol Puckett, tend to be more interested in keeping a way of life they moved to the location to enjoy), and places where people, including elected officials, believe that they personally or their community stand to gain economically.

It is safe to say that anyone with moderate experience of American society could have drawn up this list. Yet the Cerrell report has acquired the status of a smoking gun for those working against what they call systematic environmental racism. In large part, this is because plaintiffs have unsuccessfully tried to prove violation of their constitutional equal protection rights in decisions about where to site toxic facilities. Their failure has derived from an inability to demonstrate an *intent* to discriminate against them on the basis of race or ethnicity. In this context, the Cerrell report's conclusions have acquired a Solomonic status in the environmental justice movement.

The committee's final report included not the slightest recognition of Baggett's concerns or a glancing mention of those explored by Gill's subcommittee. Had they attended to Baggett's comments, however, they would have done well to focus on one of the items he reiterated from the Cerrell report: "One occupational classification which consistently demonstrates itself as a strong indicator of opposition to the siting of noxious facilities is the college educated housewife."

■ ■ ■ WHAT George Baggett and Duane Gill did was teach Martha Blackwell a basic but invaluable lesson: attack the science and faith in technology advanced by the companies. They showed her how to disentangle public relations hype from scientific explanation, and they stressed the relation between the waste fight and larger social problems in a language that was unemotional and comprehensible to lay-people.

Martha Blackwell's first opportunity to apply what she had learned came that spring day when the inimitable Ike Brown deviled her with his suggestion that a "cu-u-u-l-tural difference" left him unbothered by warmth that made her want to turn on the courthouse air conditioners. They were both at the courthouse because Ed Netherland, as part of Hughes-FTI's package of enticements for local political support, had promised the county that his fledgling hazardous waste enterprise would handle its solid waste.

The existing landfill, built in eastern Macon in a ramshackle, all-black neighborhood known as Pineywoods, was scheduled for closure because it did not comply with new federal landfill construction guidelines. Built downriver in a flood-prone area, long before more stringent regulations governing design, construction, and maintenance, the Pineywoods landfill leaked. The stuff had been thrown in together willy-nilly and stunk to high heaven for miles around in the endlessly oppressive "acres of afternoon" of a blistering southern summer, in the memorable phrase of the Alabama novelist Babs Deal.

Allen Hunter, Macon's oversized mayor, recalled that at the time the law firm of Perkins & Gowan advised local officials that FTI's promises to handle solid waste and make other civic improvements—including its vow to upgrade roads, improve the fire department, provide new hospital equipment, and underwrite emergency training for industrial disasters—"were not worth the paper they were written on, but at the time we didn't listen. Ed Netherland had done such a good selling job."

The day marked Blackwell's first public presentation advocating her new environmental politics. At a long table in front of and parallel to the judge's dais and the witness stand, the supervisors sat next to Netherland and his lawyer. Blackwell and others spoke to them from behind the court railing, where spectators sit. "It was nothing more than an intimidation thing," Blackwell recalled, still angry at the thought that the county's elected officials allowed Netherland pride of place with them.

Blackwell set out not to have her alternative proposal adopted but merely to emphasize that there were options. "It was certainly a more viable option than Ed sayin', 'I'll take care of your garbage.' " Still new to such advocacy, Blackwell stood up to address the group. She was nervous, and her voice had an emotional edge. "I said, 'Mr. Netherland doesn't even have a plan. Ya'll don't know that he won't just dump it on the side of the road. *He hasn't even given you a plan!*' " Like Attorney Gowan, she urged the board to take its time, not rush into anything.

Even in retrospect, Blackwell felt defeated by the encounter. "I don't know why I continued to get in the ring with those people. They would just make me look like an idiot. They never looked the least bit threatened by what I had to say. They just looked bored—like 'I've taken this long trip here, and now I have to listen to this woman.' Ed would just say in response, 'Surely Miz Blackwell knows that there are laws that would control us. We could not just dump it in the road.' " For her part, Blackwell knew in advance that she would not sway the board. "At that point I was still runnin' on anger and inspiration. Back then I was jumpin' into everything with two feet. I never went in there thinkin' they would take my proposal. But it was the principle of the thing. I studied it one night, and I knew more about it than they did."

Afterwards, Blackwell approached Netherland and said

something that continues to embarrass her because she felt she revealed too much of herself to him. "I walked up to him. I was so tired of him bein' so arrogant and condescending. He said something very courteous like, 'I'm just so glad you came to our meetin'—always in control. And I said, 'Ed, if you ever think I'm goin' to stop fightin' you, yer wrong. You'll be my enemy till the day I die.'" Blackwell was pleased, at least, that she "wasn't cryin'." "But I was just showin' some emotion. He can really get my dander up. He knows just how to push my buttons." Martha Blackwell and Ed Netherland never spoke to each other again.

7
IT'S NOT EVEN PAST

MARTHA BLACKWELL'S environmental education armed her to combat the waste companies at a rhetorical and public relations level. What proved much harder was freeing herself from the historical baggage of previous generations. In Noxubee County, she discovered, she was always fighting the past—not merely her own family history but Faulkner's curse of "this whole land, this whole South." Gerry Harris, PEON's secretary, offered that during the course of the Noxubee waste wars she often felt as though "we're going through a second Reconstruction." Her statement reveals the extent to which Noxubee County's white population was left untouched by the tectonic social shifts of the civil rights years, which historians of American race relations have labeled the "Second Reconstruction." It also alludes to what many whites seemed to recognize but would not say: the waste wars had become the vehicle for redistributing power among all races and classes. In the rhetoric of the Noxubee waste wars, historical metaphor was routinely, if unconsciously, used to explain events. And the past's hold on the discourse and emotions of people in the present was revealed most starkly in the ways people spoke about Ike Brown and Ed Netherland.

A common perception of Ike Brown is that, as one older white woman said to me, "he's takin' advantage of people who were less fortunate in the brain department, who hadn't been to school, who could barely read and write." Brown's adversaries, white and black, commonly believe that he exercises intimidation as well. As a white former teacher put it, "You know Ike Brown is just gonna keep those niggers from voting" when he wants to. (Brown once said that whites would not use the "n" word with me, a white outsider from up North. He was quite wrong. It was used freely and often, just as it is among northern whites.) Thus, the story usually goes, Brown supported FTI not only to foment discord among local blacks, but also to pocket a good fee.

During Reconstruction, a man named Isham Stewart came to prominence as the leader of Noxubee's black political machine. Details on Stewart are scarce, but the available record suggests a man who played a role in the county precisely analogous to the one many whites and some blacks believe Brown performs today. As one alarmed white citizen wrote to the *Macon Beacon* in October 1874:

> The Isham Stewart party is, in all conscience,
> sufficiently ignorant, sufficiently besetted, and

was wholly typical of her milieu when she insisted that, had her father been alive, there never would have been any of this mess, because "Daddy would have seen right through that carpetbagger Ed Netherland." With his "well-oiled tongue," she said, Ed was "the epitome of what Daddy hated." Netherland was depicted, to borrow the words of a local history of Noxubee County during Reconstruction, as one of that "still worse class of northerners" who were adventitiously propelled by their "only thought," namely, "to make the most of the opportunity" of the county's disarray "to better their own fortunes." Like the nineteenth-century carpetbagger and scalawag, he had descended on the county "when it became apparent how readily outsiders could obtain offices of trust." Also like Reconstruction carpetbaggers, Netherland seemed, in the eyes of many local whites, to be one of the "undesirable citizens without much character, who interfered with labor and associated with Negroes almost altogether." Some might say of him that he was one of those "others, grafters, coming south to make what money they could and staying only so long as they could do this," an adventurer "without character . . . and ready to take any chance, regardless of right or wrong." As Faulkner famously observed: "The past is never dead. It's not even past."

Netherland and his forces appropriated some of these historical images to their own advantage. One phrase uttered thousands of times in the Noxubee waste wars was "the power structure." When I inquired what the speaker meant, I typically was told that it referred to the persistence of the "plantation mentality." "The power structure" was an explanatory shorthand meaning those whites who, in another of the recurring images that accompanied the phrase, continued to keep their feet on the necks of blacks. State Representative Tyrone Ellis, a small, compact African American distinguished by his natty attire and a manner as smooth as molasses, was recruited by Ike Brown to work for FTI. Netherland acknowledged that Ellis—whose legislative district includes a portion of Noxubee—was compensated "a couple thousand a month"; a USPCI official claimed to know that it was four times that much, supposedly funneled to him through a complex web of bank accounts and corporate entities (this charge was never proven). When at a public meeting a white man angrily asked about his paid partisanship, Ellis screamed back, with barely concealed fury, "Get your foot off my head!" The image was a favorite of Ike Brown's as well: "Your people," he told me, "the Blackwells and the PEONs, put they foot on black people neck, and"—never one to stint on celebrating his own achievement—"people like me got it off."

The image of white feet on black necks inverted the recollection of a Noxubee County doctor, R. R. Wyatt, who, after Reconstruction, collected his personal history in a volume called *Autobiography of a Little Man*. Wyatt wrote that Reconstruction in Noxubee was a time of "Negro rule, or even better, black heels on white necks." This conclusion would have found many sympathetic ears among local whites 120 years later, dismayed at the political chaos fomented by FTI, as would Wyatt's observation that "with Noxubee and Lowndes counties ninety per cent Negroes who were voters, we had no chance to defeat these carpetbaggers. The Negroes realized their importance and were arrogant to the last degree."

Just who comprised "the power structure"? When pressed, Ike Brown, Tyrone Ellis, and their supporters would hurl back one name, and only one: Thomas. The irony of this, and a measure of the whopping public relations success scored by FTI's supporters, is that the Thomas family is not descended from the highest rank of its planter aristocracy, some of whom, like Gus Evans, do still live and prosper in Noxubee County. The Thomas brothers come from an old Noxubee family, but not one known for their wealth. The brothers themselves are credited with reviving the fortunes of Shuqualak Lumber, a business their father had taken over years before. When they chose to call their nascent environmental group PEON back in 1983, it was out of a very real awareness that they did not stand on the top of the county's white social ladder.

Yet the Thomases were the most vocal and therefore easily targeted opponents of a hazardous waste operation. They live a splashier, more visibly luxurious life than some of the county's older monied families—Evanses, Cavetts, Minors, and Barges. Charlie and Linda Thomas are particularly noticeable for their conspicuous consumption. Linda owns the county's only Jaguar, and their private airplane is a widespread source of gossipy envy. Tyrone Ellis and Ike Brown understood that any political effort derives strength and focus from a visible, easily ridiculed enemy. With hot tempers and extravagant personal habits, Charlie and Linda Thomas were perfect foils for their self-righteous, self-interested politics. And for representatives of those at the bottom of the social ladder, those on the second or third rung are high enough to merit attack.

The public relations firm Netherland hired in Jackson, an operation called the GodwinGroup, greedily embraced the metaphor of Reconstruction. (The GodwinGroup, which one of their representatives told me handles most Mississippi-related public relations concerns for "the southeast corridor, from Atlanta to Houston," has at one time or another represented most of Mississippi's largest industries and counts the Mississippi Manufacturers Association, or MMA, as a major client. The MMA, a major force in state politics, became a primary mover behind the probusiness pressure for in-state hazardous waste treatment capacity in 1991.) Known for its aggressive, confrontational style, the Godwin-Group did not hesitate to run with the power structure label. A junior account executive told me in a bored, slow drawl: "The problem we have is that wealthy white people with a plantation mentality are threatened by a big company, [which would cause them] to lose their power." Like every other employee I saw or talked to at the firm, the man was white and had graduated from Ole Miss, where he had fraternized with Printz Bolin and Charlie Thomas Jr. I wondered how a man with access to real power in the state of Mississippi, one who spoke on behalf of its political and economic titans *and* an affiliate of one of the world's largest corporations, could say that with a straight face.

"When you get the power in Noxubee County, just what you got? What are you controlling?" Gus Evans wondered rhetorically. Linda and Peggy Thomas seconded this point. Peggy Thomas, in her trilling voice and lovely, soft Scarlett O'Hara accent, dismissed the suggestion that they were part of a power structure: "The only possible tie that could ever be brought to the Thomas family is that the boys' grandfather was supervisor ye-yahs and ye-yahs and ye-yahs ago. And to my knowledge that's the only political office. And Captain Thomas was Sheriff of Noxubee County after the Civil Wo-wah." She giggled at the suggestion. "So that's the only two offices. I mean, the boys' daddy was on the school bo-wad. And my husband is on bo-wads that don't pay anything. Has been on the hospital bo-wad for twenty-seven years. On the bank bo-wad. But you know it's just honorable, civic duties." Still, in a place where resentments, mutual suspicions, and historical hatreds run deep, the label stuck like Super Glue.

■ ■ ■ ALTHOUGH Blackwell is typical enough of her class routinely to apply the Reconstruction images commonly used to describe Ike and Ed, she also took seriously George Baggett's words about using the debate over hazardous waste as an opportunity for racial healing. Doing so would mean convincing both blacks and whites that a hazardous waste operation threatened their mutual, long-term well-being. But besides being tainted with historical perceptions, Martha simply did not know a lot of blacks well, at least not people who would get up in a public forum and advocate a view or try to lobby others for PEON.

Blacks faced personal ridicule if they openly supported PEON, and few would identify themselves as members. This was only partly a matter of race; class was also a factor. Even among economically independent whites, getting open support was a problem. Once, in an interview with one of the county's most successful white farming families, I asked whether they were PEON supporters. They asked me to turn off my tape recorder and insisted on anonymity before admitting that they had supported PEON with substantial contributions. Why not proudly declare this fact? Things were just too fractious. The oppositional climate made possible by FTI, one carefully nurtured by Ike Brown and his supporters, made public support a risky business proposition. Public opposition by business leaders, like that demonstrated in Giles County, Tennessee, could be turned around in Noxubee County and characterized as against working people's—and especially black workers'—interests.

As a result, membership in PEON was the loosest of categories. Martha and a handful of others did most of the work. A member could be someone who gave a few dollars or attended one of the meetings scheduled as needed. PEON had an organizational structure, but it was purely a formality.

In 1991, if you asked Martha Blackwell or Gerry Harris or one of the Thomases who PEON's black members were, you were sure to be directed to one woman. Essie Spencer— a pert, pretty, diminutive grandmother with the complexion of milky coffee and a personality that belongs in a body the size of Arnold Schwarzenegger's—is someone everyone, white or black, knows. Spencer lives at the end of a little graveled drive, atop a small rise just south of Baptist Hill, the old center of black Macon. If not for the invariably poor Mississippi roads leading to her blond-brick, ranch-style house, complete with marble birdbath out front, her house presents the picture of middle-class domesticity seen in a thousand American suburbs.

Spencer is a woman seemingly without affectation or vanity. When we first met, she sat surrounded in the dark brown veneer of her spacious kitchen by various of her wigs, each atop its own manikin head. She constantly changed them, putting them on and off her head, as we spoke.

Like Ike Brown, Essie Spencer performs her own little ministry to her neighborhood. As with any visit to Brown, the phone rings constantly or people stop by to seek her counsel on some family or financial matter. One time our appointment was delayed while, for a fee, she paid the bills and balanced the checkbook of "an old boyfriend" who was illiterate. The man looked to be about fifty years old.

Spencer was an officer of PEON in the earlier fight against Chem Waste, and she rallied against FTI early on. Her involvement in the FTI fight cemented her friendships with whites, particularly with Gerry Harris, her contemporary. The two visit with one another socially, breaking another unspoken taboo. (With her songbird's vibrato of a laugh, Harris would say, "Essie comes to my house and we drink coffee and we have Co-colas and she thinks I'm trash.") As a result,

Spencer was branded by Brown and FTI's other African American supporters, in another one of their most enduring descriptions, as one of "whites' hand-picked blacks."

Essie also has the temerity to challenge Ike, and she will call his name if she thinks his actions demand criticism. This is an unusual thing. Many blacks would not criticize him on the record, for fear of retribution. To hear Spencer tell it, FTI came to the county because of Brown only. "He the one that put FTI into Noxubee County. He the one that brought 'em in here, because he found out that he had control." Like many educated blacks, Essie Spencer maintained that Ike took advantage of "the illiterate folks." She continued: "And some of them are not illiterate, they're just weak and money-hungry. . . . He is looking for a weak, black county with the most illiterate folks who will believe in somebody like him." The comment—from a black woman—is especially risky because it confirms whites' paternalistic perceptions of the limitations of "their" blacks. The precariousness of local race relations means that, in making such comments, as she does often, she can and has been depicted, with a speed and venom that would have impressed Joseph Stalin, as disloyal to black interests.

But she is at peace with herself about this. "You know, as long as you let person get by with doin' crooked shit and dirty mess, they gonna do it. But they's a stoppin' point down that road. And I have found a good way to stop it. When I set out to do somethin', I put the Lord out in front of me and I get behind. And I don't worry, I go on about my business, and I come on back, just like I lef'."

Many educated African Americans complained about political corruption. A retired woman observed disgustedly: "It's been so much dirty politics. That's why we got peoples elected to positions here in Noxubee County, black peoples that are not qualified to be there." A businessman who had lived up north for over twenty years and would not speak on the record for fear of commercial reprisals, condemned the limited education and narrower vision of the local leaders, black and white. "People are elected supervisor because they have large equipment to clear roads," he sighed. "And it should be a management position."

Another woman was more specific in her criticism: "You take the supervisor for District Three, George Robinson. He won't even show his face in front of a camera. I can get my camcorder out there, and he put a book up in front, a paper—he walk and turn his back." People throughout the county mock the way he hides his face from the camera, suggesting that this habit mirrors his concept of political office. He was widely criticized (as were his fellow supervisors Higginbotham and Joseph Stevenson, along with Noxubee's first black sheriff, Albert Walker) for refusing to be accountable to anyone asking nosy or unpleasant questions.

Through Essie Spencer, Martha Blackwell came to know her daughter, Darlene Cole, who oversees computers in the public schools. This was something of a revelation. In Nashville and Lafayette, Louisiana, Blackwell had come into contact with successful, educated, middle-class blacks, but not in Noxubee County. Here, living at once right next to her, but, until the fight against hazardous waste, a sympathetic universe away, was a woman her age who shared her aspirations and lived in comparable bourgeois domesticity. Still, there was always "that boundary"; their socializing would be limited to PEON work. More intimate socializing, emanating from activities of church and school, remained strictly among one's own. Even after fighting against hazardous waste for four years, Martha Blackwell would not recognize Cole's husband if she saw him.

Nonetheless, Martha's growing environmental justice interests forced her to confront the subtle distinctions that helped prop up the aristocracy of the soil from which she came. When she was a girl, she remembered, she was told never to call a black woman a lady or a black man a gentlemen—just a woman or a man. Whites did not wave to blacks on the road. These and similar memories came flooding back, markers of her new awareness of what helped make Noxubee so vulnerable to the predations of aspiring waste barons.

She had black people in her home to plan PEON strategy, something that her father would not have tolerated. Daddy was, she reflected, typical of his time and place in his racial views: "I mean, if there was a need, an individual need, or treating someone kindly, or somethin' that somebody needed, then they got it. But as far as an overall genuine respect for black people, you know, there was a difference."

Martha's contacts with regional environmental and civil rights groups meant that she was suddenly in their loop, the principal contact person on the ground in Noxubee. They invited her to rallies, meetings, and conferences all over the South. Often the only white, she traveled with busloads of people from Noxubee. Because of her childhood experiences, at a fundamental level she felt more comfortable with home-county blacks than with whites and blacks from the big cities they visited. On one bus trip back, she and a group laughed about how silly some urban black activists looked to them, with their dreads, nappy hair, faux kentecloth accessories, and imitation Queen Nefertiti hats. But just as her encounters with Greenpeacers had been important yet sometimes tense, so too her travels across race and class lines brought conflict. At an environmental justice con-

and other PEONs to work together and gather black support were confounded by Ed Netherland's recruiting successes. Although motivated by a cold economic calculus, Netherland aimed, if not to nurture black talent, at least to celebrate and use it to advance his company. Through Tyrone Ellis, he recruited Mississippi's most prominent African American jurist to serve on FTI's board. Reuben Anderson was the first black graduate of Ole Miss law school (in 1967) and the first black since Reconstruction to serve on the state's circuit and later its supreme court (they are both elected positions). In early 1991, he went into private practice and remains a prominent and respected figure. Ellis also appealed on FTI's behalf to an even more legendary Mississippi figure, the Reverend Aaron Henry. Henry, the longtime head of the state NAACP and a former associate of the assassinated Medgar Evers, spoke on behalf of the Mississippi Freedom Democratic Party at the 1964 Democratic National Convention. The Mississippi NAACP under Henry remained silent about the effort to site one of the nation's largest hazardous waste dumps in overwhelmingly black Noxubee County, despite simultaneous efforts by most other civil rights groups to resist such activities. According to Ellis, Henry, now a Mississippi state representative, said: "As long as the locals are supportive of it, then we have no real problems. . . . We are not gonna take a position on it." For his part, Henry scowled and waved me away when I asked him for his view on the Noxubee waste wars, insisting that "I don't know a thing about it. I don't know a thing about it."

In late January 1991, the Jackson *Clarion-Ledger* broke the news that Netherland had offered Jerry Rice, the star wide receiver for the San Francisco 49ers, $1 million in a promotional contract for FTI. Rice, who grew up the son of a bricklayer in Crawford, Mississippi, just across the northern Noxubee line, has considerable stature among Noxubee County's majority black population, who claim him as one of their own. FTI and Rice's agents both denied the story of the megacontract offer, leaked by Mississippi state representative Jim Evans, who had himself been a linebacker for fourteen years, playing for the New York Giants and other teams. They claimed that the offer to Rice was for a much less lucrative promotional deal. To this day, Evans stands by his story, one denied by Rice's handlers.

■ ■ ■ FTI's detractors depicted this as just symbolic pandering to Noxubee's black masses. The fact is, nonetheless, that whatever his motives, Netherland treated the black community as a voice to be reckoned with. On what he called the "sticky subject" of Ike Brown, Netherland insisted that despite Brown's ability to attract controversy faster than bees to a honey pot, he "understood early on that Ike could go places no white man could ever go." In his efforts to keep black support, Ike brought a number of locally eminent black people into Netherland's orbit. Their presence made it virtually impossible for PEON to get strong backing from the county's majority.

One of the most important figures Ike recruited was I. D. Conner. I. D.'s local notoriety stems only partially from the fact that he is the father of the New Orleans Saints' linebacker Darion Conner, the seventh of his eleven children. He lives in District One, the most heavily African American of Noxubee County's election districts. Now retired and on disability, he always worked outside Noxubee County after 1964, for a building supply concern in Columbus; his economic independence allowed him to speak his mind at a time when that was scarcely possible.

Conner, who turned sixty in 1994, looks as if he could have been an all-star linebacker himself. Although now slightly stooped, he presents an imposing, powerful figure, over six feet two inches tall, with hands as big as baseball gloves and skin the color of aged mahogany. Conner and his wife, Annette, a big woman herself and a quiet, watchful foil next to her affable husband, live in the X-Prairie section of the county's eastern flatlands. (Not even a local historian could explain the provenance of the X. Perhaps some homesteader had simply stopped there, slapped down an X on the map, and said, "There it is: X marks the spot on the prairie where I'm gonna put my place," after which a town grew up and the designation stuck.)

The Conners live extremely well by local standards, in a brick ranch-style house. We sat in their capacious kitchen, facing an enormous Garland stainless steel range and stove and an equally monumental refrigerator, on a wooden veneer-paneled banquette that looked out at the endless line of the prairie, drab and gray in the soft sunlight of a January afternoon. (They were the first black family in X-Prairie to have a refrigerator, a fan, a telephone, and, finally, plumbing. Still today, scattered neighbors have no running water.) I. D. wore a black sweatshirt with a cutout of the African continent emblazoned on the front and colored in red, green, and black checks—the colors of African American nationalism.

As a child, he "had some hard times coming up." He had to stop going to school in 1944. Conner was ten years old and had finished the fourth grade. "I did schemin' things like everybody else. Sellin' whiskey. Had to do it to make a livin'. Did everything but steal." In his days as a bootlegger, in the early fifties, he "put a car together for nothin'. Then bought a '39 Chevrolet and sold whiskey out of it." The car he had scrambled together was fitted with red and green lights on the dirt flaps. I. D. would follow the signal car in his Chevrolet; if the way ahead looked clear, the green lights would go on. If a roadblock was threatened, his cohort would turn on the red light to signal that the police were coming, and I. D. would head off in the other direction. In a landscape where roads are few and the distances between them vast, this allowed an easy getaway. Years later, he said: "The sheriff asked me, 'Why didn't I ever catch you?' I said, 'You're not smart enough.'"

An only child, I. D. Conner moved when he was fourteen years old. Until that year, he had lived with his mother and stepfather on Rock Hill Plantation, the Mullins's place in Prairie Point. Conner is a couple of years older than Martha Blackwell's oldest brother, Bill Mullins; they played together as children. I. D. was the preferred giver of piggyback rides to the boys from the main house. In an encounter repeated in similar form thousands of times across the South of that time, Conner remembered one day as they neared adolescence, when things changed; playmates became antagonists, master and servant. Conner recalled Bill Mullins ordering that he be called "*Mister* Billy": "And I said, 'If you want to Mister someone, Mister me. I'm older.'" For his part, Bill Mullins has no memory of either Conner or the incident.

This new tension in their relations was not to escalate. Conner's stepfather got in an argument with Mister William Sr., Martha Blackwell's father. As on every plantation, the owner would sell crops for his tenants and then "settle up," deducting expenses that had been incurred in the commissary. The settlement was an event that routinely created tension between white owners and their black tenants. In "The Revolt of Brud Bascomb," a short story by the Macon-born writer Loyle Hairston, a sawmill worker disappears after quitting his job in anger because his employer, Bull Crawford, said Bascomb "owed him back credit for stuff he bought on time from the sawmill commi'sary store. Credit were Bull Crawford's regular way of cheatin' his colored work hands. Bein he never jotted down what you bought, you had to pay whatever he said you owed; and if you wanted to keep your job you didn dare 'spute the lowdown snake." The dispute between I. D.'s stepfather and Martha's father concerned the income from the ten milk cows the former raised on Rock Hill. One day in the winter of 1948, I. D.'s stepfather challenged his overlord about the milk settlement. Conner remembers that Supervisor Mullins and his stepfather got into a vicious row that ended with Mullins ordering them to get off his property that night.

In retrospect, Conner was remarkably free of bitterness about these inequalities, which is generally true of blacks in Noxubee County, at least when speaking with a white outsider. "I don't hold it against any white folks what they used to do." Did it bother him to recall that, although blacks tentatively began registering to vote in 1959 and 1960, William Mullins and others continued to vote for their tenants? No, said Conner. "Just don't do it now. Don't put your mess on me."

Conner acknowledged that blacks' material situation had generally improved in the county since his childhood, although too often, he said, the "bossman" still holds sway over the lives of his employees, depended on to get an employee out of jail, provide for a sick relative, or help out with a loan. As for local race relations, although some aspects of blacks' lives have improved, he concluded matter-of-factly that "the coldness is still there." Conner ruefully reported, for example, that when his son was signed by his first major league team, the Atlanta Falcons—presumably an important moment in the life of not only the player and his family but also their community—there was no mention of the fact in the *Macon Beacon* or even in the larger Columbus paper, the *Commercial Dispatch.*

The "fuss" with waste arose, I. D. Conner told me, when Ed Netherland came and "talked to people," black people. "If the waste companies had never mentioned pay rates," he offered, "there never would have been this trouble." This was something, Conner and others told me, that had never happened before in Noxubee County. From the start, Netherland had advertised that FTI would pay a minimum wage of seven dollars an hour. As Eva Sherrod, the black alderwoman from Brooksville, wrote to the state's Department of Environmental Quality in support of FTI: "The jobs will pay a minimum salary of seven dollars per hour in an area where most people are making around six. The increased tax base will allow us to provide needed services to our citizens and most importantly to greatly improve our education system."

Conner "never knew of any time before where pay rates were mentioned." In short order, Netherland declared his promise of high-paying jobs and said PEON leaders—the "white power structure"—opposed his venture partly because they wanted to keep wage rates low. Although a single company's payment of higher wages could have forced others to raise their wages because of competition for the best employees, this would have been unlikely in a place like Noxubee, with high unemployment and a poorly educated workforce.

I. D. Conner's reasons for favoring FTI and agreeing to work for them—using his stature in the black churches and community groups of the prairie—existed independently of his environmental concerns. In fact, Conner lamented that there are "already so much chemicals in the world," and he reminisced about a time in Noxubee County when there was more wild, uncultivated land, and more varieties of plant and food crops. But, he said emphatically, "Jobs, that's my important. What could people get paid at? You can't even get snack food cheaply now," pointing out that a Dr Pepper costs the same in New York as in Mississippi. And, he asked rhetorically, "What does it mean to earn four or five dollars an hour?"

Conner also became, if not the direct beneficiary, then at least the conduit of Netherland's considerable largesse, of what came to seem like FTI's complimentary automated teller machine, Noxubee County branch. Conner runs a social club in a raggedy little red-brick building by the roadside near the cluster of shops that constitute what was once the hamlet of X-Prairie. The words "Country-Club" are hand painted across the top in big, blocky black letters on a white background. Conner would make the club available for people to come talk about FTI, and he would "give a snack" to visitors.

FTI started to come through with more than just a snack, too. "Lots of times I'd go to the office and ask them for a donation." The money would go to whoever was going through some hard times. "The next day a check would be there for $400 or $500." For some, this largesse was indispensable. In rural Mississippi, January and February are times for housefires. Most people lack central heating because of the generally hospitable climate and rely on portable space heaters during a cold snap. Some old models, with their exposed coils, inevitably catch fire every winter, and a handful of homes, from shotgun shacks to sturdier frame farmhouses, catch on fire in the cold months. "Ed helped building homes for people whose houses had been burned. He'd help 'em with a couple hundred dollars."

When news of this sort of beneficence would trickle out into the white community, FTI's opponents would scream, "You see! We knew they were making payoffs!" But *payoff* usually implies something illicit. Such gifts may have been morally questionable—debonair urbanite alights in impoverished farm country and starts scattering bills about like so many apples to be gathered from beneath a tree in autumn—but they were not unlawful.

The bravura theatricality of Netherland's accomplishment should not be underestimated. His visits amounted to a singular effort by a white man and his attendants to solicit the support of the county's poorest, most neglected citizens. His currency was hope, and he must have known it. For those who, like I. D. Conner, shared in dispensing FTI's bounty (many would say that he and others ate at its trough), "Ed had it in his mind that everybody would be equal, and they stopped it." They? The white power structure.

■ ■ ■ THANKSGIVING was coming. Against every prediction she might have made, Martha Blackwell had devoted an entire year of her life to fighting the company of a renegade Tennessee entrepreneur whom she had met only once. The fight strained her marriage, left her house in unaccustomed disorder, and resulted in her feeling emotionally distant from her children. Her status in the community had changed in ways she could not yet understand. She was always frazzled, torn between simultaneous demands to learn and speak and organize resistance and seek backing for her cause, even as her children grew grumpy from inattention.

Drew Blackwell would tolerate her involvement to a point, but he was bothered by the intensity of it. She would explain her feeling that the movement was an expression of her faith, a demonstration of her maternal concern for the health of her children and grandchildren. In those months, when the end still seemed close, he would relent. But the hazardous waste struggle had introduced a new tension in their marriage, one that would not disappear for the next two years.

8
OUR OWN LITTLE CIVIL WAR

THE STRANGEST YEAR IN the Noxubee waste wars was 1992, when the air was thick with charges and countercharges of corruption and foul play. Ralph Higginbotham achieved the unthinkable and ascended to the presidency of the board of supervisors. PEON bedded down with its onetime nemesis, Chem Waste. And the county's black leaders began fighting publicly with one another, thus breaking another unwritten rule of social life in "Stinking Water" County: black solidarity should be maintained in front of whites. The local NAACP chapter jumped on the Hughes-FTI bandwagon, directly countering the trend of most major civil rights organizations to oppose the siting of toxic operations in heavily black areas. Families and friends broke up and turned against one another. And a deep paranoia set in over everybody—and with good reason, because Hughes-FTI was spying on some of its opponents. People were justified in saying that the whole thing had turned into their own little civil war.

■ ■ ■ THE year was also the most important in the Noxubee waste wars: the bumbling of a haughty new governor created the opening PEON had been waiting for to attack the assumptions that another dump or incinerator was needed at all. In November 1991, the "arrogant" Democrat Ray Mabus was defeated by the state's first Republican to be elected governor since the end of Reconstruction. Kirkwood Fordice was a construction millionaire from Vicksburg, a rough-and-tumble rivertown on the other side of the state and a mental universe away from Noxubee County. With no experience in an elected office, Fordice had long been active as a fundraiser in state Republican politics, where he strongly criticized and successfully challenged affirmative action programs, as well as minority and small business set-aside programs. Alan Huffman, the journalist and former Mabus aide, said of Fordice: "He's kind of like a mean-spirited Ronald Reagan."

Fordice, a big, snarling, barrel-chested man, delights in being a bull in a political china shop. This seems only to enhance his popularity with his core supporters—conservative working- and middle-class whites. In 1992, his first year in office, he took the first in a series of steps that alienated leaders of the state's nearly 40 percent black population, proclaiming that Mississippi would not change its flag, which includes the Confederate stars and bars in its upper-left-hand quadrant. He insisted that the Confederate emblem was not a segregation symbol, but that "it goes back to our beginning." (The statement was incorrect. Mississippi was founded as a state in 1817, and like all of the other Confederate states, it did not fly the stars and bars until the Civil War. The current Mississippi flag was designed in 1894.) Several months later, Fordice attracted international attention when, at the Republican governors' conference, with his party still reeling from the divisive 1990 national convention in Houston, he publicly celebrated the fact that the United States was a "Christian nation"—a statement taken by many as veiled anti-Semitism. He stood by his guns, not only refusing to retract the statement but publicly reaffirming it three years later. Fordice's bad relations with blacks steadily worsened, culminating with his 1994 state of the state address. Most black legislators walked out in the middle of his speech when the governor called for reducing the number of legislators, implementing public school–choice programs, and building more prisons—all suggestions seen as targeted against the state's African American population.

Fordice came to office with the votes of most of Noxubee County's whites, including all of PEON's key white members: the Blackwells, the Thomases, the Chancellors, the Harrises. They liked his affable, populist style (Mabus can seem a bit prissy and technocratic) and antigovernment political line. A priority of his first term was industrial development. He appointed a former Ole Miss star quarterback, Jimmy Heidel, a man known more for his good-naturedness than his sagacity, and set about looking for business. The Mabus approach, a disinterested search for a hazardous waste treatment and disposal option appropriate for Mississippi's needs, was history. In the uncritical economic calculus applied by Fordice's new administration, any business was good business. And his politics would not countenance claims of some new liberal cause like environmental racism. Fordice's election thus set PEON on a collision course with his new administration, and the governor's unequivocal support for a Mississippi hazardous waste operation further inflamed local disputes.

■ ■ ■ IN Noxubee County, the November 1991 elections had also been contentious. Ralph Higginbotham had been reelected to the board, with the vocal support of—and, it was rumored, money from—Hughes-FTI. When the board met the following January, Higginbotham was elected its president, by the now-familiar three-to-two vote, displacing Johnny Heard, an eighteen-year board veteran and its president for the last four. Heard staunchly opposed Hughes-FTI. The change had little substantive effect: the board's president is first among equals only. Symbolically, however, the shift was monumental. Higginbotham was the board's odd man out, as the sole white Hughes-FTI supporter and the only one from the hills. Here suddenly was a stubborn, inflexible man, a man who had hauled logs, yet had been chosen to serve as the county's highest elected official. And he was, indisputably, Hughes-FTI's man.

One of the first decisions of the Higginbotham-led board was not to renew the contract with its attorneys, Perkins & Gowan. It took the board a month to settle on a replacement. In the meantime, it was forced to revisit the sorest point in its recent history, namely, its exclusive endorsement for FTI. Even though the board's membership was unchanged, reelection meant that, legally, the board was different from the one with the same people on it that had endorsed FTI a year earlier.

At a late January board meeting on the endorsement, a

cadre of angry PEONs again held the supervisors' feet to the fire. It was the last meeting at which Tim Gowan was the board attorney. Presented with the endorsement again, Gowan wearily reiterated a familiar theme: "Me or my firm makes no recommendation in regards to this document at all." At their February 3 meeting, Higginbotham immediately raised the issue for a vote and tried, as he would often do again, to block discussion. The people did not need to be heard because, he said, the matter had already been discussed; everyone understood his subtext to be, "We have already decided." Crowding around the supervisors in the little meeting room, people began heckling, demanding to voice their objections. "Martha Blackwell, of PEON," the board minutes recorded, "made a presentation how most of the promises from waste companies have never been realized in other communities." Two other whites criticized the board for, respectively, perpetuating environmental racism and not considering carefully the possible advantages of USPCI compared to Hughes-FTI.

Supervisor by Default and Hughes-FTI consultant Ike Brown spoke in favor of the board renewing its endorsement. A white woman interjected that "the Governor of Tennessee said Hughes-FTI would never be licensed in that state." And then, once again, without missing a beat, George Robinson moved and Joseph Stevenson seconded to reendorse. The board voted, and by the wholly predictable three-to-two margin, Hughes-FTI again received their support.

The board replaced Tim Gowan with Wilbur Colom, of Columbus. Colom appeared to be the ideal choice. He is black and in Noxubee County was seen to be closely tied to what whites called the Ike Brown/Reecy Dickson machine, having been the board of education's lawyer during Dickson's term as superintendent and having defended both of them. Colom represented Brown against criminal charges for false pretenses in 1983 (the charge was dropped in a plea bargain). The same year, he was Dickson's attorney in the Corilla Stallings case, in which Dickson was accused of causing the then-pregnant Stallings to lose her child in a post–school board meeting melee, when Dickson allegedly shoved Stallings in the stomach with a folded metal chair (the case was dismissed at Stallings's request years later).

Colom is nothing if not an exquisitely and self-consciously well-crafted enigma. Now in his mid-forties, Colom had been jailed three times by the time he was seventeen for his involvement in civil rights struggles. On one of those occasions, Washington, D.C.'s future mayor, Marion Barry, bailed him out. The fourteen-year-old Colom refused to leave the Capitol until the stalwart segregationist and Boll Weevil Democrat, Mississippi's Representative Jamie Whitten (a congressman for a record-breaking fifty-three years), would speak with him. Afraid for the safety of their zealous son, his parents soon sent him north, to live in New York City with family until he finished high school. (Times *have* changed.) He went on to Howard University and then to Antioch Law School, one of the country's most intellectually tumultuous and left-leaning law academies.

Colom cuts a dapper figure. He is a tall, slender, light-skinned man with an appetite for fine clothes and Chippendale furniture; he is a sailor, a pilot, and one who clearly enjoys most of the pursuits celebrated in the pages of magazines like *Travel and Leisure.* Having returned to Mississippi as a lawyer, he had lost none of his zeal for social justice, but, as he became more prosperous, he also became a zealous crusader against big government and an enthusiastic supporter of unfettered free enterprise. In a state where the Republican Party had for generations been virtually nonexistent, he became one of its leading lights, and he serves on the state's central Republican committee.

The law offices he shares with his wife, Dorothy—now a state chancery court judge for the district covering Noxubee County—occupy a stately antebellum mansion. His home is also a fine antebellum edifice. (Columbus, the town where the boy who would become Tennessee Williams played as a child, escaped the ravages of Union troops and has a concentration of some of the state's best-preserved antebellum architecture.) The walls of the waiting area, in what was the main entrance hall to the columned mansion, are filled with testimonials—from youth leagues, political clubs, the local NAACP chapter—and photos of Colom and various Republican political worthies, from Mississippians like Trent Lott and Kirk Fordice, whom he has known since the late 1970s, to Ronald Reagan, George Bush, and Haley Barbour, the GOP national chairman.

When asked about his feelings for the former presidents, however, Colom had nothing but contempt. "Reagan is the worst president we ever had," he sneered, decrying him for abandoning his fiscal conservatism and dragging the nation deeper into debt. Yet Colom's law-office waiting room is plastered with memorials catching in photographic amber his smiles and warm handshakes with political luminaries he appears to hold in contempt.

In his first action as board attorney, Colom threw the board for a loop by insisting that they hire a consultant to do a comparative review of the benefits the waste companies were offering. He did this despite the vocal opposition of the usually taciturn Ralph Higginbotham.

On April 14, Les Range, a Columbus public policy researcher hired by Colom delivered "A Report on Host Community Compensation from Hazardous Waste Facilities," to the board. The Range report came to the conclusion, clothed in bland consultantspeak, that no company promised the county a good deal. Drawing on academic writing about both NIMBY siting issues and environmental racism, Range recommended that the board overhaul the "compensation program." He urged the board to hire independent engineers to review the company's permit applications, establish a hazardous waste authority to oversee their community involvement, and require financial assurances, including a $100,000 planning-phase fee, a $100,000 guarantee to pay for county environmental monitoring costs, and creation of a contingency fund to cover the cost of any default by the building contractor hired to develop the project. These were only the sums Range recommended the county demand *before* construction.

Once the operation was up and running, Range advised Noxubee County to insist on receiving tipping fees, host fees, garbage collection, property-value protection, insurance, and health care. He entreated the board to compel a permitted company to create a $2 million mitigation and remediation fund to cover the cost of any possible environmental damage. In short, like Gowan before him, Range counseled the board to get guarantees for what they were being promised, or, in Gowan's words: "$125,000 community center? Who you kiddin'? You can't build a good house for $125,000, even in Macon. It ain't no cheaper to build a house here than anywhere else."

Range's study inaugurated a period of tense relations between the board and Colom, who, against expectations, was too smart and independent to act as their toady. This uneasiness was reflected in a worried April 30 letter from Hughes-FTI lawyer and state Democratic stalwart John Maxey to Hughes-FTI's most loyal supervisor, Higginbotham. Maxey reported that Colom had called him on April 28 to ask if Hughes-FTI "would agree to renegotiate its agreement" with the board. Clearly agitated, Maxey began by detailing what he viewed as Colom's meddlesome activities. Maxey advised Higginbotham: "Until we can obtain clarification as to the accuracy of Mr. Colom's comments and whether it is truly the Board's desire to renegotiate . . . I request that you have your Board hold in abeyance any efforts by Mr. Colom to discuss renegotiation." Maxey then described Colom's comments and his reactions. Maxey recorded Colom's complaint that the $1 million and "other monetary commitments" pledged by Hughes-FTI were a " 'pittance' when compared with payments made by other companies to their host communities in other states" and that Hughes-FTI "took advantage of the 'ignorant' people of Noxubee County to enter into this 'sham' agreement."

Maxey complained that Colom had attacked the gimmickry of his client's proposals. "Mr. Colom also stated that he thought the Center for Environmental Optimization . . . was offered as [sic] gratuitous appeal to the County but was subject to being withdrawn after the permit was granted and that any promises to construct the CEO by Hughes-FTI were not 'binding.' " Maxey used the opportunity to repeat Hughes-FTI's promises, insisting that inquiries with unnamed "professionals familiar with almost all" U.S. hazardous waste facilities had confirmed his belief that no company had paid more generous amounts to a host community than those being offered to Noxubee County by Hughes-FTI.

Maxey then reiterated Hughes-FTI's economic promises, which still lacked the guarantees that Gowan, Range, and now Colom pushed for. Although Maxey assured Higginbotham that Hughes-FTI's investment would "result in payments to the county of over $1,300,000 each year," he did not say that this sum was merely an estimate of possible earnings, dependent on the company's projected volume of toxins that would enter Noxubee.

Maxey also alluded to Hughes-FTI promises that had not received wide circulation, such as Hughes-FTI's having "agreed" to pay the salary of a community center director at approximately $25,000. Moreover, Hughes-FTI's free lunches suddenly had a price tag: "I note in passing," Maxey added, "that outside of our contractual obligations, the company," and not the Ray Danner Foundation, as Mayor Brad Moore had officially reported to the Brooksville Board of Aldermen weeks before, "purchased a police car for Brooksville and has contributed over $100,000 to various civic organizations during" the past two years. As for Colom's "insulting" suggestion that the Center for Environmental Optimization could turn out to be no more than a public relations ruse concocted to elicit support, Maxey vowed, "It is the centerpiece of this project, and you may rest assured that it will take place."

Colom minced no words in denouncing what he saw as Maxey's manipulations. The Mississippi bar still respects courtly rules of professional courtesy, and Colom's response was exceptional for its accusatory tone. Maxey's "statement that I called the people of Noxubee County 'ignorant' is simply false," he wrote Higginbotham. "A lie. He is practicing the old art of deflection from the real issue, i.e. the inadequate compensation given the people of Noxubee for the exclusive endorsement. Mr. Maxey and FTI are determined to deal with Board members without legal counsel because it is in their best interest. They have, and plan to continue, to take advantage of their superior expertise and wealth."

Colom added, "Other conduct [by FTI] causes me even greater concern, because I believe they attempted to improperly influence me." Colom's daughter Nyani was then a student at Fisk University, the largely–black school in Nashville. In late 1991, she called her father and said, "Oh, I met this guy who was a friend of yours in Nashville." The "friend" was Francis Guess, a black man who works for the Danner Company, N∍therland's principal backer. Colom hardly knew him. His daughter reported that Guess had arranged for her to fly to Jackson for the Mississippi Black Caucus dinner, on the company's private plane, so that she could see her father. He asked his daughter not to go, and they had angry words. But she accepted the ride, and the company put her in a hotel suite and entertained her at their table. Maxey also contacted Colom and told him that a bond issue would be needed to help finance the project, suggesting that Colom, as the board attorney, might make hefty legal fees on the deal. "They were always inviting me to things and offering to make contributions to candidates I supported and offering to take me to Nashville to buy tables at dinners," said Colom.

Colom concluded his rebuke of Hughes-FTI with stern advice to Higginbotham, reflecting their uneasy relations: "It is dangerous for any board member to have the appearance of a close or 'partner-like' relationship with FTI." And that is exactly what had happened.

▪ ▪ ▪ GOWAN went unheard, Range's advice was neglected, and, for Hughes-FTI's adherents, Colom was causing an unwanted fuss. The board moved to kill the messenger. As Colom recalled, Maxey "tried to get me fired." For the rest of 1992, the word was that Hughes-FTI kept the pressure on the board to get rid of Colom, who was saved time and again by the ever-indecisive Joseph Stevenson, who abandoned Ralph Higginbotham and George Robinson, the sure Hughes-FTI loyalists.

■ ■ ■ AS Hughes-FTI consolidated its grip on Noxubee County politics, PEON's image problem became ever more serious. Its sixteen-member board was neatly proportioned: half white and half black. But aside from Essie Spencer and a couple of others, PEON lacked a vocal African American presence. Hughes-FTI's successful wooing of every single African American in the top tier of the county's elected offices, along with the untestable perception that Ike Brown brought with him large numbers of black supporters, left PEON looking like a wholly white opposition. Ike sneeringly derided Martha and the PEONs: "It seems strange to me that these people hollering racism just happen to be white."

It was hard to argue with him on that point. A handful of blacks were nominally involved with PEON, but none were laboring like Blackwell. In part, this was a function of economics. The Blackwells are not prosperous, but with a substantial family home and land, Blackwell has the luxury to stay at home. What paid work she does is part-time—clerking one day a week at the antiques store, baking breads and rolls at home for a list of steady customers, minding the catfish ponds on their property, or taking an occasional interior design job to remodel a room for a well-to-do matron in town. By contrast, most middle-class blacks—people like Essie Spencer's daughter, Darlene Cole, with mortgages to pay and pensions to collect—work full-time and did not have Martha's flexibility to devote blocks of time and energy.

PEON's vice-president, Bruce Brooks—a nice, gentle man in his early thirties who works at one of the local paper mills—is black. He is pleasant, but not a commanding pres-

ence. And most of the other blacks who supported the waste
fight were older women, many in their late sixties and seventies, unlikely to rally to the cause energetically. Darlene Cole
was one of the few young African Americans drawn into the
waste wars from early on, through both her mother and her
father-in-law, Willie Cole, a retired hospital orderly who had
been vocal, in his own gentlemanly way, in the mid-1980s
fight against Chem Waste. But Darlene Cole is shy and soft-
spoken to the point of inaudibility. She would not attract
supporters.

Then John Gibson's name "kept coming up." Martha
Blackwell recalled that he came to a January PEON meeting
about environmental racism. Gibson was then assistant superintendent of the public schools. As a teacher, he had been
closely allied with Reecy Dickson and had supported her in
her fractious, winning bid to become the school superintendent in 1979. It was hard to imagine that Gibson, a severe, humorless figure whose work and social life were
almost exclusively peopled by blacks, would readily align
himself with a white-dominated fight.

This changed in the late spring, when Damu Smith, a
slick, ambitious political activist who works out of Washington, D.C., for Greenpeace and the Southern Organizing
Committee, came through Noxubee County on a southern
swing of environmental justice organizing. His thin, handsome face framed by dreads, Smith is young, energetic, opin-
ionated, and friendly with key figures in the civil rights
establishment, people like Benjamin Chavis, who was then
still head of the United Church of Christ's Commission on
Racial Justice. He knows how to work a crowd of strangers
and is ever ready to boast about his ties to People in High
Places; his speech is heavily laden with the trendy language
of empowerment. Here was a young black man speaking out

against the waste dumps in areas heavily populated by blacks, dismissing the argument that any job is a good job. He and Gibson got on well.

Smith's appeal to Gibson was unsurprising. Gibson may live in a split-level home miles away from any town, out in the prairie east of Brooksville, but for him and many others, much of the isolation of rural life is a thing of the past. A satellite dish keeps his family regularly tuned into Black Entertainment Television; when I visited his lonely home one Easter morning, a repeat of *Tony Brown's Journal* was blaring from the set. Gibson became the spokesman for the black opposition before the year was out.

During Damu Smith's visit, Martha Blackwell had long discussions with him about environmental justice. It was an education for her about the interconnection of issues in the larger, continuing fight for civil rights—of the links between the quest for decent homes and safe jobs and environmental justice concerns. Martha's lesson was not without missteps. She said to him that at last this struggle offered "an issue important for blacks and whites, and he jumped all over me," excoriating her for not realizing that all of these issues were important to blacks and whites, that as a nation we stand or fall together. "I meant," she meekly corrected, "that it was an issue on which *both* blacks and whites could work together."

That spring, her education in the civil rights concerns of African Americans did not end with Smith. Blackwell spread PEON's word to black church and neighborhood groups across the South. I saw her in action once, at a Martin Luther King Day celebration in Columbia, Mississippi, in the southern part of the state. Columbia, with a large black population, is the site of a closed wood-preservatives-manufacturing plant now undergoing a $20 million toxic chemical cleanup after a 1977 explosion and fire (the cleanup began fully ten years after the explosion, during which time children played on the property amidst 4,500 barrels of toxic chemicals). Martha drove two and a half hours, farther than anyone else there, having promised her friend Charlotte Keyes, the founder of a group called JPAP—Jesus People against Pollution—that she would try to make it. There were only five other whites among the over 100 who had come to the dilapidated community center. And Blackwell was the most at ease of any of us moving through the crowd, hugging people, and catching up like she was at a family reunion.

■ ■ ■ THERE was a price for this activity. For months PEON members had worried that their movements were being monitored, and there was a solid basis for this paranoia.

In late December 1990, the state's Department of Environmental Quality began receiving anonymous complaints about Shuqualak Lumber Company, claiming that it was dumping open chemicals used to treat lumber or that runoff from its operations had killed nearby streams. The same thing had happened in 1986, when, following PEON's success against Chem Waste, great numbers of such complaints had been received, so many that Charlie Thomas finally had to call the department and ask them to stop harassing the company at taxpayers' expense, unless there was cause to believe that his operations were really causing an environmental hazard. The anonymous callers in 1990 were never identified, although subsequent events created suspicion that it was a Hughes-FTI partisan.

Soon thereafter, Linda Thomas swore that she spied a man she believed to be a private investigator surveying her house from the driveway. The Toxic Twins repeatedly felt they were being followed while driving around Jackson. Ralph Litterst, an outspoken PEON member born and raised in Chicago who retired to Noxubee County after a peripatetic career as a financial consultant, recalled being approached at a heated meeting of the Brooksville board called to discuss the waste company plans, in late 1990. At the end of the meeting, Bruce Rubman, a local man working for Hughes-FTI, approached him and asked if he saw himself as "a law-abiding citizen."

"Well, yes I do."

"Then why," Litterst remembers Rubman quizzing him, "are you running around with an outdated truck tag?" Litterst became upset. Was he being threatened? But Ed Netherland walked up and assured him that he was not being threatened, no one was tracking his movements.

Even Charles Chisholm, the head of the Mississippi Department of Environmental Quality's Office of Pollution Control, recalled a story that his movements had been watched. A friend of Chisholm's was approached by an unidentified waste company executive who reported that Chisholm had been seen at a Perkins Restaurant in north Jackson the previous Saturday morning, at seven o'clock, with a woman. The suggestion clearly was that he could be subjected to blackmail for infidelity.

It is hard to imagine a straighter arrow than Chisholm, whose imperturbable civil servant's mien, characterless gray suits, and polyester shirts suggest a man not given in the slightest to walking on the wild side. The most prominent feature in his windowless, climate-controlled DEQ office (as are all but a handful at the agency responsible for overseeing the *natural* environment) is an encyclopedia-volume-sized, leather-bound Bible, unostentatiously placed near him on a corner of his desk. "I was," he remembers responding, "at a Perkins Restaurant in north Jackson that Saturday morning, and I was with my wife." With characteristic rectitude, Chisholm claimed to have forgotten the source of the innuendo.

PEON members started sharing their suspicions that this sort of mild bullying and veiled threat masked a comprehensive surveillance plan. People dismissed the speculations as silly. But Hughes-FTI's partisans did begin maintaining surveillance lists—records of who said what to whom against Hughes-FTI, of overheard conversations and the most idle of gossip. And unbeknownst to Blackwell and her family, among other Hughes-FTI antagonists, their movements were being watched.

Bruce Rubman is a white man who, then in his late forties, was hired by Hughes-FTI to do work out of its Macon office. Rubman became the company's secret agent. His investigative work for Hughes-FTI had a fairly comic quality; the "Secret Investigative Reports" he prepared call to mind not so much James Bond as Maxwell Smart, the bumbling, inept television detective played by Don Adams on 1960s TV.

Rubman consistently referred to himself as "Reporting Agent"; his "Informers" were identified with a "C," as in classified, and then numbered: C-1, C-2, and so on. Rubman's report of a September 1991 surveillance trip ended with the deadpan note that "this report classified SECRET in order to protect ID of individuals and informers." By early January 1992, Rubman's investigations for Hughes-FTI became more organized and systematic. Investigation Reports transmogrified into one of two forms—"Collection/Intelligence Reports," or CIRs, and "Weekly Activity Reports," or WARs (in context, an acronym both risible and unnerving).

Rubman's WAR records evidence an edgy watchfulness out of all proportion to Noxubee County's somnolent landscapes. Rubman recorded his hourly meanderings, following the military clock. "*4 February.* 0800—Commenced security monitoring of area roads." Hughes-FTI's office became "HQ," and Rubman "telephonically" contacted "HdQtrs" for "info and inst." Nothing was above suspicion. "1140—Sighted and observed a small, single engine, top wing, white plane approaching Brooksville from a northeast direction." Rubman was not up to the task, however, and in his Keystone Cops fashion, dutifully recorded his failings. "Binoculars in trunk of car and could not get to them in time to get tail #." Still, he "stood by and observed flight area for approximately thirty-five minutes. Plane did not return."

Rubman's reports for Hughes-FTI could be dismissed as the laughable reveries of a man with too much time on his hands and an overextended imagination. But they deserve to be taken seriously. What begins as inept meddling can gather a menacing momentum all its own.

■ ■ ■ SUMMER came. Reporting agent Rubman's attention began to focus on more than unknown single-engine aircraft. He turned instead to individual PEON leaders. That June, he delivered a CIR "developed after receiving information pertaining to a waste dump located on Deerbrook Farm"—run by PEON's president, Jay Chancellor—"with possible hazardous waste being burned or buried at the sight [*sic*]." The report was accompanied by a detailed map of the farm, indicating the location of offices, fields, and the "waste dump," which consisted of a few open bottles of pesticides. Photographs of this "waste dump" would circulate around Jackson in months to come, supposed proof that the PEON "power structure" was not true to its own beliefs. As with the mid-1980s anonymous complaints about the Thomases' environmental violations, there was little substance to the charge that Deerbrook was a dirty, polluting business. The official record of environmental infractions by the hog and farming operation is virtually nonexistent.

Martha Blackwell was the next target for investigation, in July. Rubman's report, again "classified SECRET due to the sensitive collecting procedures" provided photographs taken at "1405" hours on July 1 that showed both an approach to the isolated farmhouse and a close frontal view, along with a map of the property. A barn burner could not ask for a more detailed guide.

Netherland later said that Rubman was hired to do "general intelligence." In the way of big corporations, Hughes would distance itself from these and other of Hughes-FTI's most raucous exploits. Usually its officials asserted their ignorance of Netherland's goings-on. David Barclay, Hughes's African American vice-president for workplace diversity who visited Noxubee several times to promote the project, claimed that he did not know, for example, that Hughes-FTI had passed out over seven hundred job applications, adding, "I would have some problems with that." Yet it is hard to believe that the company knew nothing of what was happening. In 1992, Hughes sent Luke Lineberry, a California engineer, to live in Noxubee County and act as its liaison there. Lineberry eventually left, claiming a need to be near his family, although another reason may have been that his exacting technocrat's style clashed with Netherland's more extravagant ways.

■ ■ ■ HUGHES-FTI's beneficence helped rumors fly around the county. Of the force of rumor in the Macon of his youth, Loyle Hairston once wrote: "In town human character was acutely scrutinized. Daily. Hourly. Tongues wagged, the gossip mill rolled, tempers flared and sometimes blows were struck, by neighbors or members of the same church!" This same rumor mill still lives in Noxubee County, fueled by mutual distrust and secretiveness that has so long characterized county life. Ralph Higginbotham was said to be undertaking elaborate home renovations and to have a new Lincoln Town Car; Macon alderman Richard Brooks, a retired schoolteacher, was alleged to have been seen driving around in a new Cadillac. No one, however, could remember having personally seen the renovations or the cars. Macon's mayor, Allen Hunter, heard it said that he had accepted $200,000, delivered to him in an "unmarked" suitcase.

As the hazardous waste fight continued, the rumors became increasingly salacious. At various times I was pulled aside and told with absolute authority, for instance, that one of the waste company executives was gay, and that a prominent white supporter of another company had been blackmailed into backing the company because of his "weakness" for black women. A company's public relations firm hinted that a woman active in PEON traveled to Jackson as a cover for her extramarital escapades. A prominent white businessman asserted that Ike Brown's machine was part of a national conspiracy funded by an organization called Genesis, a subterranean network that supposedly united black political leaders and gay white businessmen to change the face of U.S. politics. Outsiders were not exempt: halfway through researching this book, a rumor started up that I was a waste company operative masquerading as a writer on environmental subjects, trying to infiltrate the opposition. Amid this thicket of rumor, it became difficult to disentangle the real from the imagined. Martha Blackwell remembered being told that Ralph Higginbotham had received $75,000, but she added, "I can't remember if I dreamed that or not."

The rumors of Hughes-FTI payoffs were particularly striking for their extravagance—at a minimum, the supposedly corrupt official received a car or a stack of cash. In fact, where expectations are as meager as they are for most blacks and poor whites in Noxubee County, the price of someone's support may be small—a nice meal or several hundred dollars contributed to help rebuild an uninsured house that had burned to the ground. The exaggerated rumors, I concluded, were a way of avoiding self-criticism: surely a person could not be so dissatisfied with life here, could not feel so underappreciated and lacking respect as to endorse a toxic waste dump in exchange for the privilege of being taken out to a nice lunch.

Ed Netherland satisfied many people's long-suppressed needs to be recognized. When the girls' basketball team from Noxubee High won the state championships, Hughes-FTI paid for a luncheon banquet at the Oak Tree Inn. Richard Brooks served as "Master of Ceremony" for the event and delivered an encomium to the team's coach, Narvell Coleman, which he titled "A Biography of Success." Money for such things simply did not come from the county's white elite, who funneled their money into programs and special events for their own struggling private school and social clubs.

The waste executives' largesse also became a means to smooth over past psychological injuries and emotional hurts. Richard Brooks moved to Noxubee County from Meridian in 1964, during the height of the civil rights movement. When he moved to Noxubee County, however, it lacked the tumult spreading through the rest of the state, and he was happy for its relative peace and quiet. Nonetheless, bitter memories of past treatment continue to inform his actions. When a friend brought him to interview for a job teaching math, the school superintendent slowly examined him, Brooks remembered: "starting at my toes and moving on up, whereupon the white administrator asked, 'Where you got this damn nigger from?'" He remembers reprimands for wearing a white shirt and tie in town, and having to take off his hat when he passed a white man. As if in quiet defiance of that time, Brooks now is almost never without a hat—usually a worn, navy blue cap that he pulls down low over his brow, covering his fluffy nest of white hair.

Unsolicited stories like this inevitably crept into my conversations with middle-aged and older blacks in Noxubee County. The continued festering of these wounds of childhood and early adulthood was, I realized, directly related to the success of Hughes-FTI. Its sponsorship of a special luncheon not only provided an opportunity to celebrate the achievement of the local girls' basketball team but also provided a retired teacher a long-denied vehicle to shine in a public forum, and thereby prop up his own sense of self-worth. It was not Ike Brown who had turned himself into Noxubee County's version of the Chicago-style, ward-heeling politician, it was Ed Netherland.

In Netherland's recollection, the support from black leaders was hard won: "We were the first people ever to come in and ask for the support of the black community. At first the black community was stand-offish." His gifts, the triple-digit bills pressed into empty hands, were merely meant to show that he and his cronies "were there just to be the right kind of people." Recalled Netherland, "I treated them right, and they trusted me." With typical grandiloquence, Netherland later explained why he pressed on. Local whites said things to him like: "They're just animals. They shouldn't be allowed to vote." "These were comments that repulsed me," he averred.

■ ■ ■ AS Hughes-FTI's profile grew, relations between family and friends in Noxubee became more strained than ever when there was disagreement on hazardous waste. Essie Spencer and Eva Sherrod, best friends since childhood, agreed never to discuss the subject, lest it ruin their friendship. At DeWitt's Cafe, the owner would order customers to shut up when the subject arose. At Brooksville Baptist Church, the congregation was so divided that Hughes-FTI supporters sat on one side of the aisle and opponents on the other. Some people switched churches just to be away from the ugliness.

Relations among the supervisors had always superficially been cordial. But Johnny Heard and Ralph Higginbotham were suddenly at each other's throats—sometimes literally. On more than one occasion, people pulled the two grandfathers apart lest they come to blows. If any family came to symbolize the divisions brought by the conflict over hazardous waste, it was the Heards. Relations between Johnny and his brother Tiny (who, in Tiny's words, had been as "stout" as any pair of brothers in Noxubee) had become strained in the mid-1980s Chem Waste fight. These feelings escalated in 1990, when Tiny's son-in-law, Brad Moore, by then Brooksville's mayor, became one of Hughes-FTI's leading supporters. Johnny's wife, Peggy, was Brooksville's town clerk when Brad was elected. As emotions escalated over waste, so too did tensions between their families.

People said it had to do with money. Johnny's brood felt that Tiny and Brad only cared about a fast buck. For their part, Tiny and Brad despised what they deemed an unprogressive social attitude, or, as Moore astringently put it: "Wanna know how to make friends in Noxubee County? Go broke. Then you're a good ole boy." The families stopped speaking when, in mid-1992, Peggy lost her fifteen-year job as city clerk. The ostensible cause was a dispute about reading meters, a minor patronage job that could have gone to Peggy's brother and son. Moore made other arrangements and they "had conversation."

"I said, Miz Peggy, as long as you do your job, you can work for me," Moore recalled. In the recriminations that followed, the incident took on a Rashomon-like quality. Peggy Heard claimed the mayor had fired her because of disagreements over hazardous waste. Insisting that the decision had nothing to do with waste, Moore said that he had asked her to resign because they could not work together. With that, Johnny and Peggy's family stopped speaking to Brad, Tiny, and their families, a rift that has persisted to this day. The thing that Martha Blackwell's friend Laurie Flora had said on the first day of Martha's involvement, back in the fall of 1990, had become true. The county's fragile social fabric had been torn apart.

■ ■ ■ IN the early summer, PEON at last seemed to gather its stride in its race against Ed Netherland. The Mississippi Department of Environmental Quality issued draft regulations covering all aspects of siting a hazardous waste facility—from geology, its effect on natural resources, endangered species, and water supplies to its proximity to homes, schools, and churches. The draft also included a provision that would allow DEQ to grant a variance if the permit applicant demonstrated, "due to the nature of the surrounding area or structures," that no "unreasonable risk" existed to the environment or the public health and safety.

For PEON, the variance provision highlighted the extent to which, if finalized, the draft regulations could be manipulated to accommodate the purported need for a hazardous waste dump. John Crawford, the group's attorney in Jackson and the state's top environmental lawyer, had his minions working overtime for the Thomases. The monthly bills—regularly one or two thousand dollars a month—collected quickly.

With Crawford's help, the men with money behind PEON took a step that threatened to derail all of Hughes-FTI's plans. In late May, they formed Noxubee Minerals, solely for the purpose of buying mineral rights on the Martin Conrad ranch. The draft regulations prohibited siting a commercial hazardous waste facility on any property for which a company did not control the mineral rights.

Noxubee Minerals planned to buy mineral rights under the Conrad ranch, some of which were owned by a Cincinnati-based insurance company. The men raised $75,000 for the purpose and pledged that sum in a sealed bid delivered to the insurance company on June 2. A June 8 meeting was scheduled in Jackson, at which bids were to be opened. That day, Crawford arrived to learn that the amount of their bid had been disclosed to Hughes-FTI, which had entered a bid for an even $100,000. Upon learning of this prior disclosure, Crawford and his clients, frustrated and angry, walked out of the meeting. Hughes-FTI was the successful bidder.

Four days after Noxubee Minerals' unsuccessful attempt to buy a large block of mineral rights, Martha Blackwell again assumed her role as complainer and agitator.

Writing to other PEON supporters, she recited PEON's view of the sorry tale. Blackwell's fury unmasked the extent to which her views of Nice Men Wearing Suits had changed in eighteen months: "Even though we have been witness to many underhanded deals since we began this fight, it is still disheartening to see how Corporate America responds to large hazardous waste companies. In this case, all it took was twenty-five thousand extra dollars on their part—a drop in the bucket to a large insurance company."

In short order, however, the House That Ed Built began to develop some cracks. Noxubee Minerals succeeded in buying mineral rights to smaller portions of the Conrad ranch, and as a result, by the end of September Hughes-FTI announced that it would "reconfigure" slightly, meaning that the company would have to reduce the size of the proposed dump from a fifty-year capacity to a ten-year capacity. Company officials brushed this off as a necessary, short-term compromise. Yet this change meant that, for Noxubee County, the economic landscape had changed significantly. If dumping was assured for only ten years, the tax revenues the county was projected to receive would correspondingly dry up. Nonetheless, no one acted to revise the Hughes-FTI endorsements; acrimony had taken hold, and reason had been banished from the discussion.

■ ■ ■ MEANWHILE, USPCI was steadily gaining ground against its rival, largely by currying favor in Jackson. In early summer, state legislative lobbying figures were released. USPCI was the fifth-highest spender for the year beginning June 1991. By comparison, Hughes-FTI spent a little over a tenth as much. Ed Netherland observed that Printz Bolin's legislative connections with the new Republican administration, cemented while performing his duties in Washington as Mr. Congeniality for Senator Lott, were paying off for USPCI: "Statewide, it became Democratic versus Republican, just as it was white/black in the county."

And although Hughes-FTI, in the fashion of its extravagant leader, was widely seen as dispensing the most favors, USPCI had been doing its bit to keep up by building community support with a steady flow of public-spirited good works. By late summer, USPCI's money had been liberally spread throughout the county—a $3,200 computer "system" for the public high school and $3,000 to the county chamber of commerce. Summoning the racial demon that fires his followers' zeal, Ike Brown claimed that PEON and powerful white interests avoided criticizing USPCI. The list of USPCI's donations would have provided him with ample ammunition to support this claim. Smaller gifts were showered on the residents of tiny Shuqualak, which had not only refused Hughes-FTI an exclusive endorsement but still had the only white-controlled board of the three towns. USPCI was generous with everything from the all-white Junior Auxiliary and Dixie Youth League (the white Little League, for which Printz Bolin served as the commissioner) to the private school's Mother Goose Parade and a publication of the determinedly white-centric historical society. The amounts were often as low as fifty dollars and so could easily be dismissed as trivial, indications of nothing but benign goodwill. But the selectivity of its beneficence in the county's white-controlled enclaves was in its way just as calculated as was Netherland's play to be Father Christmas in the county's black sections.

PEON members *would* say that they at least admired USPCI for not using Hughes-FTI's tactics. But Martha Blackwell was absolutely clear about the situation: "Some people believe one might be better than the other. But we don't operate on that premise. There's no difference in those two companies except the tactics they use." The truth was that the PEONs felt beaten down, exhausted by Hughes-FTI's relentless onslaught; USPCI often escaped their attention because its operations were relatively quiet.

In fact, from the time Martha first contacted Greenpeace in 1990, they had warned her that USPCI was the one to worry about. Through her efforts, PEON began to put the spotlight on USPCI. In mid-November, they brought Clyde Peeling, an anti-USPCI crusader in Union County, Pennsylvania, to Noxubee County. Peeling has the curious distinction of making a living as the owner of Reptiland, two petting zoos for lovers of snakes, toads, and other scaly, cold-blooded animals. He is also a leader of a collection of grassroots groups in the Susquehanna Valley called Organizations United for the Environment (OUE), which has spent over a decade opposing USPCI's efforts to build a hazardous waste incinerator. With thousands of members, a six-figure annual budget, a permanent staff, a regular newsletter, and everything for sale from posters to its own anti-incineration cookbook, OUE is the envy of similar local efforts across the nation. Peeling's message was one PEON repeated for years to come: USPCI may be quieter in Mississippi than elsewhere; but once a waste company, always a waste company. That is, he told them, your lives and families are at risk. Do whatever you can to keep them away.

■ ■ ■ THE controversy slowly began to attract national attention. Environmental wire services and industry trade publications began running stories on the Noxubee waste fight. Reporters from Indiana covered the dispute involving the Indiana University Foundation; the *Atlanta Constitution*'s Adam Nossiter came to Macon and wrote a lengthy article describing the competition between the companies to court local support. But the most important change was that Sharon Stallworth, a reporter assigned to cover environmental matters for the business section of the *Clarion-Ledger*, began to focus on the events unfolding in Noxubee County. The *Clarion-Ledger*, the state's newspaper of record, is published in Jackson. In the heyday of Jim Crow it was considered "a benchmark of racial extremism." Through the 1970s it was turned around politically by an heir to the family-owned media empire; in 1983, the onetime segregationist screed sheet won a Pulitzer Prize for coverage of an ambitious educational reform act passed in 1982 under Governor William Winter.

Stallworth, a pretty, prematurely gray woman in her early thirties with an impatient, slightly confrontational air, hammered away at the Noxubee story. Her coverage focused not only on the scientific claims for hazardous waste disposal but also on a disinterested examination of everything from changing company promises and plans to the companies' heavy reliance on public relations machinery.

Like any other visitor to Noxubee, Stallworth was overcome with rumor and innuendo. People told her dozens of stories—all of them purportedly connected to hazardous waste. She began to dig beneath the surface of the reports, but it could have taken a lifetime to verify the torrent of information she was given. But the Noxubee rumor mill, physically and mentally far from the centers of power, fed on these stories and the continuing local intrigue. In the retelling, the stories were taken as evidence of an elaborate plot worthy of a thriller by Mississippi's famous native son, John Grisham.

Stallworth also recognized that the real decisions about hazardous waste were being made elsewhere. In Jackson, the companies continued to provide the regulators who would decide to issue a facility permit with detailed models and descriptions of their plans, gathered in dozens of three-inch thick binders that slowly filled two large bookcases. Stallworth began to investigate these materials as well as the stories of the wining and dining of legislators by waste company executives, and whisperings about closed-door meetings—such as that reported between Governor Fordice and Drew Lewis, the former U.S. transportation secretary and Union Pacific's chief executive officer.

■ ■ ■ IN the last four months of 1992, three crucial events occurred that shaped the direction of the rest of the Noxubee waste wars. First and most importantly, the racial composition of the opposition changed dramatically. An audible, distinctly African American voice finally emerged to counter Ike Brown's noisy declarations of what the "black community" wanted. The increased African American presence demonstrated that the views of the county's majority were more varied than had previously seemed to be the case. The involvement of John Gibson, the former Reecy Dickson supporter and assistant superintendent of education who had warily distanced himself from the white waste opponents, proved crucial.

Gibson's involvement increased after he went to an environmental justice conference sponsored by the Indiana students on the Bloomington campus in September 1992.

"I would have gone there in a minute," Blackwell recalled, "but we felt a black person had to go." Blackwell had a hard time getting Gibson to agree to be that person.

Gibson was busy; he shouldered most of the administrative responsibility for running the county's schools. And he was being encouraged to go by the daughter of a white planter, a woman who was sending her children to the all-white private school.

In the end, he relented and went. When he returned, the usually dour, heavy-lidded Gibson—who normally manages a crooked smile, at best—seemed to Blackwell a changed man. She used a preacher's language to describe him: "Indiana was a rebirth for John," she recalled. "He didn't have a clue what he was getting into, and came back on a spiritual high. He couldn't stop talking, he was so animated." Gibson became the spokesman for black opposition in Noxubee.

Gibson had sufficient gravitas to speak against Ike Brown and attract attention. His leadership was badly needed by the end of September, when the Indiana students secured a meeting with the university foundation's officials to protest the possible sale to Hughes-FTI. The meeting was to have included agents for Hughes-FTI—in the persons of the state representative Tyrone Ellis and Macon alderman Richard Brooks. In the two days preceding the Wednesday meeting, however, flyers began appearing around the Bloomington campus that denounced the foundation's actions and criticized it for environmental genocide. They were printed in the style of nineteenth-century legal placards—in big, chunky letters, all in block capitals. One of them luridly announced that a "public sale of negroes" was to take place, with the "entire black communities of Macon and Brooksville auctioned off to the highest bidder." A second, "open letter to FTI and the IU Foundation" read: "THANK YOU FOR HELPING US TO DESTROY THE INFERIOR NIGGER RACE. WE NEVER WOULD HAVE THOUGHT OF SUCH A SLOW AND

AGONIZING GENOCIDE AS POISONING THE ENTIRE COMMUNITY WITH
TOXIC WASTE. WE ADMIRE YOUR INGENUITY. GOD BLESS THE US OF A!
SINCERELY, THE KU KLUX KLAN."

No student or campus group took responsibility for the
flyers equating the Noxubee fight with slavery.

Flyers that may have fueled the wrath of student
protestors had the reverse effect when faxed to Mississippi.
The revulsion felt by Tyrone Ellis and Richard Brooks was
profound. Ellis denounced the "ugly, vicious statements." A
more composed Brooks dismissed them as "an inappropriate
and tasteless method to gain attention." Brooks, who felt a
particular allegiance to Indiana because one of his sons had
earned a doctorate in endocrinology there, bristled at the
characterization of local blacks as manipulable. He complained that the student newspaper had "implied the black
community was ignorant and illiterate and didn't know what
they were doing."

Brooks concluded by dismissing the environmental
racism complaints. "Any environmental racism was already
here because of the fact that we have a solid waste dump in
an all-black neighborhood," referring to the Pineywoods
neighborhood on Macon's grim northwestern side. "You
can't hardly sit on the porch in the summertime." Brooks
and Ellis refused to go meet with the students; no one from
Hughes-FTI was there.

The environmental racism claims clearly had Hughes-
FTI and its supporters on the defensive. Hughes-FTI circulated a confidential memorandum that read more like a battle
plan than directions for a public relations campaign. " 'Inoc-
ulate' select audiences to minimize attention to claims of environmental racism," it instructed. Ways to do this would
vary, the memo advised Hughes-FTI partisans, depending
on the audience. For example, "minority leaders" should be

trained to say the following: " 'Notice the only people claiming 'environmental racism' are upper middle class white
people. The very same people who 20 years ago did not want
you in their schools.' " Elected officials and the news media
were to be told, by contrast, that Hughes-FTI was being vic-
timized by the very practices they hoped minority leaders
would employ: " 'These claims of environmental racism are
a prime example of race baiting—further emotionalizing an
already controversial issue. It's a convenient and 'politically-
correct' way for our opposition to dilute the issue.' " At frequent small-group meetings with minority clergy, teachers,
and law enforcement officials, Hughes-FTI partisans should
assure that "the lines of communication remain open" and
thereby "monitor and neutralize the efforts of outside agitators and insurgents to dilute the support base." In the context of a Mississippi political and social struggle, references
to "outside agitators and insurgents" recalls the opposition
to the 1960s Freedom Riders and civil rights activists.
Hughes-FTI thus cleverly tapped into this rhetorical tradition, inverting it for use by historically powerless blacks.

■ ■ ■ TWO weeks later, after the Indiana fiasco, Richard
Brooks engineered a remarkable act. On October 9, 1992, a
special meeting of the county's NAACP chapter was called.
The Noxubee NAACP has never been a hotbed of activism.
Although the national organization was founded in 1910,
the Noxubee chapter, like many others in the rural South, is
of relatively recent vintage, formed only in July 1969. Today
it is, for much of the year, more a retired men's club than
anything else. About a dozen men attended the October
meeting; the entire membership was not notified. Brooks
and Ike Brown, in his role as the chapter's "Second Vice

President," presented the group with a resolution denouncing the charges that Hughes-FTI was engaging in any environmental racism. The resolution was endorsed by everyone but Willie Cole, Darlene Cole's father-in-law. It declared "the issue of environmental racism to be inappropriate and have [*sic*] no connection with" Hughes-FTI's project.

The document allowed that allegations of environmental racism were "serious concerns requiring thorough and diligent investigation and, therefore, we have, through our members conducted [an] . . . investigation of the methods and practices of companies proposing to build hazardous waste facilities. . . ." But only Hughes-FTI had "fully informed and involved African-American citizens of this county in both the development of its proposed facility and in the role the company should take as a corporate citizen in this community." USPCI, by contrast, was seen as "likely to continue and be an instrument of the traditional oppression of African-American people within Noxubee County."

The resolution also introduced a tactic not previously seen in the Noxubee waste wars, at least not publicly. To be exact, it descended to the level of ad hominem attack:

We have ascertained that the only allegations of 'environmental racism' in connection with the activities [of Hughes-FTI] have been promoted by John Gibson, Assistant Superintendent of Education, and Martha Blackwell, spokeswoman for an organization which calls itself Protect the Environment of Noxubee ('PEON') and it is our judgment that neither John Gibson, an unelected county official, nor the PEON group has the best interest of the county, or its African-American citizenry at heart.

PEON, the resolution explained, was a group "formed and directed by a group of white business owners who, acting in concert, attempted to keep African-American citizens in Noxubee County socially and economically oppressed since the passage of the 1964 Civil Rights Act, and before, and has never taken an active role in promoting the advancement or well being or insuring the environmental safety of African-American citizens." Some of PEON's members have "in their businesses, exposed African-American citizens to environmental hazards with no regard of their well being."

The resolution amounted to one of the most incredible turns in the Noxubee waste wars. Here was the local branch of the nation's most established, staid African American civil rights organization, taking a position on the issue of environmental justice directly antithetical to that of nearly every other major civil rights group. And the tactic served no one's purposes better than Ed Netherland's. Defending his activities to a national environmental group, Netherland insisted: any claim that Hughes-FTI's "proposed site unfairly burdens African-American residents of Noxubee County" would be "totally misleading. The Noxubee County chapter of the NAACP, the nation's leading advocacy group for African-Americans, has exclusively endorsed" Hughes-FTI. The resolution's deft phrasing, linking the decision of a handful of the members of a sleepy local chapter to the reflected glory of the organization of W. E. B. DuBois and, closer to home, of Medgar Evers, was a classic sleight of hand.

In Noxubee County, few people knew of the resolution's existence. Eighteen months after it had been signed, a school board member and decades-long NAACP supporter professed never to have heard about the resolution. Adessa Bradley, the woman who for thirty-six years has directed the black office of the county's funeral home, similarly insisted that she "knew nothing about it." "We are talking," she added, her rich contralto booming out, "about a *few* local people." Essie Spencer dismissed it in characteristically pungent fashion: "The national branch of the NAACP is suppotin' us 100 percent. . . . and that little branch is ten peoples, 'cause when they drew up the resolution, somebody drew it up for them, and they called only the peoples that were members that they thought would pass it!"

Richard Brooks authored the NAACP resolution with Ben Tubb, Netherland's top local employee, and a white man. The pair then turned it over to Hughes-FTI's lawyers and public relations minions to be gussied up for wide distribution. Its pithy, tightly drafted clauses ("WHEREAS, we have concluded, based upon this investigation and our perception of recent events, that a much more serious form of racism exists in the paternalistic attitude exhibited by the PEON group and white business owners in Noxubee County") and its legalisms (such as Hughes-FTI's "responsiveness to the interests and concerns" of blacks, suggesting "a high likelihood that it would protect and be responsive to the concerns, including but not limited to environmental concerns") are not the sort of locutions commonly uttered in Noxubee County, even by a retired teacher.

Within the county, an important consequence of the resolution was to galvanize local black opposition to the waste companies. It prompted John Gibson and Essie Spencer to incorporate the African-American Committee for Environmental Justice of Noxubee County, which became simply AAEJ. AAEJ shot back with its own resolution. It avoided personal attacks on NAACP members, focusing instead mostly on the implications of the hazardous waste siting. The resolution reflected Gibson's surge of interest in and new knowledge about the environmental justice cause. It demanded that Noxubee County not become another Emelle, Alabama, or Columbia, Mississippi, or another "Cancer Alley," the grim nickname given to the black-populated corridor between Baton Rouge and New Orleans clogged with over 125 petrochemical plants.

Although the AAEJ resolution censured as "deplorable and extremely insensitive" the fact "that nine members of a local NAACP organization tainted the reputation of that prestigious [body] by endorsing Hughes-FTI's hazardous waste incinerator which threatens to poison our community with dangerous chemicals," its real targets were unidentified, menacing forces. It thus lauded those African Americans "with the courage to oppose the location of the incinerator" who had "been the target of intimidation, ridicule and slander by agents of FTI/Hughes and clandestine individuals with blind visions and vested interests," a reference understood by everyone in Noxubee as a reference to Ike Brown. The statement was strikingly self-congratulatory. John Gibson—the resolution's principal author—and Essie Spencer were the primary black targets of ridicule. The document neglected to defend others who had been pilloried, above all Martha Blackwell. Not only had she labored to involve Gibson, enduring more withering personal attacks far longer than he, but she had been the only other person denounced in the NAACP resolution.

The resolution also drew on the always volatile and ever dependable, if imprecise and distorting, suggestion that environmental injustice is but a new form of familiar oppression. Thus, "the location of a hazardous waste incinerator in predominantly African-American communities is the 1990s equivalent of the burning cross as a symbol of racism," and FTI/Hughes' attempt "to impose dominance over the economy and government of Noxubee County itself is just a disguised reversion to a new form of the sharecropper system." This rhetoric thus both articulated a new variant of the white "power structure" explanation of Noxubee's victimization and reflected lessons Gibson had learned from the activists he had met since his September trip to Bloomington. The angry images also underscored the impossibility of concerted action between Noxubee's whites and blacks, a reality mirrored in the personality and behavior of John Gibson himself.

Gibson, who has a prickly, rather didactic manner, said: "The solution is biblical. Until as people we are willing to trust or not look at race, until we bridge that gap, we will be divided." Yet for all this noble rhetoric, Gibson's actions—as evidenced by the resolution he drafted—betrayed an unwillingness to trust or look beyond race every bit as rigid that of the county's white segregationists. Where Ike Brown readily worked with and for whites in the service of his realpolitik, Gibson resisted. Gibson repeatedly distanced himself from PEON; unlike Essie Spencer, he disclaimed membership in the mostly white group. He always remained Mister Gibson to whites—even to Martha Blackwell (whom he called "Margaret")—thus inverting a small but symbolically powerful tyranny, gaining the particular satisfaction of being Mister-ed by whites while addressing them by their given names.

Gibson would say that it was necessary to form a black environmental organization separate and apart from PEON because "everything got to be a black/white issue." One of PEON's big problems, he explained, "was that it had no black officers. It would look like we were controlled by whites. And we didn't want to be labeled." But half of PEON's board, including its vice president, were black. The real reason for forming the separate group lies in the vitality of 150 years' worth of suspicion, division, and resentment, plus a refusal to work cooperatively for any goal.

For Gibson and many others like him, the inability to heed his own words and look beyond race resulted from his mixed frustration and barely concealed anger at the state of the schools. The "key to unity," he told me, "is education. A mistake was made in 1969 when schools officially integrated and private academies opened up. Big industry comes from the outside, sees schools divided and says, 'No thank you.' This sends a message that the merit of each is not valued."

Gibson's explanation then took an interesting turn, suggesting his own politics of racial separation. "Blacks came together over Reecy Dickson's election, but she ostracized the white community and then started alienating blacks. Then blacks got together to get her out." In all of this wrangling, he explained, "whites conceded" that they could not win anymore, and "we've been on an upward swing since then."

In the stinking water of the county's political life, most whites were equally wary of Gibson. When asked about the role of blacks in the waste struggles, whites offered judgments that, for their patronizing tone and evident lack of familiarity with the county's black elite, might as well have been uttered in 1953 as in 1993. As one of the key men in PEON said to me, "Do you know John Gibson? He's a *nice* black man." A nice black man: a bland judgment about someone casually encountered. There it was, once again, "that boundary."

The AAEJ resolution had minimal effect. Like PEON, AAEJ was an organization without an established constituency. Scarcely anyone in Noxubee knew of it, and most of those who did were white. In keeping with the usual order of things, whites were often hard-pressed to remember its name—"whatever-they-call-it over there in Brooksville," people would say. The "they" apparently meant John Gibson, who lives near Noxubee's northernmost town. Even Willie Cole—who cast the single vote against endorsing Hughes-FTI at the October 9 NAACP meeting—had not heard of AAEJ or its resolution two years after its formation. And his daughter-in-law Darlene was one of its nominal founders.

■ ■ ■ THE second pivotal event in late 1992 was the inauguration of the Pollution Solution, a scheme devised by a skinny white showman and sometime political organizer named Stan Flint, who runs a racetrack in Birmingham, Alabama. Jointly funded by Chem Waste and most of Mississippi's environmental groups—including PEON—the Pollution Solution was a loose affiliation of groups opposing a hazardous waste operation in the state. Its primary activity was to mount a month-long, glossy, antiwaste media blitz under the slogan "Don't Dump on Mississippi," the goal of which was to convince the intractable Fordice and his powerful legislative allies not to build an in-state toxic dump and incinerator. The campaign cost over $100,000.

The Pollution Solution was born out of Governor Fordice's inexplicable refusal to consider Chem Waste's October 29 offer to handle all of Mississippi's toxic trash for the next twenty years, either at Emelle or at any of its thirty other treatment and disposal operations nationwide. The company was visibly worried about the competition from a possible toxic dump across the Mississippi border from Emelle. Fordice refused to meet and discuss the plan. Momentum in Jackson for an in-state facility—as if it were a big, prestigious and job-generating operation like a car or airplane plant—had gained among state businesses, who were pressuring legislators to site an in-state facility. Despite the Supreme Court's ruling in the Alabama case that states could not impose limitations on the interstate shipment of wastes, Mississippi manufacturers' representatives ominously warned that other methods would be devised to leave them without access to disposal sites. They were encouraged to sound these dire warnings by an abundance of waste company lobbyists prowling the capitol throughout 1992 and 1993. (Many longtime watchers of state politics said that the lobbying onslaught in those years was unprecedented. From June 1992 through May 1993, for example, waste company lobbyists together reported over one-tenth of all expenditures for legislative lobbying in Mississippi.)

As in Noxubee County when the boards endorsed FTI and later Hughes-FTI, unsupported rumors of payoffs to the governor and various legislators were thick on the ground in Jackson. How, one unpaid lobbyist for a national environmental group asked, could a prominent state senator and Fordice confidante with no other visible means of support acquire a new car, send his three kids to private school, and buy a new house if he had not been bought off by a waste company operative instructing the politician to oppose Chem Waste's offer? (His query was prompted by the knowledge that a Mississippi legislator earns only $10,000 a year, plus legislative expenses.)

For the Fordice administration, a waste dump or incinerator was a sign of industrial progress. The argument was a simple-minded one, as Martha Blackwell tried to make clear in endless public statements. The rest of the country was deciding to try and curb the expansion of such facilities. Even if this were not the case, she would add, the suggestion that her rural, heavily agricultural state needed a facility to handle its own hazardous wastes was pernicious and misleading. One generator, Chevron, was responsible for over three-fourths of Mississippi's hazardous waste, at a plant in Pascagoula, on the Gulf Coast. In fact, the vast majority of the state's potentially poisonous material was being created on the gulf, far from places like Noxubee County. This fact called into question the notion of a national hazardous waste policy focused on individual *states'* disposal capacities, rather than focusing on *regional* waste production across state lines. Furthermore, over 95 percent of Mississippi's toxic trash was being treated on site (roughly the national average), and a significant portion of the 43,000 tons not treated on site consisted of liquid or other "specialty" wastes that could neither be landfilled nor incinerated. Thus, she argued, only about 1,600 tons were suitable for dumping in the sort of facility proposed for Noxubee County—or less than 1 percent of Mississippi's total. In short, with Hughes-FTI and USPCI proposing to handle between 200,000 and 390,000 tons a year, it was absurd to advocate a megadump and toxic burner on the grounds that they were needed to serve the needs of Mississippi industry. In the insular world of Mississippi state politics, however, the manufacturers' view, supported by the governor and his powerful legislative allies, continued to hold sway. Few listened to a woman regularly described as "well-meaning but misguided."

The Pollution Solution was a calculated effort to be heard above the chorus of waste industry lobbyists who commanded the capitol's attention. For PEON, which sent busloads of people to Jackson for a December 17 Pollution Solution rally on the capitol steps, the campaign proved to be a permanent tactical albatross because of the association with Chem Waste. Other waste companies exploited this association ruthlessly, thereafter labeling their opponents "the Chem Waste Coalition." For Martha and her PEON associates, the Pollution Solution proved to be "an unholy alliance," one that they would regret for years to come. But in the face of the waste companies' financial muscle, the unholy alliance seemed necessary at the time. As Louie Miller, the Sierra Club's legislative director for Mississippi, defensively explained: "Basically, where we are is that I've got the clothespin on my nose. There is the largest landfill in the world only a few miles from our state line, and it's owned by Chem Waste. Why, in God's name, would we want to site a megafacility in our state?"

Governor Fordice's refusal to consider the merits of Chem Waste's proposal, and his minions' eagerness to characterize the PEONs as tools of Chem Waste, inaugurated a period of sour relations between the Noxubee waste opponents and their bull-headed monarch. Relations quickly worsened. By January 1993, PEON's leaders took what in retrospect was perhaps the most decisive step in the Noxubee waste wars: they sued the governor.

PEON's activities leading to this decision constituted the third centrally important event in the last months of 1992.

■ ■ ■ ON December 1, Jay Chancellor and Charlie, Linda, Bill, and Peggy Thomas sought to have a body known as the Environmental Protection Council declared unconstitutional. A twelve-member body composed wholly of legislators, it was the council's charge to recommend to the governor both a hazardous waste capacity assurance plan and hazardous waste disposal categories (that is, incineration, as opposed to dumping or other methods). Arguing that the EPC would thus exercise an executive, and not a legislative, function, the PEON leadership declared that its recommendations would constitute a violation of constitutional separation-of-powers requirements. The Thomases, Chancellor, and their lawyer, John Crawford, sought to challenge both the EPC's substantive mission and its alleged failure to comply with state public hearings procedures. They claimed that the fifteen-day advance notice of a public hearing on the EPC recommendations was insufficient and in violation of state law. The PEON leadership's real worry was that the EPC appeared poised to urge the choice of Noxubee County as the site of a huge hazardous waste dump and incinerator. Charlie was very clear about the purpose of their tactics challenging the EPC and its procedures. The name of the game was to try and delay the permitting process: "If we wait a little while, we will at least know what direction EPA wants us to go in."

The attorney general refused to attack the constitutionality of the EPC or challenge its alleged violations of state public notice and meeting requirements. On December 11, 1992, Chancellor and the Thomases therefore filed their own suit, on a technicality: they said the public needed at least thirty days to prepare for a public hearing. Legal wrangling and the impending Christmas holidays pushed the matter over for consideration by the court until late February 1993. But on January 6, 1993, with no notice to anyone, Fordice tried to silence the PEON challenge by sending a Mississippi capacity assurance plan (CAP) to the EPA Chief Administrator, William Reilly; it included the promise to build an instate hazardous waste facility. His action directly contradicted his December promise not to submit a CAP until after he had reviewed the EPC suggestions. In fact, the CAP Fordice submitted to the EPA was nearly identical to the

EPC's draft recommendations. The governor was condemned throughout the state. The Gulfport-Biloxi paper, the *Sun Herald*, for example, denounced "the strong odor emanating from Gov. Kirk Fordice's notification to federal officials," castigating the self-styled populist for refusing to say who had prepared his plan and why he had gone back on his word to wait for the EPC's recommendations. No wonder that Fordice's autocratic executive style quickly earned him the sobriquet "Captain Kirk", as if Mississippi was his own starship *Enterprise*.

Fordice's complete disregard for the political wrangling over waste in the state courts and legislature is not without its ironies. Just a few months earlier, the governor had grandly announced his "TEAM Mississippi" campaign. His aim, he said with the mix of entrepreneurial can-do-ism and sanctimonious preachiness that is his hallmark, was to "prove that Mississippians do give a hoot about their government. There's a widespread perception that they don't." Explaining the aim of TEAM Mississippi, Fordice allowed: "It won't work unless the people are a Godly, moral people who can handle freedom. I think the lack of that is the cause of our problems." Yet he treated the PEON leaders' involvement in the statewide hazardous waste conversation, a clear demonstration that they cared about the direction of state government, with total contempt. Clearly, Captain Kirk did not have in mind the kind of mutinous opposition to his governance that originated in Noxubee in the early winter of 1992. This critical misstep provided the PEON leadership with the opening they needed. On January 28, 1993, Fordice was added as a party to the Thomas and Chancellor lawsuit. The PEON leaders claimed in the lawsuit that Fordice had violated state law by sending his CAP to the EPA without any public discussion or review. As an "administrative

9
TWILIGHT OF
THE WHITES

I F 1992 WAS THE STRANG-
est year in the Noxubee waste
wars, 1993 was the most mo-
mentous. The events of that year were extraordinary because
the local showdown between waste opponents and the companies and their supporters, an event that seemed almost
certain at the year's beginning, never happened. Larger political events intervened, multinational corporate actors
stepped in to protect their interests, and changes in the local
political landscape again heightened the mutual distrust and
suspicion that dominate county life.

The year hardly started out this way. In the first six
months of 1993, PEON reached the peak of its local influence. Not only was it beginning to attract black support, but

Martha Blackwell's growing organizational skill and the litigation muscle flexed by its top leadership also contributed to its strength.

Simultaneously, in early 1993, Hughes-FTI's Noxubee dominance looked unbeatable. Netherland was at the top of his salesman's powers; having fashioned himself into the role of hazardous waste visionary, his promises became ever grander. The week after Governor Fordice submitted his CAP, Netherland told a Rotary Club in Starkville that Hughes-FTI would be permitted to begin construction by the first of May. In early February, he announced that the company's operations would move from Tennessee to Jackson because of the "work ethic" of the Mississippi labor force (that familiar euphemism for job-hungry people who will work long hours for low wages and poor benefits); the move would bring, he promised, an annual benefit to the Jackson economy of $3 million to $4 million. This was not his only overreaching promise. In November 1990, he had promised that his efforts would bring 180 jobs and an annual payroll of more than $4.5 million for a project that would cost $60 million. By late 1992, Netherland's promises virtually doubled. Hughes-FTI officials now promised the creation of as many as 400 jobs (the number quoted was sometimes as high as 450) for a $150 million project, with a payroll estimated at between $9 million and $10 million. Company officials were more likely to stress their prediction that their average wage would be twelve dollars an hour, rather than the promise that the minimum wage would be seven dollars an hour. The only figure that remained constant was the promise of $10 million in associated goods and services.

Netherland's promises as to how much waste his facility would handle also soared. (Higher volumes, of course, mean increased tax revenues.) In 1990, Netherland had promised that FTI would handle 50,000 tons of hazardous incinerables and an always unspecified volume of landfillable hazardous waste. By early 1993, Hughes-FTI was reported to be planning annually to burn 50,000 tons and to bury another 340,000 tons of hazardous waste, with no scrutiny as to the national need for such capacity (the combined figure was twice the volume USPCI proposed to accept). Sometimes, the volume Hughes-FTI officials promised to burn and bury was as much as 450,000 tons a year, which would make the proposed facility one of the largest in the nation, nearly as active as Emelle—*if* they could get the toxic trash to handle. The degree to which these projections went unchallenged—because people wanted to believe them—is a testament to Netherland's skill.

■ ■ ■ THE governor's January 1993 surprise—his attempt to hasten the toxic dump permitting process without public involvement—helped galvanize the Noxubee County opposition. Suddenly, the likelihood of a dump and incinerator seemed imminent. Blacks and whites began meeting together more frequently, often crowding around Martha Blackwell's old oak dining table or seated along the elaborately carved Victorian couches in her narrow sitting room. The Toxic Twins and their husbands began to organize evening fundraisers once a month at the board room of the Merchants & Farmers Bank, where the region's deeper pockets were pressed for contributions to sustain the litigation. And nearly two and a half years after Martha first became involved in fighting waste, Noxubee's waste opponents planned their first public rally.

PEON and AAEJ jointly sponsored the rally, although,

as usual, the organization of it fell largely to a handful of women: Martha, Essie Spencer, Darlene Cole, and Gerry Harris. With characteristic decorousness, Martha wrote to supporters. By contrast to the neck-grabbing terror tactics used by Carol Puckett and company in Tennessee, Martha's letter could have been an invitation to a church social. "We are planning to meet outdoors on the Courthouse lawn, weather permitting, so please bring a lawnchair or blanket. A simple lunch will be served for $2.50 each." Essie Spencer circulated a more piquantly worded notice, declaring that the waste struggle represented "a challenge that will end up as life or death." She warned that the situation facing the county repeated age-old struggles: "African Americans and other minorities have always been faced with racism. Now instead of hanging us from a tree, they are using high-tech genocide. We cannot knowingly let this happen. There is unity in numbers. . . . People are putting aside their differences and joining together to keep the DREAM from becoming a NIGHTMARE. Noxubee County needs your support on April 3rd. We will be having a rally at the courthouse in Macon starting at 10:00 a.m."

Martha stayed up most of Friday night before the rally to finalize the plans. On Saturday morning, she rose early and went to the courthouse, where she finished the bulk of the antiwaste signs in her bold, sure handwriting ("OFFICIALS, YOUR TIME IS UP," "GO HOME, ED—LEAVE HOME, PRINTZ," "SAY *NO* TO *1400* TRUCKS A MONTH.") and tacking them to plywood slats. Where in Giles County such signs had been prepared by a group drawn from a cross-section of the community, the vast majority of the placards seen outside the courthouse that Saturday were Martha's handiwork. She may have been able to get people to come to meetings, but the willingness to cooperate in Noxubee extended only so far. A white

Brooksville woman and her daughter—neither of them Nox-ubee natives—did help by fashioning two banners on big sheets of light-blue plastic tarp, each about six by eighteen feet. The signs spelled out ominous messages with white duct tape; one unintentionally made an apt literary reference to Henrik Ibsen's play about the danger to a community that neglects the threat of pollution: "OFFICIALS WHO SUPPORT HAZ-ARDOUS WASTE DUMPS ARE **ENEMIES OF THE PEOPLE.** ELECTION DAY IS COMING."

One of the tarps was anchored in front of fourteen hundred plywood blocks, each about the size of a brick. The blocks snaked around the scrubby buffalo-grass lawn in front of the courthouse. About every twelfth block had a band of blue tape across its top, and the tarp bore the words: "1350 TRUCKS/MO. ONLY 158 OF THESE ARE FROM MISSISSIPPI. WHO'S BEING DUMPED ON?" John Gibson provided exhibits on waste minimization done as projects for high school science, and they were set up on boards out in front. Someone brought a trailer to serve as a platform, and by early morning Martha and students over from Starkville and down from Blooming-ton, along with organizers from Greenpeace and the South-ern Organizing Committee in New Orleans and Atlanta, were busy arranging chairs and lining up the endless piles of wooden blocks.

It was one of those glorious early spring days that draw people to the Sun Belt. The magnolias were just coming into bloom, and the large oaks framing the parking lot between the courthouse and the old jail-turned-library had just be-gun to leaf.

By 9:30, people began dribbling in, whites and blacks sitting in little pockets among their own. A group of Choc-taw men wearing synthetic simulacra of their traditional beaded and fringed tunics gathered at a distance from the crowd and stood in a circle, turned inward but not speaking. They had come to support PEON, just as they had promised when Linda Thomas, Martha Blackwell, and others had marched with them on the reservation in Philadelphia against National Disposal Systems two years before.

Shortly after ten o'clock, John Gibson began the rally for a crowd of about 100. He opened by praising at length the achievement of the local public schools in producing the state girls' basketball champions. There it was from the start: Gibson's slightly resentful, divisive, racially conscious note—celebrating what *we* are able to achieve, without your support. "This is beautiful agricultural land, and we wanna keep it." Gibson's sleepy manner did little to enliven the group. Kaye Kiker, the hefty, white anti–Chem Waste activist from Sumter County, Alabama, spoke next. "My family has been in Sumter County for 150 years. People are poor in the South, and you know you're poor when you have the best geology. Then you just become nothin' but a glorified catbox!" The crowd was beginning to warm up. A couple of older black women spoke up from the back.

"Say so! Say so!"

"Tell 'em, girl."

Kiker continued. "My county has lost population, youth, its largest employers because of the Chem Waste dump. The eyes of the nation are on this issue." (Claims Chem Waste denies.)

A cool breeze was blowing. A couple of girls from the high school got up to sing religious songs in their strong, lyrical voices. LaTanya Stevenson, a sleek, dark, striking girl with an earthy soprano, riffed on a tune of her own invention. "FTI will destroy your mah-ah-ah-ah-ahnd," she wailed. And then she got the crowd clapping rhythmically and chanting over and over again: "If you think you can do it, you can do it, you can do it." The entire morning was like this, drifting between angry denunciations of local deals with the lords of waste, bemoaning national indifference to their plight, and having inspirational interludes that show-cased local talent.

Sister Gloria Jones, a black evangelist who had traveled to Noxubee County for the occasion, delivered the day's most arresting address. She wore a characterless black shift overlain by an enormous, lacey, white shawl collar, making her look rather like a Pilgrim. Sister Gloria is tall and plain, with a chocolatey-brown complexion. Her voice began rising in the carefully modulated crescendos and decrescendos of the experienced preacher.

"Praise the Lord for the clean air, the earth and all that is in it! As it is written in Deuteronomy 3 and 18"—she opened her Bible and read in strident tones—"The LORD YOUR GOD hath given you this land to possess it." Then an instruction: "Now write the Scriptures down—so you can read them in your convenient time."

Sister Gloria's theology extended to the realities of modern technology: "If toxic waste come in, the land will be spoiled. Lest not anyone dump on us. We will not, number one, sell future generations for a few pieces of silver. What kinds of jobs do they offer? Abestos? A-BES-TOS? They sup-pos' to create jobs, and look what happened. Many people were killed because of a-bes-tos. Who's gonna pay the medi-cal bills?"

Jeremiah 9:19 provided the answer: "For a voice of wailing is heard out of Zion, How we are spoiled! We are greatly confounded because we have forsaken the land."

The Lord treasures productive work, she reminded them. But, she cautioned: "See Isaiah fifty-four and sixteen: 'Behold, I have created the smith that bloweth the coals in the fire, and that bringeth forth an instrument for his work; and I have created' "—she paused dramatically—" 'the *waster* to destroy.' " By then, about midmorning, the crowd had swelled to about 150, and they wildly began calling out their approval of her words.

Speaker followed speaker for two hours, the parking lot warmed slightly, and children began chasing one another around the edges of the crowd that had grown to about 200, playing hide-and-seek behind the memorial to the Confederate dead that sits on a corner of the courthouse lawn. Connor Bailey, a white sociologist from Alabama's Auburn University, told the crowd to trust their emotions as much as scientific evidence. Charlotte Keyes, a small black woman in her early twenties and the leader of Jesus People against Pollution, the group fighting for a swifter cleanup of the chemical mess in Columbia, Mississippi, denounced the EPA, scientific studies, and lawyers and their lies. Community organizers from around the state spoke, as did two Indiana students (one black and one white) who denounced the treachery of their university's administration, and one man who told them: "It's ironic. In Russia they just got their freedom, and here in Mississippi, we still have a dictatorship."

The last person to speak was Damu Smith, the activist from Greenpeace and the Southern Organizing Committee, who clearly intended his speech to be the rally's fiery coda. Dressed all in black except for a wildly patterned shirt and bolo tie, Smith cut an unusual figure in Noxubee County. As he spoke, his dreads springing forth from his head like so many tiny Slinkys, he jabbed his fists into the air, punctuating an angry talk about the nationwide betrayal of poor communities of color by elected officials. He concluded by asking the crowd to shout with him, in a syncopated delivery that emphasized every syllable: "Hey, hey. Let's hol-ler. We-got-the-pow-er. If-you-want-to-live-you've-got-to-fight-back-ev-ry-ho-ur. Hey, hey. Let's hol-ler. We-got- . . ." The crowd, which was about half white, haltingly began chanting and clapping with him, swaying from side to side. Smith had misjudged his audience; public displays of disquiet are not a familiar form of political behavior in Noxubee County. Just before he concluded, an older white man turned to me and asked, quizzically, "Which side are they on?"

The main rally in Macon was most striking for what it did not have, namely, speakers from Noxubee County. Aside from John Gibson, who introduced speakers and gave plugs for local talent, no local person addressed the crowd. Unlike Giles County, where the powerful white men leading the fight gave spirited attacks on FTI and Ed Netherland, the white men behind PEON—Charlie and Bill Thomas, Jay Chancellor—did not even attend. They shrugged off their nonappearance; none sought to be in the public eye on this issue. And showing up would have done more to divide than to unite, by reminding the majority of their prosperity.

As the rally disbanded, the crowd assembled to march, many picking up one of Martha Blackwell's signs from a pile at the base of the Confederate monument. As they gathered on the blacktop, facing toward Jefferson Street, the police massed their forces. The outsider may have seen the mostly older group (the predominant hair color was white) as a sweet, rather benign crowd of protestors, but Macon had never seen anything like it. Albert Walker—the county's big, portly, bearded sheriff, who is black—was there, assisted by his black and white deputies, as were state troopers, and alarm lights flashed on the roofs of their patrol cars. You would have thought Louis Farrakhan had come to town. The police monitored the slow movement of the crowd down the street the two thousand yards to Pulaski Street, where they jogged west a half block to Macon's city hall—closed, like the courthouse, on a Saturday afternoon—for another brief rally.

The same scene was repeated in Brooksville and then Shuqualak later in the afternoon. The crowd thinned out with each stop on this forty-mile movable protest.

Martha Blackwell did not speak until late in the afternoon, at the day's last stop, in Shuqualak. The remaining crowd was mostly black, young, and from out of town. Martha is a born performer, with a storyteller's gift for pacing, but she and others remembered that her earlier addresses had been disorganized, driven as much by a barely concealed fury at what she viewed as the venality of her elected officials and the predations of "carpetbaggers" like Ed Netherland as by logic and information. In the past year, she had been forced to marshall facts and figures carefully, to focus her disgust with a reasoned attack. Taking up the bullhorn, Martha began: "Today we've been criticized for bringing in outside agitators." As the marchers had moved up and down the main streets of each town, people had jeered them, claiming that mostly outsiders—students and "radical environmentalists"—were marching. The charge is one sure to put a white woman in Mississippi on the defensive, since it resonates with memories of invaders from the North preaching civil rights.

"But," Martha continued, "*they* brought in outsiders— they started this. And our response is that until their outsiders leave, we will continue to rely upon whatever support we can to make sure they leave." She then articulated what had become her central theme. Mississippi businesses needed places to dispose of their waste, but the solution was not a "megadump," which was sure, as in Emelle, to attract toxic trash from across the nation and abroad. Furthermore, she told the crowd, her voice measured and confident, Department of Environmental Quality figures showed that waste minimization was taking hold in Mississippi and across the nation. The EPA was evaluating the national need for additional waste disposal capacity. Should Mississippi not wait until the feds made a final decision?

For the conservative people of Noxubee County, the rally was a whopping success. Dramatic shifts of sentiment and experience are sometimes located in such small accomplishments. "I *never* imagined I would see Miss Mildred walking down the street with a black person—never," a middle-aged white woman gushed, referring to Mildred Cavett Taft, the doyenne of one of the county's richest planter families, the epitome of the local gentility. (When Taft was growing up on Sunshine Plantation out in the northeastern prairie in the early 1900s, her family would feast on oysters, which had been shipped up river from Mobile, at each Christmas meal. Even in landlocked Macon, two hundred miles from a seacoast, oysters were a Christmas essential because "a very old southern tradition.") John Gibson's twenty-four-year-old son, Kelvin, and his cousin, Tommy Stevenson, were similarly elated. They said that growing up in Noxubee County, they had never had white friends. "Not until we went away to college," Kelvin explained, adding that, in Noxubee "I've never seen blacks and whites together the way I did today. With this struggle, people speak to us for the first time, in a friendly way they never have before." Martha Blackwell was equally jubilant: "You can't put your finger on it, but it's a different feelin'. You become aware of so many issues that you can't ever go back to where you were."

The next day was Easter Sunday. The Gibsons' church is Drake Hill United Methodist, a plain blond-brick structure on a small rise off a back road in a heavily black section of the northern prairie. The day had become slightly cool and overcast, but Reverend James Henry, a solid, energetic man in his early sixties who travels a rural circuit from church to church, was in as sunny a mood as Martha Blackwell.

Reverend Henry began by condemning the arrogance of people who say "they made it themselves and get more and more successful" without ever thinking of how their actions were made possible by and were dependent on others. Gibson began voicing a steady stream of approval. " 'Men. A-men."

Reverend Henry decried the "idiocy," the "shortsightedness" of allowing toxic waste to enter this lovely farming country.

" 'Men. 'Men."

"I was so moved yesterday," the preacher went on, "to see white and black marching together. I couldn't have imagined that in an earlier time. Before the sheriffs would have been putting people in jail"—he paused for effect, giving the crowd a long stare. His voice rose again, and he bleated out, in celebration—"now the sheriffs are black—"

"A-men!"

"That's right!" one woman, a church elder, called out.

"And," the ebullient reverend shouted in conclusion, "it was a peaceful demon-sto-RAY-shun!"

Throughout the waste fight, black preachers used the pulpit to connect politics, morality, and spirituality, as they had done for generations. However, if Reverend Henry's words were echoed in black churches across the county that Easter Sunday, no such sentiments were heard by white worshippers. In the white churches, as the pastor of one of the county's Baptist churches put it, "they usually do not discuss politics or political things."

■ ■ ■ FOR FTI, even before the Noxubee rally, reality had begun to intrude. In March 1993, responding to the "sentiment of the public, the manufacturing and business community, and local and state officials, who said they favor the smallest feasible facility which will serve the State's needs," Hughes-FTI announced that it would voluntarily reduce the amount of waste it would accept for landfilling by 40 percent. The company nonetheless said that its capital investment, the promise of four hundred jobs and other benefits, would remain the same. Publicly, no one asked how this was possible.

And on April Fools' Day, 1993—two days before the Noxubee rally—Hughes-FTI announced that it had not exercised its option on the Martin Conrad ranch. The Indiana University Foundation issued a statement saying: "[The Conrad ranch] is now available for sale and the foundation is pursuing other potential purchasers in the hope that the property will be sold in the near future." In short order, it was learned, however, that the foundation had already optioned the property—on March 17—in a clever land transfer that helped Hughes-FTI keep its project alive and took the heat off of the foundation. Hughes-FTI's option was set to expire on March 31, and the Indiana University Foundation board had voted not to extend it past that date. The foundation promptly sold the land to Tom Merrill, the operator of a corporate farming operation near Salinas, California. Merrill in turn gave Hughes-FTI a one-year option for $50,000, renewable for a second and third year for $100,000 and $150,000, respectively. The graduated option suggested that, at long last, Netherland had acknowledged that his project would not sail through in only a few months. And, his doctors having told him that his cancer was now in remission, he settled in for what still looked, three and a half years after he had begun, like a long, hard fight ahead to build a much smaller facility than he originally hoped for.

■ ■ ■ LOCALLY, the event that most affected the direction of the Noxubee waste wars was not the courthouse rally or even the deal that gave Hughes-FTI a new option on the Martin Conrad ranch. It was Kenneth T. Misso Jr.'s sudden death of a heart attack; he was only forty-seven. Misso, a dairy farmer from an old Noxubee family, had been one of the two members of the Noxubee County Board of Supervisors who had consistently opposed Ed Netherland. Representing District Two, which stretches from Macon's eastern boundary into the prairie, he had held William Mullins's old seat. At his death, Misso was Martha Blackwell's supervisor, as his father had been before him.

When a supervisor dies, the generations-old practice across the state of Mississippi is to appoint a close relative to fill out the remainder of his (and it is almost always a man) term. For the local elite, this practice gives them an edge in maintaining control: family members become incumbents and gain an electoral advantage. The replacement can be a brother, a son, a wife. On Easter Monday, April 5, Charlie George Perkins appeared before the board to request that they appoint Misso's widow to serve out the year, until a special election to fill the vacancy. Carolyn Misso, a shy, delicate china doll of a woman, her husband dead just a week, did not appear in person to make the request. Her emissary, Charlie George, had been Mr. Kenneth, Junior's lawyer for twenty years and his friend "as far back as I can remember." When Charlie George finished articulating his request, one that emphasized the family's long service to the county, the board president, Ralph Higginbotham, whose dislike for

Charlie George was legendary—moved to table the request. The move was seconded by his ever-dependable lieutenant, George Robinson. They were joined by Joseph Stevenson, leaving Johnny Heard the sole nay vote.

The news of this slap at tradition spread throughout the county like fire lighting up a shotgun shack in the dead of winter. The board next met that Friday, April 9. The board meetings were usually attended by the supervisors, a clerk, and Ike Brown; occasionally, one or two others would show up. That Friday, over seventy-five people filed into the pews of the upstairs courtroom. The mostly older, white crowd listened attentively as Charlie George Perkins got up to eulogize his friend. Perkins speaks rather like W. C. Fields—that is, out of the side of his mouth and without looking directly at you, and he stretches out his words in a thick drawl. But no one laughed at what he had to say that day; this was for them deadly serious stuff. They knew that the board's rejection of his request would represent yet another step toward the political reconstruction of Noxubee County.

Dressed in his usual starched, white, oxford-cloth shirt open at the neck, plus his regulation blue blazer, stiffly pressed khakis, and shiny penny loafers, Charlie George began. The lawyer deliberately stated his case, again praised the Missos' long service to the county, reminded the supervisors of Mississippi custom, asked for a show of hands in favor of appointing the widow Misso (almost all raised), and waited for a motion.

A long silence ensued. Charlie George again asked that the board honor the memory of Mr. Kenneth, Junior by naming his wife to fill his seat. Ralph Higginbotham, his florid face tense, averted his gaze from Charlie George. Cameras clicked; television newsreels ran. George Robinson, as was his custom, covered his face from the image makers, like a Mafia don being led to his arraignment.

The room hung fire until the jeweler Buzzy McGuire, Blackwell's high school pal and still Macon's principal gossip channel, stood up and angrily addressed Joseph Stevenson. McGuire is professionally good-natured; his ire was wholly out of character. "Joseph, why aren't you going to do the traditional thing?" It was common knowledge that Stevenson, the perpetual swing vote, had depended on Kenny Misso Junior to loan him road equipment and work crews, essentials in fulfilling a supervisor's duties. People told stories of him weeping openly upon learning of Kenny's death. No one else spoke. After several interminable seconds, Stevenson moved to take a vote, this time casting his lot with Johnny Heard in favor of appointing Mrs. Misso. Higginbotham and Robinson again voted no. There being no majority, Higginbotham finally weighed in. "Vote's made," he said.

A jumble of voices called out. "Ralph—Ralph, explain what you're doin'—"

"Ralph, how can you—"

"We're not doin' it," Higginbotham stated firmly, looking ahead with his dull stare. He started to stand up.

From a far back corner of the long, narrow room, Martha Blackwell called out. It was Friday, her day in town to work, and she was resplendent—for Macon—in an elaborately patterned, multicolored cotton sweater, large brass disc earrings, and a vibrant shade of red lipstick. She trembled as she spoke. "Gentlemen. Ya'll are settin' a dangerous precedent. Anyone can die of a heart attack in the middle of the night. By your two votes against Mrs. Misso today, ya'll are sayin' that this same courtesy might not be extended to your own families in the event of your accidental death. Seventy-five witnesses won't forget."

With that, a sour-faced Ralph Higginbotham, his eyes clouded by his yellow-tinted sunglasses, stood up and marched out of the room. Joseph Stevenson and George Robinson followed in his wake. Still seated, a bemused Johnny Heard watched the parade and just kept shaking his head.

Amid the din of angry conversation that broke out, Charlie George Perkins tried to make sense of the scene. "The Misso family," he solemnly intoned, "is as well thought of as any in the county. Mr. Kenneth, Senior, was in office— why, I don't remember a time when a Misso was not in office. Ralph Higginbotham feels he's not obliged to anyone, and that's not how Kenny treated him." Outside the court-room, however, Charlie George's appeal for cordial treat-ment fell on mostly deaf ears. This was the same man whose partner had once defended the opposition to school integra-tion, and the very man who had represented legal efforts seen as designed to dilute black voting strength.

For Ike Brown, the vote not to appoint Misso's widow amounted to clear proof of realigned obligations. Ike re-membered: "Perkins made the statement, 'Who are you with—us or the other folks?' He said, 'Ralph, I want to know where you stand. Is you with us or these other folks?' I mean, in so many words." Brown understood the question to be a coded one, to ask " 'Are you with us or the niggers?' That's all it boil down to. The *other* folks."

The scene would be repeated four more times over the next two months—Charlie George Perkins and an entourage appearing in support of Carolyn Misso. In early May, the board received an opinion from the state attorney general informing them that they were legally obligated to fill the vacancy until a special election could be held the first week in November. The widow Misso finally appeared herself in late May, accompanied by Charlie George, but the board resisted even her imprecations.

As Martha Blackwell had promised, seventy-five witnesses did not forget. If there was anytime that Ralph Higginbotham was going to require Ed Netherland's beneficence, it would be during the next sixteen months.

■ ■ ■ BY June 1993, several events suggested that Ed Netherland's rollicking good two-and-a-half-year ride through Noxubee County was set to come to a sudden, bumpy halt. The beginning of the end came in the first week of May, when all but one of Hughes-FTI's supporters lost their seats in Macon and Brooksville city elections. In Brooksville, all of the aldermen who had supported FTI in February 1991—Eva Sherrod, John Bankhead, and Tom Mowry, two blacks and one white—lost their seats, leaving the ever more combative young mayor, Brad Moore, the sole official supporter of Ed Netherland, now his close friend. John Gibson at long last came through, cooperating with the white PEON leadership and working hard to find candidates who could outperform Ike Brown's minimachine. The entirely new five-member Brooksville board included three blacks and two whites, all of whom said they opposed hazardous waste. In Macon, Richard Brooks was the only original FTI supporter to remain on the town's Board of Aldermen. Tommy Campbell and William Rice, a white and a black alderman, respectively, both lost their seats.

PEON and AAEJ were jubilant. Here was not only vindication of their issue but also proof that Ike's rule was not supreme. The tone of the campaigns had been defiantly against the waste companies, and Hughes-FTI in particular. Essie Spencer declared that the results proved the influence of PEON and AAEJ: "Even though the people haven't stepped forward, they showed it at the polls." Added her friend and PEON's secretary, Gerry Harris, "We warned them two years ago that's what would happen." For Martha Blackwell and other whites like her, the hazardous waste issue was also evidence that racial differences could be overcome. "It still was a big deal that you had blacks and whites working together for the same slate of candidates," she reflected later. At the same time, Martha shared the discomfort of many other whites about the new black majority in Brooksville—yet another sign that the dominance of the county's aristocracy of the soil was over. There had to be a "working through between blacks and whites," she said. Echoing her father's views about ineptitude of the first black supervisor, Martha reported that Ike, Richard Brooks, and FTI were "leaning on" the new aldermen. "And they're just frightened," she said. "I imagine they wonder what they're getting themselves into. Frightened. I think *abused* is a good word. Timid. And completely inexperienced in handling a business meeting."

Suddenly Hughes-FTI, which had spent so much time contending that the views of the officials reflected the popular will, were backpedaling. The company's president, Fred Wynn, the reserved, scholarly scientist who was Netherland's second-in-command, desperately insisted: "There are lots of people in the communities who support us other than the elected officials. We're not taking it that the election sends any messages to us."

PEON had finally acquired confidence in using a confrontational, accusatory style. The spirit of Carol Puckett was suddenly evident in the ads PEON ran in the weekly *Shoppers' Guide* with the names of all the city elected officials and an indication of which side they had supported on the hazardous waste issue. At the bottom appeared a big skull and crossbones, and the explanation that the waste to be disposed of in the county "is made up of poisonous chemicals [that] would eventually poison our land and our water." It was not quite the lurid photo of a devastated landscape and sensational headline used by the opposition in Giles County, Tennessee. But in the context of the usually polite and kind public discourse of white Noxubee County, it was a radical shift in style.

After these local elections, people started saying that Ike Brown was finished, that this was a devastating defeat for his pretensions to control a political machine run on his orders. Ike is nothing if not a masterful rhetorician, able to finesse any question to his advantage. He shrugged off the loss. The new Brooksville board had three African Americans instead of the previous two, and the black man who had lost in Macon, William Rice, had in Brown's view been "replaced" by another black, Willie Dixon Jr. "I don' care what ya'll doin' as long as its all blacks," he averred, "and in Brooksville its three yaaaa-oung blacks." To Ike, every black victory is his, and so he professed complete satisfaction with the result, adding smugly, "We're turnin' the power structure on its head."

■ ■ ■ FAR more significant for Hughes-FTI than the loss of local support was the May 18 announcement by the new EPA administrator, Carol Browner, concerning hazardous waste incineration. Browner's carefully worded statement said that EPA would "make its chief permitting priority" the effort to bring existing incinerators under "permit controls" until January 1995. "This means that over the next 18 months we will give low priority to processing requests for new capacity. This will have the general effect of temporarily freezing capacity at existing levels." Despite wording that *committed* EPA to nothing at all, Browner's statement was widely viewed as implementing an eighteen-month moratorium on new hazardous waste incinerators. Moreover, with its emphasis on waste reduction, the statement cast doubt on the prospects for permitting new incineration capacity.

Browner thus confirmed that there simply was not the need nationally for new hazardous waste incinerators. Browner stressed that "the future of hazardous waste control, as well as the future of safeguarding the health of our citizens and assuring the protection of our environment" required the government to develop "policies that prevent pollution at its source, before it is ever created." In tacit recognition of arguments that critics like Peter Montague and George Baggett—and more recently, their disciples, housewives like Martha Blackwell—had been making for years, Browner acknowledged that "no system of disposal, no matter how safe or well regulated, can be as environmentally effective as minimizing the amount of wastes presently generated."

The waste companies' plans came under attack from other fronts as well. Balance sheets told the story: shares of most leading waste disposal firms' stocks were selling for less than they had three years earlier. That spring and summer, the financial and chemical industry press started to report that the nation had enough incineration and landfill capacity. These opinions came not from wide-eyed, back-to-nature environmentalists but from businesspeople. Hugh Holman, an industry watcher with Alex Brown & Sons, the national investment firm based in Baltimore, was quoted in a widely distributed *Wall Street Journal* article as saying that the nation had "abundant" capacity. In August, Holman told the trade journal *Chemical Week* that "chemical firms that see their waste stream as a process issue rather than as a garbage problem—the DuPonts of the world—don't want to do business with garbagemen, they want to do business with chemical engineers." His views were echoed by Ray Hill, a senior associate with the influential New York–based consulting firm Booz Allen & Hamilton, who stressed that because of both waste minimization and overcapacity, the industry was becoming more price based. Doubts about the future profitability of and the need for expanded hazardous waste disposal operations undercut most of Hughes-FTI's and USPCI's claims.

However, many Mississippians were to be denied much of this information. In the middle of April, not long after her thorough coverage of the PEON/AAEJ rally in Macon on April 3, a story that received front-page coverage in the state's largest-circulation newspaper, Sharon Stallworth was yanked from the environmental beat at the *Clarion-Ledger.* Stallworth had been reporting on the environment and business for nearly three years. One day in early April, she later recalled, the paper's assistant managing editor approached her and asked, "How would you like to be transferred to general assignment?"

" 'I wouldn't like it at all,' I told him. But he gave me all sorts of bullshit reasons for pulling me from the beat." The result was that Stallworth's thorough coverage of the waste fight, in all its human dimensions, suddenly disappeared. Her removal was so hasty that she was not allowed to cover a hearing on a hazardous waste–fueled cement kiln in Artesia—a town not twenty-five miles from Macon—on the night of her transfer; a series of articles on pollution in minority communities was canceled.

In fact, the previous August, in a confidential memorandum, a public relations plan for Hughes-FTI had instructed: "What we hope to avoid is a 'poverty/environmental racism' feature story highlighting the conditions in Noxubee County and accusing Hughes-FTI of attempting to exploit the locals." Stallworth was specifically targeted for attention: "Like most reporters, Ms. Stallworth is quite skeptical, so prior planning with those selected to speak with her is essential." The following February, Andy Taggart, Fordice's then powerful chief of staff and one of Mississippi's rising political stars, wrote to Duane McAllister, the paper's publisher, complaining about what he called Stallworth's "attack pieces." And Taggart admonished: "I hope that you will take some steps in response." The rumor in Jackson was that the GodwinGroup, Hughes-FTI's wily public relations team, had pressured the governor's office, which was already displeased with criticism of its handling of the issue. A frequent rumor heard in Jackson was that the GodwinGroup's head, Philip Shirley, had been heard bragging at cocktail parties that he had been responsible for getting Stallworth transferred. Shirley vehemently denied the claim: "We certainly disagreed with her and felt she made some mistakes. We were never secretive about that. We publicly challenged statements and tried to get them corrected, but her transfer was an internal affair."

Environmentalists from the state Sierra Club and other groups charged that the GodwinGroup had used its connections with their client, the Mississippi Manufacturers' Association, to threaten the paper with the loss of advertising revenues if it did not remove Stallworth or at least cut back her coverage of the hazardous waste controversy. The paper denied these claims and insisted that its personnel decisions would be kept private. Yet the environmental coverage that followed, which was irregular and less thoroughly researched

blacks, some poor whites from the hills—to get Higginbotham out of office. His refusal to let Carolyn Misso fill her dead husband's post was the last straw. Referring to more than the sultry climate, Martha Blackwell summarized the local mood when she allowed: "Things are pretty hot down here. People are in a furor over Carolyn Misso." As far as she had come in understanding the connection between environmental degradation, poverty, and racial inequality, Blackwell reacted to Higginbotham's impudent behavior with the sentiments of the planter class: "We've said all along he's way more dangerous than the two black guys in there." Higginbotham had proved himself "vindictive."

Higginbotham's explanations only reinforced the impression of his unacceptable capriciousness. He would say that an unidentified "they" put her up to it, and that Miz Misso did not really want the job anyway. People would ask him: Ralph, why wouldn't you just do the usual, the right thing? In response, his interrogators got back little more than the cryptic, "Well, it's personal." He told others that he did not vote for Carolyn Misso because she had not personally asked him for his support. When she went to him directly, he squirmed. Although a diffident, reserved woman, Misso reported: "I asked him more questions than he asked me. I said, 'Is it because I am a woman?' He said no. I asked, 'Was it my education?' Ralph said no. He complimented Kenny for being fair-minded, even when they disagreed."

With Attorney Gowan's help, PEON and its supporters in Higginbotham's district identified a way to try and punish his mule-headed intransigence. In 1956, worried that liquor and gambling interests were threatening to corrupt county officials, the Mississippi legislature passed a law creating a procedure to remove crooked public servants from office. In thirty-seven years, the law had been used in the state only once, many years earlier. The recall law requires that 51 percent of the registered voters in a politician's district sign a petition disapproving of the official's performance. Once the necessary signatures are gathered, a three-judge Removal Council must be convened to evaluate the evidence and decide whether a recall election is merited.

The removal petition circulated that summer complained: "Supervisor Higginbotham has undertaken a course which is totally unresponsive to the people of District 4 and their needs." As evidence, the petition focused first on his claimed derogation of the supervisor's central duty in the rural South: he paved the roads of his supporters and neglected those of his detractors. Further, he refused to vote for Misso's appointment to fill out her husband's term and seemed "to be under some outside direction other than the best interests of Noxubee County and the interests of his people."

Out in the remote hamlets of the western hills—into places with Choctaw names like Wahalak and Hashuqua (the last's pronunciation anglicized into "Hey Sugar")—Higginbotham's opponents, white and black, trudged up and down the red-clay roads in the intense, still heat of early summer to seek signatures. By the Fourth of July they had nearly seven hundred. This was encouraging, but they needed nearly a thousand by month's end. Martha Blackwell for one was stunned by this support, a sign that hundreds of whites and blacks, people whose names she and others born to the county's aristocracy of the soil did not know, agreed with their cause. For the rest of July, they became more aggressive. Lamar White posted a copy of the petition at his country store, imploring everyone who came in to sign. Ike Brown announced a boycott of stores in District Four, alleging that the recall was yet another example of racial intimidation by the county's white commercial elite, but his effort quietly fizzled.

At Shuqualak Lumber, the Thomas brothers called workers who lived in Higginbotham's district into their offices and urged them to sign on. By the due date in late July, the petition drive had garnered nearly eleven hundred signatures—more than enough. All the while, the rumor mill worked overtime. Higginbotham was reputed to have been offering to pay as much as $100 for people not to sign, to which one disgruntled constituent was widely reported to have responded: "A hundred dollars! He only offered me $20! I would have agreed for $100."

PEON was thrilled by the effort's success, proof positive that their star was rising. "They nailed 'em good," exulted Martha Blackwell. "We're gonna be flat testy after this." PEON's renewed sense of purpose was given a further boost the next month, when the front page of the *New York Times*'s business section reported that the NAACP had singled out Hughes Aircraft for violating federal regulations that require government contractors to diversify their management and workforce. The civil rights group said that Hughes did not award 5 percent of its subcontracts to minority-owned contractors, as required by federal law, and that blacks were "grossly underrepresented" among its fifty-five thousand employees. The NAACP claimed that the defense manufacturing behemoth systematically discriminated against and sometimes harassed its black workers. Hughes denied the allegations, which, in any event, had nothing to do with events in Noxubee County. Nonetheless, the firestorm was used by PEON and AAEJ to reinforce the impression that Netherland and the money behind him were not as black-friendly as they claimed.

In Noxubee, it was the local NAACP that struck back at

PEON and emerged as Higginbotham's most vocal defender. Incongruously, the attempt to force a recall of a white "hill-billy" was characterized by the civil rights group as the most blatant evidence yet of racial persecution in the Noxubee waste wars. Higginbotham became for some an honorary black man. Ike Brown said, "I don't know any black person who could vote better for us," and he publicly celebrated the fact that the white supervisor was a lifetime member of the NAACP. Privately, he intimated that solidarity with Higginbotham was merited because one of Higginbotham's brothers had married a black woman. Attorney Wilbur Colom explained that Higginbotham "turned into a person who really voted blacker than any of the black people on the board." Richard Brooks, the chapter president and Macon alderman, called a press conference on the courthouse steps at which he distributed a statement saying: "The Noxubee County NAACP alleges that members of the white establishment have used tactics reminiscent of the 1960s in an effort to oust Noxubee County Supervisor Ralph Higginbotham from office." Brooks claimed that elderly blacks had been intimidated or misinformed so as to surrender their signatures (exactly the charge whites routinely made about Ike Brown). Ernestine George, a black woman who terrifies many whites for her outspokenness, seconded this view: "This is the white power structure trying to keep black people in Noxubee County under their thumb, the way it has been since Noxubee County became Noxubee County. That's all it is. It's not just the waste dump."

The local NAACP and its newfound white allies—Ben Tubb, Brad Moore, and Big Tiny Heard—did their best to discredit the petition. They combed over the hundreds of signatures, identifying those that appeared to have been forged (and there were places where the petitions looked as if one person had just signed five different names in a row). They cross-checked to make sure all of the signatures were from qualified electors, and they scouted out stories of intimidation or misinformation. They secured affidavits from those who swore that the petition was something different than it turned out to be: "I wont to keep out hazard wast," one said; another claimed she thought the petition would get him to "come do the road." Still another maintained she thought the petition was "to point a Supervisor for District 2." Higginbotham's supporters identified what they said were 147 fraudulent signatures. If this number was correct, the petition would not have the needed 51 percent of qualified electors. They complained to the governor's office, but to no avail.

Governor Fordice spent most of that summer in Texas, being treated for prostate cancer. In his absence, Lieutenant Governor Eddie Briggs, a political chameleon with strong personal and business ties in Noxubee County, served as acting governor. Briggs reviewed the petition, approved it, ordered the creation of a three-judge Removal Council, and set a fall date for the hearing to consider a possible Higginbotham recall. Higginbotham's supporters cried foul: this never would have happened had Fordice not been away. Briggs, they said, was accommodating the request of his old friends, the Thomases. The removal hearing was set for Thursday, October 21. Higginbotham's team included Colom, the very man he had not so long before tried to remove as the board attorney.

On the day of the hearing—which people started to call the "Higginbotham trial," although it was not formally that—people began gathering at the courthouse by 9:30 A.M. It was a social event: members of every faction filled the benches of the shabby upstairs courtroom. Against expectations, it turned into a marathon: the three-judge panel began the hearing at 10:00 A.M. and did not conclude until 6:30 P.M.

Sixteen witnesses were heard. The one issue that dominated their sworn testimony was "the hazardous waste." The day provided a telescopic view of the events of the previous three years: the claims of influence peddling, Higginbotham's hobnobbing with the "self-interest man" Ike Brown, and the certainty that "there's money floating around offered to people for work and favors." Many of those questioned spoke of Higginbotham's choleric, stubborn character (a county worker claimed that his mercurial boss "didn't care nothing about Martin Luther's [*sic*] birthday," and "that if we wanted off a day he would give our individual birthday"). Not all of the comments were negative: some said that he regularly dragged the roads, or they assured the judges that they had known of his support for hazardous waste when they voted for him. Mrs. Azline Prince observed: "I think he seems such a nice man, and he seems to be a religious man. I don't think he would do nothing wrong."

The man himself was questioned for over an hour, longer than any other witness. Never one to favor a suit and tie, Higginbotham stepped up to the witness box wearing jeans and a striped cotton work shirt. At first, his voice was barely discernible, and his lawyer repeatedly had to ask him to speak up. Colom walked his client through the contradictory accounts: Did Mr. Higginbotham ever gravel private driveways? No sir, he did not. Did he manage his road crews in an even-handed manner? Yes sir, he did.

Higginbotham's demeanor changed entirely when Colom's questioning turned to the Misso controversy. The supervisor began to fidget in his seat, asking time and again for questions to be repeated, his recollection suddenly dim as to dates or specific events. Why had he not followed the custom and voted to appoint Miz Misso?

"Well, the customary rule is not always best for the county, I feel like. Mr. Perkins said it was the customary rule and had been for the last thirty years that this was done. I looked at what had went on in the county for the last thirty years, and the county had dropped in population from, probably, close to 30,000 to 13,000 in twenty years. That's not too good to use as a customary rule. It's time for something to be changed somewhere." What had gone on in the county for the last thirty years Higginbotham did not specify. But underneath the jumble of poor grammar and half-spoken feelings, Higginbotham revealed himself as more than a mean hillbilly. The county's population *had* declined precipitously since the enactment of the civil rights laws.

People had moved away to seek better opportunities. Landless whites and blacks had fled to seek economic advantage. Some whites surely also had left for a less black milieu. For most blacks, leaving unquestionably meant life in a less secretive, less emotionally bruised society. Whatever the reason for their flight, however, Ralph Higginbotham understood a central need for the county: things had to change.

Higginbotham fared badly under cross-examination. The board president is neither quick-witted nor eloquent, and he was unable to defend himself against a lawyer's verbal attacks. The performance confirmed for the assembled crowd that—whatever his convictions about the need to change Noxubee's politics as usual—he was a man in the grip of petty jealousies and the unaccustomed privilege of exercising political power. Why, Mr. Higginbotham, are you so resistant to Miz Misso? In response to a question he had previously answered in innumerable ways, Higginbotham offered yet another explanation—and made himself a comical figure in the process. With a facial expression some saw as a self-satisfied smirk and others as a sign of his terrified determination not to be humiliated, he explained:

"Personally, I was in office when Mr. K. T. Misso, the old man, was supervisor. He died in office. He was a good man. When he passed away, I didn't know his son that well, but I did know that if he was anything like his father, he would be a good replacement to the board and I voted for him to be on the board. Then after he passed away, I felt like that was enough Missos to die in office." It was nearing 5:00 P.M.; the hearing had dragged on for nearly seven hours, and the crowd might well have reacted loudly and violently, jeering and laughing at the absurdity of such a statement. But everyone sat silent for a few minutes. Carolyn Misso leaned over to Martha Blackwell and whispered, "I should thank him for saving my life."

Could Higginbotham be serious? Had his vote not to appoint really been meant to avoid the possibility of the widow Misso's death in office? "Well, like I say, I just felt like enough Missos had died in office. How much can any family take with their people dying in office?" The crowd sat stunned, overcome by mixed emotions of contempt and admiration for what William Faulkner—describing Abner Snopes—called the "ferocious conviction in the rightness of his own actions."

At just past 5:30, the lawyers rested and the Removal Council retired to reach its decision. At exactly 6:00 P.M., they returned and announced that they had found Higginbotham in violation of state law: as president of the board, he should have taken action to fill the vacant seat. A recall election would be held.

■ ■ ■ PEON interpreted the Removal Council's decision to hold a recall election not merely as a blow for Ralph Higginbotham but as another vindication of its ascendancy. Yet the recall election and other events of the next year confirmed that, if anything, support for "the" hazardous waste had been a means to seize political and economic power, and also to redress old grievances rather than an end in itself. This fact became even more evident during the special elections held that November to fill Kenny Misso Jr.'s seat. The challengers were Kenny Misso III, then just twenty-two years old and a part-time student at a local community college, and William "Boo" Oliver, a thirty-five-year-old black farmer. Oliver had been one of the first blacks to integrate the white public schools nearly thirty years earlier, when the voluntary integration plan was in effect and the choice was an act of immense personal courage on the part of black parents and children. One of a handful of black farmers in the area, Oliver was regarded as beholden to no special interests, including Ike Brown. Boo Oliver was seen as his own man, and he commanded respect from blacks and whites alike.

The campaign was marked by the open charges of racism that had come to characterize county politics since the start of the waste wars. In early October, Hughes-FTI's men at the local NAACP—Richard Brooks and Ike Brown—protested the list of people assigned to work at the polls in the upcoming election. "We strenuously object," they wrote to the five-member election commission, to the assignment of nine poll workers. The challenged poll workers should be dismissed, they explained: to get the "racial ratio in line." Half of their objections were to other blacks who, they wrote, harassed "illiterate black voters." Martha Blackwell was deemed unacceptable because of her "well-known racial prejudice." In the end, Blackwell and five others were replaced after a stormy series of meetings by the election commission. The vote was strictly along racial lines: three blacks for replacement, two whites against.

Both candidates for the vacant supervisor's job opposed hazardous waste. In the November 2 special election, young Kenny Misso won by thirteen votes. Ike Brown and his troops raised hell, demanding that the votes be recounted. The election commission voted to recount a dozen challenged ballots (Mississippi's loose residency requirements—an "intent to return" to Mississippi from outside the state can entitle a person to vote—create constant headaches in disputed elections). The commissioners again voted three to two in favor of a recount, as if no other margin were possible in Noxubee County. The result was an eight-vote victory for Oliver, who was sworn in as a supervisor two weeks later. His hold on the office, however, was tenuous. His opponents cried voter fraud, and Misso sued. The following September, a jury of nine blacks and three whites deadlocked; there was evidence of possible improprieties on both sides. Oliver was ordered to vacate the office. The next week, Wilbur Colom advised the board that, under state election law, they could reinstate Oliver to serve until the 1995 general elections, when he handily beat young Kenny Misso.

To everyone's surprise, Ike Brown vigorously campaigned for Oliver, even though the candidate had clearly articulated his opposition to hazardous waste and was not part of Ike's machine. Wilbur Colom warned Ike in advance that "he ain't gonna vote for you" on hazardous waste. To this Ike replied: "I don't care how he votes. He gonna vote alright, what are you concerned about?" At bottom, this was what mattered most to him: voting "alright" meant voting black in the majority-black county.

■ ■ ■ THE antiwaste cause gained further momentum as a result of events outside Noxubee in the last half of 1993. The first occurred early in the summer when, without much fanfare, a court in Jackson issued a ruling that significantly confounded the efforts of the waste companies trying to operate a hazardous waste facility in Noxubee County. On June 8, Circuit Court Judge James E. Graves Jr.—who is black, although little significance was publicly attached to this fact—issued an order declaring that the Thomases and Jay Chancellor were correct: the state Environmental Protection Council was unconstitutional. Graves agreed that the EPC was an executive agency, and therefore it was improperly constituted of elected legislators, in violation of state separation-of-powers requirements: "Ergo, any and all recommendations made by the [EPC] for both the 1989 CAP and the 1992 CAP are void." The judge added that "the acts of the Governor served to compound a pre-existing legality" and ordered him—as a state agency—to comply with the state administrative procedures law. In conclusion, Graves held that state environmental regulators were "expressly prohibited from processing hazardous waste treatment facilities permit applications or evaluating those permit applications." Although the bull-headed, imperious Fordice would continue to try and get around Graves's ruling, well into late 1995 it continued to impede the best efforts of the waste companies to push their plans forward. By then, most of the players who had actively campaigned for a Noxubee facility were long gone from the scene.

The second pivotal event was a novel complaint made on AAEJ's behalf by the Sierra Club Legal Defense Fund regional office, out of New Orleans. The complaint—in the form of a letter requesting action by the U.S. Commission on Civil Rights—was delivered in late September. In the letter, the group implicitly conceded that proof of a discriminatory *intent* to site toxic operations in poor communities of color was virtually unattainable. Instead, their letter aimed to show that the permitting process was discriminatory in *impact.*

A third event providing momentum to the anti–hazardous waste forces was a lawsuit filed in Jackson by a brash, decisive white woman named Deirdre McGowan who, two years before, had been Executive Director of the Mississippi Civil Liberties Union. McGowan obtained minimal funding and an office for a new enterprise she called the Environmental Justice Project, with a vaguely stated purpose ("dedicated to block environmental racism in Mississippi by serving as a central resource and communication link to those groups concerned with this issue on both local and state levels"), but which specifically focused on Noxubee and three other Mississippi counties. Like the lawsuit filed by the PEON leadership, McGowan's complaint presented a highly technical set of arguments focusing on the role of the governor's office and attacking Fordice for having settled important public policy questions in informal, back-room deals.

■ ■ ■ THUS, by the end of 1993, Governor Fordice had two lawsuits filed against him personally and one civil rights complaint challenging his environmental policies. And all of these legal efforts were the direct result of the governor's assumption that he could unilaterally dictate the state's hazardous waste policy, in much the same way he had always made private business decisions.

The governor's office had for several months also been working on other fronts to hasten the approval of a Mississippi toxics operation—and an end to controversy. Behind the scenes, the administration had been pushing to end the rivalry between the two companies vying for a Noxubee permit. Between them, the cost of the fight for a Noxubee permit had cost them by the end of 1993 an astonishing $26 million (at least, that is the sum they publicly admitted to having spent). (Such a sum could have had a transformative effect on schools and social services in Noxubee County.)

In short, three years after Netherland had first shown up in Noxubee, it looked no more likely than in 1990 that one company would receive a permit. Printz Bolin remembers receiving a call from Jimmy Heidel, the governor's director of economic development, who convinced him "that the only way the process was going to go forward was for there to be one application." Bolin, "dead set against" the merger, blamed Netherland's exploitative public relations tactics for poisoning the well of local feeling against USPCI; several months earlier he had told a friend that he would walk on water before joining forces with Hughes-FTI. But the astronomical costs of this little war had become so onerous that, by early December, the companies agreed to a merger.

■ ■ ■ THE merger had been rumored since late summer and was signaled throughout the fall by the steady disintegration of Ed Netherland's efforts. After the Brooksville elections that replaced a pro-FTI board with an anti–hazardous waste slate, mayor and real estate agent Brad Moore came under increasing attack for his connections to Netherland and FTI. In November, he announced his resignation. By the end of the year he and his wife—both of whom had lived their entire lives in Noxubee County—moved with their boys to suburban Memphis. This was only the most visible sign that Netherland's hopes were evaporating, but there had been others: Hughes-FTI's offices had been largely closed for months, and the staff had slowly and quietly been let go.

In fact, Hughes-FTI had little choice but to agree to the merger. General Motors (Hughes' parent company) had been asked to give an unconditional guarantee as to liability. The company initially agreed but later balked. Some people close to the merger negotiations insisted that the Danner Company—the money behind Netherland's largesse—began to feel that Netherland had given away too much with no result. On December 2, Ben and Betty Tubb, Hughes-FTI's last employees in Noxubee, received a fax informing them that they would both be terminated the following day. The deal gave Hughes-FTI an option to gain up to 50 percent of a share in the company that might eventually obtain a permit to operate a Noxubee toxic dump. Netherland agreed to keep a low profile when in Noxubee; his antagonists grandly claimed that he had been ordered to keep out of the county.

The shock was not that the companies merged but that their corporate marriage locked out the people Netherland had cultivated so assiduously. Ben Tubb felt "absolutely" betrayed by Netherland and FTI. Macon's mayor, Allen Hunter, admitted: "I just felt like that they made some promises that they didn't have any intention of keeping. I'll give you an example: They said, 'Look, if you'll all help us and ya'll endorse us, we're goin' to carry through and we're goin' to do this right.' And when they merged with USPCI? They said that all the promises, all the guarantees that they were gonna give to the cities and the county . . . didn't apply anymore. But we'd already laid the groundwork for 'em to try and get the permit, see?" To the coolly realistic Ike Brown, however, it was a predictable example of the governor's political gamesmanship. "Fordice and them forced the merger" because they supported USPCI. Netherland was just a businessman, one who tried to do business "the right way" by cultivating the majority of the population. He failed because larger political interests resisted him. For Ike Brown, Ed Netherland's departure was merely another casualty in his ongoing campaign for majority rule in Noxubee County.

Despite his sense of betrayal, Ben Tubb reflected the view of many when he admitted that Netherland's enthusiasm and go-gettum-ness had been the secrets of his near-success: "Ed told us we were all going to be millionaires. Most of the people I know never believed it. But I think Ed actually believed that a permit was always only months away."

■ ■ ■ IF Netherland physically disappeared from the scene, the brush fires he helped start were not extinguished; the taste of power and influence is not easily forgotten. It was eventually revealed that the NAACP had paid a portion of the legal fees Higginbotham racked up in the effort to fight the recall. The amount was at least $25,000—and probably well over that, in the estimation of Wilbur Colom, the partial beneficiary of those funds. The legal fees had been channeled to the NAACP in contributions from Hughes-FTI and others, including the Ray Danner Foundation, a life member of the local chapter. The rich irony of this—given that Danner himself, in sworn deposition testimony, had not denied using the word *nigger* and had just paid a settlement of over $130 million for systematic racial discrimination in his businesses—was scarcely noted in Noxubee.

People were too busy getting agitated about new developments in the waste wars. On December 2, Richard Brooks sent a letter on NAACP stationery to USPCI, bemoaning his "utter confusion as to what you are proposing" to the county's black majority. "There have [*sic*] not been any educational training, history, or clear explanations with respect to your proposed facility's functions and operation." What would USPCI promise Noxubee's African Americans in the short and long terms? "In a gesture of good faith," would USPCI "be willing and able to set aside" $250,000 in an escrow account for "the African-American Community?" If USPCI did not get a permit, Brooks proposed, the money would be "divided between" the county's blacks. The creation of such an account, he intimated, would result in the NAACP giving USPCI its endorsement.

Brooks's letter was intended to be private and may have followed USPCI's request for NAACP support, but it was leaked by an anonymous source to papers across the state. In short order the letter was turned against him: the NAACP was made to look like it was soliciting a bribe in exchange for its support. Indignant, Printz Bolin piously insisted: "We're gonna work with the black community just like we work with anybody here. We're not gonna give them a check. We're not gonna give them a monthly retainer—that's just not the way we're gonna do it." For his part, Ike Brown was clear about the nature of the letter: "If you read it, you know the letter is no big deal. It jus' ask a lot of 'pecifics." Only at the end, he pointed out, did it ask USPCI to consider a money gift. And who, he reasoned, would make a request for a bribe in writing? Thus, for Ike the affair was "an example of racism in the works, because it was blown out of proportion. The newspapers jumped on everybody, you know. Jus' a person trying to get the best for they people, isn't askin' anything for themself."

Netherland's shadow again hung over Macon six months later, when Higginbotham's recall election finally happened. The vote had originally been scheduled for early February. But Ike Brown summoned the interest of his friend Nancy Sardeson, a Department of Justice attorney in Washington, D.C. To enforce the Voting Rights Act, the Justice Department has the right to postpone any election where there is suspicion of any irregularities or the need for special monitoring. In heavily black counties like Noxubee with a long history of voter fraud and intimidation, this preelection scrutiny can be particularly intense (820 federal election observers have been sent to observe county elections since June 1966). The Justice Department ruled that preclearance would be necessary and changed the date to late June.

A week before the election, "An OPEN LETTER To the Voters of District 4 from Ike Brown" ran in the local *Shopper's Guide* and in the *Beacon*. Self-consciously a martyr-in-the-making, Brown's missive began by referring to the fact that he had been indicted for federal tax fraud, for his work as an income tax preparer: "Even in my 'time of trouble,' I MUST continue on my job of being vigilant . . . despite 'death threats,' obscene phone calls and even ugly looks—I WILL NOT be silenced!" He then linked his woes to Higginbotham's: "Again I must warn you that the **same people** who are attempting to **frame me** are the **same people** who are in the process of trying to RAILROAD Supervisor Ralph Higginbotham from his duly elected office. **DO NOT . . . I Repeat, do not vote** IN A FRAUDULENT ELECTION!!" Most ominously of all for his political antagonists, he promised, "I will personally be at the polls to see who is standing with me," and added that any voting improprieties should be reported to him for handling by federal election monitors. **"AS LONG AS YOU STAND WITH ME . . . I WILL KEEP FIGHTING !!!!!!!!!"** he promised. He signed the letter "Your friend in Christ, Ike."

June 21 was a mild day—humid but not oppressively hot, the clouds low and black, threatening rain. The polls opened at 7:00 A.M. About a dozen election monitors from the Justice Department, with clipboards in hand, spent the day quietly pacing in front of the polling places. They shed their jackets, loosened ties, or unbuttoned their blouse collars as the storm clouds of early morning gave way to the brilliant, blazing heat of midafternoon.

Ike Brown began his day at 8:30 A.M. and spent most of it like a turkey vulture, crossing back and forth in front of the main polling place, in front of Shuqualak's raggedy city hall. He dressed for the occasion all in brilliant purple, the color of royalty: In his bright polyester trousers and tropical-patterned, short-sleeved shirt he could not be missed. This day would be his. He paraded in front of the precinct until midafternoon, as if it were his realm. At the end of the block, near the rail sidings that look over to Shuqualak Lumber in one direction and Gus Evans's office in the other, Ralph Higginbotham paced nervously, huddling in anxious conversation with his mostly black road crew–turned–advisors. A black teenage girl acted as his scout, and every half hour he would send her over to Ike for an update on the numbers reported in each precinct; merely showing up was viewed as a vote against the supervisor. A young white woman who had come into town to work the polls said to me: "I live out in the country and don't mix much in town. So it's real interesting to see people you know a long time come out to take a stand." But, I protested, you don't know how they vote. "Tha's true, but you jus' have a feelin'."

Bill and Charlie Thomas and their family spent the day ferrying people back and forth to the polls. Midmorning, Ike's pal from Justice, Nancy Sardeson, arrived. Sardeson, who is white, is what my grandmother would have called "a big-boned gal." She was arrayed in a purple shift, as if fitted to be Ike's Queen for a Day. The ever-volatile Charlie Thomas complained to her and the other Justice Department monitors that Ike's presence in front of the polls was sure to intimidate voters, that he needed to be stopped. But Sardeson was adamant: their mandate was to enforce the Voting Rights Act, which meant taking note of any improprieties and listening to complaints about possible irregularities that affected members of historically oppressed classes of voters. If necessary, complaints would be investigated later. When I asked Brown what he thought of the Thomas brothers' worries that he would intimidate elderly voters, he was uncharacteristically laconic: "They can go to hell."

Charlie Thomas approached Ike Brown. The men had words.

"Ike, you shouldn't be so close to the polling place."

"Are you a lawyer?"

"No, but I know the law, and you are too close."

"There is one place you can go," Ike yelled, excited, "and it isn't heaven!"

Furious, Charlie stomped off.

Later, Ike, delighting in his ability to enrage, laughed about the incident. The Thomases were the ones getting into an illegal mess, he maintained. They had, he had reliably been told, offered the Brandons—a huge black family who live out by Calyx, near Robert Field's place—an air conditioner if they would vote. "That's true," Charlie Thomas admitted, but only "if they'd *vote*, not one way or the other. Just vote."

Flush with success in irritating the steady stream of whites and a few blacks who arrived that day to oppose Ralph Higginbotham, Ike would call out effusive greetings. To Johnny Kinard, an older white man and one of the leaders of the recall effort, he gave an especially enthusiastic welcome. Kinard turned and gave him a sour glare. "We've got 'em on the squeeze," Ike exulted. Blacks who arrived to vote merited only his contempt: they were, for him, accomplices in propping up white control.

By four o'clock, it was clear that Higginbotham would remain. Minutes before the polls closed at five, Brad Moore zoomed up. Behind the wheel of his shiny new white Cherokee Jeep, dressed in a suit and tie, he looked suddenly out of place in the county where he had lived all but a few months of his life. Moore had come down from Memphis just to show support for his new friend from the waste wars, Higginbotham. For the next hour, he stood around with Ralph and Ike and Ben Tubb, and Higginbotham's black road crew and exulted in their success. It was a "big victory for the people" said Noxubee's master of the sound bite, Ike Brown. "The power structure could not restore themselves."

The supervisor's victory was made final at the courthouse the next day. Only 461 ballots had been cast. Although 395 of them represented voters who wanted Higginbotham out, that was far from the simple majority of voters in District Four needed to expel him from office.

The next day, I called Broox Sledge, the county's de facto historian. Sledge, who is in his early seventies, answered my questions about early settlement on the Noxubee and Tombigbee Rivers. Discussion then drifted to the just-finished election. It was, he reflected matter-of-factly, "the twilight of the whites." It is a judgment V. O. Key Jr. might have endorsed, marveling at the rich irony that the sun set on Noxubee's once-powerful white planter class in a dispute over the political sympathies of a renegade white man from the hills.

■ ■ ■ IN Ed Netherland's absence, Printz Bolin and USPCI became the new target of PEON's anger. People started to pun on Bolin's first name—"Printz Edward" they called him, suggesting that he was nothing better than a less abrasive version of his Tennessee antagonist. The two men disliked each other intensely, and the epithet stung: Bolin loves to be liked. Powerful whites were strongly against him by then. The merger, said PEON's Linda Thomas, would mean that the community would figuratively "slit his little throat." The Ike Brown machine opposed him just as vigorously. Ike remained "totally negative" on the merger, on the grounds that USPCI had never catered to the African American community.

The specter of the hazardous waste wars continued to hang over many other encounters as well. The congregation at Brooksville Baptist Church remained divided by hurt feelings over hazardous waste partisanship. USPCI closed its Macon and Shuqualak offices in May 1994, but a suspicious fire tore through the Macon office six months later. A letter bomb made its way to Ralph Higginbotham's mailbox that October as well, and most people thought it was further fallout from the hazardous waste controversy. By October, USPCI confirmed that the entire company was for sale and that it would be ending its effort to get a Mississippi permit. By January 1995, Printz Bolin quit and moved to Austin, Texas, where he began working as a lobbyist for a division of Union Pacific, determined never to be involved in hazardous waste again. Bitter and hurt by the events of the previous "three fun-filled, blissful years," he thus left behind the home to which he had so eagerly returned.

Printz is hardly a social reformer, and his politics remain firmly anchored in the far right of the Republican Party. Nonetheless, his return to Macon had changed him.

In his last two years there, he began to share the sentiments of many of the county's black majority. He even went so far as to take the heretical position that the private school should close: "Have to start somewhere," he said. "They are absolutely gonna strangle the county." *They?* Did he mean that the white majority—his people—had not acted in the best interests of all? Bolin retreated somewhat. By *they* he meant "everyone—blacks and whites. The blacks don't want integration anymore than the whites. In anything."

Printz was quite "convinced that if it wasn't hazardous waste it would be something else." He said: "Hazardous waste stirred it up a little bit more than usual, more than the norm. A good friend of mine, lives in Laurel now, grew up here and lived here. And he came back here and I was talking to his wife, and she said, 'There's nowhere like it.' And it is, it's an interesting place," he concluded, shaking his head and wincing slightly.

EPILOGUE

IN MARCH 1994, JUST ONE month short of Ike Brown's fortieth birthday, a federal grand jury in his hometown of Canton had indicted him on twenty-five counts of tax fraud. The allegations charged that in 1987 and 1988, in his role as an income tax preparer, Brown had taken spurious deductions for his clients—such as child-care credits for a pair of octogenarians. For this malfeasance, he had typically charged his clients about fifteen dollars. Shortly thereafter, a federal investigation of claims about Hughes-FTI's payoffs to elected officials commenced as well. Ike insisted that he had not been responsible for funneling payments to any politicians.

On December 29, Ike was convicted on nine of the original counts, and on January 6, 1995, he was sentenced to two years in a minimum security prison in Montgomery,

Alabama. He was scheduled to report on Monday, March 6, at 1:00 P.M. His departure was surprisingly upbeat, and was something of a political happening. Noxubee's state legislators—Representative Reecy Dickson and Senator Sampson Jackson—both turned up to see him off, as did a gaggle of other friends and admirers. They gathered outside Brown's Video, a combination video-rental store and pool hall that he had opened on Macon's main street in the first months of 1994. Together they helped him map out his route to Montgomery (to what he braggingly called "Club Fed") and waved goodbye as he left at 10:00 A.M. sharp, in his shiny new green Oldsmobile Cutlass.

Within a few months, Ike began to cry foul, suggesting that he was being martyred because that old bugaboo, "the power structure," wanted him out of commission. By his second month in jail, he came forward and said that the money had "flowed" from FTI during the waste wars, maintaining that at least $2 million in illegal funds had been passed to elected state and local officials. He would not name names and could not document the claims (who bribes by check?), although he did offer to take a polygraph test, an offer the U.S. attorney did not jump to accept.

For his confession, Ike suddenly gained credibility in the eyes of many who were once among his fiercest detractors; they rejoiced that Ike's admission confirmed what they had known all along. Martha Blackwell did not gloat: "I think, personally, Ike talked because he's frightened. He realized that he's gonna be the fall guy."

Ike is gone from Noxubee for the present, but only physically. The county held local elections at the end of 1995. By the late spring, he had begun working the elections from prison, receiving a steady stream of Noxubee visitors to decide on a slate of black candidates and, after that, a strategy for getting them elected. It would be, he predicted, a "watershed" election; with Supervisor Johnny Heard's retirement, blacks looked likely to occupy four of the five seats, with Ralph Higginbotham the only possible remaining white. All other offices, including the important and powerful position of chancery clerk, which has always been held by a white, would go black. In many races, the competitors were all black.

In midsummer, Ike made his personal choices and announced them in a letter addressed "TO THE BLACK VOTERS OF NOXUBEE COUNTY," which was distributed throughout his strongholds in Macon and out in the country. "Lest We Forget," he portentously began, "We are not free yet."

> As I am imprisoned, so could you, but in a different
> manner. They thought by getting rid of me they
> could fool you. Don't let them carry you back to the
> old days, when blacks were found dead in the jail,
> you couldn't even go in the courthouse, you weren't
> even respected. I help bring a change in Noxubee
> County, and I will be back soon. You must win this
> one yourself. I am asking you to remember me by
> supporting these candidates who have pledge to keep
> the dream alive.

He did not say so, but it is hard to resist the speculation that Ike was modeling himself after Martin Luther King Jr., whose passionate and philosophical letter from a Birmingham jail a generation earlier had become one of the classic texts of the civil rights movement.

Most curious of all, Ike made no recommendations for supervisor in Districts Three and Four—respectively, George Robinson's and Ralph Higginbotham's beats. Why was he suddenly estranged from his old FTI cronies? "My recommendations are based on what the people tell me, and they are not doing what the people want." The pair needed, he said, to be taught a lesson.

In white Noxubee, people were jubilant. Some said that his absence was the beginning of a new era: they thought it would be the end of his brand of the politics of historical revenge, and they hoped a torrent of absentee ballots would not come pouring in from his machine (they were wrong). But as his letter showed, he was very much involved. Even had he not been, Noxubee's deeper problems—the gulf between black and white, hill and prairie—remained. As Larry Miller, a white farmer who was raised as a Mennonite and now helps run one of the county's few racially mixed churches, acknowledged: "This is still not an open county and not willing to discuss sore spots, our disease points."

That this continued to be the case was clear as the results of the 1995 elections came in. Ike had urged people to vote against Ralph Higginbotham, and it was big news that he lost in the Democratic primary—to a white truck driver—as Ike had urged. Ike's own supervisor, George Robinson, withstood the political tactician's rebuke, however, and was reelected. The remaining "FTI supervisor," Joseph Stevenson, lost to another black man, ending his long tenure. These results made transparent the fact that black political dominance in Noxubee was at long last assured: not only was the hill district now the only one represented by a white man but most other powerful offices—including that of chancery clerk, charged with the critical task of maintaining land records—also went to black candidates. After the November final elections, Noxubee County's only white supervisor was a working man from the hills. The new board soon chose Boo Oliver as its president. The political transformation of the county was complete; the reign of its aristocracy of the soil had finally passed.

Nonetheless, the usual acrimony continues, this time on the subject of crooked elections. Instead of an open conversation about their divisions, people continue to point fingers across racial and class lines, much as they have since the county's founding. Whites and some blacks loudly complain that a fair election is impossible in Noxubee; in November 1995, they pointed above all else to the high number of absentee ballots (nearly 20 percent), many of them suspiciously discovered in large batches just as the votes were to be counted. For many blacks this was seen as yet another effort to deny them their due. What no one is perhaps willing to acknowledge is that unfair elections are a legacy of Noxubee's secretive culture, one that has tainted everybody. The practice of ballot tinkering has a long, if not venerable, heritage in the black belt. Today's tactics may be unscrupulous, but they are hardly of recent invention.

■ ■ ■ ABOUT the time Ike was indicted, Martha Blackwell, nearly thirty-nine, learned that she was pregnant again—surprising no one more than herself and her husband. In early 1995, just before the birth of Martha Claire, I called her to go over her recollections of several events, including her nerve-wracking first run as an environmentalist, when she urged the supervisors to try something other than the solid waste disposal Ed Netherland promised to provide if the county would only let him become its toxic waste king. She could not speak when I phoned, but she was in a reflective mood when she got back to me the next day.

"I was thinkin' about the solid waste meeting you called about, and started thinkin', one by one, where are all of those people now. It was really strange to think through. Kenny Misso's dead. Johnny Heard's not runnin' again because of stress. Ralph Higginbotham went through reelection by teamin' up with Ike, a twice-convicted felon. Stevenson and Robinson have big-time opposition." Ed Netherland was gone—"at least for the moment," she qualified—as was Brad Moore. "All the people there were just so changed. It just totally took over my life. I'm just so glad my marriage is intact and my kids are okay. I was literally on the phone all night and all day. With me just bein' emotionally gone for three years—if not physically gone, and I was gone a lot."

She paused to collect her thoughts and then concluded. Her pregnancy had been a difficult one, she explained, and Drew had had to take care of her. It had been a time for them to get close again and to reach an accommodation on the hazardous waste: she was to spend no more than regular business hours on it and was also to manage other family activities. The hours of late-night calls, the endless trips to Jackson and across the South—they all had to end. She readily agreed to this plan. Martha was exhausted; the fight's toll on her personally had been enormous. Drew—once jealous of the time she gave to her advocacy and suspicious of her motives—became more accepting of her zeal. "I just feel very fortunate to feel the way I do," Martha concluded. "I wonder how many people feel that way who were at the meeting that day."

Ed Netherland for one. He is back in his hometown of Murfreesboro, Tennessee, making a bundle (half a million in 1994, he boasted to me). And he is still involved with the merged and resold entity that began as FTI, working on "international projects." "I'm real proud of what we did down there." Did we do it for profit? Yes. For personal gain? You bet. For ego? Absolutely. But, he also said, "we did it to change Noxubee County," too. His cancer is in remission, and he has lost none of his sense of personal destiny—what others saw as his arrogance. "Maybe God put me there to change Noxubee County," he solemnly reflected. "I may have been His vehicle, His instrument."

Others would not take such a sanguine view. The board of supervisors briefly looked into suing Hughes-FTI for breach of promise. Netherland left behind a trail of bitter employees and others shaken by what they saw as his duplicity. Ben Tubb, for example, angry at having given so much of his good name working on FTI's behalf, returned to training dogs for a living. Sharon Stallworth left journalism altogether—largely as a result of her experiences reporting on the hazardous waste wars—and went to cooking school in New Orleans.

Martha's life has also changed as much as anyone else's at that meeting. She broadened her world of experience in Noxubee in ways that most people only talk about: by summer she would be out working for black and white candidates, which is still, as she said, "a big deal" in Noxubee (and, she might have added, much of the rest of the country). If the fights over Ralph Higginbotham's term in office and Boo Oliver's hold on his position had signaled the twilight of the whites, it was a dramatic step forward that she and other whites could find common ground to work together with blacks like John Gibson, something her parents could not have imagined. To be sure, she has emerged from the waste wars with a fuller sense of how all the people of Noxubee have to work together to cure their ills. "The thing that's come out in this whole thing," she reflected "is that it's come down to, if the good people aren't going to work together, stand together, then the bad people are just gonna sink us all." Gerry Harris, who had become her closest advisor through all of the waste business, seconded this view: "This whole thing has made me realize how many different kinds of people there are in every race." These are simple but important moments of self-understanding. Of course, the shift in political power in Noxubee means that its whites now require the approval of its black majority in a way they never did before, and the waste fight made clear that it is now in the interest of the white minority—the remnants of Noxubee's aristocracy of the soil—to recognize different shades of black. Nonetheless, because whites still have most of the economic power, the efforts of Martha and Gerry and a few like them to work not only with but also for their neighbors provides the best chance for resuscitating the county's fortunes.

Martha's life has also changed because she is now plugged into a national network of environmental activists. Most are college-educated homemakers like herself, but some are full-time activists, fixtures in the civil rights community. One measure of how much she has changed in five years is that she now counts black leaders in the environmental racism movement as her teachers and friends. Her description of Connie Tucker, a black organizer out of Atlanta, is typical of her new outlook. The characterization is interesting because of the slight note of race fear on which it begins, nonetheless ending with a warm endorsement. With Connie, she said, "you have to go through a period of wading through the dreadlocks and all that"—"all that" meaning the rhetoric of the historical oppression of blacks—"but she's brilliant and has a heart of gold."

She acknowledges, too, the divisions that the separate public and private schools help perpetuate in Noxubee; like most of us, she balks at the search for solutions. "I guess I've really avoided the issue," she said. Meanwhile, the Noxubee schools, public and private, have continued to decline. The enrollment of the private school is back down below three hundred—about what it was when Central Academy opened in 1968—and is again graduating about a dozen students each year. In 1995, metal detectors were installed in the Noxubee public schools to keep students from bringing guns and other weapons to class. Other signs of what people think of as urban pathologies are making a steady advance in Noxubee as well: people worry about a growing teenage drug problem, and the county has had a couple of drive-by shootings.

The hope is that people like Martha Blackwell can use what they have learned in the waste wars to work for Noxubee's future—not just in avoiding environmental threats but, more important, on healing the causes of its vulnerability. The unanswered questions are whether its aristocracy of the soil can take that step, and whether its embittered black majority will let them. On the one hand, Martha worries that the waste companies will be back, and she laments the reason for this: "We have successfully raised a generation— we have no support under eighteen. The outcome is you've bred ignorant people and you're just goin' to be plagued over and over." Yet the ignorance of which she spoke referred only to environmental awareness. The future task for people like her will be to commit to correcting ignorance in the largest sense, not only in working with people of different backgrounds but also in improving access to education and employment opportunities for all of Noxubee's citizens. It is easy enough to blame corporations and bureaucrats for our ills, and it is sometimes appropriate. But the starting place for preventing their worst excesses must begin at home, across the neighbor's fence, down the road.

This is not just, or even fundamentally, a matter of money. A former state education official, who is white, observed to me that the Noxubee public schools do not fare badly by comparison with other Mississippi counties in per-pupil expenditure. But, he grimly explained: "They're very suspicious of any outsider group cummin in. They're very suspicious. And you know, not only blacks, but it goes back to the whites, too." Ending Noxubee's secretive, suspicious culture may be the biggest challenge the county will ever face.

Luckily, there is some hope that this will start to happen. The purchase of the *Beacon* by Scott Boyd, a white journalist and photographer from Jackson, who is in his mid-thirties, has meant that Noxubee's paper of record finally aims to examine the lives of everyone in the county. For the first time, stories about blacks appear next to those about whites. Although Ike Brown and other blacks do not hesitate to label Boyd the power structure's toady when it suits their interest, whites who long for the days when the paper was mostly a white social calendar have also denounced him for being a "nigger lover." He seems to be doing something right. Moreover, the example of Giles County, Tennessee gives hope. In Giles County, a fight against white supremacists educated the community on coming together, and thus enabled them to fight the very different opponents of an ill-considered environmental policy and the entrepreneurs who sought to implement it. This example suggests that, in the long run, the Noxubee waste wars may have given people living close to but separate from one another the experience they needed to achieve an essential accommodation.

The longer Noxubee and similar communities tolerate division, the harder healing becomes. During the middle of the waste wars, George Robinson's sister spoke for many blacks when she warned the county's whites that "it's pay-back time." One way to diffuse such hardened anger would be to pursue less sectarian politics. This would require the unthinkable for the county's whites—talking to, working with, and respecting the contributions of Ike Brown and his forces. Ike gathers strength from opposition, and, as Larry Miller said: "Ike is more of a prophet than he is a leader." A prophet may be a bit of an overstatement, but Ike is a squeaky wheel, and one that many want to continue to ignore. Because he scares some and is seen by others as so hopelessly corrupt that cooperating with him taints his collaborators, this is unlikely. But listening to him and then engaging him in discussion would be crucial steps in moving beyond the divisive aspects of his rhetoric. Brown is fully aware of this effect, too. After the merger that left him and his forces suddenly making an about-face and opposing a hazardous waste operation, he wondered why the PEON leadership—and, specifically, Martha Blackwell—had not called him: "She can't pick the phone up and call me and say, 'Look, we may be in agreement on this issue, let's see if we can work together'?"

Even imperfect prophets like Ike Brown may have a message worth hearing—like his emphasis on the need for improved infant and child health, integrated education, and shared economic power. And if his antagonists do not agree to work with him, to break down the mistrust on which the political culture is based, Noxubee's future is grim. Otherwise, a corrupting and destructive struggle for control of the black prairie belt is likely to continue, not lifting the curse on the land that began with the white usurpation of the Choctaw.

To break this cycle, maybe someday Martha Blackwell or someone like her will pick up the phone and call Ike

Brown, or whoever follows in his footsteps. In late 1995, Martha, Gerry Harris, and other PEON leaders began pressing the state attorney general to reopen official inquiries into Hughes-FTI's alleged bribery of local elected leaders. Ike Brown and Wilbur Colom were among those who supported such investigations. And although the sometime antagonists did not work together for this end, Martha noted hopefully on New Year's Day, 1996, how "interesting" it was that you "get two diametrically opposed people"—by which she meant herself and Ike—"taking the same side on what was happening,"

■ ■ ■ THE specter of the waste wars continues to hang over Noxubee. In mid-1995, the state NAACP, under the leadership of Bea Branch, the commissioner of human services in the Mabus administration, finally disciplined the Noxubee chapter, ostensibly for its heavy involvement in the Higginbotham recall, and specifically for paying the white supervisor's legal fees. Branch ordered that its officers, including the longtime president and FTI partisan, Richard Brooks, vacate their offices.

The victorious lawsuit brought by the Thomases and Jay Chancellor meant that Governor Fordice could resubmit his CAP to the EPA, but the likelihood of a megadump and incinerator in Noxubee seems increasingly dim, if only because industry is at long last cutting down on the volume of hazardous waste it produces, precipitating a financial crisis in the toxic waste disposal business that makes building a new facility an increasingly unattractive proposition. In July 1994, the EPA tacitly acknowledged as much when it told state environmental regulators that the nation had more than enough waste disposal capacity in every treatment category. Nonetheless, the now-merged companies that once duked it out in "Stinking Water" County have spent too much money merely to abandon ship. On December 31, 1994, Laidlaw (another one of the giants in the hazardous waste management business) finalized its purchase of USPCI. In May 1995, John Maxey, Ed Netherland's old lawyer, wrote on Laidlaw's behalf to Mississippi's environmental regulators to request that permit review recommence, a request that was denied pending resolution of some legal issues connected to the Thomas lawsuit. And in September 1995, the EPA's Civil Rights Office finally got around to visiting Noxubee for fact-finding in connection with the Sierra Club Legal Defense Fund's complaint that Noxubee would be unequally burdened by a massive toxic dump.

The fact is that much of the environmental controversy in Noxubee could have been avoided. The decline in the need for waste "management" was not an unforeseeable surprise. Business analysts and environmentalists alike had for years been urging adoption of federal waste-minimization strategies instead of toxics disposal policies predicated on providing disposal capacity.

Yet if Noxubee County and places like it do not get hazardous waste dumps and incinerators, they will get the next worst thing. A seventy-five-bed prison work center opened in the spring of 1996, and a new chicken-processing plant (easily one of the most unsavory possible ways to earn minimum wage) is now operational, providing more jobs than a hazardous waste facility ever would have. Were it not inland, Noxubee's demographics make it a likely location for a casino (by state law, gambling is currently restricted to riverboats). In early 1995, a clothing manufacturer based in nearby Neshoba County decided it would not open in Noxubee because of the "disappointing" labor pool; at the same time, Wal-Mart politely declined the effort by Eva Sherrod and other leading black citizens to have it open a Noxubee store. And in April 1996, in a pre-dawn raid, 50 heavily-armed state narcotics officers broke a major crack cocaine ring—arresting 15—operating out of Noxubee's eastern prairie. Noxubee is no pastoral idyll.

Yet like the seemingly intractable dilemma of school integration, the related question of how to reshape the community so as to make it more attractive to industry remains largely unaddressed. This is a point that a range of people— everyone from Duane Gill to Damu Smith—urged Martha and her forces to examine, but to little apparent effect. But such issues may go unexplored in Noxubee because the world outside remains as indifferent as the county's white elite to its continuing backwardness.

POSTSCRIPT
ON ENVIRONMENTAL
JUSTICE

Whether or not Ed Netherland and other waste company executives understood that Noxubee County was overwhelmingly African American and poor, one would be hard pressed to find a place that better substantiated claims of environmental racism. This postscript will explore the evidence of environmental racism with respect to the choice of Noxubee as a toxic dump and incineration site. However, before examining the evidence, it is important to ask: What is the nature of the fight against environmental racism?

Benjamin Chavis, the short-tenured executive director of the NAACP, is usually credited with coining the term *environmental racism* in 1982, although civil rights organizations throughout the country had long before concerned themselves with the growing awareness that real and perceived environmental hazards were unevenly distributed in American society. Wendell Paris, a grassroots labor and civil rights organizer for the Minority People's Council in west-central Alabama, remembers that his group began looking at environmental concerns in the mid-1970s. Their push culminated with efforts to address worker safety and environmental problems at the newly opened hazardous waste dump at Emelle.

From the start, those who questioned the social justice of environmentally sensitive decisions realized that some activism would be needed outside of the usual legal channels. It quickly became clear that traditional civil rights remedies—specifically, challenges under the equal protection clause of the Fourteenth Amendment to the Constitution—would be of little help in addressing concerns about environmental racism. In 1979, residents of a predominantly black Houston neighborhood challenged in federal court plans to build a solid waste disposal facility in their neighborhood, claiming not only that their community would be irreparably changed for the worse if a permit to build was granted but also that their area had been disproportionately burdened with such waste sites. This practice amounted, the plaintiffs argued, to a violation of the equal protection clause, passed in 1868 in the wake of the Civil War, which provided that no state shall "deny to any person within its jurisdiction the equal protection of the laws." This phrase has formed the basis of much subsequent civil rights law.

After eleven days of testimony involving detailed evidence of the claimed discrimination and volumes of statistical evidence, the court (in the person of Gabrielle McDonald, an African American woman appointed to the bench by President Carter) showed great ideological sympathy with the plaintiffs and their predicament. However, the judge also concluded regretfully, "This Court [might] very well have denied this permit." She added: "It simply does not make sense to put a solid waste site so close to a high school, particularly one with no air-conditioning. Nor does it make sense to put the land site so close to a residential neighborhood." However, McDonald concluded that because a finding of a constitutional equal protection violation requires a showing of *intent* to discriminate, the plaintiffs had no good legal claim.

Despite this precedent, similar court challenges followed, as did the obstacle of proving discriminatory intent. Until as late as 1991, plaintiffs unsuccessfully advanced court challenges alleging discrimination in the siting of environmentally threatening activities in black and Latino neighborhoods. The cases, all of which originated in the Southeast, failed for the same reason: an inability to find a smoking gun that proved intent to discriminate with regard to race.

But the failed equal protection challenges did demonstrate the need to collect a solid statistical record in order to prove that environmental injustice was in fact occurring. Robert Bullard, in the late 1970s a sociologist teaching in Houston and the husband of Linda McKeever Bullard, the lawyer who brought the Houston equal protection case, has played a key role in that effort. Robert Bullard, who is black, began his demographic and sociological analysis of the environmental harms suffered by communities of color at his wife's request; as a young legal services attorney, Linda Bullard lacked funds to pay expert witnesses to substantiate her clients' claims of racial discrimination. She lost that case, but her husband's findings inspired him to produce a steady stream of material documenting instances of environmental racism nationwide.

Legal efforts to combat environmental racism did not occur in isolation. In the early 1980s, large-scale political organizing around environmental justice issues began to take root as well. In 1982, Chavis and other civil rights leaders, including the former congressman Walter Fauntroy of the District of Columbia and Joseph Lowery, the president of the Southern Christian Leadership Conference, were arrested in Warren, North Carolina, along with hundreds of others. The men were in Warren to protest North Carolina's ultimately successful effort to site a dump for polychlorinated biphenyls (PCBs) in a predominantly black neighborhood. (PCBs are a highly toxic class of compounds that were widely used after the Second World War; they are extremely stable and so make excellent coolants and fire retardants when used in industrial electrical equipment. Congress banned their production in 1976.) The Warren incident helped fuel the consolidation of grassroots efforts by civil rights and church groups opposing what they said was the unfair share of environmental hazards borne by communities of color, and primarily African American and Latino communities.

Two subsequent studies proved central to the growing awareness about environmental justice and helped fuel the grassroots movement. The first was a 1983 report prepared by the U.S. General Accounting Office at the request of James Florio, then a U.S. representative, "to determine the correlation between the location of hazardous waste landfills and the racial and economic status of the surrounding communities." The GAO study looked only at offsite dumps in the Southeast and found a high correlation between census areas containing offsite toxic dumps and majority poor, black populations. The second and more influential study was issued in 1987 by the Commission for Racial Justice of the United Church of Christ, then headed by Chavis, and it is now widely credited with catapulting claims of environmental racism to widespread national attention (see chapter 5). Like Robert Bullard's work, the report contained statistical data indicating, if not actual intent to discriminate, at least a troubling correlation between race and proximity to environmental threats. *Toxic Waste and Race in the United States: A National Report on the Racial and Socio-Economic Characteristics of Communities with Hazardous Waste Sites* analyzed census tract information for all hazardous waste sites in the nation. Its most noted finding was that "although socio-economic status appeared to play an important role in the location of commercial hazardous waste facilities, race still proved to be more significant." The UCC report was updated in 1994, correcting some methodological problems of the original and finding that the problem had grown even more severe from 1980 to 1993.

The UCC report helped pave the way for a national debate. In the late 1980s and early 1990s, the movement also put the major national environmental groups on the defensive, particularly the "Big 10" national organizations, such as the Environmental Defense Fund, the National Wildlife Federation, and the Natural Resources Defense Council. Civil rights activists began loudly to denounce what they saw as the neglect of the environmental problems of poor people of color by these largely white groups focused on what they called an elitist agenda concerned more with conserving wilderness than with protecting human health due to environmental problems.

This activism led to the establishment in July 1990 of an official U.S. Environmental Protection Agency workgroup to study the issue and, subsequently, an EPA Office of Environmental Equity. The Big 10 environmental groups began to give the issue attention in the form of staff and funding. Federal and state legislation was introduced that would have required social justice concerns to be incorporated into environmental policy decisions. Although some states have passed such legislation, this has not happened at the federal level. In early 1994, President Clinton even issued an executive order directing that "to the extent practicable and permitted by law, [a federal agency] shall make achieving environmental justice part of its mission by identifying and addressing, as appropriate, disproportionately high and adverse human health or environmental effects of its programs, policies and activities on minority populations and low-income populations in the United States." In short, in the years that Ed Netherland and Printz Bolin were leading the charge to create a huge new hazardous waste dump in one of the poorest, blackest counties in the nation, concern was being raised at the highest levels of government about the ethical and social implications of such businesses to an extent that had never been true before.

■ ■ ■   IF there is any place that resoundingly proves the view that environmentally undesirable activities follow poor people of color—it is Noxubee County, Mississippi. Noxubee is the country's fifty-third poorest county; only seventeen counties have higher African American populations. In 1991, when the waste wars were at their peak, per capita income was only $8,618. A litany of other statistics tells the tale of Noxubee's sorry social and economic state, supporting the claims of environmental justice activists.

To understand Noxubee County's woes more thoroughly, at least to the extent they are revealed in facts and figures, I compared it to the seven surrounding Mississippi counties. It should be remembered that this region of east-central Mississippi is the second poorest region—next only to the Delta—in what is by many measures the nation's poorest state.

Comparing Noxubee County to seven surrounding Mississippi counties—Clay, Kemper, Lowndes, Monroe, Neshoba, Oktibbeha, and Winston—what is striking is the extent to which Noxubee uniformly scores worse by nearly every measure, including welfare (and its likely corollary, the fertility rate among unmarried women), infant mortality, unemployment, literacy, and per capita income. This grouping is especially relevant because many of these counties, including Clay, Kemper, Lowndes, Monroe and Oktibbeha, contain the Selma chalk that Ed Netherland, Printz Bolin, and their superiors and associates maintained was the primary reason to site a hazardous waste operation in Mississippi, and the central reason they had chosen Noxubee County. (I included the two counties without Selma chalk—Neshoba and Winston—because they are hill counties with cultures and demographic makeups similar to those of western Noxubee County's pineywoods.)

When I mapped out all of these measures for the region, Noxubee stood alone: a big sore thumb, throbbing with unrelieved social and economic pain. To find counties with a comparable incidence of poverty and its attendant bleak prospects, one would have to go to the Delta—the other region of the state with consistently high rates of poverty, illiteracy, and unemployment among African Americans. Small wonder that Cathy Johnson, Hughes-FTI's black secretary, would warn her superiors that the company needed to reassure the county's majority of its commitments: "These people are scared," she wrote, "because they don't have anything to rely on."

In the 1990 census, Noxubee's per capita income was only $6,654, by far the lowest in its region (its nearest competitor was Kemper County, at $8,033). By comparison, the per capita income in Giles County, Tennessee, in 1990, the year of FTI's fiasco there, was $10,983.

Among the eight counties in Noxubee County's region, for over ten years from 1983, it consistently scored far higher percentages of food stamp dependence (see chapter 3). In those years, the percentages of people on food stamps were nearly 100 percent higher in Noxubee County than in all but two surrounding counties, Clay and Winston, both of which registered figures about two-thirds of Noxubee's. In a state that in the mid-1980s had the highest percentage of food stamp dependence and emergency food assistance of any state in the nation, Noxubee County was always at least twelve percentage points higher than any county in its region from 1983 to 1994.

The comparative picture of welfare dependence is no happier. (Chapter 3 also contains a discussion of Noxubee's AFDC figures.) Between 1983 and 1993, AFDC payments were received by between 10 percent and 15 percent of Noxubee's residents (and usually closer to 15 percent received the assistance), and the county routinely registered rates two to three times higher than those in all of the seven surrounding counties but two, Clay and Winston. Moreover, neither Clay nor Winston distributed monies to 10 percent of their populations during those years; 9.6 percent was the highest figure registered for either county (9.6 percent in Clay, for 1991 and 1992).

Comparisons of the birthrates among unmarried black women are correspondingly dismal. From the last year of Jimmy Carter's presidency through the second year of Bill Clinton's, Noxubee County registered the highest percentage of births to unmarried African Americans—in six years, more than any other of the eight counties in its region. The percentage of live births to unmarried black women in Noxubee was at least 50 percent in each of those years and often amounted to two-thirds of the county's black mothers. In only one out of fourteen years was the rate of births to unmarried African Americans lower in Noxubee County than in any other county in its region. Even then, the figure was not encouraging. In 1990, fully 62.4 percent of the African American babies born in Noxubee County were to unmarried women, a figure that escalated in the years of the local waste wars: 71.5 percent in 1991; 76.3 percent in 1992; 74.4 percent in 1993, and 73.4 percent in 1994.

The rate of births to unmarried whites also increased throughout this region for the same years, sometimes at a more dramatic rate than for blacks. For instance, the birthrate to unmarried whites in Neshoba County went from 1.2 percent in 1980 to 15.4 percent in 1994, an increase of over 1,100 percent. By comparison, the highest increase among blacks for this period was just under 125 percent, in Kemper County. The only exception to this comparison was Noxubee County, where the birthrate to unmarried whites remained relatively low, fluctuating between 1.6 percent and 7.3 percent for the period, and going into double digits (14 percent) only once, in 1990. For nine out of the fourteen years, Noxubee County registered the lowest percentage of live births to unmarried white women in its region. This suggests that Noxubee's white elite tends to be the most socially conservative in its region, where the norm of "traditional" married families continues to prevail.

The evidence of a relatively privileged white elite living among a highly disadvantaged, impoverished black majority is again evident in infant mortality statistics. In all but three out of fourteen years, Noxubee had black infant mortality figures well above the state average, as high as 35 percent (1980) and usually about 20 percent. In fact, while the health statistics reporting the life experiences of African Americans in east-central Mississippi are particularly grim, those for its white citizens are far more encouraging. Noxubee's white infant mortality rate for the same period was, until 1993, less than half of that for blacks; and in the years that Ed Netherland occupied center stage there, the rate of white infant mortality was about a fifth of that for blacks. Admittedly, these figures require qualification. Because Noxubee is more thinly populated than other counties, the numbers of births and deaths in Noxubee County are correspondingly smaller and so may be unrepresentative. Nonetheless, this and other gloomy statistics that reveal the comparative gulf between the well-being of whites and the well-being of its blacks—a gulf that is wider than in most of the surrounding counties—make it hard for any observer to escape the distinct conclusion that the majority of its citizens are, as the British would say, hard done by.

An alarming feature of these statistics is that, for Noxubee County at least, the figures for blacks and whites appear to have remained proportionally static. In 1925, J. D Green, the county health officer, reported on local mortality and "mortibility" rates. That year the state of Mississippi registered white mortality of 9.5 percent and black mortality of 15 percent. By contrast to the 1990s, Noxubee County scored better in both areas, but, strikingly, even seventy years ago the differential between white and black mortality was greater in Noxubee County than for the rest of the state. While Noxubee County's white death rate was 6.3 percent, its "colored rate" was 13.9 percent—over 100% greater, as opposed to a statewide average differential of slightly over 60 percent.

Of course, the comparison is inexact: 1925 mortality figures for the entire county's population are not the same as infant mortality statistics for the same place seventy years later. But the figures do help support, however imperfectly, the claim many people in Noxubee County made to me time and again, directly or indirectly: the county is locked in time and has not progressed with the world around it.

From 1970 through 1993, Noxubee County also had the highest annual average unemployment rate in its region for just under half of that period—once again, more than any of the eight counties. And it always ranked among the top three counties in its region for high unemployment. From 1975 until 1993, the unemployment rate was not in double digits for only three years, all of them in the late 1970s; in 1975, 1982, 1983, and 1985 the annual unemployment rate was over 15 percent.

One reason for Noxubee County's comparatively poor employment figures unquestionably stems from the county's appallingly high rate of functional illiteracy (also discussed in chapter 3). And unless something dramatic happens in Noxubee, this is unlikely to change: just 51.34 percent of its adults have a high school diploma.

In sum, a company peddling what, to most communities, would be an undesirable business activity would have to look long and hard to find a place more desperate to consider anything at all than Noxubee County.

In public statements, as with most such operations that the public perceives to be dangerous, Hughes-FTI and USPCI maintained that it chose Noxubee County for three reasons only: its geology, the transportation access, and "a large buffer zone," meaning a large tract of land surrounding the location of the actual facility. In support of this claim, waste company publicists routinely pointed to a 1974 EPA study that identified counties with Selma chalk as "ideal" for toxic waste dumps. However, I have also never met a waste company spokesperson—from Chem Waste, Hughes-FTI, or USPCI—who had actually seen that study. In fact, the 111-page report was primarily devoted to the problems of hazardous waste management and advocated passage of a statute very much like the federal hazardous waste management law enacted two years later. Only in the report's sixth appendix—two-thirds of the way through the lengthy document—did it list seventy-four sites across the country that might be appropriate for hazardous waste disposal. The sites were scattered across thirty-six of the lower forty-eight states and included several notable omissions; no sites were mentioned in North Carolina, today the location of several commercial hazardous waste facilities, as well as the controversial PCB dump in Warren that ignited national civil rights groups' attention in 1982. Provided a site was at least 250 miles from an identified industrial center, the criteria for site selection, in order of importance, were as follows: earth science (e.g., geology and hydrology), transportation (including risk and economics), ecology, and "human environment and resources utilization." The only site listed for Alabama was Sumter County, where Emelle sits, less than 250 miles from that state's major industrial centers of Montgomery and Mobile. The only Mississippi county named in the report was Lincoln County, which sits about an hour directly south of Jackson on the interstate—about as far from Noxubee as you can get in Mississippi. The fact was never noted during the Noxubee waste wars.

Noxubee County's example therefore begs the need for

systematic rethinking of our location and regulation of toxic industries. One promising approach is disparate impact analysis—the tactic tried on AAEJ's behalf by the Sierra Club Legal Defense Fund (see chapter 9). The Sierra Club LDF's arguments relied on Title VI of the 1964 Civil Rights Act, a provision of which requires in part that no person, "on the ground of race, color, or national origin, be excluded from participation in, be denied benefits of, or be subjected to discrimination under any program or activity receiving Federal financial assistance." Because the Mississippi Department of Environmental Quality's hazardous waste section receives most of its funding from the federal government, this provision could be said to apply to its permitting process.

The Sierra Club LDF argued that the practical effect of Mississippi's hazardous waste permitting regulations was to discriminate against poor and mostly black communities. For example, "the Mississippi siting criteria themselves essentially push hazardous waste facilities toward areas that are majority African-American." This was true because of the focus on siting in counties with low population density, which "are in general those with the highest population of non-white citizens."

At first blush, most Americans endorse the idea of putting hazardous waste where there are the fewest people. In Noxubee, even after the havoc wreaked on the community by the waste fight, PEON supporters regularly suggested to me that the stuff should be sent to Utah, Nevada, or, most oddly, to Japan. On reflection, however, the rationale is not so clear. The environmental researcher Peter Montague has argued only half facetiously that there is no more reason to put a landfill in the remote countryside than in the city. He reasons that if toxic operations are truly believed to be safe, they should go where we can keep an eye on them. He thus proposes an elevated landfill, built anywhere except on soils that may shift and so cause a structure to crack. In his scheme, a landfill would be built of twelve-inch-thick reinforceable concrete slabs on top of walkways that would allow constant inspection to assure that nothing is leaking. Montague has few illusions about the effect: "Of course they'd be ugly. But why kid ourselves? . . . I'd emboss the exterior walls with huge skull and crossbones to get the message across to enthusiasts and critics alike—this building is a deadly tomb for technical hubris and dumb ideas."

The Sierra Club LDF complained that Mississippi's environmental regulators never made public the grounds for choosing the factors it did, "or explained its failure to adopt additional criteria designed to reach a non-discriminatory result." This criticism could be applied almost anywhere in the nation. It was the complaint Martha Blackwell first heard from George Baggett and Duane Gill: concerns about environmental safety aside, siting a toxic operation sends a psychological message as well, reflecting the larger society's valuation of the importance and worth of a community and its citizens.

In addition to disparate impact lawsuits, other possible approaches include solutions like tax incentives for cleaner industrial processes, as well as those that demonstrably reduce their generation of dangerous materials. Surely we need not accept environmentally dangerous businesses merely because they are a necessary cost of living the good life. Instead, we need to cultivate habits that do not require dirty living. This is above all true because the evidence so compellingly suggests that the people who most often bear the dangers of living near the excreta of our acquisitive industrial society are the very same ones who have been most abused throughout our history. Thus, the environmental justice movement not only asks us to find solutions in the service of our shared health and environment but also asks us to confirm our commitment to a truly just society.

ENDNOTES

These endnotes are not a comprehensive accounting of every source used in the preparation of this book. Instead, they are designed as a bibliographic resource for use by general readers, and therefore mostly direct attention to easily obtained material. References are not given for interviews conducted by the author or materials from most local Mississippi, Alabama, and Tennessee sources, such as newspapers and official or private correspondence. References are provided for national and regional newspapers and other periodicals obtainable in most public libraries or on widely used electronic databases. Thus, for example, there are no references to the Macon, Mississippi *Beacon* or the Columbus, Mississippi *Commercial-Dispatch*, but there are references to the *New York Times* and the *Atlanta Journal and Constitution*, as well as to Mississippi's newspaper of record, the *Clarion-Ledger*, and the state's principal financial newspaper, the *Mississippi Business Journal*, both published in Jackson. The exception to this rule is published material of historical or archival interest, even when not readily accessible.

INTRODUCTION

page ix
" 'The unearthly stench . . .' " Gordon Hansen, *Noxubee County Historical Trail* (Macon: Noxubee County Chamber of Commerce, 1992). The volume contains no page numbers.

page x
"Names are the consequences of the things . . ." Mark Musa, ed., *Dante's* Vita Nuova: *A Translation and an Essay* (Bloomington: Indiana University Press, 1973), chap. 13, p. 22 (". . . since, as has often been said, names are the consequences of the things they name: *Nomina sunt consequentia rerum*"). I am indebted to Albert Pesant for this reference.

page xi
"While researching for a consumer . . ." Paul Kemezis, "Three proposals in Mississippi," *Chemical Week*, Apr. 24, 1991, p. 22.

page xiii
"I knew, too, that the movement . . ." In fact, environmental scientists routinely argue that hazardous waste disposal operations pose a relatively low risk to public health and safety by comparison to problems that are of much less concern to the general public, such as indoor air pollution. See, for instance, Joel Makower, *The E Factor: The Bottom-Line Approach to Environmentally Responsible Business* (New York: Times Books, 1993), p. 19; U.S. Environmental Protection Agency Science Advisory Board, *Reducing Risk: Setting Priorities and Strategies for Environmental Protection* (Washington, DC: GPO, 1990) and *Unfinished Business: A Comparative Assessment of Environmental Problems* (Washington, DC: GPO, 1987).

page xv
"The best explanation I found came from . . ." Peter Montague is the editor and publisher of *Rachel's Environment and Health Weekly*, formerly *Rachel's Hazardous Waste News*, issued weekly by his Environmental Research Foundation, in Annapolis, MD. The views described here mostly draw from his essay "The Limitations of Landfilling," in Bruce Piasecki, ed., *Beyond Dumping: New Strategies for Toxic Contamination* (Westport, CT: Quorum Books, 1984).

page xvi
"Landfills give further cause for concern . . ." *Rachel's Hazardous Waste News*, no. 370 (Dec. 30, 1993) and no. 71 (Apr. 4, 1988).

page xvii
". . . call the precautionary principle . . ." An endorsement of this approach from an unusual source appears in Gordon K. Durnil, *The Making of a Conservative Environmentalist* (Bloomington: Indiana University Press, 1995).

"In the face of such criticism, hazardous waste . . ." The legal definition of a *hazardous substance* is one that demonstrates any one of several different properties, such as materials that are flammable, combustible, corrosive, irritant, likely to generate pressure through decomposition or other processes, or toxic. See 15 U.S.C. Sec. 1261(f). Because in everyday parlance *hazardous* and *toxic* are often used synonymously, I have done so here. Readers with a professional interest in this material should keep in mind, however, that there are technical and legal differences between different kinds of hazardous substances.

page xviii
"This is becoming . . ." Waste reduction efforts are succeeding in individual states, including Mississippi. The promising results of one such effort appear in an unpublished report from the early 1990s titled *Demonstration Project for Waste Minimization for a Metal-Finishing Industry* (Starkville: Mississippi State University, n.d.). These issues are discussed generally in Barry Commoner, *Making Peace with the Planet* (New York: New Press, 1992). See also Michael B. Gerrard, *Whose Backyard, Whose Risk: Fear and Fairness in Toxic and Nuclear Waste Siting* (Cambridge, MA: MIT Press, 1994), p. 148.

"In a 1937 autobiographical essay . . ." Richard Wright, "The Ethics of Living Jim Crow," in *Uncle Tom's Children* (New York: HarperPerennial, 1993), p. 15.

page xix
". . . famously dubbed Jim Crow's 'strange career.' " C. Vann Woodward, *The Strange Career of Jim Crow*, 3rd rev. ed. (New York: Oxford, 1974).

CHAPTER 1
page 6

"Canton, the heavily black seat . . ." Civil rights activism in Canton and elsewhere is discussed in Anne Moody's affecting memoir, *Coming of Age in Mississippi* (New York: Dial Press, 1968).

"(Charles Evers, . . ." The campaign is discussed in Adam Nossiter, *Of Long Memory: Mississippi and the Murder of Medgar Evers* (Reading, MA: Addison-Wesley, 1994) and Maryanne Vollers, *Ghosts of Mississippi: The Murder of Medgar Evers, the Trial of Byron de la Beckwith, and the Haunting of the New South* (Boston: Little, Brown, 1995).

page 8

"Even today, . . . 81 percent white." "School Sketches," *Commercial Appeal* (Memphis, TN), Mar. 8, 1995. A protracted court challenge to the still-segregated universities suggests that sentiment for keeping the less distinguished black universities may be as strong among African Americans as among whites. Ronald Smothers, "Mississippi's University System Going on Trial," *New York Times*, May 9, 1994, p. A10; Andy Kanengiser, "NAACP Will Help Fund Ayers Case," *Clarion-Ledger* (Jackson, MS), Feb. 22, 1994, p. 1A. This is hardly a new phenomenon; W. E. B. DuBois discussed it, in "Does the Negro Need Separate Schools?" 4 *Journal of Negro Education* (1935): 328. See also Claude M. Steele, "Race and the Schooling of Black Americans," *Atlantic*, Apr. 1992, p. 68, and James Traub, "Can Separate Be Equal?" *Harper's Magazine*, June 1994, p. 36. Major rulings in the over-ten-year-old federal case seeking to desegregate Mississippi universities include: *Ayers v. Fordice* 879 F. Supp. 1419 (N.D. Miss. 1995), and *Ayers v. Fordice*, 970 F.2d 1378 (5th Cir. 1992).

page 15

"A local history reports that, in 1797, Barnett . . ." John A. Tyson, *Historical Notes of Noxubee County* (Macon: Noxubee County Historical Society, 1985), p. 255. The volume reprints material originally collected by Tyson in 1928 and taken from his regular column for a local newspaper, *The Macon Beacon*.

"In the early 1850s, . . ." *Ibid.*, p. 254.

page 16

"The Calhoun Institute was . . ." Susie V. Powell, supervisor, *Source Material for Mississippi History: Noxubee County*, vol. LIII, pt. 2 (Works Progress Administration [MS] State Wide Historical Research Project, 1936-1938; reprint of an 1858 brochure), p. 64. *Source Material*, vol. LIII, consists of two separate volumes of typescript, marked as parts 1 and 2. The two are invaluable sources on life in Noxubee County until and during the Great Depression; similar volumes were prepared under WPA guidance for each Mississippi county. The copies I consulted are the property of the Office of Chancery Clerk, Noxubee County, MS. Neither volume contains place of publication data.

" 'People were too aristocratic to . . . undignified." *Ibid.*, p. 63.

page 17

"William Faulkner once wrote that . . ." William Faulkner, "Mississippi," reprinted in Dorothy Abbott, ed., *Mississippi Writers: Reflections of Childhood and Youth*, vol. 2 (Jackson: Univ. Press of Mississippi, 1986), p. 245. This view did not originate with Faulkner. For example, the Greenville, Mississippi, writer David Cohn wrote that "the Mississippi Delta begins in the lobby of the Peabody Hotel in Memphis and ends on Catfish Row in Vicksburg" (quoted in James W. Loewen and Charles Sallis, eds., *Mississippi: Conflict and Change* [New York: Pantheon, 1974], p. 15).

page 18

"(In 1920, the name was changed . . ." The DUB-ya went coed in 1982, in a U.S. Supreme Court case won by the lawyer Wilbur Colom, who would later play a key role in Noxubee County's waste wars. The case is *Mississippi University for Women v. Hogan*, 458 U.S. 718 (1982).

page 19

"In it a local writer . . ." *Source Material*, pt. 2 (cited above in note for page 16), p. 141. The entire passage, written in the late 1930s by one Mrs. Laura H. Griffin, of Macon, reads as follows:

"Land of Ideals"
    The history of Noxubee County is an amazing record of achievement and disillusion, happiness, and despair; a gripping drama of romance and adventure. Rich in the

traditions established by an intellectual and cultured citizenship of the Old South, Noxubee is a land of ideals, tenaciously adhered to down through the years since the early days of the nineteenth century.

Noxubee is a story of an aristocracy of the soil. The characteristics of the great Black Prairie-Line lands have fought for expression since long before the coming of the white man. It has been successfully the chosen home of the Choctaws, the most intelligent and agricultural-minded of American Aborigines; the "Granary of the Confederacy" during the War between the States, and today, it aspires to the distinction of being the "Dairyland of Dixie."

page 22

"In fact, an early chronicler of the event . . .". Tyson reported but rejected this story. *Historical Notes of Noxubee County* (cited above in note for page 15), p. 315.

"Historians of the event agree that . . ." For example, see Robert B. Ferguson, "Treaties between the United States and the Choctaw Nation," in Carolyn Keller Reeves, ed., *The Choctaw before Removal* (Jackson: Univ. Press of Mississippi, 1985), pp. 223–24.

". . . 'bought with the white man's money . . . forfeited ours.' " William Faulkner, "The Bear," reprinted in *Three Famous Short Novels* (New York: Vintage, 1961), pp. 244–45.

page 25

"The Tombigbee River, once . . . in 1938." Jeffrey K. Stine, *Mixing the Waters: Environment, Politics and the Building of the Tennessee-Tombigbee Waterway* (Akron, OH: Univ. of Akron, 1993).

page 26

"But the state was growing . . ." I visited a capacious plantation house deep in the Delta, on the other side of the state from Noxubee County, that had been purchased as a mail-order kit and shipped downriver from Cincinnati for assembly in Mississippi. For a discussion of the erratic patterns of agricultural and industrial growth in the Mississippi Delta, despite its "tremendous wealth-producing potential," see James C. Cobb, *The Most South-*

ern Place on Earth: The Mississippi Delta and the Roots of Regional Identity (New York: Oxford, 1992).

page 27
"In 1860, on the eve of . . ." U.S. Bureau of the Census, *Population of the United States in 1860: Compiled from the Original Returns of the Eighth Census under the Direction of the Secretary of the Interior* (New York: N. Ross, 1990), pp. 264–73. And in a world where people were property, it seems safe to assume that the antebellum figures may significantly undercount the slave population, since the reported numbers were in control of owners who, for personal and financial reasons may have distorted them.

page 29
"Tyson reported that . . . abundant.' " *Historical Notes of Noxubee County* (cited above in note for page 15) p. 31.

page 33
"But with emancipation . . ." Eric Foner, *Reconstruction: America's Unfinished Revolution, 1863–1877* (New York: Harper & Row, 1988), p. 78.

CHAPTER 2
page 36
"In 1987, the Mobro garbage barge . . ." William E. Sauro, "Garbage Barge's 155-Day Odyssey Comes to an End," *New York Times*, Aug. 25, 1987, p. B4. On the "poo-poo choo-choo," about which Mike Goff told reporters: "We don't want it here. We're going to do what we have to do to get it out of here," see Fern Shen, "Mississippi Turns Up Nose at Md. Sludge," *Washington Post*, Nov. 10, 1989, p. B6; "Baltimore Waste Arrives in Mississippi," United Press International, Nov. 3, 1989.

page 37
"The growing sense of crisis . . . 'pay toilet.' " The phrase came from Jimmy Evans, then an aggressive Alabama prosecutor and rising political star whose unconventional ways were profiled by CBS's *60 Minutes*, in a segment titled "Jimmy Evans," which was broadcast on Dec. 15, 1985.

"The Emelle landfill . . ." Emelle has long been the focus of criticism in environmental circles. For instance, see Conner Bailey and Charles E. Faupel, "Environmentalism and Civil Rights in Sumter County, Alabama," in Bunyan Bryant and Paul Mohai, eds., *Race and the Incidence of Environmental Hazards: A Time for Discourse* (Boulder, CO: Westview, 1992), pp. 140–52; William E. Schmidt, "When the Neighbor Is a Toxic Landfill," *New York Times*, Oct. 16, 1985, p. A18.

page 38

"The Holley bill challenged . . ." CAPs were introduced by the Superfund Amendments and Reauthorization Act of 1986 (SARA). Public Law 99-499, Oct. 17, 1986, 100 Stat. 1613. Key sections of the Superfund law, which is formally known as the Comprehensive Environmental Response, Compensation and Liability Act of 1980, are codified at 42 U.S.C. Secs. 9601-9661. The specific section referred to here is 42 U.S.C. Sec. 9604(c)(9).

"In an August 1990 opinion, . . ." The Holley bill was struck down as unconstitutional by *National Solid Waste Management Association and Chemical Waste Management, Inc. v. The Alabama Department of Environmental Management et al.*, 910 F.2d 713 (11th Cir. 1990)(a related case appears at 924 F.2d 1001 [11th Cir. 1991]). The Holley-bill case also involved challenges to state regulations that further aimed to restrict waste shipments to Emelle. The federal district court ruling which Chem Waste appealed was 729 F.Supp. 792 (N.D. Ala. 1990).

"It was not until June 1992 that . . ." The decisions on the out-of-state tax law are *Chemical Waste Management, Inc. v. Guy Hunt, Governor of Alabama et al.*, 504 U.S. 334 (1992), reversing 584 So. 2d 1367 (Supreme Court of Ala. 1991). In the Supreme Court, Chief Justice Rehnquist dissented, eloquently stating what, later in this chapter, is characterized as the "states' rights" view of hazardous waste disposal. The chief justice wrote: "[T]he Court today gets it exactly backward when it suggests that Alabama is attempting to [isolate itself]. To the contrary, it is the 34 states that have no hazardous waste facility whatsoever, not to mention the remaining 15 States with facilities all smaller than Emelle, that have isolated themselves."

page 39

"Danner, the quintessential . . . controversy." For instance, see Steve Watkins, "Racism du jour at Shoney's," *Nation,* Oct. 18, 1993, p. 424; Brett Pulley, "Strained Family: Culture of Racial Bias at Shoney's Underlies Chairman's Departure," *Wall Street Journal,* Dec. 21, 1992, p. A1. A federal case discussing the consent decree reached in the discrimination case is *Haynes et al. v. Shoney's Inc., Danner et al.,* No. 89-30093-RV (N.D. Fla. 1993). A related decision is *Haynes et al. v. Shoney's Inc., Danner et al.,* 803 F.Supp. 393 (N.D. Fla. 1992).

page 47

"Stephen Gaskin . . . nearby" Don Lattin, "Retro Religion: The Hippie, Jesus Movements Continue to Thrive in the '90s," *San Francisco Chronicle,* Nov. 28, 1992, p. 9D.

page 49

"The six young men who dreamed up . . ." Nelle Roger Cohen, *Pulaski History, 1809–1950,* rev. ed. (Pulaski, TN: Giles County Historical Society, 1986), p. 19.; see also Mr. and Mrs. W. B. Rommie, *A Story of the Original Ku Klux Klan* (Pulaski, TN: Pulaski Citizen, 1924); William L. Katz, *Invisible Empire: The Story of the Ku Klux Klan, 1866–1871* (Washington, DC: Open Hand, 1986).

"In 1869, retired Confederate general . . ." Several years later, Congress enacted the Klux Klan Act of 1871, which prevents any one citizen from depriving another of his rights through intimidation and coercion. Sections of the act are scattered throughout the U.S. Code, but see especially 42 U.S.C. Secs. 1983, 1985, and 1986.

". . . the writer who, in 1951, wrote that the Klan . . ." *Pulaski History,* p. 23.

page 50

"Giles Countians boast that . . ." *Finding Our Past: History of Black Education in Giles County, 1920–1970* (Pulaski, TN: Giles County

Historical Society, 1986) explains, in chapters 4 and 5, the local history of integration.

CHAPTER 3
page 72

"It was as if they worried that latter-day . . ." The best account of the Philadelphia, Mississippi, civil rights murders is by Florence Mars, a Philadelphia native, in her book *Witness in Philadelphia* (Baton Rouge: LSU Press, 1977). I am grateful to Philadelphian Allen Payne for recommending that I read Mars's book. Another contemporary account is William Bradford Huie, *Three Lives for Mississippi* (New York: Signet Books, 1968).

page 73

"The typical white student in Mississippi . . ." Gary Orfield, *The Growth of Segregation in American Schools: Changing Patterns of Segregation and Poverty since 1968; A Report of the Harvard Project on School Desegregation* (National School Boards Association, 1993).

"Mississippi has a black population . . . African-American legislators." The percentage of legislators is based on U.S. Bureau of the Census, *Statistical Abstract of the United States, 1994* (Washington, DC: GPO, 1995), p. 284; see also Reed Branson, "Redistricting Changing the Face of Mississippi Politics," *Commercial-Appeal* (Memphis, TN), July 16, 1995, p. 1B; "Lott Not Surprised at Flap over Vote to End King Day Funds," *Commercial-Appeal*, May 26, 1994, p. 17A.

". . . (this is the state, after all . . ." Miss. Code Ann. Sec. 3-3-7. The federal Memorial Day holiday is also celebrated in Mississippi as Jefferson Davis's birthday. The state observes Confederate Memorial Day on the last Monday in April.

page 74

"In the end, the prodigal son/daughter . . ." The names are pseudonyms. These facts bear an uncanny similarity to the fictional situation imagined by playwright Ed Graczyk in his play, *Come Back to the 5 & Dime Jimmy Dean, Jimmy Dean* (Samuel French: New

York, 1976). The play was produced on Broadway in 1982 and made into a movie that year by the director Robert Altman.

page 75

"W. E. B. Dubois's color line, . . ." W. E. B. DuBois, "Of the Dawn of Freedom," in *The Souls of Black Folk* (New York: Library of America, 1990), p. 35.

page 77

"For nearly two decades, Noxubee's level . . ." State data indicate that Noxubee County always posted the highest figures in its region, with percentages two to three times higher than in all but one of the seven surrounding counties. These figures are discussed in greater detail in the Postscript.

page 80

"In November 1958, Medgar Evers . . ." Medgar Evers, "Why I Live in Mississippi," reprinted in *Mississippi Writers* vol. 2 (cited above in note for page 17), p. 210.

page 81

"If, for example, you stopped in . . ." William Stanley Hoole, ed., *Reconstruction in West Alabama: The Memoirs of John L. Hunnicutt* (Tuscaloosa: Confederate Publishing Co., Inc., 1959).

" If you visited the library . . ." Ward grew up among Stowes and other abolitionists in Litchfield, Connecticut. In Macon, he achieved minor fame as the author of "Come to the South" and similar inspirational verse:

> We call you, O men of the kilt and the tartan,
> > From highland and lowland, from mountain and mere—
> Though you feel for your country the love of a Spartan,
> > A sunnier home and a welcome is here . . .

Locally, Ward acted as a conciliator between Union and Confederate interests:

> And so they share—the brave and the true,
> > The glory of that fateful day;
> The Gray the glory of the Blue,
> > The Blue the glory of the Gray.

William Ward, *The Poems of William Ward* (Macon: Macon Beacon Press, 1933), p. 16. Williams's best-known historical novel, *House Divided* (New York: Houghton Mifflin, 1947), was about the Civil War.

page 82
"You will certainly not hear about . . ." W. E. B. DuBois quoted an African American contemporary of Davis's who said that the Reconstruction lieutenant governor "had made a creditable record as member of the Legislature, but he was not a strong man." DuBois, *Black Reconstruction in America, 1860–1880* (New York: Atheneum, 1992), p. 445.

page 83
"As a young man, Hairston attempted . . ." Loyle Hairston, "Growing Up in Mississippi," reprinted in *Mississippi Writers* vol. 2 (cited above in note for page 17), p. 311.

page 85
"But one aspect . . ." William Winter, Mississippi's progressive Governor from 1980-1984, and one who made educational reform a priority, referred to his years as a state legislator when he later explained: "For twenty years we had spent most of our energy seeking ways to forestall the implementation of the Brown decision." The recollection was shared with one of his aides—Martha Blackwell's first cousin, Andy Mullins. Andrew P. Mullins Jr., *Building Consensus: A History of the Passage of the Mississippi Education Reform Act of 1982* (Jackson: Mississippi Humanities Council, 1992), p. 2. In Noxubee County, in substance if not in form, the resistance of which he spoke continues today.

"Despite the Supreme Court's 1955 order . . ." *Brown v. Board of Education of Topeka*, 349 U.S. 294, 300 (1955).

"In August 1968, on the eve . . ." *Adams v. Mathews*, 403 F.2d 181, n. 3 (5th Cir. 1968).

page 86
"His opinion reiterated . . ." *Ibid.* (quoting *Green v. County School Board of Kent County, Virginia*, 391, U.S. 430, 438 [1968]).

page 88

"In the summer of 1969, the U.S. Court of Appeals . . ." *U.S. v. Hinds County School Board et al.*, 417 F.2d 852, 855 (5th Cir. 1969). During this period, the federal court also issued injunctions prohibiting further intimidation of African Americans in Noxubee County who tried to take advantage of freedom-of-choice plans and send their children to formerly white schools. See *U.S. v. Farrar*, 414 F.2d 936 (5th Cir. 1969). Data on the incidence of racial harassment in Noxubee County were used in the preparation of an influential assessment of the Voting Rights Act in the decade after its passage. *The Voting Rights Act: Ten Years After. A Report of the U.S. Commission on Civil Rights* (Washington, DC: GPO, 1975).

"At the time this decision . . ." *U.S. v. Hinds*, *ibid.*, p. 859.

"The court ordered that freedom of choice . . ." *U.S. v. Hinds*, *Ibid.*, p. 856.

page 89

"By early November 1969, . . ." *U.S. v. Hinds County School Board et al.*, 423 F.2d 1264, 1268 (5th Cir. 1969).

page 90

"Its account of this latest development . . ." Careful readers will note the discrepancy between the numbers reported in the *Hinds* decision and those used by the *Macon Beacon* (taken from the federal Department of Health, Education and Welfare). I have no explanation, although I am more inclined to trust the statistics that appeared in the official court record. In any event, the discrepancy does not affect the substance of the analysis.

page 91

"Memories of the boycott, . . ." In a subsequent decision, the federal court did mention—if fleetingly—the boycott: "Although not a part of the evidence at this hearing, the Court takes judicial notice of the fact that the Negro students of [the Noxubee County] school district, in toto, refused to accept their assignments under the modified plan and boycotted the schools for the remainder of the 1969 term." *U.S. v. Hinds County School Board et al.*, 433 F.2d 619, 620 (5th Cir. 1970).

page 92
"Twenty years ago, the constitutional law scholar . . ." Derrick A. Bell, "Racial Remediation: An Historical Perspective on Current Conditions," *Notre Dame Lawyer*, 52 (1976): 5. Bell has spent his career examining these issues. Much of his thinking is summarized in two highly accessible books, *And We Are Not Saved: The Elusive Quest for Racial Justice* (New York: Basic Books, 1987) and *Faces at the Bottom of the Well: The Permanence of Racism* (New York: Basic Books, 1992).

page 103
". . . runs counter to the idea that . . . would naturally be expected.'" V. O. Key Jr., *Southern Politics in State and Nation*, rev. ed. (Knoxville: Univ. of Tennessee, 1984), pp. 5–9. Key's chapter on Mississippi (pp. 229–53) also includes an invaluable introduction to the politics of the black belt.

page 105
"Richard Brooks, the retired schoolteacher . . ." Richard Brooks, *Noxubee County, 1985–1877: The Rebirth, 1960* (Macon: Noxubee County NAACP, 1993).

page 106
"In 1975, Joseph Wayne was reelected . . ." *Ibid.*

CHAPTER 4
page 113
"Despite the fact that Mississippi . . ." These figures are drawn from U.S. Environmental Protection Agency, *List of Large Quantity Generators in the United States: The Biennial RCRA Hazardous Waste Report (Based on 1991 Data)* (Washington, DC: GPO, 1994). Mississippi was that year the ninth-largest generator in the nation, producing 8,050,831 tons in 1991. (By comparison, Texas, the largest generator of hazardous waste that year, produced 104,000,000 tons of hazardous waste in 1991.) Mississippi's ranking was much emphasized by the waste companies; but this attention obscured a key detail, namely, that 6,600,000 of those tons were produced by a single generator far away from Noxubee County, on the Gulf Coast—Chevron's Pascagoula facility.

page 122
"WMX's story is one of . . ." For basic information on WMX, see Council on Economic Priorities, *Hazardous Waste Management: Reducing the Risk* (Washington, DC: Island Press, 1986), pp. 168–72; Will Collette, Gabrielle Katz, Brian Lipsett, Sybil Peterson, and Karen Stults, *Waste Management, Inc.: A Corporate Profile* (Arlington, VA: Citizens' Clearinghouse for Hazardous Waste, 1989).

page 123
"In 1977, Alabama Governor George C. Wallace's . . ." Questions surrounding the transaction were investigated by Diane Sawyer in the CBS *60 Minutes* segment referred to above in note for page 37.

"In 1976, Congress passed . . . RCRA . . ." Public Law 94-580, Oct. 21, 1976, 90 Stat. 2795. The law is codified at 42 U.S.C. Secs. 6901-6987.

"Only about 4 percent of the nation's waste stream . . ." *Whose Backyard, Whose Risk* (cited above in note for page xviii), p. 148.

page 124
"A 1980 study by the Conservation . . ." Reported in a special investigative edition of *The Advertiser* [Montgomery, AL], p. 24 (December 1984) prepared by Booth Gunter and Mike Williams and entitled "Alabama: The Nation's Dumping Ground".

page 140
"The amounts were not sufficient to cause . . ." Federal standards provide that concentrations of fifty parts per million or above should cause alarm (40 Code of Federal Regulations ("C.F.R.") Part 761.1). Others are not so sanguine that any concentration is acceptable; see, for example, *Rachel's Hazardous Waste News*, no. 327 (Mar. 4, 1993) and no. 329 (Mar. 18, 1993).

CHAPTER 5
page 143
"The issue had achieved national prominence . . ." The influential United Church of Christ report, issued by the church's Commission for Racial Justice, was titled *Toxic Waste and Race in the*

United States: A National Report on the Racial and Socio-Economic Characteristics of Communities with Hazardous Waste Sites (New York: United Church of Christ Commission for Racial Justice, 1987). The Postscript discusses the report and related matters in greater detail.

page 146

"This role has done little to endear him . . ." For example, Ernest L. Brown represented the Noxubee County School District in the case of *U.S. v. Hinds County School Board et al.*, 417 F.2d 852, 855 (5th Cir. 1969) and the then-sheriff of Noxubee County, Emmett W. Farrar, in an integration-related harassment case, *U.S. v. Farrar*, 414 F.2d 936 (5th Cir. 1969). Charlie George Perkins represented Noxubee County defendants in a case involving an effort to declare unconstitutional a 1962 Mississippi statute that allowed for the at-large election of aldermen on the grounds that it "was conceived and designed by the legislature as a purposeful device to invidiously discriminate against black voters in municipal elections by diluting black voting strength." *Stewart et al. v. Waller*, 404 F.Supp. 206 (N.D.Miss. 1975).

page 152

"County unemployment was then at its . . ." The 15 percent figure is based on the 1990 U.S. Census, which calculated that Noxubee's "civilian labor force" had 4,930 people. U.S. Bureau of the Census, *1990 Census of Population and Housing: Mississippi*, 1990 CPH-3-26, Table 18 (Washington, DC: GPO, 1993).

page 153

"The last new commercial hazardous waste operation . . ." *Whose Backyard, Whose Risk* (cited above in note for page xviii), p. 3.

"More recently, an Ohio hazardous waste incinerator . . ." Liane Clorfene-Casten, "E.P.A. Fiddles while W.T.I. Burns," *Nation*, Sept. 27, 1993. Terri Swearingen, the former high school cheerleader at the center of the opposition, is described in Keith Schneider, "For Crusader against Hazardous Waste Incinerator, a Bittersweet Victory," *New York Times*, May 19, 1993, p. A14; Alan A. Block, "Into the Abyss of Environmental Policy: The Battle over the World's Largest Hazardous Waste Incinerator in East Liverpool, Ohio" (paper prepared for presentation at the American Society of Criminology Annual Meeting, New Orleans, LA, 1992).

page 156

"In the story 'Barn Burning' . . ." Dorothy Abbott, ed., *Mississippi Writers: Reflections of Childhood and Youth*, vol. 1 (Jackson: Univ. Press of Mississippi, 1985), p. 161.

page 162

"A cousin had taught at 'the DUB-ya' . . ." On the achievements and history of Mississippi State College for Women, see "Save the W," *Wall Street Journal*, May 6, 1994.

page 164

"Keeping a colored shack on the property . . ." A celebrated study of that world and its intricate web of obligation is Allison Davis, B. Burleigh, and Mary R. Gardner, *Deep South: A Social Anthropological Study of Caste and Class* (Chicago: Univ. of Chicago Press, 1941).

page 166

". . . becoming the 'czar of economic development in Indian country.' " Susan Traylor, "Mississippi Choctaw Chief Pushing Formation of Native American Office," Gannett News Service, Apr. 10, 1991. Some of Chief's Martin's pregaming endeavors are recounted with admiration by Robert White, in *Tribal Assets: The Rebirth of Native America* (New York: Holt, 1990).

". . . had an unemployment rate as high as 70 percent" Chris Gilmer, "Choctaws Sign Casino Agreement with Vegas Group," *Mississippi Business Journal*, Mar. 22, 1993.

". . . he earned over $97,000 in 1992 . . ." Scott Morrison, "Highest Paid Tribal Leader Gets Raise," *News from Indian Country* 6 (Dec. 1992): No. 24.

"The pregaming per capita income . . ." Adam Nossiter, "Proposed Toxic Waste Dump Divides Choctaws, Alarms Environmentalists," *Atlanta Journal and Constitution*, Feb. 5, 1991, p. 2.

page 172
"Like Chem Waste, USPCI expanded . . ." A somewhat dated profile of the company (preceding its purchase by Union Pacific) appears in *Hazardous Waste Management* (cited above in note for
page 122), pp. 165–68. Organizations United for the Environment,
based in Allenwood, Pennsylvania, produced a series of studies on
USPCI's corporate history and environmental compliance record.
The volumes were researched and compiled by Lynn E. Moorer
and published by OUE between November 1991 and April 1993.

CHAPTER 6
page 195
"I asked him about an article . . ." Kevin Jones, "Companies Court
Noxubee County for Waste Site: FTI/USPCI Employ Different
Strategies to Gain Support," *Mississippi Business Journal*, Sept. 30,
1991, p. 1.

page 197
"It was as if he had read . . ." Faith Popcorn, *The Popcorn Report*
(New York: Doubleday, 1991), pp. 17–18.

"In that capacity, Britain's *Economist* magazine . . ." "NASA's
Troubles; Truly Messed Up," *Economist*, Feb. 22, 1992, p. 102.

page 208
"The core group behind the petition . . ." Susan Traylor, "Choc-
taw Members Protest Waste Dump, Chief Martin," Gannett News
Service, Apr. 2, 1991; "Choctaw Dumping Decision Worried Other
Tribes," Gannett News Service, Apr. 1, 1991.

"This led South Dakota's Senator Tom Daschle . . ." Ronald
Smothers, "Future in Mind, Choctaws Reject Plan for Landfill,"
Sunday New York Times, Apr. 21, 1991, pt. 1, p. 22. On the national
concerns of tribes around this issue, see, for example, Peter H.
Eichstaedt, *If You Poison Us: Uranium and Native Americans* (Sante
Fe, NM: Red Crane Books, 1994); Seth Mydans, "Tribe Smells
Sludge and Bureaucrats," *New York Times*, Oct. 20, 1994, p. A18;
Matthew L. Wald, "Nuclear Storage Divides Apaches and Neigh-
bors," *New York Times*, Nov. 11, 1993, p. A18; Richard A. DuBey,
Mervyn T. Tano, and D. Grant, "Protection of the Reservation En-

vironment: Hazardous Waste Management on Indian Lands," *Environmental Law* 19 (1988): 449. However, Native Americans do not uniformly oppose such projects, as noted in Kevin Gover and Jana L. Walker, "Escaping Environmental Paternalism: One Tribe's Approach to Developing a Commercial Waste Disposal Project in Indian Country," *U. Of Colo. Law Rev.* 63 (1992): 933.

page 214
"In the wake of the EPA's 1974 report . . ." U.S. Environmental Protection Agency, *Report to Congress: Disposal of Hazardous Waste*, Pub. No. SW-115 (Washington, DC: GPO, 1974). The report is discussed in greater detail in the Postscript.

page 217
". . . or even 99.9999 percent nontoxic . . ." The 99.9999 percent figure is based on federal destruction standards. See 40 C.F.R. Sec. 264.463 (stating hazardous waste destruction and removal efficiency standards). The "99.99" figures have been widely derided by environmental activists such as Barry Commoner. See *Making Peace with the Planet* (cited above in note for page xviii), p. 16.

page 221
"Underfunded and pressed for time, . . ." Gill subsequently supervised a master's thesis addressing some of the social and economic issues involved in Noxubee County. Richard Brian McGee, "Determinants of Levels of Approval for a Hazardous-Waste Facility in Noxubee County, Mississippi: A Comparison of the Effects of Cognitive, Socioeconomic and Demographic Factors" (master's thesis, Mississippi State University, 1993).

page 222
". . . a California environmental consulting firm, . . ." Cerrell Associates, *Political Difficulties Facing Waste-to-Energy Conversion Plant Siting* (1984), cited in Luke Cole, "Empowerment as the Key to Environmental Protection: The Need for Environmental Poverty Law," *Ecology Law Quarterly* 19 (1992): 619, 629.

page 224
". . . in the endlessly oppressive 'acres of afternoon' . . ." Quoted by Howell Raines, "Grady's Gift," *New York Times Magazine*, Dec. 1, 1991, p. 89.

CHAPTER 7

page 228
"As one alarmed white citizen . . ." The material on Isham Stewart and Reconstruction in Noxubee County is drawn largely from *Source Material* pt. 1 (cited above in note for page 16), pp. 285–86.

page 230
"As Faulkner famously observed . . ." Quoted in *Mississippi: Continuity and Change* (cited above in note for page 17), p. 6.

page 231
"The image of white feet on black necks . . ." *Source Material*, pt. 1 (cited above in note for page 16), p. 301. The quotation comes from an account of a black riot in 1888, which started when "a Negro refused to give Henry Maury the right-of-way when they passed each other on the road and the Negro was impudent to him." The riot was quieted only with the intervention of Ike Brown's spiritual ancestor, Isham Stewart. Similarly, blacks and whites reported to me the memory of a lynching a generation ago when a black man, Lanky Tensleigh, failed to give a white man right-of-way across a bridge. I was unable to verify the story in any published account.

page 243
". . . a short story by the Macon-born writer Loyle Hairston . . ." Loyle Hairston, "The Revolt of Brud Bascomb," in *Mississippi Writers* vol. 1 (cited above in note for page 156), pp. 250-261. A classic examination of the settlement between plantation owner and tenant is in *Deep South* (cited above in note for page 164), pp. 369–400.

CHAPTER 8

page 250
". . . the state's first Republican to be elected governor . . . " Elizabeth Kolbert, "Mississippi's Governor Beaten by a Newcomer," *New York Times*, Nov. 6, 1991, p. A22.

"He insisted that the Confederate emblem . . ." The quotation appeared in "Mississippi Governor Won't Scrap Rebel Flag," *USA Today*, June 4, 1992, p. 5A.

page 251

"The current Mississippi flag . . ." See "Blacks Sue over State Flag, *Sacramento Bee*, Apr. 20, 1993, p. A10.

"Several months later, Fordice . . ." See, for instance, Moshe Kohn, "In God We Trust," *Jerusalem Post*, Feb. 12, 1993; Jacob Neusner, "A Christian Nation? We Could Do Worse," *Wall Street Journal*, Nov. 25, 1992, p. A12.

page 262

"Columbia, with a large black population, . . ." Sharon Stallworth, "Activists Link Toxic Cleanup Delay, Racism," *Clarion-Ledger* (Jackson, MS), Mar. 28, 1993; Marianne Lavelle and Marcia Coyle, "Unequal Protection: The Racial Divide in Environmental Law," *National Law Journal*, Sept. 21, 1992, p. S1. Lavelle's and Coyle's articles appear in a prize-winning twelve-page special supplement, which they cowrote and researched. The report has become a touchstone for much environmental justice writing and activism.

page 264

". . . At the end of the meeting, Bruce Rubman . . ." *Bruce Rubman* is a pseudonym.

page 267

"Of the force of rumor in the Macon . . ." "Growing Up in Mississippi," (cited above in note for page 83), p. 318.

page 277

"The Clarion-Ledger, the state's . . ." Adam Nossiter, *Of Long Memory* (cited above in note for page 6), p. 83.

page 290

"The Pollution Solution was a calculated effort . . ." The Pollution Solution was the major focus of an article by the chief environmental reporter for the *New York Times*. See Keith Schneider, "Plan for Toxic Dump Pits Blacks against Blacks, *New York Times*, Dec. 13, 1993, p. A7. For his coverage, Schneider—who spent one and a half days there—is not warmly remembered by black and white opponents of hazardous waste in Noxubee, many of whom told me that they thought his article caricatured a complicated situation by stressing black/black conflict, and boosted the companies' position as a result. The influential reporter has in the past been criticized by environmentalists for what they perceive to be his probusiness views. See Vicki Monks, "See No Evil," *American Journalism Review* 15 (June 1993): 18.

page 291
"A twelve-member body composed wholly . . ." The governing statute at the time was Miss. Stat. Ann. Secs. 49-29-1 through 49-29-11. This statute was revised in 1993 and recodified at Miss. Stat. Ann. Secs. 5-3-151 through 5-3-167.

page 292
"On December 11, 1992, Chancellor and the Thomases . . ." *Thomas et al. v. Gunn et al.*, No. 92-74-38 (Hinds County Circuit Court, First Judicial District).

CHAPTER 9
page 299
"The signs spelled out messages . . ." Henrik Ibsen's play; *An Enemy of the People*, was written in 1882, and involves the threat to a community's health by income-generating baths that a local doctor insists must be shut down due to water contamination.

page 305
"(When Taft was growing up on Sunshine Plantation . . ." *Noxubee County Historical Trail* (cited above in note for page ix).

page 314
"Browner's carefully worded statement . . ." "EPA Administrator Browner Announces New Hazardous Waste Combustion Strategy," *EPA Environmental News*, May 13, 1993. In addition, see "Guidance to Hazardous Waste Generators on the Elements of a Waste Minimization Program, May 28, 1993," 58 Federal Register 31114 (May 24, 1993). Browner's report is discussed in detail in Philip L. Comella, "EPA Cancels Invitations to Its Own Program: The Agency's New Hazardous Waste Combustion Strategy," *Environmental Reporter* 24 (July 1994): 10380. See also Viki Reath, "Uncer-

tainty Clouds New EPA Policy on Hazardous Waste," *Environment Week* 6 (May 20, 1993): No. 20; Paul Kemezis, "U.S. Hazardous Waste Incineration Boom Becomes A Bust", *Environment Week* 6 (September 6, 1993): No. 35.

page 315
"Hugh Holman, an industry watcher with . . ." Jeff Bailey, "Environment: Managing Waste: Pay-as-You-Throw Cuts Garbage Volume," *Wall Street Journal*, Apr. 30, 1993, p. B1; Ray Pospisil, "Radical Change for Hazardous Waste Services, *Chemical Week*, Aug. 18, 1993, p. 26. A key event at the time was the decision of Chemical Waste Management to withdraw its application to build a hazardous waste incinerator in Kettleman City, California—deep in a majority-Spanish-speaking section of the San Joaquin Valley. The announcement followed a successful challenge to Chem Waste's plans in the California courts, in a major environmental justice case, *El Pueblo Para El Aire Y Agua Limpio v. County of Kings*, No. 366045 (Cal. Super. Ct., Sacramento County, Dec. 30, 1991). The text of the decision appears at Vol. 22, *Environmental Law Reporter* 20357. See also Casey Bukro, "Waste's Firm's Future a Burning Issue," *Chicago Tribune*, Sept. 13, 1993, p. 1C; and Jeff Bailey, "Slump at Hazardous Waste Dumps Raises Concerns," *Wall Street Journal*, Aug. 5, 1994, p. B5.

page 319
"In 1956, worried that liquor and gambling interests . . ." Miss. Code Ann. Secs. 25-5-1 through 25-5-33.

page 321
"PEON's renewed sense of purpose . . ." Calvin Sims, "N.A.A.C.P. Says Hughes Is Violating Diversity Rules," *New York Times*, Aug. 8, 1993, p. D1.; Calvin Sims, "Hughes Fails to Convince N.A.A.C.P.," *New York Times*, Aug. 12, 1993, p. D4.

page 325
"The county's population *had* declined . . ." Higginbotham's figures were wildly exaggerated. Noxubee's population decline was hardly so precipitous: as in much of the rural South, Noxubee's population has been in steady decline since the Great Depression, with the great northern exodus of African Americans. In

1930, for example, the county was nearly 80 percent African American, with a reported 20,138 black and 5,432 white citizens. *Source Material,* pt. 2 (cited above in note for page 16), p. iii. *Source Material* cited to the 1930 U.S. Census. In 1940, the total reported population was 26,669; in 1950, 20,022; in 1960, 16,826. U.S. Bureau of the Census, *Census of the Population: 1960* (Washington, DC: GPO, 1963), pp. 26–13. From 1960 to 1990, Noxubee lost another 4,222 residents, a decline of about another 25 percent. U.S. Bureau of the Census, *1990 Census of Population and Housing: Summary Population and Housing Characteristics: Mississippi* (Washington, DC: GPO, 1991) 1990 CPH 1-26, Table 1, p. 11. On the migration north, see Nicholas Lemann, *Promised Land: The Great Black Migration and How It Changed America* (New York: Knopf, 1991).

page 326
". . . what William Faulkner . . ." See above note for page 156.

page 329
"The first occurred early in the summer when, ..." Environmental justice activists are giving increased attention to the use of Title VI, and the government has begun to take such complaints more seriously. For instance, see Christopher Boerner and Thomas Lambert, "Environmental Injustice: Industrial and Waste Facilities Must Consider the Human Factor," *USA Today* (magazine), Mar. 1995, p. 30; Luke W. Cole, "Community-Based Administrative Advocacy Under Civil Rights Law: A Potential Environmental Justice Tool for Legal Services Advocates", *Clearinghouse Review* 29 (1995): 343.

"The second pivotal event . . ." The case was *State of Mississippi ex re. McGowan v. Fordice,* Civ. No. 93-77-196 (Hinds County, Mississippi Circuit Court, First Judicial District).

page 335
"To enforce the Voting Rights Act . . ." The Voting Rights Act, Public Law 89-100, was passed on August 16, 1965, and it has been amended many times since then. It appears at 42 U.S.C. Secs. 1971–1973gg-10.

EPILOGUE

page 343

"He did not say so, but it is hard to resist . . ." See Martin Luther King, Jr., "Letter from Birmingham City Jail" (dated April 16, 1963), reprinted in Clayborne Carson, David J. Garrow, Gerald Gill, Vincent Harding, and Darlene Clark Hine, general eds., *Eyes on the Prize Civil Rights Reader* (Penguin: New York, 1991), pp. 153-158.

page 345

"What no one is perhaps willing to acknowledge . . ." *Reconstruction in West Alabama* (cited above in note for page 81), pp. 73–9.

page 349

"It is easy enough to blame corporations . . ." In the environmental justice movement, the tendency is to do just that. For example, I asked John McCown, an African American organizer for the Sierra Club, who works out of Birmingham, Alabama, if he thought communities bear any responsibility for the situations in which they find themselves and the choices they face. "No," he answered, "industries and government are exploiting a bad situation. The culprit is government and industry." See also Charles Lee, "Beyond Toxic Wastes and Race," in Robert D. Bullard, ed., *Confronting Environmental Racism* (Boston: South End Press, 1993), pp. 41–52.

POSTSCRIPT

page 357

"Benjamin Chavis, the short-tenured . . ." Marcia Coyle, "When Movements Coalesce; Empowerment: Civil Rights Meets Environmental Rights," *National Law Journal*, Sept. 21, 1992, p. S10. Chavis has perhaps received more than his due of credit for originating the animating ideas of the environmental justice movement. Many were thinking along the same lines at least as early as he. See, for instance, Charles W. Bowser, "Prerogatives of the Powerful—Plight of the Poor, *Villanova Law Review* 19 (May 1974): 705.

"In 1979, residents of a predominantly black . . ." *Bean v. Southwestern Waste Management Corp.*, 482 F. Supp. 673 (S.D. Tex. 1979) affirmed by 782 F.2d 1038 (5th Cir. 1986). Subsequent equal protection/environmental justice cases of note include *East Bibb Twiggs Neighborhood Association v. Macon-Bibb County Planning and Zoning Commission*, 706 F. Supp. 880 (N.D.Ga. 1989), affirmed by 896 F.2d 1264 (11th Cir. 1989), and *R.I.S.E., Inc. v. Kay*, 768 F. Supp. 1144 (E.D. Va. 1991), affirmed by 977 F.2d 573 (4th Cir. 1992).

page 358
"Robert Bullard, in the late 1970s . . ." Bullard has become one of the most prolific and influential of environmental justice scholars. Books edited by him include *Confronting Environmental Racism* (cited above in note for page 349) and *Unequal Protection: Environmental Justice and Communities of Color* (San Francisco: Sierra Club Books, 1994). He is the sole author of *Dumping in Dixie: Race, Class, and Environmental Quality* (Boulder, CO: Westview Press, 1990) and *Invisible Houston: The Black Experience in Boom and Bust* (College Station: Texas A&M University Press, 1987). A sampling of his articles includes "Race and Environmental Justice in the United States," *Yale Journal of International Law* 18 (1993): 318; and "Examining the Evidence of Environmental Racism," *Land Use Forum* 2 (Winter 1993): 6–11.

page 359
"The first was a 1983 report . . ." U.S. General Accounting Office, *Siting of Hazardous Waste Landfills and Their Correlation with Racial and Economic Status of Surrounding Communities* (Washington, DC: GPO, 1983). In the early 1980s, the EPA came under repeated criticism from the GAO for failure to execute its regulatory duties, as, for example, in the GAO's *EPA Is Slow to Carry Out Its Responsibility to Control Harmful Chemicals* (Washington, DC: 1980).

"The second and more influential study . . ." See above note for page 143.

page 360
"The UCC report was updated in 1994 . . ." Benjamin A. Goldman and Laura Fitton, *Toxic Wastes and Race Revisited: An Update*

Achieving Sustainability with Environmental Justice (Washington, DC: National Wildlife Federation, 1993); Richard J. Lazarus, "Pursuing 'Environmental Justice': The Distributional Effects of Environmental Protection," *Northwestern University Law Review* 87 (1992): 787. In some of those articles, a revisionism of the just-born academic sub-discipline of environmental justice studies attacked the UCC's 1987 report. Vicki Been, a young, white New York University Law School professor, is one of the most outspoken of these revisionists, and has questioned the suggestion that minority neighborhoods are targets of hazardous waste companies and the purveyors of other services perceived as environmentally dangerous. Been has urged those who decry environmental racism to consider the effects of various forces, including the "free market", suggesting that people may have come to an undesirable land use—because land is cheap—as easily as the undesirable use having come to them. Her views are outlined in Vicki Been, "Locally Undesirable Land Uses in Minority Neighborhoods: Disproportionate Siting or Market Dynamics?" *Yale Law Journal* 103 (1994): 1383, and "What's Fairness Got to Do With It? Environmental Justice and the Siting of Locally Undesirable Land Uses," *Cornell Law Review* 78 (1993): 1001. Been was later given a $155,000 grant by the U.S. EPA to test these conclusions. Some of her results are reported in Vicki Been, "Analyzing Evidence of Environmental Justice", 11 *Journal of Land Use & Environmental Law* (1995): 1-36. Because of the neoconservative ring to Been's exhortations, her critics have accused her of being a corporate apologist. They ask, for example, what it means to speak of a "free" market when poor people of color move to an area near an environmentally undesirable site. Presumably, the invisible hand of free choice in a capitalist market is a useful concept only when people have real choices. Other, probusiness writers on the subject of environmental justice include, for example, Thomas Lambert and Christopher Boerner, *Environmental Inequity: Economic Causes, Economic Solutions*, Policy Study No. 125 (St. Louis: Center for Study of American Business, 1995); and *Environmental Justice?* Policy Study No. 121 (St. Louis: Center for Study of American Business, 1994). See also Charles J. McDermott, "A Waste Manager's Perspective," *Land Use Forum* 2 (Winter 1993): 12–17.

page 362

"Among the eight counties in Noxubee County's region, . . ." It must be noted that for two of the years on which my discussion is based—1987 and 1990—there were no county-by-county statistics collected by the Mississippi Department of Human Services, due to factors such as new methods of agency data collection procedures and political change. However, because there was so little variation in the figures for the surrounding years, I assumed that, had county-by-county figures been available, these years would not have proven exceptions to the claims advanced in the text.

page 364

"In 1925, J. D. Green, the county health officer . . ." *Historical Notes of Noxubee County* (cited above in note for page 15), p. 208.

page 365

"In support of this claim, . . ." U.S. Environmental Protection Agency, *Report to Congress: Disposal of Hazardous Waste*, Pub. No. SW-115 (Washington, DC: GPO, 1974), p. 255.

page 366

"The Sierra Club LDF's arguments relied . . ." The statutory authority relied upon by the Sierra Club LDF was 42 U.S.C. Sec. 2000d.

"The environmental researcher Peter Montague . . ." *Rachel's Hazardous Waste News* no. 260 (Nov. 20, 1991).

ACKNOWLEDGMENTS

DURING THE GREAT Depression, the Mississippi writer Eudora Welty worked on a Works Progress Administration bookmobile, travelling all over her home state. For a girl from a relatively sheltered background, the extremes she saw—of wealth, of racial difference—filled her with surprise. Welty took a camera with her, taking snapshots of what she saw. The photographs are remarkably honest, unstudied, amazed. She later wrote that "In taking all of these pictures, I was attended, I now know, by an angel—the presence of trust. In particular, the photographs of black persons by white persons may not testify soon again to such intimacy. It is trust that dates the pictures now, more than the vanished years."

During the course of preparing this book, I was haunted by Welty's words. Our nation's tortured racial history, more complicated still since Welty traveled across Mississippi in a WPA bookmobile, hung over all of my efforts. As a northerner, I was greeted with suspicion by whites tired of sanctimonious finger-pointing. As a white, many blacks eyed me warily as I sought to understand their world. Further complicating any project like this one is the fact that in our media-saturated age most of us are now poised and ready for our 15 minutes of fame, constantly calling into question the authenticity of what we say to a relative stranger. As a result, I am above all indebted to the people of east-central Mississippi who gave me their trust, especially inasmuch as each of them will, I suspect, disagree with at least some of what is written here. In particular, I am grateful to Printz Bolin, Martha and Drew Blackwell, Richard Brooks, Ike Brown, Wilbur Colom, I.D. and Annette Conner, Tim Gowan, Geraldine Harris, Brad Moore, Essie Spencer, Peggy and Linda Thomas, and Ben Tubb. Scott Boyd and *The [Macon] Beacon* also deserve my thanks for their interest in and support of this project. Jeanette Floore Craig and her staff at the Noxubee County Circuit Clerk's office graciously provided me access to county archival material. Ann Leach of the Mississippi Department of Public Health, and Barbara Spann of the Mississippi Department of Human Services were extraordinarily accommodating in helping me locate statistical data. In Giles County, I am especially obliged to Carol and Chuck Puckett and Jerry and Pat Miles for their cooperation.

Two people were indispensable to the creation of this book and merit special thanks. Chandler Crawford, my sister, was unfailingly encouraging and supportive, both emotionally and materially. I will never be able to thank her enough for her faith in me and her steady counsel. My agent Faith Childs is, as another one of her author's appositely put it, "a queen among women." An empress, even? She believed in the worth of this project from the very start and lit the fire that got me started, giving me time and attention well beyond my due. Whatever merit this text may have was greatly enriched by what I have learned from her. Thanks also to her able assistants: Emily Bernard, Debbie Goodison, and Arlene Stoltz.

Very special thanks also go to Erica Marcus, who went well beyond the call of friendship in advising, criticizing, handholding, and editing portions of the book at various stages. She endured endless queries about possible titles as well, and for her forbearance, intelligence, and humor I will always be grateful.

For the better part of two summers, Chandler Crawford and Fred Chapman made available a beach apartment that made work on this book infinitely more comfortable than it would have been in a sweltering city apartment. The manuscript took shape in Omi, New York, and I am deeply indebted to Francis Greenburger and the Board of Directors of Ledig House International Writer's Colony for a residency there and the rare opportunity to work without interruption in bucolic, nurturing surroundings. Thanks go also to the colony's Executive Director, Elaine Smollins-Sruogis, who, along with her husband Saulius, helped make my stay a comfortable one, and to Roy Harvender, who kept me and the other writers so well fed. Final corrections were made in the peace and quiet of The Writer's Room, New York City, and I greatly appreciate the chance to work there.

At Addison-Wesley, I appreciated Don Fehr's initial interest. Henning Gutmann was a model editor: intelligent, probing, supportive, always accessible. He was an absolute delight to work with, as were his assistants Jack Dew and Albert DePetrillo. Bill Patrick's belief in this project at a trying time provided welcome reassurance. Art Director Jean Seal was invariably patient and encouraging (and don't let's forget to go rabbit-hunting). Thanks also to Alison Pratt, for her enthusiasm, and to Robert Dancy, for his meticulous legal review. I am also grateful to my outstanding, unflappable project supervisor, Tiffany Cobb, and to the thoughtful work of my copy editor, Sharon Sharp.

I am delighted to have the work of the extraordinary Mississippi photographer Birney Imes and the Best Designer in the World, Alexander Knowlton, on the cover of this book, and want to thank both of them for their contributions. Typically, Addison-Wesley accommodated my wishes to work with both artists, and for this I am grateful. Karen Savary's book design added nicely to their work.

Jess Bravin, the late Diane Cleaver, Bettina Drew, Stacy Leigh, and Albert Pesant gave me helpful criticism on drafts of the proposal that became this book. Kenneth Scott fed me a steady diet of information on the environment. As the manuscript reached completion, Jessie Allen, Eve Cary, and Andrea Schwan provided detailed, thoughtful comments on my ideas and organization, as did Tennessean Victor Flatt, who read chapter 2 with special attention, for which I am in his debt. Lars Waldorf read the manuscript with extraordinary care and a sharp, critical eye (you can take the boy out of the editor's chair, but you can't take the editor out of the man). Frank Rouda tolerated with good humor my questions about syntax and diction. Lloyd Marks fed me sushi at an unexpected, and much appreciated, moment. Christopher Booker and Jerusha DeGroote did needed research. Professor Joseph C. Robert provided illuminating historical background material on Noxubee County. Gwendolyn Applewhite helped keep me organized. Rosemary Campagna, Linda Holmes, and above all Jean Jablonski provided indispensable library assistance with unwavering good cheer. Heide Lange and John Chaffee helped make this book possible through their very special generosity. I am thankful to all of them.

INDEX